Lecture Notes of the Institute for Computer Sciences, Social Informatics and Telecommunications Engineering 147

More information about this series at http://www.springer.com/series/8197

Amos Nungu · Bjorn Pehrson
Julianne Sansa-Otim (Eds.)

e-Infrastructure
and e-Services
for Developing Countries

6th International Conference, AFRICOMM 2014
Kampala, Uganda, November 24–25, 2014
Revised Selected Papers

 Springer

Editors
Amos Nungu
Dar Es Salaam Institute of Technology
Dar Es Salaam
Tanzania

Julianne Sansa-Otim
Makerere University
Kampala
Uganda

Bjorn Pehrson
KTH/ICT/TSLab
Kista
Sweden

ISSN 1867-8211 ISSN 1867-822X (electronic)
Lecture Notes of the Institute for Computer Sciences, Social Informatics
and Telecommunications Engineering
ISBN 978-3-319-16885-2 ISBN 978-3-319-16886-9 (eBook)
DOI 10.1007/978-3-319-16886-9

Library of Congress Control Number: 2015937498

Springer Cham Heidelberg New York Dordrecht London

Printed on acid-free paper

Springer International Publishing AG Switzerland is part of Springer Science+Business Media
(www.springer.com)

Preface

Africa is a continent of diversity that is going through dramatic changes in its social, political, and economical environments. Deploying efficient and effective infrastructures and solutions when limited resources are available is a challenging task, but a key-enabler for the diffusion of ICT.

AFRICOMM conference addresses the communication part of this deployment, which is characterized by transformation from satellite based to a terrestrial infrastructure, starting from the intercontinental submarine cables to the national backbones and then on to the distribution and access networks, not least into rural areas. In the end, the potential users need to adapt their working procedures to take advantage of the benefits of ICT.

The economical challenges include reducing operational and capital cost to provide affordable connectivity to all. Services must be adapted to local needs, and business concepts must meet local requirements. The technical challenges include not only the ICT aspects, but also reliable power supply.

The aim of the AFRICOMM 2014 conference was bringing together international researchers, students, public officers, policy makers, and practitioners in ICT to discuss issues and trends, recent research, innovation advances, and on-the-field experiences related to e-Infrastructures and e-Services with a focus on developing countries. Thus, the conference is a platform where new ideas are tested, evaluated, discussed, and challenged.

This volume of papers testifies to the exemplary diversity of the various topics presented and discussed, providing a unique insight into appropriate technology and practice. Let these conference proceedings of be a milestone and empowerment for cultural aligned practices in e-Infrastructure and e-Services in developing countries.

November 2014   Amos Nungu

Organization

AFRICOMM 2014 was organized by the College of Computing and Information Sciences, Makerere Univeristy in cooperation with European Alliance for Innovation (EAI).

Steering Committee

Chair

Imrich Chlamtac   CREATE-NET, Italy

Members

Salomao Julio Manhica	UTICT, Mozambique
Fausto Giunchiglia	University of Trento, Italy
Paolo Traverso	FBK, Italy

Conference Organizing Committee

General Co-chairs

Julianne Sansa Otim	Makerere University, Uganda
Bjorn Pehrson	Royal Institute of Technology, Sweden

TPC Chair

Amos Nungu   Dar es Salaam Institute of Technology, Tanzania

Workshop Chair

Mathias Kretschmer   Fraunhofer FOKUS, Germany

Publication

Karl Jonas	Bonn-Rhein-Sieg University of Applied Sciences, Germany
Steven Mutaawe	Makerere University, Uganda

Publicity

Marion Alina	Makerere University, Uganda
Tony Bulega	Makerere University, Uganda
Philip Lutaaya	Makerere University, Uganda

Poster

Ruth Mbabazi Mutebi	Makerere University, Uganda
Paddy Jr. Assimwe	Makerere University, Uganda
Tom Kamya	Makerere University, Uganda

Industry Forum

Isaac Kasana   Research and Education Network of Uganda,
Uganda

Local Chair

Dora Bampangana   Makerere University, Uganda

Website

Maxwell Omwenga   Makerere University, Uganda

Exhibition

Grace Kamulegeya   Makerere University, Uganda
Mary Nsabagwa   Makerere University, Uganda

Conference Manager

Ruzanna Najaryan   European Alliance for Innovation, Italy

Technical Program Committee

Amos Nungu	Dar es Salaam Institute of Technology, Tanzania
Bjorn Pehrson	Royal Institute of Technology, Sweden
Julianne Sansa-Otim	Makerere University, Uganda
Mathias Kretschmer	Fraunhofer FOKUS, Germany
Zaipuna O. Yonah	NMAIST, Tanzania
Isaac Kasana	Research and Education Network of Uganda, Uganda
Karl Jonas	Bonn-Rhein-Sieg University of Applied Sciences, Germany
Finian Mwalongo	Visualisierungsinstitut der Universität Stuttgart, Germany
Jim Yonaz	Institute of Financial Management, Tanzania
Chomora Mikeka	University of Malawi, Malawi
Kenedy Greyson	Dar es Salaam Institute of Technology, Tanzania
Sam Anael	NMAIST, Tanzania
Ruth Mbabazi Mutebi	Makerere University, Uganda
Edephonce Ngemera Nfuka	Open University of Tanzania, Tanzania
Josephine Nabukenya	Makerere University, Uganda

Solomon Mangeni	Swansea Univesity, UK
Msumba John	Dar es Salaam Institute of Technology, Tanzania
Masinde Muthoni	Central University of Technology, South Africa
Petro Ernest	Dar es Salaam Institute of Technology, Tanzania

Sponsoring Institution

MTN Uganda

Contents

Health

IoT, Cloud Computing and TVWS

ICT4D Applications

Access to Information

ICT4D Miscellaneous

Communication Infrastructure

Throughput Performance of Interference Mitigation Techniques in Cognitive Femtocell Networks

Peterson Mwesiga[✉], Julius Butime, and Richard Okou

Department of Electrical and Computer Engineering,
CEDAT, Makerere University, P.O. Box 7062, Kampala, Uganda
mwesigapeter@cedat.mak.ac.ug

Abstract. The exponential growth in demand for higher data rates and other services in wireless networks require a more dense deployment of base stations which results in more demand of the radio spectrum. Due to the scarcity of radio spectrum and the under-utilization of assigned spectrum, government regulatory bodies have started to review their spectrum allocation policies so as to implement opportunistic spectrum access (sharing) through cognitive femtocells. The cognitive femtocell technique is however challenging due to uncertainties associated with co-tier and cross-tier interference, adjacent channel fading, path loss, and other environment dependent conditions that bring about a progressive degradation of the signal coverage. In this paper, we review the different interference solutions and prioritize the Optimal Static Fractional Frequency Re-use (OSFFR) approach. We analyze the system performance with different metrics such as throughput, number of free channels and Bit Error Rate. Simulation results show that the proposed OSFFR shows an improved result compared to other frequency reuse schemes.

Keywords: Cognitive femtocell · Interference mitigation · Hetnet · Optimal static fractional frequency Re-use (OSFFR) · Soft fractional frequency reuse (SFFR)

1 Introduction

With the advent of LTE, big data era and the emergence of new hand-held devices such as tablet PC and smart phones, data intensive applications like online video streaming and network gaming have inexorably occupied many users' focus. LTE-A calls for higher data rates to provide quality services and better user experience. Studies have suggested that this rapidly increasing demand for high data rate is chiefly generated from indoor environments in urban and sub-urban areas [1]. In an effort to meet increasing data traffic demand and enhance network spectral efficiency, cellular network operators can densify their existing networks using cognitive-capable femtocell access points in a cognitive femtocell architecture. In addition, joint deployments of

---

This paper was presented at AFRICOMM 2012 in Younde, Cameroon.

© Institute for Computer Sciences, Social Informatics and Telecommunications Engineering 2015
A. Nungu et al. (Eds.): AFRICOMM 2014, LNICST 147, pp. 3–12, 2015.
DOI: 10.1007/978-3-319-16886-9_1

femtocells and macrocells can enhance the energy efficiency of cellular networks by hugely boosting data rates at a small energy cost [2]. Cognitive radio is an intelligent and adaptive wireless communication system that enables more efficient utilization of the radio spectrum [3]. The use of cognitive radio technology requires frequent sensing of the radio spectrum and processing of the sensor data which would require additional power with a proportional increase in co-tier interference.

However, efficient spectrum usage is not the only concern of cognitive radio. Actually, in the original definition of cognitive radio by J. Mitola, every possible parameter measurable by a wireless node or network is taken into account (Cognition) so that the network intelligently modifies its functionality to meet a certain objective [4]. It has been shown in recent works that structures and techniques based on cognitive radio reduce the energy consumption, while maintaining the required quality-of-service (QoS), under various channel conditions [5]. There are a number of other technologies and techniques which have been developed so as to quantify energy savings in cognitive femtocells through mitigation of interference which include; defining the interference [3], interference cartography [6], frequency overlay, frequency under lay, cognitive femtocell power control, contention schemes [7], adaptive uplink algorithm, frequency bandwidth dynamic division, clustering algorithm, interference signature, and cognitive femtocell network controller. Hence, a roadway to the future would be striving for more feasible, less complex, and less expensive schemes of mitigating interference within the scope of cognitive radio. The remaining part of the paper is organized as follows: The system model is described in Sect. 2. Section 3 presents the Het-net interference mitigation techniques. Our evaluation methodology is described in Sect. 4, and the analysis and simulation results presented in Sect. 5. We conclude the paper in Sect. 6.

2 System Model

Figure 1 shows a Heterogeneous Network (HetNet) where a Master enhanced Node B (MeNB) is overlaid with one Picocell and several Home enhanced Node B (HeNBs). In this network, each UE device usually communicates on a specific subchannel corresponding to the base station (BS) from which it receives the strongest signal strength, while the signals received from other BSs on the same subchannel are considered as interference. We focus on a two-tier HetNet comprising macrocells and femtocells. Two types of interference occur in such a HetNet. Co-tier interference occurs between neighboring femtocells. For example, a femtocell UE device (aggressor) causes uplink co-tier interference to the neighboring femtocell BSs (victims). Each MUE is interfered by all neighboring macrocells and femtocells that use the same sub-bands assigned to its serving macro BS.

The signal-to-interference-plus-noise-ratio (SINR) for downlink transmission to MUE x_m from MeNB m on sub-channel k, SINR is given by

$$SINR^k_{x_m,m} = \frac{P^k_m h^k_{x_m,m} G^k_{x_m,m}}{N_0 \Delta B + \sum_{m' \in M'} P^k_{m'} h^k_{x_m,m'} G^k_{x_m,m'} + \sum_{f \in F} P^k_f G^k_{x_m,f}} \tag{1}$$

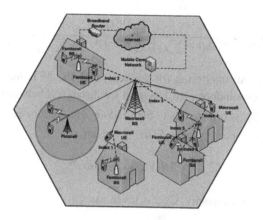

Fig. 1. Cognitive femtocell interference scenario

where; P_m^k is the transmit power from MeNB m on sub-channel k. $h_{x_m,m}^k$ is the exponentially distributed channel fading power gain associated with sub-channel k, $G_{x_m,m}^k$ is the path loss associated with sub-channel k between MUEx_m and MeNB which is given as

$$G_{x_m,m}^k = 10^{-PL_{outdoor}/10} \qquad (2)$$

where $PL_{outdoor}$ is the outdoor pathloss modeled as [8];

$$PL_{outdoor} = 28 + 35 \log_{10}(d) \text{ dB}$$

with d as the Euclidean distance between a base-station and a user in meters. However, $G_{x_m,f}^k$ is affected by both indoor and outdoor path-loss. In this case, d would be the Euclidean distance between a HeNB f and the edge of the indoor wall in the direction of MUE x_m. After the wall, the pathloss is based on an outdoor path loss model. In (1), M' is the set of interfering MeNBs, which depends on the location of the MUEs and the specific FFR scheme used. F is the set of interfering HeNBs. Here, the adjacent HeNBs are defined as those HeNBs which are inside a circular area of radius 60 m centered at the location of MUEx_m. N_0 represents noise power spectral density and ΔB represents sub-carrier spacing. The maximum achievable capacity for a MUEx_m on sub-channel k is then given by;

$$C_{y_m,m}^k = (\Delta B. \log_2(1 + \alpha SINR_{y_m,m}^k) \qquad (3)$$

Where α is a constant defined by;

$$\alpha = \frac{-1.5}{\ln(5 X BER)} \qquad (4)$$

Here, BER represents the target Bit Error Rate (e.g., 10^{-6}). For an FUE y_f communicating with the HeNB f on sub-channel k, the downlink $SINR$,

$$SINR_{y_f,f}^k = \frac{P_f^k G_{y_f,f}^k}{N_0 \Delta B + \sum_{m \in M} P_m^k h_{y_f,m}^k G_{y_f,m}^k + \sum_{f' \in F'} P_f^k G_{y_f,f'}^k} \tag{5}$$

where F' is the set of all interfering (or adjacent) HeNBs, M is the set of interfering MeNBs, $G_{y_f,f}^k$ represents indoor path loss gain for distance d between the FUE and its serving HeNB and $G_{y_f,m}^k$ corresponds to both indoor and outdoor path loss model. The maximum achievable capacity for an $FUE_{y\ f}$ is given as;

$$C_{y_f,f}^k = (\Delta B . \log_2 (1 + \alpha SINR_{y_f,f}^k)) \tag{6}$$

The average network capacity, C_{avg} is given as:

$$C_{avg} = \frac{\sum_{x_m \in X_m} \sum_{k \in K} \Gamma_{x_m,m}^k C_{x_m,m}^k}{MUE_{total}} + \frac{\sum_{f \in F_A} \sum_{y_f \in Y_f} \sum_{k \in K} \Gamma_{y_f,f}^k C_{y_f,f}^k}{FUE_{total}} \tag{7}$$

Where, in general, $\Gamma^k = 1$ when a sub-channel k is assigned to a UE, otherwise it is set to zero. The spectral efficiency η in digital communication systems is defined as;

$$\eta = \frac{C}{W} \tag{8}$$

Where C is the channel capacity (in bits/second) and W is the channel bandwidth in Hz. Shannon showed there is a fundamental tradeoff between energy efficiency and bandwidth efficiency for reliable communications [9]. If we let $\eta = C/W$ (the spectral efficiency), then we can re-express in terms of $\frac{E_b}{N_o}$ as;

$$\frac{E_b}{N_o} = \frac{2^\eta - 1}{\eta} \tag{9}$$

3   Conventional HetNet Interference Mitigation Techniques

A. Interference Avoidance Techniques: Interference avoidance techniques include; power control, Game Based Resource Allocation in Cognitive Environment (GRACE), Coverage Adaption, Frequency Bandwidth Dynamic Division and Clustering Algorithm. Q-Based Learning algorithm [10], cognitive sniffing, and contention control [7].

B. Interference Cancellation: Interference cancellation refers to a class of techniques that demodulate/decode desired information, and then use this information along with channel estimates to cancel received interference from the received signal. It aims at demodulating and canceling interferences through multi-user detection methods so as reduce and cancel interference at the receiver end [11]. Interference cancellation schemes include; successive interference cancellation (SIC), and parallel interference cancellation (PIC).

C. Interference Randomization: These techniques aim at randomizing the interfering signals and thus allowing interference suppression. Randomization averages the interference on user equipment by randomly hopping between channels [12]. Interference randomization policy therefore spreads the user's transmission over a distributed set of subcarriers in order to randomize the interference scenario and achieve frequency diversity gain. Such schemes include IDMA and interference averaging [13].

D. Interference Alignment: Interference alignment (IA) is a linear beam forming technique used to align beam forming matrices at the transmitters such that the interference at each receiver is aligned in an interference subspace. This leaves the desired signal to transmit in an interference-free subspace whereas at the receivers, a simple zero-forcing (ZF) receiving vector to project the desired signal onto the interference-free subspace, which is sufficient for signal detection is employed [14]. This includes; Distributed Algorithm Interference Alignment [15], Opportunistic Interference alignment, Lattice Alignment, Blind Interference Alignment, Retrospective Interference alignment, Asymptotic Interference Alignment, Linear Interference alignment [16].

E. Interference Suppression: This scheme employs signal noise projection and conventional maximum likelihood techniques to decode both the interference and desired signals at the receiver using the euclidean and hamming distances between the code words received.

F. Interference Coordination: This approach capitalizes on efficient radio resource management techniques to coordinate the channel allocation in nearby cells and minimize the interference level. Interference co-ordination techniques include; Fractional Frequency Reuse, Soft Frequency Reuse, Optimal Fractional Frequency reuse [17], and Coordinated Frequency Reuse Table 1.

Table 1. Summarized comparison of key interference techniques

	Complexity	Mitigation efficiency	Channel State Information	User capacity	Spectral efficiency
Avoidance	Low	High	Not Required	High	High
Cancellation	High	High	Required	Low	Medium
Coordination	Low	High	Not Required	High	Low
Alignment	High	High	Required	Low	Low
Randomization	Low	Medium	Not Required	Medium	Medium

We now consider various interference mitigation techniques based on complexity, mitigation efficiency, channel state information, user capacity and spectrum efficiency. Interference avoidance combined with interference coordination techniques such as fractional frequency reuse with power control show a high performance with regard to co-channel interference mitigation, spectrum efficiency and capacity, compared to other techniques reviewed above.

1) **Soft Fractional Frequency Reuse:** This uses a cell partitioning technique similar to that of the strict FFR scheme. However, the center-zone MUE devices of any

cell are allowed to use the sub bands of cell-edge-zone MUE of the neighboring cells within the cluster. For a cluster of N cells, the total number of available sub channels in a cell is divided into N sub bands with one sub band assigned to each edge zone. One of the major advantages of soft FFR is that it has better spectrum efficiency than strict FFR. Similar to strict FFR, a HeNB located in the center zone may select the sub band that is used by the MUE in the edge zone, and if the HeNB is located in the edge zone, it chooses the sub bands that are used by the MUE in the center zone [17].

2) **Optimal Static Fractional Frequency Reuse:** The macrocell coverage is partitioned into the center zone and edge zone with six sectors in each zone, the center zone MUE devices (i.e., the UE situated within the optimal center-zone radius of the cell) are allocated sub band A with the number of sub-channels in this sub band obtained from the solution of the optimization problem. The rest of the available sub channels are divided into six sub-bands (B, C, D, E, F, and G), each of which is allocated to one of the edge-zone sectors [17]. Figure 2 shows the OSSFR channel allocation mechanisms.

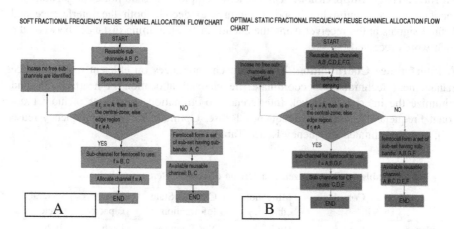

Fig. 2. SFFR and OSFFR channel allocation schemes

4   Evaluation Methodology

A. Number of free channels (local sensing at CFAP): Due to random deployment of the cognitive FAP, local sensing is performed based on Monte Carlo simulations using energy detection spectrum sensing technique. This approach is repeated for different fractional frequency reuse schemes to evaluate the performance as the number of deployed femtocells increases with increase in center radius.

B. User capacity performance: By continuously changing the FUE location, we evaluate the SINR and user capacity at all possible locations within the coverage areas of all macrocells and femtocells. This is justified by the fact that fading is averaged out and an AWGN channel is assumed. Using Monte Carlo Simulations, we simulate the available user capacity to the HeNB as the location of the Femtocell varies from the center-zone to the edge-zone. FAP distance is varied within the MeNB for three schemes while the user capacity is obtained.

C. Throughput performance: For a random femtocell deployment, the user capacity of both MUEs and FUEs is calculated using (7) at all possible locations. Average capacity of MUEs and average capacity of FUEs are then calculated. The overall average FUE capacity can express the average throughput performance of the whole network. This is repeated for all the respective schemes.

D. Bit Error Rate performance: BER performance is evaluated based on the Shannon bandwidth-energy efficiency relationship in (9). This shows the quality of radio signal received per cognitive femtocell user.

5 Simulation Analysis

5.1 Simulation Environment

We assume that the HeNBs operate in closed access mode (i.e. only registered FUE devices will be able to access the HeNBs). The MUE devices are uniformly distributed while FUE are randomly distributed in the network. The MUE and FUE are randomly allocated with available sub-channels from the designated frequency bands corresponding to each sub-area for each scheme and also continuously change positions. A FUE is considered as a cell-edge one if its distance from the center is more than 70 % of the cell radius. The numbers of HeNBs are varied up to 40 in one Macrocell coverage area but we take a sample of 4 FUEs in the network. We also assume that all the neighboring macrocell base stations always transmit at full power over all the available sub bands.

5.2 Simulation Parameters

We take two scenarios into account to compare the performance of OFDMA based communication networks using the proposed OSFFR scheme with those using other frequency reuse techniques such as the SFR scheme, and the classical reuse-1 scheme. 4G LTE-Advanced wireless standard is simulated with the parameters shown in Table 2.

5.3 Simulation Results

Figure 5 shows that at low SINR values such as 5 dB, the throughput is well below 1Mbps but increases with a greater SINR value for the OSFFR scheme. In addition, OSFFR energy efficiency is 73.33 % and SFR energy efficiency is 25.93 %. This is due to the fact that the edge-zone secondary users of the FAP, the FAP under observation, are not interfered with by any other MeNB of the first-tier network. Figures 3 and 4 show that OSSFR gives a better performance, compared to SFR. At a given distance of

Table 2. Simulation parameters

Parameters	Value used
Bandwidth	10 MHz
FDD-LTE	OFDMA
Number of sub-channels	512
Carrier Frequency	800 MHZ
Number of thin walls	4
Sub-carrier Spacing	15 kHz
Radius of the femtocell	30 m
Radius of the MeNB	280 m
CR Threshold	-111.6 dB
Noise Spectral Density	-174 dBm/Hz
Indoor penetration loss	20 dB
FAP TX Power	20 dBm
Number of subcarriers	600
Number of FUEs	4
Antenna Gains	MeNB: 14 dBi, FAP: 5 dBi, Users: 0 dBi
Target SNR	20 dB
Noise spectral density Shadowing standard deviation	Macro: 10 dB, Femto: 4 dB
Modulation	QPSK

0.4 km from the centre-zone (Fig. 4), OSFFR shows 80 % increment in number of free channels while SFFR indicates a 62.5 % increment. In Fig. 6, we note that at higher E_b/N_O, the probability of error reduces for all schemes hence higher data rates for the femtocells in the network. For example at a $E_b/N_O = 9$ dB, we observe a lower probability of error at 10^{-5} for the OSFFR scheme. It can also be observed that SFFR possesses a higher bit error rate performance. This is accounted for by the increased number of sub-channel division it has as compared to FFR 1.

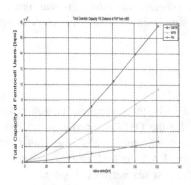

Fig. 3. Total capacity

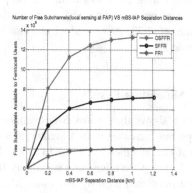

Fig. 4. Number of free channels

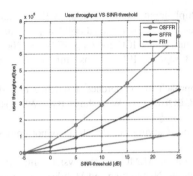

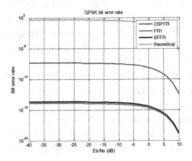

Fig. 5. Throughput performance   **Fig. 6.** BER performance

6 Conclusion

We have compared different cognitive femtocell interference mitigation techniques. Results show that the ICIC schemes offer superior performance to other state-of-the-art interference mitigation schemes. Based on Shannon's energy-bandwidth efficiency relationship, a performance evaluation by means of event driven Monte Carlo simulations was presented, and OSFFR compared with SFFR. The proposed OSFFR scheme achieves the best tradeoff between user capacity, downlink throughput, and number of free channels obtained after local sensing. Furthermore, OSFFR can provide more flexibility, improved BER performance and robustness than the SFFR scheme. Our results demonstrate that the OSFFR radius that maximizes system throughput and the number of free channels obtained after local sensing, is a more efficient mechanism to realize energy savings in cognitive femtocell under heterogeneous LTE–A systems.

References

1. Kebede, G.M., Olayinka, O.: Performance Evaluation of LTE Downlink with MIMO Techniques. (ed.) Blekinge Institute of Technology, Karlskrona, Sweden (2010)
2. Liu, Y., et al.: Deploying cognitive cellular networks under dynamic resource management. IEEE Wirel. Commun. **20**, 82–88 (2013)
3. Haykin, S.: Cognitive radio: brain-empowered wireless communications. IEEE J. Sel. Areas Commun. **23**, 201–220 (2005)
4. Mitola, J.: Cognitive radio architecture evolution. Proc. IEEE **97**, 626–641 (2009)
5. Akyildiz, I.F., et al.: NeXt generation/dynamic spectrum access/cognitive radio wireless networks: a survey. Comput. Netw. **50**, 2127–2159 (2006)
6. Alaya-Feki, A., et al.: Informed spectrum usage in cognitive radio networks: Interference cartography. In: 2008 IEEE 19th International Symposium on Personal, Indoor and Mobile Radio Communications. PIMRC 2008, pp. 1–5 (2008)
7. Chen, Z., et al.: Interference modeling for cognitive radio networks with power or contention control. In: 2010 IEEE Wireless Communications and Networking Conference (WCNC), pp. 1–6 (2010)

8. Soma, P., et al.: Analysis and modeling of multiple-input multiple-output (MIMO) radio channel based on outdoor measurements conducted at 2.5 GHz for fixed BWA applications. In: 2002 IEEE International Conference on Communications. ICC 2002, pp. 272–276 (2002)
9. Verdú, S.: Spectral efficiency in the wideband regime. IEEE Trans. Inf. Theor. **48**, 1319–1343 (2002)
10. Bennis, M., Niyato, D.: A Q-learning based approach to interference avoidance in self-organized femtocell networks. In: 2010 IEEE GLOBECOM Workshops (GC Wkshps), pp. 706–710 (2010)
11. Sen, S., et al.: Successive interference cancellation: Carving out mac layer opportunities. IEEE Trans. Mob. Comput. **12**, 346–357 (2013)
12. He, C., et al.: Co-channel interference mitigation in MIMO-OFDM system. In: 2007 International Conference on Wireless Communications, Networking and Mobile Computing. WiCom 2007, pp. 204–208 (2007)
13. Feng, W.: Intercell interference mitigation based on IDMA. Tsinghua University, Beijing (2007)
14. Nguyen, T.M., et al.: Interference alignment in a Poisson field of MIMO femtocells. IEEE Trans. Wirel. Commun. **12**, 2633–2645 (2013)
15. Gomadam, K., et al.: Approaching the capacity of wireless networks through distributed interference alignment. In: 2008 IEEE Global Telecommunications Conference. IEEE GLOBECOM 2008, pp. 1–6 (2008)
16. Jafar, S.A.: Interference alignment: A new look at signal dimensions in a communication network. Now Publishers Inc., Hanover (2011)
17. Saquib, N., et al.: Fractional frequency reuse for interference management in LTE-Advanced HetNets. IEEE Wirel. Commun. **20**, 113–122 (2013)

Inclusive Ubiquitous Access - A Status Report

Amos Nungu[1](✉), Robert Olsson[2], Björn Pehrson[2], Jiawei Kang[2],
Daniel Kifetew[2], and Alisher Rustamov[2]

[1] Dar Es Salaam Institute of Technology (DIT), P.O. Box 2958,
Dar Es Salaam, Tanzania
amosnungu@dit.ac.tz
[2] Royal Institute of Technology (KTH), KTH/ICT/TSLab,
Forum 120, 164 40 Kista, Sweden

Abstract. The development towards ubiquitous network access requires innovative solutions to get remote areas included, especially rural areas of developing regions. We report on recent progress in the Serengeti Broadband Network, one of the first pilots established in the Tanzania ICT for Rural Development programme with the mission to design and validate a method to establish sustainable broadband markets in under-served areas. The challenges include ownership and leadership, sustainable business models, robustness of network components and poor or non-existent supply chains, including power supply.

1 Introduction

We report on experiences and results from the Serengeti Broadband Network (SBN) established in the Tanzania ICT for Rural Development (ICT4RD) programme [1, 2]. The mission of the programme is to design and validate a reproducible and scalable method to establish sustainable broadband markets in areas with demand but no supply of services. The method involves local communities in demand-driven first mile social business initiatives in order to speed up the deployment of commercial last mile connectivity [3]. The method aims at reducing all sorts of risks by demonstrating feasibility and start building local supply-chains. While everybody is invited to use the network and contribute to the running costs, the strategy to facilitate infrastructure investments is to primarily target basic public services prioritized in regional, national and local strategies, such as healthcare, education and local administration, including environment monitoring, climate change adaption, support to local entrepreneurs, etc. These services are taken as the starting point for iterative pre-commercial procurements in which local government specifies needs and requirements and issues calls for tenders, including invitations to form time-limited public private partnerships regarding services that cannot yet be considered commercially available and need to be developed before a next procurement. Since local communities often lack the competence and experience necessary to initiate and drive this process, they need to team up with independent advisers that can also facilitate capacity building. The method tested in the ICT4RD program is to use

© Institute for Computer Sciences, Social Informatics and Telecommunications Engineering 2015
A. Nungu et al. (Eds.): AFRICOMM 2014, LNICST 147, pp. 13–22, 2015.
DOI: 10.1007/978-3-319-16886-9_2

local research and higher education institutions, such as universities or colleges, as such advisers, since they are clearly independent, can engage senior students that soon are available on the labor market and can easily themselves get support from more resourceful peers at a global level, e.g. via the recently formed Technology Transfer Alliance of universities facilitating involvement of their faculty members and students in development cooperation projects for academic credit. SBN is an example of a network designed and deployed by PhD and senior MSc students in cooperation with other stakeholders. Their work also includes deployment of services, evaluation of usage, etc. There are efforts to take the lessons from the ICT4RD project in Tanzania to extend it to neighbouring countries under the African Great Lakes Rural Broadband Infrastructure (AGLARBRI) proposal [4].

The challenges include, on the business side, ownership and leadership issues, sustainable business models, awareness of the benefits of ICT, especially regarding local communication needs vs Internet access, how to combine a top-down and a bottom-up approach and lack of confidence in the community caused by the "consultant knows everything" syndrome [5]. On the technical side, the main challenges are robustness of network components, poor or non-existent power supply [6, 7] and lack of trained human resources and financial resources to organise efficient network and service maintenance. There is also a lack of experience from how to organize pre-commercial procurements and public private-partnerships among stakeholders [8].

Positive developments include District Commissioners in both districts who are interested and supportive of ICT issues, and an increasing availability of data communication services provided by mobile operators. There are still, however, needs for services that the mobile networks cannot provide, which motivate further development of demand-driven inclusive ubiquitous access approach.

2 Background

The SBN backbone uses an optical fibre cable deployed in the medium-voltage power line between the capitals of the Bunda and Serengeti districts in northern Tanzania and includes a node in the Nata village between the capitals. SBN implements an IP-network on top of 1 Gbps Ethernet links. Initially, SBN was implemented as a single switched Ethernet as a proof of concept regarding transmission and applications. To make the network more scalable from a traffic aspect and sustainable from a power supply aspect, the backbone switches are being replaced by low-power routers. Two switches have been replaced by 12VDC routers consuming considerably less power than average routers of comparable performance. These routers are based on open source software and commercial off-the-shelf hardware components, selected to provide ISP-grade quality and the highest possible number of packets routed per energy unit (J) at a power level (W) low enough to facilitate the use of renewable sources. The routers have an integrated power management system accepting power from any 12–24 V power source, controlling the charging of a backup battery as well as the operation of

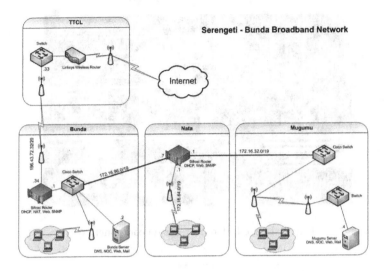

Fig. 1. Serengeti broadband network topology

the load to facilitate graceful shut-down when no power is available. The integration is part of our research aiming at extending the digital system architectures to include a power supply bus connected to a micro-grid with power sources, storage and loads in which energy can be routed on a demand and supply basis. Recently, the low-power routers were complemented with solar cells and a wireless sensor network measuring insolation, temperature and wind data. SBN end users are so far all connected via wireless links (WiFi). First mile fibre links are being discussed [2]. There are some 130 users connected, 100 in Bunda and 30 in Serengeti, including some local companies. The current network topology is shown in Fig. 1.

3   The System Improvements

Recently, new solar-powered routers with built-in power controller were introduced [6]. Three senior M.Sc. students were engaged in upgrading the SBN network and setting up Network Operating Centres (NOC) at DIT and KTH.

3.1   Deploying Low Power Hardware

The changes and additions introduced to the new low-power router include:

- *Modified cooling system:* Unlike the previous version, the new one has no active cooling components (fans). Cooling is done using heatsinks adherent to the top cover as shown in Fig. 2. This contributes to the reduction of power requirements and eliminate needs due to fan problems.
- *Improved charge controller:* The new router is capable of connecting two complementing power sources, e.g. solar panel and AC-adapter.

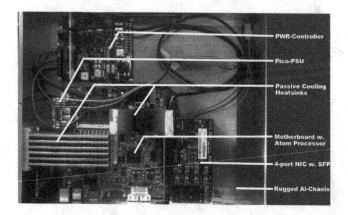

Fig. 2. Low-effect router, inside components

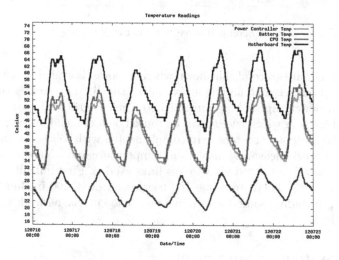

Fig. 3. Temperature reading, 7 days at Nata

– *Router Statistics:* Digital Optical Monitoring (DOM) statistics, including optical output and input power, laser, temperature and bias current can be collected from the optical transceivers in real-time. This facilitates troubleshooting optical communications and fibre status.

  Given the harsh environmental conditions where the equipment is installed, it is important to monitor temperatures to prevent overheating that may damage and shorten the life of all electronic components as well as of back up batteries. Temperature is read from the charge controller, sensors are installed near the battery, in the router chassis, outdoors and from the motherboard and CPU using IPMI, see Fig. 3.

3.2   Alternative Power Sources

In Bunda, a maintenance free battery with a capacity of providing 12 v/100 Ah is used as a backup power source for the router. The battery is charged by the main power supply grid and serves as a backup power source during a blackout or power disruption. In Nata, two lead acid batteries are used as a backup power sources. A 65 W solar panel and an AC-adapter are used to charge these batteries.

3.3   Power Controller

The power controller works as a battery charge and discharge manager. It controls the charging of the battery from the input sources, AC-adapter and solar panel, and concurrently regulates the power supply to the router. When there is no input power, typically in case of failure of the power grid and solar power it not available, the battery will supply power to the router until the power sources are back or a Low Voltage Disconnect (LVD) limit is reached. In the latter case, the load (router) is disconnected in order to protect the battery from being fully discharged, which would shorten is lifetime. To facilitate parameter setting, monitoring, data collection and debugging, the power controller can be reached via a USB connection to the router.

Figure 4 shows the data collected via the power controller over a period of 24 h. The yellow line illustrates the battery current. It is positive when the battery is being charged and negative when the battery is being discharged. Between 18:45 to 21:10, there is no power from the AC-adapter or the solar panel and the router/load is then powered from the battery as is illustrated by the battery current going negative.

When the power sources are available, the power controller adjusts the battery voltage to "floating voltage" (approximately 13.5 V). The charging algorithm periodically boosts the voltage to approximately 14.5 V to prevent sulfurization. This is indicated with red line. When the boost threshold is reached, the charge voltage is decreased to the floating value, The battery current changes to small negative periodically. The green line shows the low disconnect voltage (12 V). To prolong the lifetime of the battery, the float and boost voltages are temperature compensated based on readings from a dedicated temperature sensor.

3.4   The Backoffice Network Operations Center

To support the local administrators with monitoring and troubleshooting, back-office NOCs are set up at DIT and KTH. The web-based network management tools, Nagios and Cacti are used for monitoring. Wifi access points, routers, switches and server operation statuses are monitored by Nagios, which is installed in both the Bunda and Serengeti Servers. Nata and Bunda routers are also connected to Cacti that uses RRD tool for data logging. It allows for alerting and data graph access in case any routers become inaccessible. Data is being collected via the industry standard SNMP protocol as well as via scripts pulling data from the routers every 5 min. Collected data is being plotted in graphs that

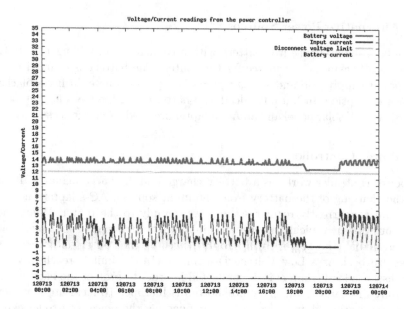

Fig. 4. 24 h data readings from the power controller (Color figure online)

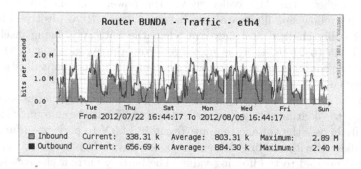

Fig. 5. Eth4 bandwidth utilization - Bunda router

are available in daily, weekly, hourly and yearly formats. Graphs being plotted include traffic information per each active interface, CPU usage, memory usage, temperature and charge controller stats. Figure 5 is an example illustrating the bandwidth utilization from the eth4 interface on the Bunda router.

3.5 Environment Monitoring via Wireless Sensor Networks

Some of the SBN routers have been instrumented for data collection via Wireless Sensor Networks (WSN) to gather site and environmental data. This is an experimental set-up to gain experiences and test equipment. In total five sensors are installed, three at DIT and two in the Bunda power station.

A WSN sink mote is connected to the router via USB collecting data from all the motes in the WSN network. Data fields are tagged and all data are

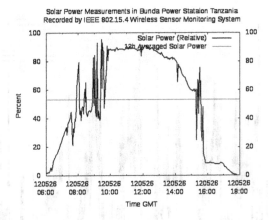

Fig. 6. Solar power measurement in bunda

sent and stored in ASCII format on the router. This WSN implements RIME [9], a broadcast scheme forming a simple auto-configured topology. The data is collected and directly made available via web access as raw data. In some cases plot and graphs are processed directly for instant analysis and monitoring. In Bunda, an insolation solar power meter is tested. This is a low budget solar power meter based on a small photo-voltaic (PV) solar panel loaded with a 50 Ohm resistor to report power via a WSN mote. The mote is reporting the voltage over the resistor. Another PV solar panel is powering and charging two NiMh AAA batteries to power the mote.

Our insolation measurements, Fig. 6 indicate a 12 h average about 50 % of the nominal solar panel power. A 1 kW panel would thus produce 0.5 kWh/h, 6 kWh/day, 2190 kWh/year. As a comparison, 800 kWh/year has been reported for Stockholm. With more data we will get the variation over time, which will affect the dimensions of the solar panel and battery back-up for a 24 h system.

At DIT, temperatures and relative humidity are collected from the Server room and selected offices. Sensors for measuring soil moisture is tested in collaboration with Swedish University of Agricultural Sciences (SLU).

3.6 The Applications

Both Bunda District (www.bunda.go.tz) and Serengeti District (www.serengeti.go.tz) websites are based on Content Management Systems (CMS) to provide information from district government, blogs and news feeds. Mail services were implemented in Bunda and Serengeti severs using open source applications (Postfix, Dovecot, Squirrel-Mail and Postfix Admin) to overcome the shortcoming of slow and unreliable Internet access. Sending and receiving emails within the local area network is more efficient.

Drug Management Application. A Drug Management Application (DMA) was designed and is about to be field tested. The objective is to minimize delays

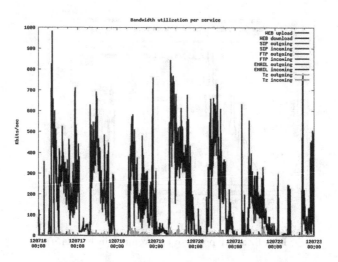

Fig. 7. Traffic utilization, 7 days in Bunda

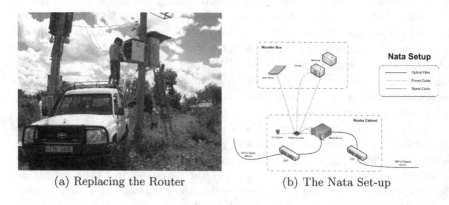

(a) Replacing the Router   (b) The Nata Set-up

Fig. 8. Installations in Nata (a) and (b)

in the logistic chain involving stock-taking, ordering and delivery of medical drugs to get a better balance between demand and supply of drugs. Orders can be sent to a drug distribution centre via a client-server application that runs on computers or android tablets or phones via HTTP or SMS. The application is expected to significantly improve current drug distribution process within local hospitals and healthcare centres. Tests on site regarding the technical aspects have been concluded successfully. Local authorities involved in the drug distribution chain are involved in the planning of a field test with end-users.

Traffic Statistics. Traffic statistics is being collected in both the Bunda and Nata routers via an iptables rule filtering out data in the following categories:

Tanzania: traffic destined to/from IPs allocated to Tanzania; Web: traffic to/from ports 80, 8080, 443; SIP: traffic to/from ports 5060–5070; FTP: traffic to/from ports 20, 21; and Email: traffic to/from ports 25, 110, 143, 587, 993, 995

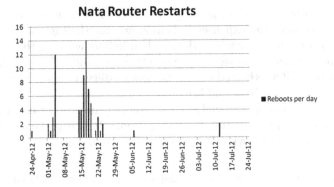

Fig. 9. Number of restarts per day

As seen in Fig. 7, the major part of the bandwidth is used by web applications. Note that the Bunda router is the Ingress and Egress point for Both Nata and Mugumu distribution points.

In order to reduce the bandwidth consumption, Squid is implemented as a proxy server in Bunda, so that webpage content is cached in the server and useless information such as advertisement and access to bad sites are blocked. Also, the proxy server facilitates collection of more traffic for further analysis.

4 Discussion

The current phase of the ICT4RD efforts has brought significant improvements in the availability, reliability and accessibility of SBN and the end-user services. Technically, the main improvements include more efficient monitoring and management due to the data collection and the support of the back-office NOCs. Stable power supply/backup is another major improvement. The combined performance of the deployed low power hardware, alternative power source and power controller is being evaluated based on the number of restarts happened per day before and after the new set up has been put in place, Fig. 8.

Figure 9 shows the number of restarts that have occurred on the router at the Nata station in the past three months. The router had restarted more frequently, even reaching up to fourteen times per day, in May, before the new set up was put in place. The number of restarts has significantly reduced in the next months, as a result of improved power management.

The network up-time has increased leading to a more reliable and dependable infrastructure. Note that, though most of the restarts was due to power disruption, some of the restarts are accounted for maintenance.

5 Conclusion and Future Plans

Still there are many challenges, both technical and non-technical in maintaining the network. The challenges range from decentralized management, awareness, hardware failures to power supply issues.

The decentralized management sometimes makes it difficult to have a common vision especially since the expenses in Bunda are not the same as in Mugumu. There are many connected users in Bunda than in Serengeti, on the other hand, there are more running expenses in Serengeti than in Bunda. Bunda don't pay for electricity as their NOC is hosted within the power utility company while Serengeti must pay for two nodes: Nata and Mugumu.

Device failure is another crucial issue as replacements are not easily available. There is no store/supplier within or nearby towns. It is necessary to have own stock to avoid long delays when there is a device breakdown.

Acknowledgement. We acknowledge support from Costech, LiTECH, SPIDER, Tanesco and other important stakeholders.

References

1. Information and Communication Technology for Rural Development (ICT4RD) Tanzania. http://www.ict4rd.ne.tz/
2. Nungu, A.: Towards sustainable broadband communication in under-served areas: a case study from Tanzania. Ph.D. Thesis. KTH, Stockholm (2011)
3. Pehrson, B., et al.: A First Mile Initiative, presented at UN Broadband Commission Working Group on Broadband and Science, Paris, France (2011)
4. Kahiigi, P., Kariuki, E., Kyalo, V., Masinde, M., Ngarambe, D., Nungu, A., Sansa-Otim, J., Pehrson, B.: African great lakes rural broadband research infrastructure. In: IST-Africa Conference (2012)
5. Nungu, A., Brown, T., Pehrson, B.: Challenges in sustaining municipal broadband networks in the developing world. In: Yonazi, J.J., Sedoyeka, E., Ariwa, E., El-Qawasmeh, E. (eds.) ICeND 2011. CCIS, vol. 171, pp. 26–40. Springer, Heidelberg (2011)
6. Nungu, A., Olsson R., Pehrson, B.: On powering communication networks in developing regions. In: Proceedings of the 16th IEEE Symposium on Computers and Communications (IEEE ISCC), Kerkyra (Corfu), Greece (2011)
7. Nungu, A., Olsson, R., Pehrson, B.: On the design of inclusive ubiquitous access. In: Proceedings of the Third International Conference on Ubiquitous and Future Networks (IEEE ICUFN), Dalian, China (2011). Received excellent paper award, extended version to be published in journal of wireless personal communication (2012)
8. Ngowi, H.P.: Public-Private-Partnership (PPP) in the management of municipalities in Tanzania issues and lessons of experience. Afr. J. Public Adm. Manag. **XVII**, 1–18 (2006)
9. Dunkels, A: Rime - a lightweight layered communication stack for sensor networks. In: Proceedings of the European Conference on Wireless Sensor Networks (EWSN), Poster/Demo session, Delft, The Netherlands (2007)

Performance Evaluation of Scheduling Algorithms in Fixed WiMAX Network

Okus Paul$^{(\boxtimes)}$, Karim Djouani, Anish Kurien, and Thomas Olwal

French South African Institute of Technology (F'SATI), Tshwane University of Technology (TUT), Private Bag X680, Pretoria 0001, South Africa
pauloo213.okus@gmail.com,
{djouanik,kurienam,olwalto}@tut.ac.za

Abstract. Scheduling Algorithm performance in Worldwide Interoperability for Microwave Access Network (WiMAX) or IEEE802.16 promotes a huge success due to its current availability in the network, providing multiple and high rate capabilities. However, several algorithms have been proposed and designed, in order to achieve high quality of service (QoS) in the network. Not all can be selected to implement in real WiMAX, rather a need to know and choose the best ones for real WiMAX development. In order to do this, the study employs simulation scenario of considered different scheduling algorithms in order to measure their performances such as the loss rate. Their behaviours are investigated using MATLAB simulation tool and the results are compared. The end to end loss rate experienced with all the considered algorithm is high compared to International Telecommunication Union (ITU) standard. Our contribution is to minimize and improve the Algorithms as a result of the shortcomings experienced. The number of channels created in this layer to reduce the end to end loss rate is realized using the Reconfigurable Optical add-drop Multiplexer (ROADM) technique in the MAC layer. This is because MAC layer supports data communication and routing. This technique generate channels, controls and monitors flow rate of data in the MAC layer using a mathematical model to reduce the loss rate in the network. The results achieved from the qualitative analysis show that the performance of the improved algorithm is accomplished as result of low loss rate as a result of increasing the number of channels in the MAC layer. High throughput is attained due to high flow rate of real time application and more so, fair sharing of resources is achieved in different scenarios with different times and sizes.

Keywords: IEEE 802.16d · QoS · Throughput · Scheduling algorithms

1 Introduction

WiMAX also known as IEEE 802.16 is the future of wireless technology designed to provide fast mobile Internet access to the rural and urban areas. It is a wireless broadband technology which allows Point-to-Multi Point (PMP) broadband wireless access [1]. This application request can be variable for resources and dormancy requirements. Therefore, 802.16 are required to be dynamic for a variety of different traffic models. Base Station (BS) supports a lot of parallel connections and judgments are required to be completed within WiMAX frame time [2], the scheduling algorithms must be easy,

© Institute for Computer Sciences, Social Informatics and Telecommunications Engineering 2015
A. Nungu et al. (Eds.): AFRICOMM 2014, LNICST 147, pp. 23–31, 2015.
DOI: 10.1007/978-3-319-16886-9_3

speedy and use least resources as memory. The similar condition is also applicable to Subscriber Stations (SSs) [2, 3].

Currently, available uplink (UL) and downlink (DL) scheduling schemes at Subscriber Stations (SSs) in WiMAX experience resource wastage and high access delay for the different present service flows in WiMAX [4]. Scheduling algorithms are of utmost importance in WiMAX network for the efficient use of radio resources. The scheduling algorithm has to determine the allocation of bandwidth among the users and their transmission order. One of the most important tasks of the scheduling algorithm is to satisfy the QoS and enhance the QoS requirements of its users while efficiently utilizing the radio resources and available bandwidth. The Scheduling algorithms designed and discussed are Strict Priority (PQ), Round Robin (RR), Weighted Round Robin (WRR), Weighted Fair Queuing (WFQ), Modified Weighted Round Robin (MWRR) and Modified Deficit Round Robin (MDRR).

There have been a lot of research going on the designing of an efficient scheduling algorithm [5] for the optimized usage of the resources, but mostly are not capable to utilize resources with low computational overheads.

Thus, this paper focuses on improving and modifying scheduling algorithms, which will highly optimize the usage of the resources in WiMAX networks which will be computationally simple. In this paper, performance of existing scheduling algorithms for IEEE 802.16 networks applicable for SSs are evaluated quantitatively and qualitatively. We evaluated the performance of various scheduling algorithms quantitatively and the best performed algorithms are further evaluated qualitatively.

In this work, our contribution is to improve the one of the best performed algorithms so as to be used in other networks a part from a fixed WiMAX network. Due to the end to end loss of packets in the network, there is a need to improve the loss experienced as a result of congestion. This is carried out by increasing the number of channel in MAC layer using the ROADM technique in order to reduce the end to end loss rate and by evaluating performances using MATLAB simulation tool. It is revealed that the loss rate and complexity experienced according to the International Telecommunication Union (ITU) standard during measurement are high and as a result the QoS expected is not achieved. We also improve the loss and compare the performance of the modified and existing algorithms. The objectives of our study also extend towards reducing the time consumption during the transmission of resources in the queue and as well as minimizing shortage of resources in the network. The rest of the paper is organized as follows. In Sect. 2, the related works are discussed and described. The design and modeling of improved scheduling algorithms are presented in Sect. 3, Sect. 4 shows the simulation results, comparison of the improved and existing scheduling algorithms and finally, Sect. 5 concludes the paper.

2   Related Work

Gakuba et al. [1] put forward a MDRR-based (Modified Deficit Round Robin) scheduling algorithm to maintain QoS requirements among heterogeneous traffic. The study is limited to performance and comparison of the enhanced MDRR-based algorithm with the existing MDRR algorithm measured in throughput in an evenly-distributed and mixed traffic scenario in a single channel. Chung-Hsien et al. [6] investigated the performance of the MCDRR scheduling algorithm for a multi-channel link with tunable transmitters and fixed receivers, using the DRR and also considering the single-channel scheduling algorithm. In this work, the DRR is extended to the case of multi-channel scheduling to efficiently utilize the network resources (i.e., channels and tunable transmitters) by overlapping rounds, while maintaining its low complexity (i.e., $O(1)$). The nearly perfect fairness result achieved in MCDRR which has not thoroughly proven the behavior of this proposed algorithm.

Chih-Wei et al. [5] proposes the channel awareness and cross-layer cooperation between physical and MAC layers and have been extensively debated in radio environments, like either cellular systems or generic wireless systems. However, despite the wide literature on interesting proposals for WiMAX uplink and downlink scheduling, aspects related to the effect of impairments in the radio channel on WiMAX scheduling are not sufficiently stressed. This study is focused on the performance of different algorithms on a single channel and the performance of the algorithms considered could not be fully accepted based on standard.

Sleem et al. [7] focused on the channel aware scheduling algorithms and modifications for RR (Round Robin), WRR (Weighted Round Robin) and DRR (Deficit Round Robin) scheduling algorithms and detailed simulations study are performed. Analysis and evaluation of the performance of each scheduling algorithms to support the different QoS classes were performed. The simulation results show that the purposed channel aware modified DRR scheduler can provide higher service standards to support the QoS in terms of packet loss ratio and bounded delay, which is required by different types of traffic in a time varying channel which is limited to single channel.

Andrews et al. [3] proposed new scheduling algorithm for IEEE 802.16 Broadband wireless Metropolitan Area Networks in TDD mode. The proposed algorithm focuses on an efficient mechanism to serve high priority traffic in congested networks. A detailed simulation study is carried out for the proposed scheduling algorithm and its performance has been compared with some known algorithms such as Proportional Fairness (PF), Adaptive Proportional Fairness (APF) and Round Robin (RR). For performance evaluation and comparison with existing algorithms, we used OPNET 14.5 modeler simulator. The results show that the proposed algorithm is capable of dealing with different users' requirements under congestion conditions. However, in this study, the performance of the existing scheduling algorithms have not been carried out to meet the requirements according to ITU standard. Hence, we envisaged to evaluate the performance of the existing scheduling algorithms quantitatively and qualitatively. The results are compared. This study is done to know the best performed algorithm to use and also improved the algorithm to meet the requirements for Mobile WiMAX Networks standard as required.

3   QoS-Based Scheduling Algorithms

In this section, a quantitative work is considered on the scheduling algorithms using various metrics and results are recorded for further study. More so, in other to realize scope of the study, the qualitative effort is carried out to describe the behaviours of scheduling algorithms such as Weighted Fair Queuing (WFQ), Modified Weighted Round Robin (MWRR) and Modified Deficit Round Robin (MDRR) and result shows that Modified Deficit Round Robin (MDRR) performed better than the other scheduling algorithms using the end to end loss rate, end to end delay and throughput as the parameters to achieve the results. The results simulated in MATLAB environment shows that MDRR has low loss rate, low end to end delay and high throughput based on the ITU standard.

Our contribution in this study is evaluate the performance of the existing scheduling algorithms and the performance of MDRR. We consider to reduce the end to end loss rate of MDRR so as to be used in Mobile WiMAX Networks.

In other to achieve this, we envisage that number of channels in the MAC layer is increased using the ROADM techniques which is designed using a mathematical model. This technique creates, controls and monitors the flow of data in the channel of inside the MAC layer and ensure that no congestion occurs that lead to delay during transmission. The following features of ROADM is as stated below

- Add new channels and monitors the existing channels, it decides on how to provide service to flows depending on their channel conditions.
- A compensation technique and Prioritization of real time applications in other to make the BS aware of the channel state as well as to avoid losing high sensitive packets in a bad channel.
- Separate per-class packet queues used to support rtPS, UGS, nrtPS, and BE traffic flows.

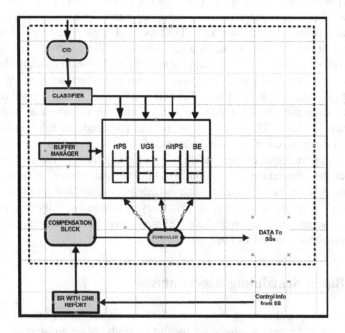

Fig. 1. Scheduling design in fixed WiMAX base station

In order to accomplish our aim, the MAC layer protocol is restructured using the ROADM technique embedded in the modified scheduling algorithms and implemented in the MAC layer of Fixed WiMAX Network. The design is achieved in a way such that as more resources are transmitted in the network, channels are created to avoid congestion or delay that lead to loss and this guarantees QoS and per-flow resource assignment. The Flow-level resources are controlled through the management of per-class queues according to the Frame based Scheduling Algorithm, which is enhanced with a per-flow channel error compensation and ROAM technique in the MAC layer.

The ultimate aim of the algorithms are to provide, in any channel condition, the target QoS in terms of high throughput and reduced packet loss to each WiMAX service class, while achieving fairness in the treatment of traffic flows belonging to the same class as described in the Fig. 1 below:

4 Simulation Setup and Results of Scheduling Algorithms

In this section, the quantitative analysis is accomplished from the result of the existing carried out by previous researchers using the following performance metrics and simulation parameters. The qualitative study is attained in the MATLAB environment using end to end delay, end to end loss and throughput performance metrics to examine the behaviours of the algorithms in Fixed WiMAX Network. Based on the simulation arrangement, MDRR performs than the other algorithms and this tend to improving MDRR scheduling algorithm by minimizing the end to end loss rate during transmission. The reduction in the loss rate is realized by the broad simulation for the Multi-channel scheduling algorithms is conducted by using MATLAB. In the simulation, an IEEE 802.16d WMAN-OFDM network composed of one BS and up to 50 SSs with Rayleigh flat fading channel is configured. The simulation parameters are given in Table 1. The simulations had been repeated over 400 times with different random seeds and the average value was calculated. The assumptions employed in simulations are:

Table 1. Simulation parameters

SIMULATION PARAMETERS	VALUES
FREQUENCY BAND	3.5 GHz
CH. FADING MODEL	RAYLEIGH
Tx POWER	15 dBm
DUPLEX MODE	TDD
DATA RATE	10 MHz
MAC FRAME DURATION	5 ms
UL SUBFRAME DURATION	2.5 ms
UGS TRAFFIC MODEL	CBR
rtPS TRAFFIC MODEL	VBR
nrtPS TRAFFIC MODEL	VBR
BE TRAFFIC MODEL	VBR

A1: The wireless channel quality of each connection remains constant on a per-frame basis; that is, the BS assumes that the report sent by the SS at the frame beginning is valid for the entire duration of the subsequent frame. The channel quality is allowed to vary from frame to another. This corresponds to a block-fading channel model, which is suitable for slowly varying wireless channels: Perfect channel state information is available at the BS, i.e., CINR reports are correctly received.

The outcome justification presented work is validated via the comparison with the previous published work in [8]. In [7, 8], performance evaluation of scheduling algorithms are carried out as discussed above and Modified Deficit Round Robin and results shows that during evaluation, MDRR scheduling algorithms outperforms other algorithms by 95 % at end to end loss rate, end to end delay and throughput. Based on the result reached, the downlink scheduler implementation in WiMAX has supported WiMAX QoS by providing each QoS class average delay value as it should be.

Figure 4 shows the loss of rtPS traffic class experienced is low compared to other classes. This is because of the prioritization and multichannel which results high flow rate of data. Hence, low loss rate experienced as users increased.

The performed simulation aimed to show the importance of Multi-channelization in Fixed WiMAX network as well as on the scheduler performance. The following parameter monitored is the loss. Loss indicates the ratio of both packets that missed their deadlines and also packets that discarded due to the queue size.

The results in Fig. 5 show the loss rate by varying the buffer size for the scheduler. The rtPS traffic class achieves the minimum loss among other traffic classes. This is because rtPS is variable bit rate (VBR) and its high demand from the end users and as a result, emphasis is laid on it to reduce loss experienced by increasing the channel to increase the flow rate and as a result high throughput is attained as shown in Fig. 5 below.

Results show that Multi-channel MDRR achieves the minimum loss rate than the existing MDRR (Figs. 2 and 3).

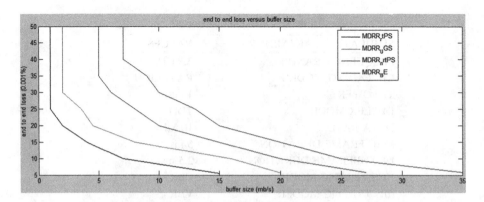

Fig. 2. Loss rate versus buffer sizes for MDRR

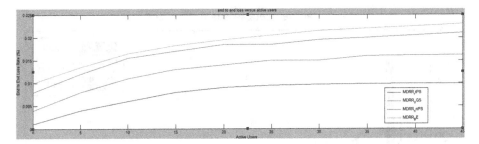

Fig. 3. Loss rate versus active users for MDRR

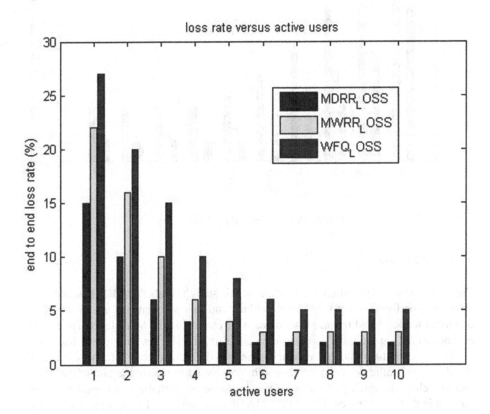

Fig. 4. Loss rate versus active users

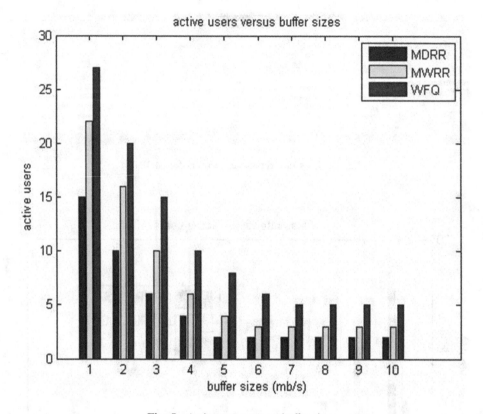

Fig. 5. Active users versus buffer sizes

5 Conclusion

The performance of scheduling algorithms in this study reveals that MDRR scheduling algorithms performs better than the algorithms and its improvements as our contribution using the ROADM technique to increase the channel in the MAC layer. The results enhance to reduce the error compensation coupled with the low end to end loss rate.

More so, for the purpose of enhancing the QoS differentiation and fairness in uplink and downlink traffic delivery, the algorithm considered to realize the aim of the study and as well as the quality of service (QoS) in the network traffic is achieved based on the standard. The improved Scheduling Algorithms feature is of extreme importance in Fixed WiMAX architectures point-to-multipoint.

We validated the opportunity of redesigning the MAC and introducing a Multi-channel scheduler with compensation and ROADM mechanism that dynamically increases channels and reassigns resources virtually allocated by the error-free scheduler to each traffic flow according to the knowledge of the channel status. The followed approach proved to be effective, and a set of encouraging simulation results witness the positive effect the transmission of Fixed WiMAX traffic can be derive from its adoption under non-ideal channel conditions.

P Okus: received a B.Tech degree in Computer Engineering at Ladoke Akintola University of Technology (LAUTECH) in Nigeria. He is currently pursuing an M'Tech degree in Telecommunication Engineering at Tshwane University of Technology (TUT) South Africa.

His research interest is on Performance Evaluation of Scheduling Algorithms in Fixed (IEEE 802.16d) WiMAX Networks.

References

1. Kumar, B., Gupta, P.: Scheduling algorithms in a WiMAX network. In: 2012 Second International Conference on Advanced Computing & Communication Technologies (ACCT), pp. 457–462 (2012)
2. Gakuba, M., Mjumo, M., Kurien, A.M.: An enhanced WiMAX scheduling algorithm for QoS guaranteed. In: Southern Africa Telecommunication Networks and Applications Conference (SATNAC) 2009, 30 August– 02 September 2009, Royal Swazi Spa, Ezulwini, Swaziland
3. Andrews, M., Zhang, L.: Scheduling algorithms for multicarrier wireless data systems. IEEE/ACM Trans. Netw. **19**(2), 447–455 (2011)
4. Haghani, E., Ansari, N.: VoIP traffic scheduling in WiMAX networks. In: Global Telecommunications Conference on 2008, IEEE GLOBECOM 2008. IEEE (2008)
5. Fu-Min, C., Chih-Yu, W., Shang-Juh, K.: A Slot-based BS scheduling with Maximum Latency Guarantee and Capacity First in 802.16e networks. In: 2010 40th International Conference on Computers and Industrial Engineering (CIE) (2010)
6. Chih-Wei, H., Shiang-Ming, H.: OLM: opportunistic layered multicasting for scalable IPTV over mobile WiMAX. IEEE Trans. Mob. Comput. **11**(3), 453–463 (2012)
7. Chung-Hsien, H., Kai-Ten, F.: Predictive interference-based scheduling mechanism for direct communications in IEEE 802.16 networks. In: Wireless Communications and Networking Conference (WCNC), 2012 IEEE (2012)
8. Sleem, M.Y., ElBadawy, H.M.: Two layer channel aware scheduling for QoS support in IEEE 802.16/WiMAX networks. In: 2011 Eighth International Conference on Wireless and Optical Communications Networks (WOCN) (2011)
9. Xu, L., Xiaosong, Y.: Resource scheduling and congestion control for WMN. In: 2009 IEEE International Conference on Communications Technology and Applications, ICCTA 2009 (2009)
10. Jakimoski, K., Janevski, T.: Priority based uplink scheduling scheme for WiMAX service classes. Int. J. Inf. Technol. Comput. Sci. (IJITCS) **5**, 66 (2013)

Enhancing Performance in Cognitive Radio Networks

Roseline Nyongarwizi Akol[(⊠)] and Solomon Muhumuza

Department of Electrical and Computer Engineering, CEDAT,
Makerere University, P.O. Box 7062, Kampala, Uganda
rnakol@cedat.mak.ac.ug, muhumuzasol@gmail.com

Abstract. Cognitive radio (CR) has been fronted as technology for spectrum sharing. For a CR to work efficiently and effectively, the secondary user (SU) should without any reasonable doubt detect the presence or the absence of the primary user (PU). Therefore, spectrum sensing is core to the performance of cognitive radio networks and it is shown in this paper that deploying multiple input multiple output (MIMO) at the SU, improves the performance. In addition, this paper deploys multi-slots and cooperative spectrum sensing to enhance detection in CR networks. Results show that the probability of detection increases while the probability of false alarm decreases for a MIMO implementation. An overall performance improvement in the network throughput is realized by increasing the number of antennas, sensing time slots and the number of users.

Keywords: Cognitive radio · Spectrum sensing · MIMO · Multi-slots spectrum sensing · Cooperative sensing

1 Introduction

Cognitive radio (CR) has emerged as a promising technology to enable the access of the intermittent periods of unoccupied frequency bands, called white spaces or spectrum holes, and thereby increase the spectral efficiency [1–3]. The fundamental task of each CR user in CR networks, in the most primitive sense, is to detect the licensed users, also known as primary users (PUs), if they are present and identify the available spectrum if they are absent [5]. This is usually achieved by sensing the RF environment, a process called spectrum sensing [6, 13]. There are two main objectives of spectrum sensing include: Firstly, CR users should not cause harmful interference to PUs by either switching to an available band or limiting its interference with PUs at an acceptable level. Secondly, CR users should efficiently identify and exploit the spectrum holes for required throughput and quality of service [3]. Thus, the detection performance in spectrum sensing is crucial to the performance of the CR networks.

The detection performance can be primarily determined on the basis of two metrics: (1) probability of false alarm, which denotes the probability of a CR user declaring that a PU is present when the spectrum is actually free, and (2) probability of detection, which denotes the probability of a CR user declaring that a PU is present when the spectrum is indeed occupied by the PU [2, 3, 6]. Since a miss in the detection will cause

© Institute for Computer Sciences, Social Informatics and Telecommunications Engineering 2015
A. Nungu et al. (Eds.): AFRICOMM 2014, LNICST 147, pp. 32–42, 2015.
DOI: 10.1007/978-3-319-16886-9_4

interference with the PU and a false alarm will reduce the spectral efficiency, it is usually required for optimal detection performance that the probability of detection is maximized subject to the constraint of the probability of false alarm [3, 6].

Many factors in practice such as multipath fading, shadowing, and the receiver uncertainty problem may significantly compromise the detection performance in spectrum sensing. The main idea of introducing MIMO in cognitive radio networks is to enhance the spectrum sensing performance by exploiting the spatial diversity in the observation of the primary signal [4, 6–9]. Also demonstrated in the literature, use of multiple time slots and cooperation from several secondary users for sensing can greatly improve the probability of detection and false alarm [10].

In this paper, we combine the use of multiple antennas for the cognitive radio user, multiple time sensing slots and cooperation during the detection process. Simulation results show that there is a tremendous performance improvement as number of antennas, sensing time slots and cognitive radio users' increase.

The remainder of this paper is organized as follows: Sect. 2 presents the system model illustrating how MIMO technique and multiple time slots are used for spectrum sensing in cognitive radio. In Sect. 3, the analytical model, outlining how MIMO, multiple time slot and cooperative spectrum sensing are combined is presented. Simulation results are presented in Sect. 4 and a conclusion drawn in Sect. 5.

2 System Model

Assume a system model where the primary transmitter P_{TX} relays information to the primary receiver P_{RX} through a mobile channel h_r. The secondary or cognitive radio user employs several transmit and receive antennas as demonstrated in the Fig. 1. The channel from the PU to the SU is a multiple channel $h_1, h_2, \ldots\ldots, h_M$, where M is the total number of transmit antennas. Due to the practical constraint on the distances between antennas to ensure independent fading, we mainly considered a case where SUs are equipped with two transmit antennas and in some cases up to a maximum of four transmit antennas. Note that during sensing time, the primary transmitter behaves as a receiver. Therefore, the SU detects the presence or absence of the PU under the following conditions respectively

$$H_1 : X(n) = S(n) + W(N) \tag{1}$$

$$H_0 : X(n) = W(n) \tag{2}$$

where $X(n)$, $S(n)$, $W(n)$ is the received signal at the SU, the PU signal and additive white Gaussian noise (AWGN) during the nth time slot for a frame of $L(1 \leq n \leq L)$ slots (symbols) respectively. In this paper, multiple discontinuous mini sensing slots spread across the entire frame [10] are used as opposed to using one block sensing time slot [11]. Each frame therefore will consist of one data transmission slot and multiple mini sensing slots. In some instances, distributed cooperative spectrum sensing is deployed.

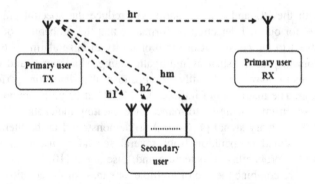

Fig. 1. Employing MIMO technique in spectrum sensing [9]

3   Analytical Model

To evaluate the performance of MIMO, an optimal detector is used. The assumption is that the optimal detector needs to know the noise (AWGN) σ_n^2, PU signal variance σ_s^2 and channel gains. It is assumed that the signals are Gaussian distributed with zero mean and the channel is independent in this case.

For the optimal detector in Neyman-Pearson sense, we need to compare log likelihood ratio (LLR) function given in [9] with a threshold

$$\frac{tr(x)^2}{2\sigma_n^2}\left(\frac{1}{1+\frac{\sigma_n^2}{\sigma_s^2}}\right) - \frac{L}{2}\ln\sigma_s^2 \underset{>}{\overset{<}{\gtrless}} \eta \tag{3}$$

Where x is the received matrix defined in (1) and (2) for L frame symbols, σ_s^2/σ_n^2 is the signal-to-noise ratio (SNR) of the signal of the PU, $tr(x)$ is the trace of the received signal matrix at the SU, and η denotes the detection threshold obtained by solving $F(\eta) = 1 - P_{fa}$, P_{fa} denotes the probability of false alarm and $F(\eta)$ is the cumulative distribution function (CDF) of the decision statistic [9]. The detection thresh hold is

$$\eta = \frac{\eta_1 + L\ln\left(\frac{\sigma_n^2}{\sigma_s^2}\|h\|^2 + 1\right)}{\left(\frac{\sigma_n^2}{\sigma_s^2}\|h\|^2\right)\sigma_n^2}, \tag{4}$$

where η_1 is the decision threshold for spectrum hole detection and h is the channel matrix. For the independent channels in MIMO, the probability of false alarm (P_{fa}) and the probability of detection (P_d) can be expressed as [6, 9]

$$P_{fa} = \frac{\Gamma\left(L, \frac{\eta}{\|h\|^2\sigma_n^2}\right)}{\Gamma(L)}, \tag{5}$$

$$P_d = \frac{\Gamma\left(L, \frac{\eta}{\|h\|^2\left(\|h\|^2\sigma_s^2 + \sigma_n^2\right)}\right)}{\Gamma(L)}. \tag{6}$$

where $\Gamma(L,)$ is an incomplete gamma function, $\Gamma(L)$ is a complete gamma functions and h is the channel matrix. In terms of SNR, the probability of detection is as follows:

$$P_d = \frac{\Gamma\left(L, \frac{\eta}{\|h\|^2\sigma_n^2(1+\gamma)}\right)}{\Gamma(L)} \tag{7}$$

The SNR γ of the received primary signal as observed by the SU is

$$\gamma = \frac{\|h\|^2\sigma_s^2}{\sigma_n^2}. \tag{8}$$

3.1 Multiple Slot Spectrum Sensing

At the medium access control (MAC) layer, each frame consists of one sensing slot [10, 11] with a period τ and one data transmission slot with a period $T - \tau$. In this paper the sensing slot in each frame is split into multiple discontinuous mini-slots. The concept is as illustrated in Fig. 2. For a single frame, if S is the number of mini-slots, τ_1 the sensing time for each mini-slot and T the duration for the entire frame, then the total sensing time in each frame is $\tau = s\tau_1$ and the number of samples for each mini-slot is $L_1 = L/S$. The probability of detection and false alarm for different mini-slots while using data fusion with MIMO under consideration is given in [10] and can be expressed as (9) and (10) respectively. The SNR γ is calculated from (8) so as to compute the probabilities that are dependent on MIMO.

$$P_{fa} = Q\left(\beta Q^{-1}(P_d) + \gamma\sqrt{\frac{L_1}{S}}\sum_{i=1}^{S}|h_i|^2\right) \tag{9}$$

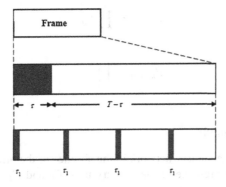

Fig. 2. Cognitive radio network frame structure with multiple sensing slots

$$P_d = Q\left(\frac{1}{\beta}\left(Q^{-1}(P_{fa}) - \gamma\sqrt{\frac{L_1}{S}\sum_{i=1}^{S}|h_i|^2}\right)\right) \tag{10}$$

where $\beta = \sqrt{1 + \frac{2\gamma}{S}\sum_{i=1}^{S}|h_i|^2}$, γ is the same SNR given in (8). Considering a special case where $h_i = 1$ for all i, the probability of false alarm P_{fa} for a given target probability of detection $\bar{P}_d$ is given in [10] and is

$$P_{fa} = Q\left(\sqrt{2\gamma + 1}Q^{-1}\left(\bar{P}_d\right) + \gamma\sqrt{SL_1}\right) \tag{11}$$

3.2 Cooperative Spectrum Sensing

In addition to MIMO and multi-slot time sensing, this paper also considers the use of cooperative spectrum sensing with multiple distributed secondary users. Suppose there are Y secondary users in a cognitive network, the probability of detection $P_d^{(y)}$ and probability of false alarm $P_{fa}^{(y)}$ of the yth cognitive radio user as given in [10] as;

$$P_d^{(y)} = Q\left(\left(\frac{\eta}{\sigma_n^2} - \gamma|h_y|^2 - 1\right)\sqrt{\frac{L}{2\gamma|h_y|^2 + 1}}\right) \tag{12}$$

$$P_{fa}^{(y)} = Q\left(\left(\frac{\eta}{\sigma_n^2} - 1\right)\sqrt{L}\right) \tag{13}$$

Each cognitive radio user's data is processed separately and individual decisions are made hence decision fusion [10–12, 14]. The final cognitive radio network decision is made by fusing the individual decisions thus using the Logic-AND rule [10, 15], to calculate the network probability of detection and false alarm in (12) and (13) respectively as

$$P_{d(net)} = \prod_{i=1}^{Y} P_d^{(i)} \tag{14}$$

$$P_{fa(net)} = \prod_{i=1}^{Y} P_{fa}^{(i)} \tag{15}$$

3.3 Sensing Throughput

The throughput of the secondary network in the absence of the primary user is denoted as C_0 and as C_1 in the presence of the primary user. C_0 and C_1 can be expressed as;

$$C_0 = \log_2\left[det\left(\mathbf{I}_N + \frac{SNR_s}{M}\mathbf{hh}^*\right)\right] \tag{16}$$

$$C_1 = \log_2\left[det\left(\mathbf{I}_N + \frac{SNR_s/M}{1+SNR_p}\mathbf{hh}^*\right)\right] \tag{17}$$

where SNR_s and SNR_p (given by (8)) is SNR for the SU and PU respectively, h is $M \times N$ channel matrix for the SU wth M transmit and N receive antennas. For a given band of interest, $P(H_1)$ is the probability for which the primary user is active and $P(H_0)$ is the probability for which the primary user is passive, then $P(H_0) + P(H_1) = 1$. The two scenarios under which the secondary network operates at the primary user's frequency band to achieve the following throughput are: when the primary user is not present and no false alarm is generated by the secondary user, therefore the achievable throughput of the secondary link is $\frac{T-\tau}{T}C_0$. Secondary when the primary user is active but it is not detected by the secondary user, the achievable throughput of the secondary link is $\frac{T-\tau}{T}C_1$. The probabilities for which scenario one and scenario two happens are $(1 - P_{fa})\,P(H_0)$ and $(1 - P_d)P(H_1)$ respectively. Therefore the total throughput of the secondary network under the absence and presence of the primary user is respectively given (18) and (19)

$$R_0 = \frac{T-\tau}{T}C_0\left(1 - P_{fa}\right)P(H_0) \tag{18}$$

$$R_1 = \frac{T-\tau}{T}C_1(1 - P_d)P(H_1) \tag{19}$$

and hence the average throughput of the secondary network is

$$R = R_0 + R_1 \tag{20}$$

The normalized throughput of the secondary network while using multi-slot spectrum sensing is given in [10] as

$$B = \frac{T-\tau}{T}\left(1 - \tilde{P}_f\right) \tag{21}$$

where $\tilde{P}_f$ is the average probability of false alarm over all frames.

4 Simulation Results

This Section presents results for a distributed MIMO cooperative, multiple slot spectrum sensing obtained using Matlab version 7.9 runing on windows 7. The performance parameters used are the probability of detection, probability of false alarm and the MIMO CR network throughput. The signal variances of the PU observed at the SU considered for the simulation were taken from [16] and are as follows: $1\sigma_n^2$, $1.3634\sigma_n^2$, $1.6112\sigma_n^2$ and $1.7802\sigma_n^2$ for a CR user with one, two, three and four antennas respectively. The PU signal was assumed to be BPSK modulated with a bandwidth of

6 MHz and a target probability of 0.9. BPSK modulated signal were used in the Alamouti space time block codes (STBC) to generate multiple data streams transmitted across several transmit antennas of the SU. The SNR for the PU and the SU was set to 0 dB and 20 dB respectively.

The decision threshold η_1 for spectrum hole detection in (4) is found using

$$\eta_1 = gammaincinv([1 - P_{f(g)}], b) \times 2 \tag{22}$$

The probability of failed spectrum hole detection$P_{f(g)}$ depends on the number of failed spectrum hole detection probabilities $f(g)$ that have been used, with b representing the bandwidth time factor which is assumed to be one for the simulation.

Figure 3 depicts a case when the sensing slot in each frame is split into multiple discontinuous mini-slots. The total sensing time in each frame is divided equally among the multiple mini-slots, and the normalized throughput is obtained from (21) by substituting for probability of false alarm P_{fa} in (11).

It can be seen from Fig. 3 that the more the number of mini-slots used, the lesser the sensing time needed to obtain a higher throughput. However, the sensing time for MIMO system is much shorter than that of a single input single output (SISO).

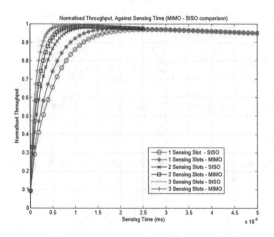

Fig. 3. Normalized throughput against sensing time for multi-slot spectrum sensing

Results in Fig. 3 present a significant improvement in throughput of up to 0.95 with a total sensing time of 0.57 milisecond for a MIMO system using 3 sensing slots as compared to results in [10], where the maximum throughput obtained was 0.94 with a total sensing time of 3.6 ms for a SISO system using 5 sensing slots. This is possible because combining MIMO and multislot techniques greatly improves spectrum sensing in CR networks as evidenced by the results in Fig. 3.

Figures 4 and 5 shows the probability of detection P_d and probability of false alarm P_{fa}. The probabilities are based on (5) and (6).

It can be seen from Figs. 4 and 5 that the probability of detection increases and the probability of false alarm decrease with increasing number of antennas. Note that the

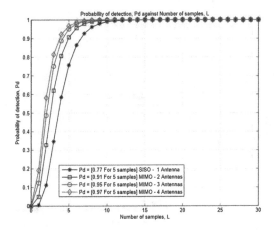

Fig. 4. Probability of detection against number of samples

probability of detection improves from 0.77 for a one antenna to 0.91 for two antennas, 0.95 for three antennas and 09.7 for four antennas at five samples. The probability of false alarm for five samples decreases from 0.23 for one antenna to 0.09 for two antennas, 0.05 for three antennas and 0.03 for four antennas. Results in [9] present the probability of detection and probability of false alarm using 5 samples as 0.95 and 0.04 respectively for a two-antenna system only. Comparing the results of the two-antenna configuration, results in Figs. 4 and 5 give a minor performance decline of 0.04 and 0.05 for probability of detection and probability of false alarm respectively which may be due to the difference in the simulation environments. Results in Figs. 4 and 5 also show that the performance improvement margin significantly reduces after the two antenna MIMO configuration system. This observation cannot be deduced from the

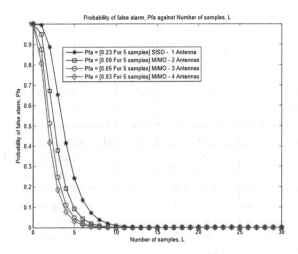

Fig. 5. Probability of false alarm against number of samples

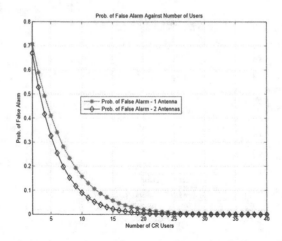

Fig. 6. Probability of false alarm against cognitive radio users

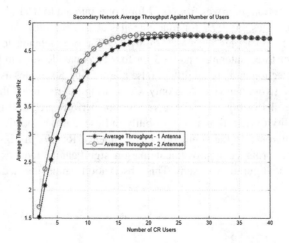

Fig. 7. Network average throughput against cognitive radio users

simulation results in [9] since they are not exhaustive or are of a limited data set for such a conclusion.

Figure 6 shows results for the probability of false alarm $P_{fa(net)}$ in (15) for Y secondary users in a cognitive radio network obtained by substituting (13) in (15). This paper investigated the performance improvement in the probability of false alarm with an increasing number of cooperating CR users which was not covered in [10] and yet offers a better understanding of the CR network performance. From Fig. 6, it can be seen that the probability of false alarm decreases with increasing number of users. After a total of 20 CR users, there is a negligible increase in the probability of false alarm margin. Its also noted that the probability of false alarm decreases more repidly for MIMO than SISO system in Fig. 6.

Figure 7 presents the average throughput of the secondary network against the number of users. The results were based on (20), by substituting the probability of dection $P_d^{(y)}$ in (12) and probability false alarm $P_{fa}^{(y)}$ in (13) into (14) and (15) respecitively.

It can be seen from Fig. 7 that the average throughput increases with increasing number of CR users, however, the average throughput increases more rapidly for a MIMO than a SISO system.

5 Conclusion

Radio frequency spectrum efficiency is one of the major concerns in wireless communication systems today. CR technology has emerged as solution which enables opportunistic spectrum sharing and usage. It has been demonstrated in this paper through simulations that by combining MIMO, multiple time slots distributed over a frame and cooperation amongst the CR user's provides a degree of certainty about the behavior of the PU in CR network. This enhances spectrum sensing and therefore provides improvement in the performance of CR network. MIMO cooperative cognitive radio systems deploying multiple time slots during spectrum sensing increase the probability of detection decrease the probability of false alarm and increase network throughput.

References

1. Federal Communications Commission, Spectrum policy task force, report, ET Docket no. 02-135, November 2002
2. Mitola, J., Maguire Jr., G.Q.: Cognitive radio: making software radios more personal. IEEE Pers. Commun. Mag. 6(4), 13–18 (1999)
3. Fette, B.: Cognitive Radio Technology, 1st edn. Elsevier, Burlington (2006)
4. Muhumuza, S., Emeru, T., Akol, R.N.: Performance of MIMO cognitive radio networks. In: 2nd National Conference on Communications, Kampala, Uganda (2012)
5. Wyglinski, A.M., Nekovee, M., Hou, T.: Cognitive Radio Communications and Networks, 1st edn, pp. 6–8. Academic press, Elsevier Inc (2010)
6. Taherpour, A., Nasiri-Kenari, M., Gazor, S.: Multiple antenna spectrum sensing in cognitive radios. IEEE Trans. Wirel. Commun. 9(2), 814–823 (2010)
7. Biglieri, E., Galderbank, R., Constantinides, A., Goldsmith, A., Paulraj, H., Poor, H.V.: MIMO Wirelesss Communications, 1st edn. University Press, Cambridge (2007)
8. Rohde & Schwarz: Introduction to MIMO, application note (Unpublished)
9. Rathi, S., Dua, R.L., Singh, P.: Spectrum sensing in Cognitive radio using MIMO Technique. Int. J. Soft Comput. Eng. 1, 259–265 (2011)
10. Liang, Y., Zeng, V., Peh, E., Hoang, E.: Sensing-throughput Trade off for cognitive radio networks. IEEE Trans. Wirel. Commun. 7(4), 1326–1337 (2008)
11. Akyildiz, I., Lo, B., Balakrishnan, R.: Cooperative spectrum sensing in cognitive radio networks: a survey. Phys. Commun. 4(1), 40–62 (2010)
12. Lee, J., Baek, J., Hwang, S.: Collaborative spectrum sensing using energy detector in multiple antenna system. In: International Conference on Advanced Communication Technology (ICACT), pp. 427–430 (2008)

13. Danijela, C., Mubaraq, S., Brodersen, R.: Implementation issues in spectrum sensing for cognitive radios. In: IEEE 38th Asilomar Conference on Signals Systems & Computers, vol. 1, pp. 772–776 (2004)
14. Akyildiz, I., Lee, W., Vuran, M., Mohanty, S.: Next generation/dynamic spectrum access/ cognitive radio wireless networks: a survey. Comput. Netw. **50**, 2127–2159 (2001)
15. Loyka, S.: Channel capacity of MIMO architecture using the exponential correlation matrix. IEEE Commun. Lett. **5**, 369–371 (2001)
16. Ustok, R.: Spectrum sensing techniques for cognitive radio Systems with multiple antennas. Msc. Thesis, Izmir Institute of Technology (2010)

Enabling Converged Satellite and Terrestrial Access Networks

Christian Niephaus[1,3], Mathias Kretschmer[2], Gheorghita Ghinea[3], and Senka Hadzic[4(✉)]

[1] Fraunhofer FOKUS, St. Augustin, Germany
christian.niephaus@fokus.fraunhofer.de
[2] DeFuTech UG, Hennef, Germany
mathias@defutech.de
[3] Brunel University, London, UK
george.ghinea@brunel.ac.uk
[4] ERCIM Fellowship, St. Augustin, Germany
senka.hadzic@fokus-extern.fraunhofer.de

Abstract. Rural and remote areas, particularly in emerging countries, often lack broadband connectivity mainly due to economic constraints. This limits the access to existing and novel application and services, which often require a high connection speed. At the same time satellite systems have evolved significantly during the last decade leading to a tremendous decrease in cost per bit. In fact, satellite systems can provide very high bandwidth links. However, mainly due to the high signal propagation time, the latency on those links is significantly higher than in terrestrial networks. Simultaneously using terrestrial access technologies, such as, or cooperatively, in parallel to new high speed broadband satellite systems is believed to be a promising option to enable broadband connectivity to rural and remote regions. However, typically used load distributing methods, commonly used multi-homing environments might do more harm than good due to the heterogeneity of the technologies and in particular the higher latency of the satellite systems. This could affect service quality for especially latency sensitive applications. In this work we identify the key building blocks required to realize a converged satellite terrestrial network. Moreover, we present an easy to implement approach based on packet sizes that takes the satellite specifics into account and allows for providing broadband connectivity while maintaining a high QoS for the user.

Keywords: QoS · Satellite terrestrial network convergence · Load distribution

1 Introduction

The importance of broadband Internet access has increased significantly over the last decade and is nowadays considered to be "a crucial factor to realize economic

© Institute for Computer Sciences, Social Informatics and Telecommunications Engineering 2015
A. Nungu et al. (Eds.): AFRICOMM 2014, LNICST 147, pp. 43–52, 2015.
DOI: 10.1007/978-3-319-16886-9_5

growth", enabling the development of new services and applications. However, Africa still shows the worlds lowest Internet penetration. While the potential of improving the quality of life is higher via Internet access, Africa shows the worlds lowest penetration. According to ITU [1] only 16 % of all Africans will have accessed the Internet in 2013 (at least once within the year) and only 7 % of these households are actually connected. Particularly providing broadband connections to rural and other difficult-to-serve areas is a challenging task due to typical economical constraints in these areas [2]. Moreover, current access networks, if available, are very unlikely being able to cope with the tremendous increase in IP traffic in the next years, as predicted in [3].

At the same time, satellites links provide ubiquitous coverage and are therefore able to reach rural and remote areas more cost effectively than many terrestrial alternatives. Next generation of fixed satellite systems, which are scheduled to be operational by 2020, are even targeting the Terabit/s aggregated capacity [4]. These systems will lower the cost per bit significantly. However, satellite links using satellites will still increase the latency on connections, making it difficult for users to perceive a high user when latency intolerant applications are being used. For example, and other interactive applications should be serviced with a latency of not more than 100 ms and a latency variation (jitter) below 50 ms, whereas a video streaming application can easily tolerate a latency around 1 s [5]. Obviously, the latter can be achieved with satellite systems while the first cannot.

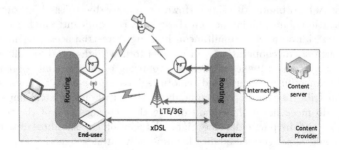

Fig. 1. Multiple connection scenario overview

The authors believe that there is a significant opportunity that will arise when satellite and narrow-band terrestrial networks, wired and wireless, converge into a common network infrastructure, which enables broadband connection in rural and remote areas with a high service quality but at a fraction of the capital cost of deployment. Effectively exploiting multiple heterogeneous access networks in parallel, as depicted in Fig. 1, can be a potential solution to provide the required bandwidth to the end users in rural and remote areas while still allowing for a high level of for all types of applications [6]. By having a converged network infrastructure utilizing transparently all available technology also higher availability and reliability can be provided.

As can be seen from the aforementioned example, intelligently distributing the traffic on the available links is essential to benefit from having multiple access networks available with different characteristics. Hence, in this paper we focus on load distribution in converged satellite terrestrial environment. The remainder of the paper is structured as follows we first analyze the related work in load distribution and identify the key building blocks required to realize the multiple connection scenario. Afterward, we present our approach and evaluate it by using MATLAB/Simulink simulations. Finally, we conclude and present the planned future work.

2   Related Work

Load distribution itself is a long-standing research issue in the scientific community. A comprehensive survey and comparison of different Load Distribution algorithms has been done in [7]. The authors classify different approaches of load distribution into adaptive and non-adaptive models. While the non-adaptive models distribute the links statically and thus cannot react on dynamically changing conditions, adaptive models are able to react on variations in traffic- or network conditions. Typical examples for non-adaptive models are round-robin or hash-based approaches, which distribute the load on a per-packet or per-flow basis, without being aware of neither the specifics of the satellite link nor the -requirements of the traffic. As shown in [8], such approaches are not able to exploit the benefits of the aforementioned scenario. Moreover, [7] also analyzed adaptive models, which are either Network-Condition-Based or Traffic-Condition-Based or both. While Network-Condition-Based models can adapt to changing network conditions, such as delivery time or network utilization in terms of packets/s or bytes/s, Traffic-Condition-Based Models consider traffic characteristics, e.g. flow- or packet size, packet arrival time, etc., when performing load distribution. However, while terrestrial connections usually have a considerable latency only when they are operated at their capacity limit, e.g. due to queuing, the signal propagation latency on a satellite link is already higher than most interactive applications can tolerate. Those huge differences in latency is to the best of the authors knowledge not considered by any of the current load distribution approaches.

3   Key Building Blocks

In the following we describe the key building blocks that have been identified being required to realize a converged satellite and terrestrial network. These are depicted in Fig. 2 and described as follows: the heart of the system is the Load Distribution algorithm itself, which selects the most optimal link for a particular traffic unit based on different parameters. In order to do that properly, mechanisms are required to identify both the capabilities and characteristics of the different networks and the requirements of the various kinds of traffic. That is, before the traffic is distributed on the available links it first needs to be classified. Compared to typical traffic classification this not necessarily include identifying the concrete application or application type but rather its tolerance against latency. Interactive and real-time application usually cannot cope with the high latency of satellite systems and, thus, must be routed via the terrestrial link. Moreover, in order to not overload a link the available capacity must be known. However, particularly in wireless networks, which rely on a shared medium, this might change frequently and requires a constant monitoring. It should be noted that in this work we focus on the actual link selection, hence we assume that both the latency tolerance of traffic and the current capabilities of the links is known.

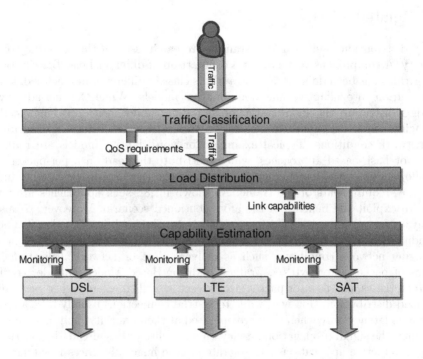

Fig. 2. Key building blocks of QoS-aware link selection

4   Approach

In this work we present an easy to implement approach with low computational overhead. Code Listing 1.1 shows the pseudo code of our algorithm: First, each packet is classified into *elastic* and *real-time* traffic. As previously mentioned, how this classification is realized is out of scope of this document. If a packet belongs to a real-time flow it is sent via link with the lowest delay. In contrast to that, elastic traffic is always sent via the satellite link, if the packet size is above a certain threshold Θ. If the packet size is below Θ it is sent via the link with the lowest delay.

Listing 1.1. "Link Selection"

```
1 Link function path_selection(Packet p, LinkVector ←
     availLinks)
2 {
3   //get traffic class of packet
4   tc=p.tc();
5
6   if (f.realTime)==true)
7     return lowest_latency_link();
8   else
9   {
10    th=determine_current_threshold();
11    if (size>th)
12      return satLink;
13    else
14      return lowest_latency_link();
15  }
16 }
```

The threshold Θ that distinguished whether packets are sent via the satellite or the lowest latency link depends on the queue limit Λ and the current queue size λ of the lowest latency link as well as maximum packet size Γ. It is determined as shown in Eq. 1.

$$\Theta = \Gamma(-\frac{\lambda}{\Lambda} + 1) \qquad (1)$$

Both Λ and λ are, as well as the lowest_latency_link() function, determined by the Capability Estimation block. Γ is assumed to be 1500 bytes, which is a typical value in Ethernet-based networks.

5 Evaluation

In order to test the size-based load distribution algorithm MATLAB/simulink simulations have been conducted. Our model focuses, without loss of generality, only on transferring traffic in one direction, i.e. either from the end user towards the Internet or vice versa. Moreover, only one terrestrial and one satellite link is considered in this model.

5.1 Key Performance Indicators

In order to evaluate different load distribution approaches often he overall achievable throughput is used as the main, e.g. in [7,9]. However, for several services the pure throughput is not the only criteria to achieve a good service quality. Eventually, high user satisfaction is the most meaningful metric, which is usually referred to as perceived by the user. A common metric for is the, which is difficult to determine as test users and extensive test setups are required in order to gain reproducible and reliable values [10]. The is influenced by several factors including the type of device, the user profile and parameters such as throughput, latency, jitter or packet loss. Unfortunately there is no simple mapping between and values. However, [11] has shown that in fact latency and jitter do not negatively impact the user's ability to assimilate the information yet it significantly impacts the and, thus, it is essential to provision at an appropriate level to achieve a high [12]. Thus, besides the overall throughput we define the numbers of so-called violations. A violations occurs if the overall latency is above 80 ms for the real-time QoS class or above 5 s for the elastic QoS class. Moreover, we also consider the packet loss rate as another.

5.2 Simulation Model

The main characteristics of the used model are as follows: The capacity of the satellite link has been configured to 10 mbps and a one-way latency of 300 ms, while a link provides a capacity of just 1 Mbps but only a one-way latency of 10 ms. A packet generator model generates packets of the two different QoS classes, namely Real-time and Elastic. The packet generation time for elastic and real-time traffic is assumed to be exponentially distributed, with a mean of 1 ms and 20 ms, respectively. The packet size is similarly defined: Packets sizes of the real-time traffic class are uniformly distributed between 30 and 200 bytes, whereas the packet size for the elastic traffic is arbitrary discrete distributed with a value vector [32 96 192 384 768 1271] and a probability vector [0.2 0.07 0.2 0.02 0.01 0.5]. Besides the packet size and QoS Class, all packets contain a sequence number, which is unique within the scope of QoS class, in order to detect reordering. A Link Selection function implements the size-based Load Distribution. Finally the received packets are logged to the MATLAB workspace with sequence number, QoS class and packet size, and overall transmission time, so that results of the simulation can be evaluated offline.

5.3 Simulation Results

In order to have reference values for testing the size-based link selection algorithm, we first run the test with a simple round-robin path selection, which is often used in nowadays networks. Afterwards we run the same test again but with our packet-size based load distribution approach.

Figure 3 depicts the ratio of traffic sent via the satellite link. As can be seen in Fig. 3(a) approximately 70 % of the traffic of each traffic class is sent via the satellite network, which was expected due to the round-robin approach. It should be noted, that in this ratio lost packets are not accounted for. Since the loss rate on the UMTS link is quite high due to a link overload, as can be seen later on, more than 70 % of the received traffic was sent over the satellite and not 50 % as could have been expected. In contrast to that our approach utilizes the satellite link only for the elastic and not for the real-time traffic. However, more than 80 % of the elastic traffic is sent via the satellite link, as shown in Fig. 3(b).

Moreover, due to the high amount of traffic sent via the satellite link, the amount of QoS violations is also above 70 % for the real-time traffic class when

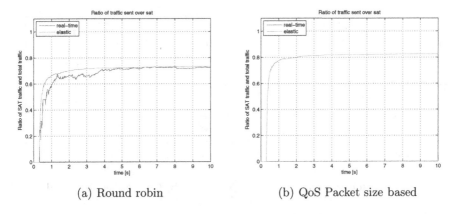

(a) Round robin   (b) QoS Packet size based

Fig. 3. Ratio of traffic sent via the satellite link

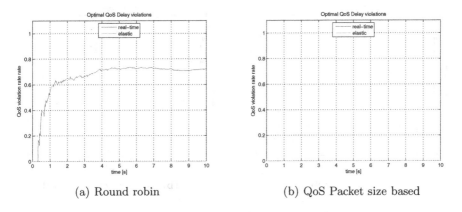

(a) Round robin   (b) QoS Packet size based

Fig. 4. Violations

the round robin distribution is used, as depicted in Fig. 4(a). That is, 70 % of the packets experienced more than 80 ms latency and corespondent with the previously shown ratio of traffic sent via the satellite link. It should be noted that the elastic traffic class can tolerate 5 s of latency. Hence, even if packets are sent over the satellite link the tolerable latency is not exceeded.

In contrast to that our packet size based approach takes into account the maximum tolerable latency and, thus, does not route real-time traffic via the satellite, leading to zero violations and eventually a higher, as depicted in Fig. 4(b).

This is also reflected in the packet loss rate (see Fig. 5). Whereas the in round robin approach leads to approximately 30 % packet loss for both classes of traffic, as shown in Fig. 5(a) the packet size based approach has virtually zero packet losses (see Fig. 5(b)), since the current load on the link is considered and overload situations are avoided.

These characteristics of the based packet size approach leads to an increase of overall throughput as well. Figure 6 shows the throughput for both real-time and

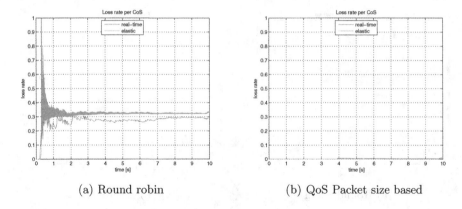

(a) Round robin   (b) QoS Packet size based

Fig. 5. Packet loss rate

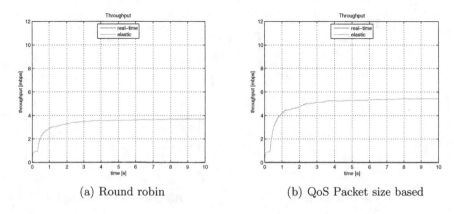

(a) Round robin   (b) QoS Packet size based

Fig. 6. Throughput per traffic class

elastic traffic. Due to the high packet loss caused by link overload the throughput for the round robin approach (see Fig. 6(a)) is significantly lower than for the packet size based approach (see Fig. 6(b)).

It should be noted, that the amount of packets generated in both test does not exceed the aggregated capacity of both links (11 mbps).

6 Conclusion and Future Work

In this work we advocate for convergence of satellite and terrestrial networks into a uniform communication network. We believe that narrow-band terrestrial networks, such as, complemented by novel high capacity satellite systems are particularly suited to provide high capacity broadband connectivity to rural and other difficult to serve areas, given that a tremendous decrease in cost per bit on the satellite system is expected within the next year. Such a convergence can help to enable new services and application in Africa and other emerging areas, which require resilient, high speed connection. However, mainly due to the high (fixed) latency on satellite links load distribution algorithms commonly used in multi-homing environments are not suitable when satellite and terrestrial links are used in parallel, as shown in this work. Instead novel load distribution mechanisms are required that are able to take into account the specific characteristics of a satellite link. Moreover, we have developed an easy to implement algorithm that is considering different classes and distributes traffic based on packet sizes. By using MATLAB/Simulink simulations we have shown that end user and eventually can highly benefit from our approach.

Future work will further test and enhance the packet size based load distribution by sending specific packets over the terrestrial connections to also increase the performance of delay tolerant elastic traffic, for example by sending TCP Acknowledgments via a terrestrial path. We will also further investigate the impact of having multiple narrow-band terrestrial connections complemented by a single satellite links. Finally, we will explore closer integration between satellite and terrestrial networks, which encompasses not only the data plane but also control and management mechanisms.

Acknowledgment. This work has been supported by the BATS research project which is funded by the European Union Seventh Framework Programme under contract n317533. The views and conclusions contained here are those of the authors and should not be interpreted as necessarily representing the official policies or endorsements, either expressed or implied, of the BATS project or the European Commission.

References

1. ITU: The world in 2013: Ict facts and figures, Technical report (2013)
2. Henkel, D., Englander, S., Kretschmer, M., Niephaus, C.: Connecting the unconnected - economic constraints and technical requirements towards a back-haul network for rural areas. In: GLOBECOM Workshops (GC Wkshps), 2011 IEEE, pp. 1039–1044, December 2011
3. Cisco Cooperation: The zettabyte era-trends and analysis (2013)
4. Evans, B., Thompson, P., Castanet, L., Bousquet, M., Mathiopoulos, T.: Concepts and technologies for a terabit/s satellite. In: SPACOMM 2011. Budapest, Hungary (2011)
5. I. T. Recommendation: "Y.1541: network performance objectives for IP-based services," international telecommunication union, Technical report (2003). http://www.itu.int/itudoc/itu-t/aap/sg13aap/history/y1541/y1541.html
6. Peters, G., Perez-Trufero, J., Watts, S., Wall, N.: The bats project. In: 2013 Future Network and Mobile Summit (FutureNetworkSummit), pp. 1–8 (2013)
7. Prabhavat, S., Nishiyama, H., Ansari, N., Kato, N.: On load distribution over multipath networks. IEEE Commun. Surv. Tutor. **14**(3), 662–680 (2012)
8. Niephaus, C., Kretschmer, M., Ghinea, G.: Towards qos-aware load distribution in heterogeneous networks. In: 2013 IEEE Malaysia International Conference on Communications (MICC), pp. 151–156, November 2013
9. Mkel, A., Siikavirta, S., Manner, J.: Comparison of load-balancing approaches for multipath connectivity. Comput. Netw. **56**(8), 2179–2195 (2012). http://www.sciencedirect.com/science/article/pii/S138912861200093X

10. Kilkki, K.: Quality of experience in communications ecosystem. J.UCS **14**(5), 615–624 (2008)
11. Gulliver, S., Ghinea, G.: The perceptual and attentive impact of delay and jitter in multimedia delivery. IEEE Trans. Broadcas. **53**(2), 449–458 (2007)
12. Stankiewicz, R., Jajszczyk, A.: A survey of qoe assurance in converged networks. Comput. Netw. **55**(7), 1459–1473 (2011). http://dx.doi.org/10.1016/j.comnet.2011.02.004

Empirical Path Loss Models for 802.11n Wireless Networks at 2.4 GHz in Rural Regions

Jean Louis Fendji Kedieng Ebongue$^{(\boxtimes)}$, Mafai Nelson, and Jean Michel Nlong

Computer Science, University of Ngaoundéré,
P.O. Box 454, Ngaoundéré, Cameroon
{jlfendji,mnelson,jmnlong}@univ-ndere.cm

Abstract. The prediction of the signal path loss is an important step in the deployment of wireless networks. Despite the plethora of works on this field, just a little is addressing rural environments at 2.4 GHz. In this work, we consider empirical path loss models in wireless networks at 2.4 GHz, using off-the-shelf 802.11n. We define three scenario usually observed in rural environment: free space, raised space and built space. Afterwards, we do a measurement campaign and compare results to selected prediction models. After analysing the results, Liechty model provides a better precision than the others. This model is further improved by considering the distance between the transmitter and the first breakpoint. We obtain predictions with mean errors less than 2.4 dB which is inferior to 4.00 dB predicted using Liechty model.

Keywords: Path loss · Empirical model · 802.11n · Rural area

1 Introduction

In rural regions, wireless networks appear as a suitable solution to bridge the digital divide between rural and developing regions. Although they can be more easily setup, especially in hostile environments, wireless networks can provide very bad performance if they are not well planned. The difficulty is to predict the quality of links by estimating the attenuation of the signal. To predict the quality of the signal, empirical path loss models are generally used. But empirical models are usually tied to particular environment with particular conditions such as the type of equipment, the frequency of the signal, the height of tower and the range of the signal. Despite the plethora of empirical models on signal path loss [1–8, 10], just few are considering rural environment at 2.4 GHz [9]. But with off-the-shelf technologies like IEEE 802.11b, g and n, wireless networks at 2.4 GHz and 5 GHz represent currently an appealing solution to connect rural regions. Therefore, there is a need to predict the signal path loss at these particular frequencies in rural environment.

In this work, we try to provide a more precise empirical model for predicting signal path loss at 2.4 GHz using off-the-shelf 802.11n in outdoor. Therefore, we do a measurement campaign in three different scenarios: free space, raised space and built

© Institute for Computer Sciences, Social Informatics and Telecommunications Engineering 2015
A. Nungu et al. (Eds.): AFRICOMM 2014, LNICST 147, pp. 53–63, 2015.
DOI: 10.1007/978-3-319-16886-9_6

space. Afterwards, we compare the results to the path loss predicted by selected empirical models. Liechty model [9] shows itself as the more precise empirical model with a mean error of 4.22 dB in raised space and 4.35 dB in built space. Finally, we improve this model to obtain a better prediction model by considering the distance to the first breakpoint. Finally we obtain a mean error of 2.33 dB in raised space and 2.36 dB in built space.

The rest of the paper is organised as follows: Sect. 2 presents relevant empirical models for this study; in Sect. 3, we present our methodology, material, scenario and data collection. Section 4 is for the numerical analysis of data and Sect. 5 presents the proposed new model.

2   Related Work on Prediction Models for Wireless Networks

There exists numerous works trying to predict path loss in wireless network and they are split into two groups: deterministic models also called theoretical methods and empirical models. Because of their complexity, deterministic models are usually set discarded in favour of empirical models which are based on statistics and probability.

There are several empirical loss models presented in literature. Each of them is designed for a particular environment, in Line Of Sight (LOS) and/or Non-Line Of Sight (NLOS), in indoor or outdoor propagation, at different frequencies. Table 1 provides a list of most common empirical path loss models.

Table 1. Most common empirical path loss models:

Models	Condition
-Free space	
-Egli	$f \in {]}30; 3000[$
-One-slope	
-Log Normal Shadowing	
-Dual-slope	
-Partitioned	
-Liechty	$f \approx 2400$
-Okumura	$f \in {]}150; 1920[; d \in {]}1; 100[; htx \in {]}30; 200[; hrx \in {]}3; 10[$
-Okumura-Hata	$f \in {]}150; 1500[; d \in {]}1; 10[; htx \in {]}30; 200[; hrx \in {]}1; 10[$
-COST 231 Hata	$f \in {]}150; 2000[; d \in {]}1; 20[; htx \in {]}30; 200[; hrx \in {]}1; 10[$
-Hata-Davidson	$f \in {]}150; 1500[; d \in {]}1; 300[; htx \in {]}30; 200[; hrx \in {]}1; 10[$
-Rural	$f \in \{160; 400; 900\}$
-ITU-R	$1.5 < f < 2; 1 < d < 10; 30 < htx < 200; 1 < hrx < 10$
-ECC-33	$700 \leq f \leq 3500; 1 < d < 10; 20 < htx < 200; 1 < hrx < 10$
-Erceg	$f \approx 2000; 1 < hrx < 2$
-SUI	$2500 < f < 2700; 0.1 < d < 8; 20 < htx < 80; 2 < hrx < 10$

f: frequency (MHz);   d: distance between the transmitter and the receiver (Km)
htx: height of transmitter antenna (m);   hrx: height of the receiver antenna (m)

In general, all these empirical models attempt to predict the propagation attenuation of the signal as the ratio in decibels between the transmitted power and the received power. The basic equation is the one of Friis:

$$PL_{fs} = 10log_{10}\frac{(4\pi d)^2}{G_t G_r \lambda^2} \tag{1}$$

With PL_{fs}: Signal attenuation in free space (dB)

d: distance between the transmitter and the receiver (Km)
Gr: Gain of the receiver antenna (dBi)
Gt: Gain of the transmitter antenna (dBi).

When considering the antennae as isotropic (Gt = Gr = 1) we obtain (2)

$$PL_{fs} = 20log_{10}\frac{(4\pi d)}{\lambda} \tag{2}$$

With $c = \lambda f$, f frequency in Hz and $c = 3.10^8 m.s^{-1}$, we finally obtain (3)

$$PL_{fs} = -147.56 + 20log_{10}d + 20log_{10}f \tag{3}$$

Basic empirical path loss models are based on (3) taking into consideration the distance between transmitter and receiver and the frequency of transmission. Some models also consider the obstacles between transmitter and receiver and the height of antennae.

In this work, we compare five models:

(1) One Slope Model:

$$PL_{1slope} = PL(d_0) + 10nlog\left(\frac{d}{d_0}\right) \tag{4}$$

$PL(d_0)$: attenuation of the signal in free space at the distance d_0 (dB)
d: distance between the transmitter and the receiver (m)
d_0: distance of reference (m)
n: path loss exponent of the environment.

(2) Dual-slope Model:

$$PL_{2slope} = PL(d_0) + \begin{cases} 10n_1 log_{10}d & \text{with } 1m < d \le d_{bp} \\ 10n_2 log_{10}\frac{d}{d_{bp}} + 10n_1 log_{10}d_{bp} & \text{with } d > d_{bp} \end{cases} \tag{5}$$

$PL(d_0)$: attenuation of the signal at the distance d_0 (dB)
d: distance between the transmitter and the receiver (m)
d_0: reference distance (m)
d_{bp}: distance between the transmitter and the first obstacle (m)
n_1: path loss exponent for $d \le d_{bp}$
n_2: path loss exponent for $d > d_{bp}$.

(3) Log Normal Shadowing Model:

$$PL_{sha} = PL(d_0) + 10nlog\frac{d}{d_0}\chi_\sigma \tag{6}$$

$PL(d_0)$: attenuation of the signal at the distance d_0 (dB)
d: distance between the transmitter and the receiver (m)
d_0: reference distance (m)
χ_σ: shadowing effect (dB)
n: path loss exponent of the environment.

(4) Partitioned Model:

$$PL_{parti} = PL_{fs}(d_0) + \begin{cases} 20logd & with\ 1m < d \leq 10m \\ 29 + 60log\dfrac{d}{20} & with\ 20m < d \leq 40m \\ 20 + 30log\dfrac{d}{10} & with\ 10m < d \leq 20m \\ 47 + 120log\dfrac{d}{40} & with\ d > 40m \end{cases} \tag{7}$$

$PL(d_0)$: attenuation of the signal at the distance d_0 (dB)
d: distance between the transmitter and the receiver (m)
d_0: reference distance (m).

(5) Liechty Model:

$$PL = PL(d_0) + 10nlog_{10}\left(\frac{d}{d_0}\right) + \sum_i nbre_i * a_i \tag{8}$$

$PL(d_0)$: attenuation of the signal at the distance d_0 (dB)
d: distance between the transmitter and the receiver (m)
d_0: reference distance (m)
$nbre_i$: number of obstacle of type i
a_i: attenuation of obstacle of type i (dB)
n_1: path loss exponent for $d \leq d_{bp}$
n_2: path loss exponent for $d > d_{bp}$.

In all these models, the reference distance is the minimal distance for measuring the signal and the path loss exponent is the attenuation factor indicating how quickly the signal attenuation increases with the distance.

3 Methodology

3.1 Environment and Tools

Figure 1 present the environment of study. From this environment, we define three scenarios: Free space, Raised space shown in Fig. 2 and Built space shown in Fig. 3.

- **Free space:** This environment covers a distance of 600 m. Measurements of signal strength are taken straight to each interval of 50 m.

- **Raised space:** In this space, all trees have an average height of 6.5 m. Measurements of the signal strength are taken at different points as shown in Fig. 2.

- **Built space:** In this space, the heights of the houses are 3.5 m (the average height of the houses). Measurements of the signal strength are taken at different points as shown in Fig. 3.

In all scenarios described above, measurements are made with an USB wireless 300 Mbps Dodocool SL-1504N (Chipset Realtek 8191, driver RTL8188SU/8191FEB28 antenna gain 2 dBi) compliant to the IEEE 802.11n standard. An ALFA Network N2 compliant to the IEEE 802.11n standard (power 30 dBm, integrated antenna 12 dBi) serves as access point. A laptop, to which the USB wireless adapter is connected, is driven away from access point to geographical coordinates (latitude and longitude) determined using a USB GPS (Navilock NL-464US 60122, sensibility: −159 dBm). The signal intensity at each point is measured using Vistumbler version 9.8.

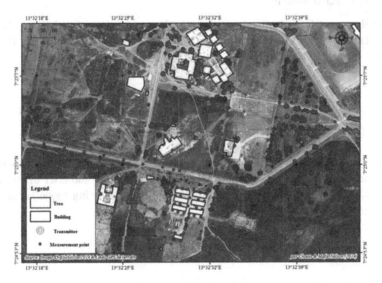

Fig. 1. Environment of study

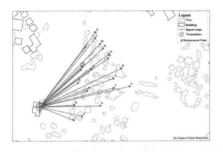

Fig. 2. Raised space scenario

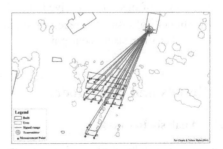

Fig. 3. Built space scenario

3.2 Data Collection

During the measurements, the USB wireless adapter was connected to the USB port of the laptop. Throughout the measurements, the antenna of the wireless USB adapter is oriented towards the sky. In this study, the positioning mode used is the Single Marker Measurements [9]. In this method, measurements are made at each location chosen randomly. So with the help of Vistumbler software, this method has been used in all the different scenarios previously described.

3.3 Numerical Analysis

The analysis is done in five steps: 1. Calculate the mean loss of signal measured in the field. 2. Use the least squares method to determine the fitting curve. 3. Evaluate the attenuation exponent n, using the fitting curve. 4. Calculate the σ parameter of Log Normal Shadowing Model. 5. Compare the mean loss measured with the loss calculated by the selected models.

1. Using the curve fitting to evaluate the path loss exponent n for the models One-slope, Dual slope, Log-normal shadowing and Liechty. This is done using the least squares methods (9).

$$y = ax + b$$

$$so\ that \begin{cases} \sum_i (A_i P_i)^2 = \sum_i (e_i)^2 & is\ minimal \\ A_i P_i = e_i = y_i - (ax_i + b) & 1 \leq i \leq n \end{cases} \tag{9}$$

2. Determining the value of the attenuation of the obstacle i for Liechty model: the difference between the mean loss of signal obtained before and after the obstacle.
3. Evaluating the value of parameter σ of Log-normal shadowing model. It is determined using (10):

$$\sigma^2 = \frac{\sum_i (\overline{P_m} - \overline{P_r})^2}{k} 1 \leq i \leq k \tag{10}$$

With:

$\overline{P_m}$: power of measured received signal
$\overline{P_r}$: strength of estimated received signal
k: number of measurement point.

4 Results and New Model

4.1 Analysis Results

Comparative results of selected models are illustrated in Figs. 4, 5 and 6.

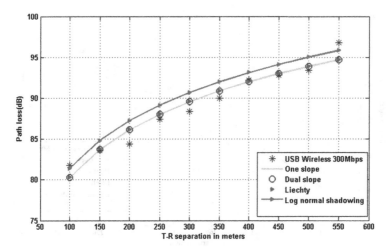

Fig. 4. Comparison of path loss in free space between selected models

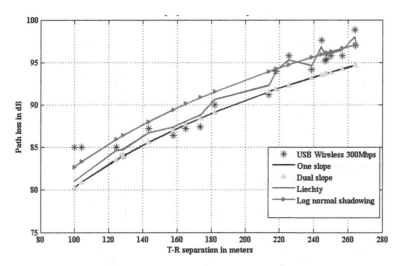

Fig. 5. Comparison of path loss in raised space between selected model

In Table 2 we have the path loss prediction of selected models. From this table, Lietchy model provide the less path loss. This is provable by looking Figs. 4, 5 and 6. In these Figures, Lietchy model is more close to measured points.

4.2 New Empirical Path Loss Model

Liechty model takes into account the number of obstacle between the transmitter and the receiver and their attenuation on the signal. But, the distance of each attenuation point also influence the quality of the signal. So considering the distance from the

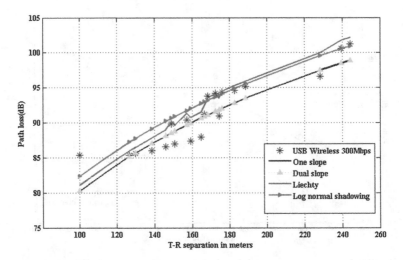

Fig. 6. Comparison of path loss in built space between selected models

Table 2. Comparative results between selected Models:

Models		Mean error (dB)	Standard deviation (dB)
Free space	One slope	0.90	1.12
	Dual slope	0.90	1.12
	Lietchy	0.90	1.12
	Log normal	1.54	1.68
	Partitionned	141.03	142.89
Raised space	One slope	1.97	2.41
	Dual slope	1.97	2.41
	Lietchy	0.94	1.35
	Log normal	1.54	1.81
	Partitionned	116.73	117.32
Built space	One slope	1.73	2.10
	Dual slope	1.73	2.10
	Lietchy	1.60	2.03
	Log normal	1.97	2.49
	Partitionned	109.71	109.93

transmitter to those points during the prediction could improve the prediction of the signal. However, since it is difficult to consider the distance from the transmitter to all those points, we just consider the distance to the first obstacle, the so-called breakpoint. We assume that the attenuation at this point has the greatest impact on the signal.

The optimization is done by adding to Liechty model the parameters of the Dual slope model. This results in Eq. 10:

$$PL_{new} = PL(d_0) + \begin{cases} 10n_1 log_{10}d & with\ 1m < d \le d_{bp} \\ 10n_2 log_{10}\dfrac{d}{d_{bp}} + 10n_1 log_{10}d_{bp} + \displaystyle\sum_i num_i * a_i & with\ d > d_{bp} \end{cases}$$

$$(11)$$

Where:

$PL(d_0)$: attenuation of the signal at the distance d_0 (dB)
d: distance between the transmitter and the receiver (m)
d_0: reference distance (m)
d_{bp}: distance from the transmitter to the first obstacle (m)
$nbre_i$: number of obstacle of type i
a_i: attenuation of obstacle of type i (dB)
n_1: path loss exponent for $d \le d_{bp}$
n_2: path loss exponent for $d > d_{bp}$.

Figures 7 and 8 show a comparison between the two models on measured data respectively in built space and raised space. From these Figures it is clear that the new model is more close to measured data than Liechty model both in raised space and in built space.

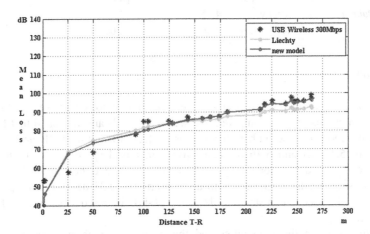

Fig. 7. Path Loss in built space Lietchy and new model

From Table 3 the new model provide a better prediction of the path loss of the signal. In raised space we obtain a mean error of 2.33 dB and a standard deviation of 4.02 dB and in built space a mean error of 2.36 dB and a standard deviation of 4.01 dB.

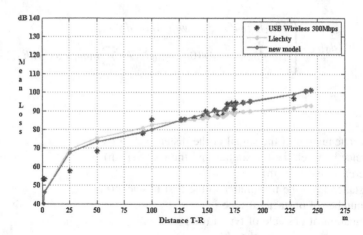

Fig. 8. Path Loss in raised space Lietchy and new model

Table 3. Comparative results between Lietchy Model and the new model

Models		Mean error (dB)	Standard deviation (dB)
Raised space	Lietchy	4.22	5.12
	New model	2.33	4.02
Built space	Lietchy	4.35	5.46
	New model	2.36	4.01

5 Conclusion

In this work, we defined three scenario tied to rural regions and we conducted a measurement campaign. We compared five selected models and we found that Liechty model is the more precise with a mean error of 4.22 dB and 4.35 dB and standard deviation of 5.12 dB and 5.46 dB respectively in raised space and in built space. Further, we improved this model by considering the distance to the first breakpoint. We obtained a better prediction model with a mean error of 2.33 dB in raised space and 2.36 dB in built space, and a standard deviation of 4.02 in raised space and 4.01 dB in built space.

Usually, between the transmitter and the receiver, we observe more than one breakpoint. To be more precise, all those different breakpoints should be taken into consideration. But thinking like this should make the model more complex and difficult to handle. The next step of this work is to study the impact of other breakpoints on the precision of the path loss model. And we will also compare the new model to more other empirical path loss models in more different scenario.

References

1. Sumit, J.: Outdoor propagation models : a literature review. IJCSE **12**(2) (2012)
2. Egli, J.: Radio propagation above 40 mc over irregular terrain. Proc. IRE (IEEE) **45**, 1383–1391 (1957)
3. Alam, D., Khan, R.H.: Comparative study of path loss models of WIMAX at 2.5 GHz frequency band. Int. J. Future. Gener. Commun. Netw. **6**(2), 11–23 (2013)
4. Rakesh, N., Srivatsa, S.K.: A study on path loss analysis for GSM mobile networks for urban, rural and suburban region of Karnataka state. Int. J. Distrib. Parallel. Syst. (IJDPS) **4**(1), 53–66 (2013)
5. Chebil, J., et al.: Comparison between measured and predicted path loss for mobile communication in Malaysia. World. Appl. Sci. J. **21**, 123–128 (2013). (Mathematical Applications in Engineering)
6. Kumari, M., et al.: Comparative study of path loss models in different environments. Int. J. Eng. Sci. Technol. **3**(4), 2945–2949 (2011)
7. Erceg, V., Greenstein, L.J., Tjandra, S., Parkoff, S.R., Gupta, A., Kulic, B., Julius, A., Jastrzab, R.: An empirically based path loss model for wireless channels in suburban environments. In: GLOBECOM 1998, vol. 2, pp. 922–927 (1998)
8. Medeisis, A., Kajackas, A.: On the use of the universal Okumura-Hata propagation prediction model in rural areas. IEEE. Veh. Technol. Conf. Proc. **3**, 450–453 (2000)
9. Liechty, L.C.: Path loss measurements and model analysis of 2.4 GHz wireless network in an outdoor environment. Master's thesis, Georgia Institute of Technology (2007)
10. Hata, M.: Empirical formula for propagation loss in land mobile radio services. IEEE Trans. Veh. Technol. **1**(29), 317–325 (1980)
11. Tummala, D.: Indoor propagation modeling at 2.4 GHz for IEEE 802.11 networks. Master's thesis, University of North Texas (2005)

Quantifying the Effects of Circuitous Routes on the Latency of Intra-Africa Internet Traffic: A Study of Research and Education Networks

Josiah Chavula[1]([⊠]), Nick Feamster[3], Antoine Bagula[2], and Hussein Suleman[1]

[1] Department of Computer Science, University of Cape Town, Private Bag X3,
Rondebosch 7701, South Africa
jchavula@cs.uct.ac.za

[2] Department of Computer Science, University of Western Cape, Private Bag X17,
Bellville 7535, South Africa

[3] School of Computer Science, Georgia Institute of Technology, 266 Ferst Drive,
Room 3348, Atlanta, GA 30332, USA

Abstract. Despite an increase in the number of Internet eXchange Points (IXP) in Africa, as well as proliferation of submarine and terrestrial fibre optic cable systems, the level of peering among Africa's Internet service providers remains low. Using active network measurements, this work characterizes the level of interconnectivity and peering among Africa's National Research and Education Networks (NRENs), and examines the performance of traffic exchange in terms of latencies. This paper shows that over 75 % of Africa's inter-university traffic follows circuitous inter-continental routes, and is characterised by latencies that are more than double those of traffic exchanged within the continent.

Keywords: Round-trip time · Latency · Peering · Active topology measurements · Internet exchange points · National Research and Education Networks

1 Introduction

Latency, measured as round trip time (RTT) for traffic to move from source to the destination, and for the acknowledgement packet to be received by the sender [1], is an important characteristic of Internet connectivity that affects the performance and responsiveness of Internet applications, especially real-time and interactive ones. This is particularly important for National Research and Education Networks (NRENs), where many education and collaboration oriented applications are used. High latency makes it difficult for research communities to make use of Internet-based collaborative tools such as real-time remote lectures or sharing of virtualized resources such as computer processors [2]. Furthermore, many scientific research facilities, such as the Large Hadron Collider (LHC) and other astronomical observatories, generate lots of data at high speed that needs

© Institute for Computer Sciences, Social Informatics and Telecommunications Engineering 2015
A. Nungu et al. (Eds.): AFRICOMM 2014, LNICST 147, pp. 64–73, 2015.
DOI: 10.1007/978-3-319-16886-9_7

to be exchanged among research centres around the world. These applications necessitate low latency networks among the research community.

In Africa, interconnectivity and peering among Internet Service Providers (ISPs) remains low [3]. With many of universities obtaining Internet connectivity from such ISPs [2,4], traffic exchanged among African NRENs traverse higher tier transit providers and global Internet Exchange Points (IXP) through long intercontinental links, resulting in high latency and data transmission costs.

The contribution of this work is two fold; first through active topology measurements, it takes a fresh look at the logical topology of the African Internet, with a specific focus on education and research networks. As detailed in Sect. 3, topology measurements are carried out from 5 vantage points targeting a selected set of 95 universities. The results are presented in the form of AS-level and PoP-level maps, presented in Sect. 4. The second contribution is the performance analysis for traffic that uses inter-continental links, and this paper shows that links connecting Africa to other continents contribute over 50 % of the latency for the traffic that uses those links. As presented in Sect. 4.2, more than 75 % of intra-Africa traffic utilizes inter-continental links.

2   Background and Related Work

The Internet is an interconnection of many privately managed networks known as Autonomous Systems (ASes) [5]. Traffic exchange among ASes is facilitated through the Border Gateway Protocol (BGP), a single path routing system that conveys AS-level paths between domains, enabling them to interconnect and exchange traffic. Any two ASes can exchange traffic if they have some direct logical connection between them, or if they both have access to other higher level providers that can transit traffic between them [6]. Due to this hierarchical structure of the Internet, traffic whose source and destination networks are geographically close may sometimes have to traverse circuitous remote links in search of interconnecting paths - a phenomenon know as boomerang routing.

To obtain a better understanding of an internetwork, topology discovery techniques are used to obtain data for network visualization. Internet topology discovery techniques can largely be grouped into two: passive techniques and active techniques [7]. Passive techniques involve analysing network management data such as BGP routing tables in order to infer the network topology in terms of logical relationships among ASes. Active measurements, on the other hand, rely on sending specially crafted packets into the network with the aim of soliciting topology information [8]. Active measurement techniques attempt to exploit network management protocols such as SNMP and ICMP to solicit responses from a set of network destinations, and then analyse such responses to infer topological characteristics such as route paths, round-trip-times (RTTs) and packet loss.

Recent work on the African Internet topology [3] has shown that about 66 % of traffic between South African Internet vantage points and Africa-based Google cache servers is routed outside the continent. The same work also characterized the IXP peering situation in Africa and showed that most African

ISPs do not peer among themselves at national or regional IXPs, but rather prefer to peer at larger European IXPs such as London and Amsterdam, presumably to achieve better economies of scale with access to global networks. Gilmore et al. [9] also carried out topology measurements on the African Internet from a South African vantage point, and showed that routes originating from the South African Tertiary Education Network were mostly routed via the UK, Scandinavia and the USA.

3   Dataset

This work used active network topology discovery techniques to characterise the performance of the traffic whose source and destination is within Africa, and also to obtain a logical connectivity map of the African NRENs. In particular, this work performs active Internet measurements from 5 vantage points that are part of the CAIDA's Internet measurement platform - Archipelago, and are located in North, West, East and Southern Africa (Morocco, Gambia, Senegal, South Africa and Rwanda). The Archipelago measurement platform is based a network measurement tool called Scamper [10], which implements Paris-traceroute [11], a variant of traceroute based on Multi-path Discovery Algorithm (MDA) [12,13].

3.1   Traceroute Measurements

In this work, Internet path traces were performed to a set of 95 university campus IP addresses across 29 African countries. Traceroute probes from 5 vantage points to each of the IP addresses were repeated daily for 14 days from 6 April to 20 April, 2014.

Of interest from each of the traces is the round-trip time for each source-destination pair, as well as the geo-location of the IP path hops used. Another interest is to compare the latency of the traffic that is routed through intercontinental links (boomerang traffic) in comparison to locally routed traffic. For this purpose, traces from each vantage point are grouped into two; intercontinental traffic that gets routed at Points of Presence (PoPs) outside Africa, and intra-Africa traffic that gets routed within the continent. For the inter-continental traffic, a further interest is to quantify the effect of the inter-continental links (i.e., latency from the vantage point to remote inter-continental gateway) on the overall RTT.

To observe the extent of inter-continental link utilization from each vantage point, traceroute traces are grouped by source and destination pairs. From each vantage point, the traces for each source-destination are analysed as follows: starting from the source (vantage point), the next hop and its corresponding RTT is extracted; using MaxMind's GeoIPLite database, each hop's geographical location (country and longitude/latitude coordinates) are obtained; if the extracted hop is located outside Africa, then the traffic trace is categorised as inter-continental. For each inter-continental route, the first hop outside Africa, together with its corresponding RTT, is recorded as the inter-continental gateway RTT for the route.

The RTT for each source-destination pair is taken as the RTT of the last responding hop. However, since not all probes reach the end point (among others due to blocking by routers [7]), only probes that reach the destination network are considered valid RTT values for each source-destination pair. To determine if the destination network is reached, the last responding hop's autonomous system number (ASN) and country is compared with that of the probe destination. Finally, the RTT values for each source-destination pair are computed as the mean of the multiple RTTs.

3.2 Dataset Limitations

Although the topology measurements were carried out from multiple vantage points, the drawback is that the paths discovered are only forward paths from the vantage points to the destinations. This is the case because Internet traffic is largely asymmetric, i.e., forward paths are not necessarily the same as reverse paths [5]. Therefore, the maps obtained from outgoing traceroute measurements are still incomplete. A more complete picture can be obtained by increasing the number and distribution of vantage points [14].

Another major challenge on the analysis of the dataset is the inaccuracy of the geolocation information for the IP addresses. Maxmind's free geolocation database - GeoLite2 - reported to have about 80 % accuracy for IP to city resolution (within 40 km) for most countries [15]. For example, the accuracy level reported for South Africa's IP to city database is 71 %, whereas for Kenya it is reported to be as low as 55 %. However, the accuracy for IP to country resolution, on which route categorisation is based, is higher at 99.8 %.

4 Results

4.1 Circuitous Logical Links

A key observation from the traceroute data is that a larger percentage of traffic originating in Africa and destined for African universities gets routed through PoPs that are outside the continent. On average, 75 % of the traces from African vantage points to African NRENs traversed inter-continental links through PoPs in Europe, such as Amsterdam, London, Lisbon, and Marseille. However, depending on the geographical location of the vantage points, different levels of inter-continental traffic is observed. For example, the vantage points along the north-west coast of Africa used inter-continental links for as much as 95 % of the traces, whereas vantage points in central and southern Africa had a relatively lower usage of inter-continental links. From the Rwandan vantage point, 70 % of the traceroute traffic used inter-continental links, while the South African vantage point had only 60 % of the traffic using inter-continental links. The lower usage of inter-continental links by the South African vantage point can be attributed to the direct logical links observed between South Africa and some of its neighbouring countries, such as Mozambique, Zambia and Zimbabwe, as well as links to East Africa, such as the EASSY submarine fibre-optic cable.

Figure 1 shows the PoP-level connectivity map for traffic originating at the five vantage points to the addresses in the sample.

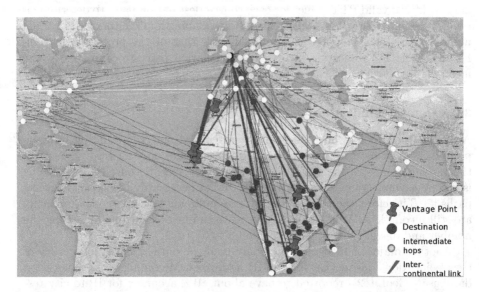

Fig. 1. Logical paths for African traffic, showing logical links interconnecting in Europe and North America

4.2   Round-Trip Times (RTT)

Results from the traceroute measurements show that inter-continental traffic from Africa to African universities experiences an average RTT of 300 ms, in contrast to an RTT of 139 ms for traffic that did not leave the continent (intra-Africa). Inter-continental RTT has a standard deviation of 120 ms while the intra-Africa RTT has a standard deviation of 82 ms. The standard deviations in both cases show an overlap in latencies obtained by the two sets of traffic, indicating that, for certain source-destination pairs, better performance is obtained by using exchange points outside Africa, while for other traffic, better performance is obtained when traffic is routed within the continent. Figure 2 shows a scatter plot of the RTTs for both cases and shows an overlap of performance between the two sets of traffic.

4.3   AS-Level Peering

Using Maximind's database and the WHOIS database, IP hops in the traced paths are mapped to their corresponding Autonomous System Number (ASN). Each ASN is represented as a node in a graph, and edges are created where

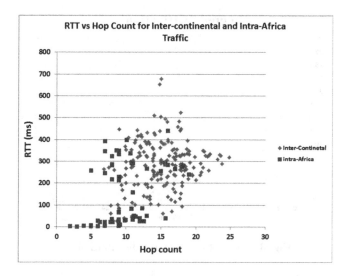

Fig. 2. Scatter plot showing the distribution of RTT for intra-Africa traffic and inter-continental traffic.

there is direct link between ASes. The observed interconnection among the African NRENs is largely through ASes that peer at global IXPs in Europe, such as Cogent Communications (ASN 174), TATA (ASN 6453), Level3 (ASN 3356) and Seacom (ASN 37100). These ASes peer mainly at the London Internet Exchange (LINX), Amsterdam Internet Exchange (AMS-IX), and Frankfurt Internet Exchange. There is also high connectivity to the UbuntuNet Alliance (ASN 36944) peering at LINX and AMS-IX.

The AS-level graph shows that there is minimal peering within Africa, as most of the probed networks have direct AS-level paths to the ASes in Europe, resulting in high node degree (ranging from 18 to 32) at the European ASes, and low node degree (between one and three) for Africa-based ASes. The AS-level graph indicates an overall network diameter of 8, an average path length of 3.37, and an average clustering coefficient of 0.180. On the other hand, a path length of 3.37 would suggest a densely interconnected AS-level topology, a low clustering coefficient of 0.180 suggests that, overall, the AS-level topology is sparse. This finding is consistent with the previously reported low peering among Africa based ASes and a high connectivity to the global IXPs [3]. Figure 3 shows the degree distribution of the AS-level topology.

5 Discussion

5.1 Effect of Inter-continental Latency

Round-trip times as well as geographical distribution of routes for inter-NREN traffic in Africa reveals a lack of peering among the African service providers.

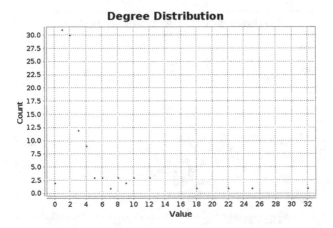

Fig. 3. AS-level node degree distribution.

Despite a growing number of national IXPs in Africa, there is still limited inter-connection at regional IXPs to facilitate cross-border peering. As a result, inter-NREN traffic in sub-Saharan Africa follows circuitous inter-continental routes, resulting in much higher latencies compared to traffic exchanged within the continent. The physical length of the transmission medium travelled by the packets (linearised path) has a significant contribution to the internet path delay. This delay is relative to the signal propagation time, which is bounded by the speed of light, i.e. the speed cannot be greater than the speed of light (299.792 km/ms) [16]. In practice, however, the speed of light in a fibre optic cable is slower at about 200 km/ms.

We observed that traffic to countries with no direct fibre connection from the vantage points[1] experienced much higher latencies. For example, traffic from Johannesburg to Malawi is routed first through London, then Maputo Mozambique, before being forwarded to Lilongwe, and experiences RTT of around 380 ms. Traffic from southern Africa to southern Africa routed via London, covers a distance of roughly 30,000 km, hence a round trip of about 60,000 km (the West Africa Cable System fibre-optic cable from Cape Town to London is about 14,530 km long). At optic speed of 200 km/ms in fibre cable, this translates to a minimum RTT of about 300 ms. The observed RTT for this round-trip is around 370 ms, which suggests that about 80 % of the RTT in this case is due to the linearized distance factor alone. The effect of inter-continental routing is demonstrated further in the case of universities within the same country that achieve remarkably different RTTs due to where their traffic is routed. For example, in Kenya, one university has its traffic from Johannesburg South Africa routed via Amsterdam (AIMS-IX), then back to South Africa (CINX, Cape Town) before being forwarded to Kenya, and achieves an RTT average of about 400 ms.

---

[1] http://afterfibre.net/.

In comparison, another university in the same country (Kenya) has a direct logical link from Johannesburg to Kenya and achieves an RTT of only 80 ms.

Lower latencies are observed between countries where direct fibre cable connection and peering exists. For example, the Zambia NREN (ZamREN) recently established a direct connection to the Johannesburg IXP where it is peering with the UbuntuNet alliance, and using this link, traffic from South Africa to ZamREN experiences a low latency of 55 ms. Other locations achieving low RTT from the South African vantage point are in the neighbouring countries such as Mozambique (45 ms) and Namibia (80 ms). The countries have direct fibre links to South Africa. Furthermore, where functional NRENs are present and traffic is routed locally within national IXPs, much lower latency is observed. For example, within South Africa, members of South African NRENs (SanRen) are linked though a fibre-optic backbone and exchange traffic locally at national IXPs - the Johannesburg Internet Exchange (JINX) and the Cape Town IXP (CINX). In the experiments, traffic from the vantage point located within the SanRen, to other SanRen members achieved an average RTT of 20 ms.

Further more, vantage points experience varying degrees of delay on the inter-continental link depending on their proximity to their remote gateways (i.e., the first hop outside Africa). For example, Morocco, which is closest to Europe among all the vantage points used in this study, had an average RTT of 39 ms to its remote gateways, whereas the South African vantage point had an average RTT of 170 ms to its remote gateways. The highest latency for reaching the remote gateway was from the Rwandan vantage point, which was at 199 ms. In general, vantage points with a higher inter-continental link latency obtained higher overall RTT, which shows that the high latency for inter-continental traffic is largely due to the delay on the egress and ingress links. On average, the RTT from the vantage points to the remote gateways is 150 ms, almost half the average RTT obtained for inter-continental traffic. This is also more than the average RTT of 139 ms obtained for traffic exchanged within Africa.

5.2   Improving the Routing and Traffic Engineering Environment

One solution that is used to reduce latencies and the circuitous route problem is the use of Internet Exchange Points (IXPs) [17], which can enable ASes to establish mutual peering agreements for direct exchange of local traffic. For end-to-end communication, the challenge is that selection of Internet route paths is mostly influenced by routing policies that are optimized for interests of individual autonomous systems. Such policies do not provide guarantees for optimal end-to-end connections and sometimes result in packets not traversing the shortest paths to their destinations. To deal with this challenge, inter-domain traffic engineering (TE) techniques aim to optimize resource utilization and internetwork performance through mechanisms that identify and dynamically use optimal low-latency paths. This requires routing systems that are able to learn and make use of inter-domain topology information in choosing routing paths.

Solving the problem of circuitous routes also requires effective TE techniques. With multiple end to end paths, it is possible to optimise usage of inter-continental links as well as cross-border terrestrial links. One challenge however, is that the inter-domain routing protocol, BGP, being a single-path system, is inflexible with regard to multi-path routing and inter-domain TE. On the other hand, novel hierarchical routing protocols such as the Locator/Identifier Separation Protocol (LISP) [18], provide new opportunities for inter-domain traffic engineering by allowing networks to announce multiple gateways (route locators) for reachability, making it possible to have multi-path routing. Furthermore, Software Defined Networking (SDN) protocols allow for dynamic and remote configuration of traffic forwarding paths. These protocols can make possible collaborative routing and dynamic peering among edge networks, by allowing ASes to exchange multiple routing paths and to dynamically respond to varying network path conditions and QoS requirements. Furthermore, networks could employ remote peering strategies, dynamically selecting and peering at optimal open exchange points. For example, SEACOM[2], a major fibre cable operator in Africa, provides open peering points that allow networks to peering remotely.

6   Conclusion

This paper has looked at the effect of circuitous inter-continental IP routes on the performance of traffic exchanged between education and research institutions in Africa. Traceroute probes on a sample of 95 African IP addresses has shown that on average 75 % of the traffic originating in Africa and destined for African universities traverse links outside the continent, thereby performing with a latency that is more than double that of the intra-Africa traffic. Future work will evaluate how this actually affects the performance of the African Internet, and will undertake further monitoring of the actual Internet traffic to determine how much traffic is actually exchanged between the African NRENs.

Acknowledgement. We are thankful to the Hasso-Plattner-Institute (HPI) for their financial support towards this work.

References

1. Ahmad, M., Guha, R.: Evaluating end-user network benefits of peering with path latencies. In: 2012 21st International Conference on Computer Communications and Networks (ICCCN), pp. 1–7, July 2012
2. Barry, B., Barton, C., Chukwuma, V., Cottrell, L., Kalim, U., Petitdidier, M., Rabiu, B.: eGY-Africa: better internet connectivity to reduce the digital divide. In: IST-Africa, pp. 1–15. IEEE (2010)
3. Gupta, A., Calder, M., Feamster, N., Chetty, M., Calandro, E., Katz-Bassett, E.: Peering at the internet's frontier: a first look at ISP interconnectivity in Africa. In: Faloutsos, M., Kuzmanovic, A. (eds.) PAM 2014. LNCS, vol. 8362, pp. 204–213. Springer, Heidelberg (2014)

---

[2] http://seacom.mu/services-solutions/.

4. Steiner, R., Tirivayi, A., Tirivayi, N., Jensen, M., Hamilton, P., Buechler, J. Jeffries, A., Emdon, U.H., Ibrahim, I.A., et al.: Promoting african research and education networking. In: International Development Research Center, January 2005
5. Shavitt, Y., Weinsberg, U.: Quantifying the importance of vantage point distribution in internet topology mapping (extended version). IEEE J. Sel. Areas Commun. **29**, 1837–1847 (2011)
6. Ahmad, M., Guha, R.: Internet exchange points and internet routing. In: 2011 19th IEEE International Conference on Network Protocols (ICNP), pp. 292–294 (2011)
7. Donnet, B., Friedman, T.: Internet topology discovery: a survey. IEEE Commun. Surv. Tutor. **9**, 56–69 (2007)
8. Govindan, R., Tangmunarunkit, H.: Heuristics for internet map discovery. In: Proceedings of the Nineteenth Annual Joint Conference of the IEEE Computer and Communications Societies, INFOCOM 2000, vol. 3, pp. 1371–1380. IEEE (2000)
9. Gilmore, J., Huysamen, N., Krzesinski, A.: Mapping the african internet. In: Proceedings Southern African Telecommunication Networks and Applications Conference (SATNAC), Mauritius, September 2007
10. Luckie, M.: Scamper: a scalable and extensible packet prober for active measurement of the internet. In: Proceedings of the 10th ACM SIGCOMM Conference on Internet Measurement, pp. 239–245. ACM (2010)
11. Augustin, B., Friedman, T., Teixeira, R.: Multipath tracing with paris traceroute. In: Workshop on End-to-End Monitoring Techniques and Services, E2EMON 2007, pp. 1–8. IEEE, Munich (2007)
12. Augustin, B., Friedman, T., Teixeira, R.: Measuring load-balanced paths in the internet. In: Proceedings of the 7th ACM SIGCOMM Conference on Internet Measurement, pp. 149–160. ACM (2007)
13. Augustin, B., Friedman, T., Teixeira, R.: Measuring multipath routing in the internet. IEEE/ACM Trans. Netw. (TON) **19**(3), 830–840 (2011)
14. Shavitt, Y., Shir, E.: Dimes: let the internet measure itself. ACM SIGCOMM Comput. Commun. Rev. **35**(5), 71–74 (2005)
15. Shavitt, Y., Zilberman, N.: A geolocation databases study. IEEE J. Sel. Areas Commun. **29**, 2044–2056 (2011)
16. Landa, R., Araujo, J., Clegg, R., Mykoniati, E., Griffin, D., Rio, M.: The large-scale geography of internet round trip times. In: IFIP Networking Conference, pp. 1–9, May 2013
17. Chatzis, N., Smaragdakis, G., Feldmann, A., Willinger, W.: There is more to ixps than meets the eye. ACM SIGCOMM Comput. Commun. Rev. **43**(5), 19–28 (2013)
18. Li, K., Wang, S., Wang, X.: Edge router selection and traffic engineering in lisp-capable networks. J. Commun. Netw. **13**, 612–620 (2011)

Towards Centralized Spectrum Allocation Optimization for Multi-Channel Wireless Backhauls

Michael Rademacher[1], Senka Hadzic[2]([✉]), Philipp Batroff[2],
Osianoh Glenn Aliu[2], and Mathias Kretschmer[3]

[1] Hochschule Bonn-Rhein-Sieg, Sankt Augustin, Germany
michael.rademacher@h-brs.de
[2] Fraunhofer FOKUS, Sankt Augustin, Germany
senka.hadzic@fokus-extern.fraunhofer.de,
{philipp.batroff,osianoh.glenn.aliu}@fokus.fraunhofer.de
[3] DeFuTech UG, Hennef, Germany
mathias.kretschmer@defutech.de
http://defutech.com

Abstract. With the growing potential of wireless backhaul technologies for outdoor environments and rising interest in unlicensed bands for broadband delivery, dynamic channel assignment and improved spectrum utilization is re-emerging as a research topic. In this paper we describe a centralized channel assignment optimization for our wireless backhaul architecture WiBACK. In order to efficiently utilize wireless channels in heterogeneous networks, we propose an improvement to the current frequency planning scheme using 802.11 as an example. The contributions in this paper can improve broadband access for emerging areas, often lacking required telecommunication infrastructure.

Keywords: Channel assignment · Frequency planning · Wireless backhaul · Spectrum optimization · Rural areas · Mesh networks

1 Introduction

A backhaul network bridges the gap between the backbone and the access network. Different technologies can be used for the backhaul, such as Ethernet, digital subscriber line (DSL), synchronous/plesiochronous digital hierarchy (SDH/PDH) interfaces or wireless technologies. Today, wireless backhaul networks are used to extend, complement or even replace traditional operator equipment, to relay end-user traffic from access points to the backbone. Wireless Backhauls (WiBACKs) goal is to extend the Internet coverage while keeping

---

S. Hadzic—This work was carried out during the tenure of an ERCIM "Alain Bensoussan" Fellowship Programme. The research leading to these results has received funding from the European Union Seventh Framework Programme (FP7/2007–2013) under grant agreement n° 246016.

A. Nungu et al. (Eds.): AFRICOMM 2014, LNICST 147, pp. 74–83, 2015.
DOI: 10.1007/978-3-319-16886-9_8

the investment cost low. Wireless backhaul deployments provide a solution for broadband access especially in rural areas, where the lack of sufficient profitability prevents operators to invest in infrastructure. Another characteristics of rural areas that impose challenges are the lack of energy access, shortage of skilled labor, huge distances and low population density. All these factors contribute to very high OPEX/CAPEX. WiBACK, a wireless backhaul solution developed at Fraunhofer FOKUS makes use of heterogeneous multi-radio nodes, forming point-to-point links in order to extend the broadband coverage. Details on WiBACK will be provided in Sect. 2.1.

In multi-radio networks, smart channel assignments are desirable for several reasons. The most common motivation is to minimize the interference from external networks, but also to improve the capacity when some links are heavily used, and thereby balance the load over different channels. With the growing adoption of outdoor Wireless Local Area Network (WLAN) and its integration as an essential part of future heterogeneous networks, particularly for traffic offload and backhaul for small cells, new challenges on the opportunistic usage of these channels have to be addressed. Furthermore, channel bonding mechanisms in 802.11n/ac for example, enable the use of wider channels but also increase the likelihood of co-channel interference. Channel occupancy in the unlicensed Industrial, Scientific and Medical (ISM) or Unlicensed National Information In-frastructure (U-NII) band is increasing due to the immense opportunities and applications it can be utilized for. With no rigid regulation on accessibility of channels in this spectrum, it has become pertinent to include a dynamic channel assignment scheme for wireless backhaul networks operating in this ISM band. Therefore we intend to extend our current frequency planning scheme in WiBACK.

The remaining of the paper is organized as follows: In Sect. 2 we present state of the art solutions for channel assignment in multi-radio wireless networks, the current channel assignment implementation in WiBACK and the motivation for our new approach. We propose a solution to improve the existing implementation in Sect. 3 and evaluate the proposed method with results in Sect. 4. Finally, Sect. 5 concludes the paper and gives an overview of our intended future work.

2   Related Work

The simplest approach to multi-radio channel assignment is the Common Channel Assignment (CCA) [1], which assigns channel 1 to the first radio interface of each node, channel 2 to the second radio interface of each node, and so on. This approach demands no coordination among nodes and retains network connectivity. However, it also leads to a high degree of interference and only works with omnidirectional antennas. For this reason, the fixed assignment method CCA usually serves as a baseline for performance comparison. Some papers consider the joint channel assignment and routing problem. Rainwala et al. [2] proposes an iterative routing algorithm based on traffic profiles, using only local traffic load information. It is shown that even with just two network interface cards on each node instead of a single radio, it is possible to achieve up to 8 times higher network throughput.

In general, temporary topology alterations should be avoided or at least minimized, since they may lead to suboptimal routing or even network partitioning. In order to guarantee that the network will remain connected after channel assignment, [3] proposes the use of a default channel, over which the data flow is redirected during resource allocation. The channel assignment problem can be formulated from different perspectives, but mostly used tools are graph theory, multi-objective optimization and game theory. The majority of approaches make use of graph theory to model the interference relationship between multi-radio nodes in a wireless mesh network. The edge coloring problem is formulated as follows: nodes are represented as vertices, and the links form the edges of the graph. A pair of nodes has a link between them in the undirected connectivity graph if they are located within each others transmission range. The graph coloring problem consists in finding the k minimum numbers of colors to paint the edges of a graph so that two adjacent edges are assigned different colors. It is a well known NP[1] hard problem [2]. Semidefinite and linear programming solutions have been proposed to reduce the time complexity of the channel assignment problem. A multi-radio conflict graph, an extension to the regular conflict graph model, has been proposed in [3] to model the interference between multi-radio nodes in a mesh network. Instead of links between nodes, links between single radios are represented as graph edges. Problems arise when the number of interfaces on a node exceeds the number of available channels.

Channel assignment can be seen as a multi-objective optimization problem for which several objectives can be defined with various conflicting constraints and requirements. The problem is in general NP-hard and many heuristics have been proposed [2,4], providing suboptimal solutions. An overview of channel assignment approaches using multi-objective optimization is given in [5].

Both cooperative and non-cooperative game theory can be used as a tool to model the channel assignment problem [6]. In [7] a non-cooperative game is formulated where wireless interfaces act as players, and the player's strategy set is represented by channels available to each player. The utility function is defined to minimize co-channel interference from other players. In practice, most evolutionary algorithms based on game theory and artificial intelligence are not widely adopted by industry due to known issues with their stability [8].

Our proposed solution is thus inspired by existing graph coloring schemes which have been shown to be suboptimal. We therefore define and prioritize a set of objectives including constraints based on real deployments and regulatory issues.

2.1   Current WiBACK Approach

WiBACK is a self managing wireless backhaul network, with deployment scenarios ranging from last-mile service provisioning to wide-area coverage in emerging

---

[1] Non-deterministic Polynomial-time.

areas and developing countries. The WiBACK architecture is technology agnostic, making it able to exploit features of low cost off-the shelf hardware like IEEE 802.11 radios to form long distance point-to-point links among multi-radio nodes. In order to meet the QoS requirements, these links must operate on low-interference channels.

The WiBACK architecture can be positioned between access and backbone networks. Controller nodes and Access Points (AP) form the WiBACK interface to external networks. WiBACK can be used to complement existing operator networks, but may also be deployed as a cost-effective low-energy alternative to conventional backhaul networks. Its technology-independent nature allows WiBACK to integrate any type of radio network technology, provided that an appropriate abstract control interface is available. The network control plane is inspired by IEEE 802.21, but extends it to a media independent service platform.

The channel assignment in WiBACK is currently implemented during the ring-based topology forming and is not a centralized process [9]. After a node joins the network, it scans on all free interfaces and choses a frequency depending on the scan results. This is used as input for radio planning since new nodes will scan the spectrum and join on the free interface on the previously defined frequency [10], and therefore acts only on local knowledge without any option of the controller to interfere in case of link degradation. If there are multiple available interfaces to join, a WiBACK node attempts to assign the least utilized channel with the highest Signal-to-noise ratio (SNR).

2.2 Motivation for a New Approach

Existing frequency planning schemes based on graph coloring aim to minimize interference in multi-radio networks. We want to further ensure a high throughput for long distance point-to-point links in a typical WiBACK deployment is achieved. In case of 802.11 long distance links, the major constraint limiting the range is the SNR needed for higher modulations, leading to an increased throughput. However, the SNR is mainly reduced by the Free-space path loss (FSPL) and the effects of Fresnel zone. Moreover, common WiFi-cards operate in the ISM band which is under regulatory restrictions by different organizations and governments. In certain frequency bands, regulatory restrictions might require a maximum allowed transmission power, so it is of interest to use particular frequencies for long range links in order to maximize the throughput. A frequency assignment algorithm for long distance wireless backhaul networks should care that following objectives are met (in descending order):

1. No local interference
2. Maximize the Modulation and Coding Scheme (MCS) used
3. Maximize the guard interval
4. Minimize the number of frequencies used for transmission.

To the best of the authors knowledge there is no solution addressing all these goals under the premise of long distance wireless backhaul links operating in the ISM or U-NII band.

3   Proposed Solution

The fundamental priority of the algorithm is to ensure that links are void of interference from transmission by multiple interfaces at the same node. Based on these unique assignments, we aim to maximize the MCS used for each link based on its distance for throughput maximization. We have provided a detailed mapping of the MCS and throughput in [11]. Maintaining a sufficient guard interval is required as shown in [12]. In the 5 GHz ISM band, Adjacent Channel Interference (ACI) is a problem resulting in SNR degradation and the medium is incorrectly sensed busy. Therefore we maximize the guard interval during the channel assignment, taking into account possible interferences in the spectrum as well as locally used frequencies on the other interfaces. Additionally, we are trying to reuse frequencies in order to improve spectrum utilization.

3.1   Algorithm Design

The algorithm works on the principle of graph edge coloring, with the assigned frequencies represented by the colors. Figure 1 is a flow chart of the steps and decisions taken in the algorithm. We need a regulatory database [13] to know which frequencies can be utilized with which power, to be able to calculate the maximum possible MCS with a given distance at the links. Since we are using a centralized approach, we start at the controller (see Sect. 2.1) and from there on we iterate over all available nodes. At each node we check whether the edges have already a frequency assigned. If that is the case, we can continue to the next edge.

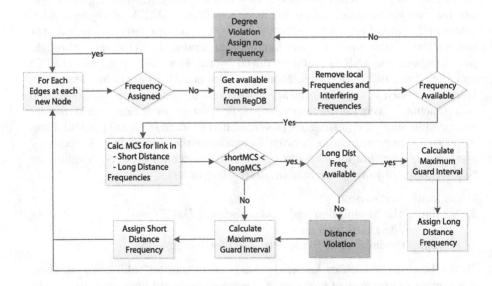

Fig. 1. Flow chart of the algorithm steps

Otherwise we get the available frequencies from the country specific regulatory database and remove the locally interfering frequencies from the other
links of the node, as well as the frequencies on the link from possible external
interferences.

If no more frequencies are available at this point, we leave the link unassigned
and count it as a *Degree Violation* for the validation. If there are frequencies
left, we calculate the maximum MCS for the link in the short distance and
long distance frequency pool. If the short distance MCS is smaller than the
long distance MCS, we use the long distance frequencies, otherwise we apply
short frequencies for the link. Then we calculate the maximum guard interval
considering the interfering frequencies at the link and the chosen part of the
spectrum and assign the resulting frequency. This results in an implicit frequency
reuse if the neighbouring nodes have the same amount of interfaces, see Fig. 2.

In case we have to use long distance frequencies but do not have any in the
spectrum available, we assign a frequency from the short distance pool with
maximum guard interval and denote this edge as a Distance Violation.

4   Verification

We evaluate the performance and reliability of our solution by testing its quality
under different simulated network topologies. We create random graphs utilizing
the networkx python library [14] based on the concept of a randomized tree which
is the common case in existing deployments. It is generated in the simulation
by starting at the controller node and adding a random number of edges at the
consecutive nodes. For all random processes we use the Linux built-in random
device as seed. Every random graph is specified by the number of nodes and the
maximum possible degree, and an example is provided in Fig. 2. We assign a random link distance in the range from 1 to 10 km to each link, based on experience
in our real deployment scenarios. Interferences are generated randomly on each
link as non-available channels for the algorithm, the upper bound being 50 % of
the overall available frequencies. Without considering the added advantages of
using directional antennas and the vast amount of white spaces in rural areas, we
have chosen a worst case scenario to demonstrate the reliability of our solution.
To accurately evaluate the maximum possible MCS we calculate the link budget
based on the well known concept of FSPL as well as an additional margin of
5 dB[2]. We consider typical hardware currently used for 802.11 based WiBACK
nodes. This includes 802.11n WiFi cards (Mikrotik R11e-5HnD), antennas (26 dB
gain) and loss occurring from the needed high-frequency cables (1.5 dB) [11].
Because of plans for future build-ups we choose the country of South Africa
for our simulation. This especially implies the care and attention of the regulatory restrictions [13] for the 5 GHz ISM band. Two bands with a different
maximum possible Equivalent isotropically radiated power (EIRP) are available:
5170–5330 MHz using 20 dBm EIRP and 5490–5710 MHz using 27 dBm EIRP.

---

[2] The additional margin may be used for compensating a possible Fresnel Zone violation or reflexions.

This leads to a total amount of 21 frequencies assuming a bandwidth of 20 MHz, and 11 for 40 MHz. In our simulation, 1000 random topologies were generated for each combination of input parameters. We evaluate three different output values to measure the quality of our algorithm which are strongly related to the goals mentioned in Sect. 2.2. *Degree Violation* represents a case where the algorithm was unable to assign a free frequency to the current link. *Distance Violation* occurs when the algorithm uses a low power frequency in the case a high power frequency was needed. We quantify this value as percentage of all links. Strongly related to this parameter is the value of *Lost MCS* which describes the overall missed MCS due to *Distance Violations* compared to the maximum possible MCS for a perfect frequency assignment.

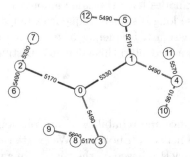

Fig. 2. Example of generated graph. Number of nodes = 13, maximum degree = 3. Low Power links = green, high power links = red (Color figure online).

4.1 Results

In this section we present the results of our algorithm considering two different cases. First, we assume a fixed channel bandwidth of 20 MHz. Afterwards, we conduct the same experiments for 40 MHz channel bandwidth which halves the number of available channels but doubles the throughput as described in [11].

20 MHz Channel Bandwidth. For the case of 20 MHz bandwidth we could not obtain any Degree and Distance Violations for networks sizes of 25, 50 and 100 nodes and a maximum degree ranging from 3 to 9. However, a maximum degree of 9 is unlikely in real deployments. Our algorithm was always able to assign a high power frequency where needed and therefore maximizes the possible MCS on each link.

Figure 3 shows for the same amount of nodes and degrees the number of available and assigned frequencies as well as the average guard interval between local links at nodes. In all cases the algorithm did not exhaust all possible frequencies. However, the needed frequencies increase with the network size as well as with the maximum degree of the network. An important result is that the algorithm assigns frequencies in a way that there is an adequate average guard

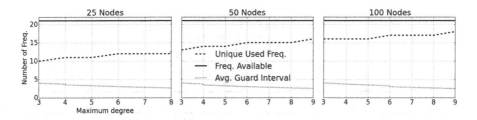

Fig. 3. Results with channel bandwidth 20 MHz. Average link distance: 5,5 km

interval even for high degrees and large networks. The average guard interval ranges from 2.5 (50 MHz) to 4.5 (90 MHz) channels. These values are sufficient to avoid SNR degradation as described in [12].

The average assigned MCS can be observed through the dotted line in Fig. 4. Since the algorithm always assigned the maximum possible MCS for an average link distance of 5.5 km, the average value is constant at 6.4. For lower average link distances or higher available maximum EIRP this value theoretically moves closer to 7.

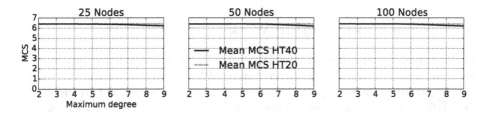

Fig. 4. Average assigned MCS for HT40 and HT20. Average link distance: 5,5 km

40 MHz Channel Bandwidth. A channel bandwidth of 40 MHz is more challenging for the algorithm since a decreased number of channels are available for assignment. This is observable in the results presented in Fig. 5. However, the top row shows again that the algorithm assigned no Degree Violation so there is no local interference for all different network sizes and maximum degrees. This is a surprising result taken into account the high number of simulated interferences and the maximum degrees. However, Distance Violations and the associated Lost MCS occur. This effect is especially evident for a higher degree and for an increased amount of nodes. For the worst-case scenario (network size of 100 nodes, maximum degree of 9) the algorithm assigned at 10 % of the links a short distance frequency where a long distance frequency was preferable. This leads to an overall loss of 15 % of physical throughput in the complete network. However, since 40 MHz channels doubles the possible throughput as described in [11] it is still a preferable choice. The lower row shows a sufficient width of guard interval between one (40 MHz) and two (80 MHz) channels.

The straight line in Fig. 4 shows the average assigned MCS for 40 MHz bandwidth. It can be observed that this value is slightly descending for higher degrees

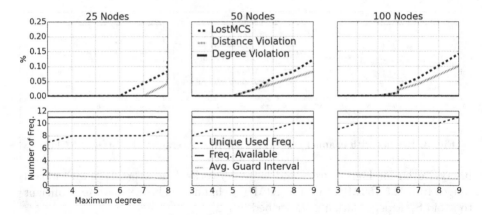

Fig. 5. Results with channel bandwidth 40 MHz. Average link distance: 5,5 km

to a minimum of 6.2. This decrease relates to that Lost MCS in Fig. 5 for higher degrees. However this is still located between the two highest possible MCS, which is a good result for the worst case scenarios used.

5   Conclusion and Future Work

In this paper, we presented a centralized spectrum allocation scheme for wireless backhaul networks using 802.11 as an example. We showed that local interference can be avoided while keeping a guard interval between assigned frequencies. Depending on the number of interfaces at each node and the overall network size, a minimum number of frequencies can be assigned. We showed the difference between an assignment for 20 MHz and 40 MHz channels in the country of South Africa for a large amount of different topologies. We showed that the average assigned MCS is well above 6 for an average link distance of 5.5 km.

As an outcome of this work, several future work items have been identified. While we considered operation on the 20 MHz or 40 MHz channels, a mixed operation may be desirable. Instead of using the MCS for distinguishing between long and short distance links we intend to use the approximated layer 3 throughput as described in [15]. The influence of directional antennas [11] on local interference in combination with geographical location of the nodes may be an interesting approach as well. A centralized spectrum management allows us to incorporate other technologies into our algorithm such as TV-White Spaces (TVWS). Additionally continuous optimization, error handling and Dynamic Frequency XSelection (DFS) restrictions need to be considered.

References

1. Adya, A., Bahl, P., Padhye, J., Wolman, A., Zhou, L.: A multi-radio unification protocol for IEEE 802.11 wireless networks. In: BroadNets 2004, pp. 344–35, October 2004

2. Raniwala, A., Gopalan, K., Chiueh, T.: Centralized channel assignment and routing algorithms for multi-channel wireless mesh networks. SIGMOBILE Mob. Comput. Commun. Rev. **8**(2), 50–65 (2004)
3. Ramachandran, K.N., Belding, E.M., Almeroth, K.C., Buddhikot, M.M.: Interference-aware channel assignment in multi-radio wireless mesh networks. In: IEEE INFOCOM 2006, pp. 1–12, April 2006
4. Subramanian, A.P., Gupta, H., Das, S.R.: Minimum interference channel assignment in multi-radio wireless mesh networks. In: 4th Annual IEEE Communications Society Conference on Sensor, Mesh and Ad Hoc Communications and Networks, SECON 2007, pp. 481–490, June 2007
5. Benyamina, D., Hafid, A., Gendreau, M.: Wireless mesh network planning: a multi-objective optimization approach. In: 5th International Conference on Broadband Communications, Networks and Systems, BROADNETS 2008, pp. 602–609, September 2008
6. Gao, L., Wang, X.: A game approach for multi-channel allocation in multi-hop wireless networks. In: Proceedings of the 9th ACM International Symposium on Mobile Ad Hoc Networking and Computing, MobiHoc 2008, pp. 303–312. ACM, New York (2008)
7. Yen, L.-H., Dai, Y.-K., Chi, K.-H.: Resource allocation for multi-channel multi-radio wireless backhaul networks: a game-theoretic approach. In: WCNC, pp. 481–486. IEEE (2013)
8. Aliu, O.G., Imran, A., Imran, M.A., Evans, B.: A survey of self organisation in future cellular networks. IEEE Commun. Surv. Tutor. **15**(1), 336–361 (2013)
9. Kretschmer, M., Batroff, P., Ghinea, G.: Topology forming and optimization framework for heterogeneous wireless back-haul networks supporting unidirectional technologies. J. Netw. Comput. Appl. **36**, 698–710 (2013)
10. Kretschmer, M., Horstmann, T., Batroff, P., Rademacher, M., Ghinea, G.: Link calibration and property estimation in self-managed wireless back-haul networks. In: 2012 18th Asia-Pacific Conference on Communications (APCC), pp. 232–237, October 2012
11. Rademacher, M., Kretschmer, M., Jonas, K.: Exploiting IEEE 802.11n MIMO technology for cost-effective broadband back-hauling. In: AFRICOMM 2013, Blantyre, Malawi (2013)
12. Angelakis, V., Papadakis, S., Siris, V.A., Traganitis, A.: Adjacent channel interference in 802.11a is harmful: testbed validation of a simple quantification model. IEEE Commun. Mag. **49**(3), 160–166 (2011)
13. CRDA regulatory database. http://wireless.kernel.org/en/developers/Regulatory
14. Hagberg, A.A., Schult, D.A., Swart, P.J.: Exploring network structure, dynamics, and function using NetworkX. In: Proceedings of the 7th Python in Science Conference (SciPy 2008), Pasadena, CA, USA, pp. 11–15, August 2008
15. Rademacher, M., Jonas, K., Kretschmer, M.: DCF modeling and optimization of long-distance IEEE 802.11n point-to-point links. In: ITG-Fachbericht-Mobilkommunikation-Technologien und Anwendungen (2014)

Towards a Practical Cognitive Channel Allocation Scheme

Dennis George Ozhathil[(⊠)], Geoffrey Mark Kagarura,
Dorothy Kabagaju Okello, and Roseline Nyongarwizi Akol

College of Engineering, Design, Art and Technology,
Makerere University, Kampala, Uganda
{odennis, gmkagarura, dkokello, rnakol}@cedat.mak.ac.ug

Abstract. The actual implementation of an intelligent system that can well manage and utilize the scarce spectrum is a major difficulty towards cognitive radio deployment. By integrating spectrum usage characteristics in Uganda, we develop a hybrid protocol to select optimal channels for use by the cognitive radio. It uses physical layer characteristics of signal to interference and noise ratio and interference power to legacy users to achieve a higher layer goal of maximizing network throughput. The fuzzy logic approach effectively reduces the protocol stack to a hybrid form that considers only the parameters that directly impact on the desired goal. The multiple pertinent variables can be suitably represented in a common linguistic language and solved as a multi-objective optimization problem. The resulting hybrid protocol shows high efficiency in selecting the channel while also maximizing the network throughput.

Keywords: Cognitive radio · Spectrum · Channel allocation · Fuzzy logic · Protocol · Signal to interference and noise ratio · Interference power · Network throughput

1 Introduction

Traditional fixed spectrum assignment approaches of allocating RF spectrum to users has led to its underutilization as different studies report [1, 2]. Techniques to better utilize the spectrum vacancies integrating cognitive radio technology (CRT) have been widely proposed. At the heart of CRT lies an entity that can interact with its environment, learn and adapt its states to operate within the prevalent conditions. Smart and adaptive radios therefore require an efficient artificial intelligence (AI) in cognitive radio (CR) design to better identify spectrum holes, more optimally utilize and vacate bands when a primary user (PU) appears. To improve the CR's cognitive capability, this paper proposes the use of a fuzzy logic (FL) based technique based on a cross-layer protocol design [6].

Development of a FL based protocol using selected physical (PHY) layer variables i.e. signal to interference and noise ratio (SINR) and the interference power (IFP) to legacy users to develop a channel allocation decision process (and subsequent hybrid protocol) based on spectrum usage statistics in Uganda is as follows:

© Institute for Computer Sciences, Social Informatics and Telecommunications Engineering 2015
A. Nungu et al. (Eds.): AFRICOMM 2014, LNICST 147, pp. 84–92, 2015.
DOI: 10.1007/978-3-319-16886-9_9

- Determine nature of RF spectrum usage in a local scenario, to analyze the temporal spectral holes as well as obtain its statistical characteristics.
- Develop a spectrum allocation model for the secondary user (SU) transmitters that utilizes a FL based optimization technique integrating the PHY and network layers of the communication protocol.
- Determine the efficiency of the FL based technique with the design objective of maximizing the network throughput.

We first describe the problem scenarios and physical environment then perform analysis of the current radio frequency (RF) spectrum usage that underpins the FL technique parameters. Development of the FL based protocol to solve the problem follows. We then describe the operation of the simulation, its results and analysis.

2   Channel Access Model for the Cognitive Radio

2.1   Proposed System Layout

We consider a network consisting of M radio channels, labeled c_1, c_2,..., c_M. Every channel has an identical amount of bandwidth, B (for $M = 5$) which are non-contiguous blocks of spectrum that the SU can utilize on the range of 100–1000 MHz. At any time any channel can be only used by one user, the PU or an SU. The PU's activity is assumed to use a synchronous time-slotted basis i.e. a PU is either present or absent in a channel during the whole slot duration. The occupancy measurements discussed in [4] utilize the duty cycle (DC) i.e. the average occupancy of the spectrum in a given number of time samples. The performance of the hybrid protocol was evaluated for the different indoor and outdoor scenarios with the path loss exponent values of $\alpha = 4$ and 2.7 respectively. We assume stationary PUs and SUs and the channel occupancy is modeled by the DC based on distributions from a prior spectrum study [4].

2.2   The FL Protocol Design Basis

As a wireless environment offers a broadcast, multi-access medium, it is rather difficult to maintain a strict modular design or layered protocol stack like is the case for wired systems [3, 8]. To cope with dynamics of a wireless environment, a cross layer design (CLD) has been suggested [3, 7–10] which permits protocols at non-adjacent layers to interact, share information and other parameters [6]. Cross layer optimization is therefore a design objective for improved performance of such a network where the SU operates in [11–13]. To implement a CLD, it is necessary to have much interaction between different existing protocols, protocol layers and FL provides a multi-fold benefit by decoupling the operations of dependent outcomes from the underlying and dependent technology. Each communication protocol layer processes different types of information e.g. numeric or subjective such as pertaining to the quality of service. Whereas there are many CRT approaches to channel allocation, such as wave-shaping, hand-off management, interference mitigation, we propose a CLD that interfaces the PHY and network layer protocols using FL that achieves an overall objective of maximizing the network throughput.

Since spectrum contention involves complex relations between such approaches, it is difficult to obtain a single mathematical expression or model to describe these relations [3, 14]. FL is suited to such uncertainty modeling using approximate or vague information [14–16]. Decision making can then be made basing on FL rules, which generally require less complex computational resources [6] resulting in enhanced node performance.

Similar work using FL and SINR and IFP characteristics include these. A SINR model of a multi-hop multi-channel CRN is shown in [17] to study the cross-layer throughput optimization problem where it uses a heuristic method to maximize the end-to-end flow throughput. Capacity in CR networks is studied in [18] with SINR models using a mixed integer non-linear program to relate power control, scheduling and routing from the PHY, medium access control (MAC) and network layers respectively. A two-stage local spectrum sensing approach where each CR performs and combines the result of spectrum sensing i.e. energy, matched filter and cyclostationary detection is discussed in [19] where it uses FL to deduce the presence of a primary transmitter.

2.3 Spectrum Usage Analysis

Local RF spectrum usage for indoor and outdoor cases at Makerere Hill in Kampala with parameters as in [4] was used. To understand the statistical characteristics of the spectrum usage that the SU could potentially utilize in a realistic situation, received power was measured using an RF spectrum analyzer and the power spectral density (PSD) plots were developed and statistics obtained as shown in Figs. 1, 2 and 3.

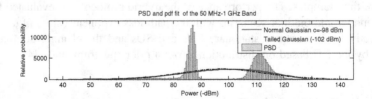

Fig. 1. PSD probability density fitting of selected indoor measurements

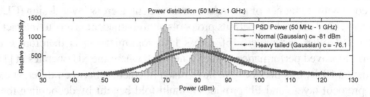

Fig. 2. PSD probability density fitting of selected outdoor measurements

Kampala spectrum usage can be characterized by high power, medium power users and noise for the indoor and outdoor cases. The DC for selected high-power frequency modulation (FM) and television (TV) bands varies between 49.4 % and 63.4 %. Further statistical and noise analyses (Fig. 3) more accurately reflect the setting and data

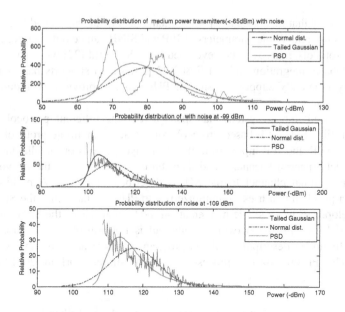

Fig. 3. Comparison of signal and noise distributions

obtained for a realistic scenario used in the model. A normal distribution fit is proposed and compared with closer fit tailed Gaussian distribution. The means obtained for medium users are −99.3 dBm and (−109 dBm) for tailed and normal Gaussian respectively, in top plot of Fig. 3, both with a standard deviation of 6 dB.

Medium power users have −76.4 dBm (−80.2 dBm) means. The noise threshold at −99.3 dBm (−109 dBm) in the middle plot of Fig. 3 shows mean −105 dBm (−111.1 dBm) for TV bands. Average noise from a threshold on actual PSD values is −115.0 dBm, consistent with the distributions to within 3.39 % (3 dBm). The normalized received power at any SU shows that a lower DC reflects a lower spectrum occupancy but higher DC yields higher occupancy. However a lower DC does not imply a lower power scenario since high power transmission can occur even when the DC is low for example having a lone TV station (transmitter) operating nearby (low DC and high power). Statistics mitigate uncertainty involved in determining the future state of the environment but channel allocation decisions are based on varying and often incomplete information hence the possibility of using a FL based system to process such information. For a worst case estimate of this uncertainty, a DC of 1 i.e. 100 % occupancy is added to the test scenario. The FL hybrid protocol seeks to identify such spectrum vacancies and allocate them for use by a potential SU.

3 Proposed Fuzzy Logic Based Protocol

The optimization technique and subsequent channel selection is implemented through the operation of the FL protocol linking the PHY and network layers of the communication stack. The source layer dynamics (SINR and IFP values) are utilized as inputs to the FL protocol that then uses it for subsequent channel allocation and to achieve the necessary throughput. While parameters of IFP and SINR can be obtained for a number of existing protocols, moreover the developed IEEE 802.11af [22] which supports geo-location database integration and IEEE 802.22 [23] which supports base station-like control, they inherently support sensing of PUs and can provide the required input network parameters.

The FL based hybrid system that spans across the different protocol layers is illustrated in Fig. 4. The FL based protocol extends across multiple protocol layers; it receives the SINR and IFP inputs from the PHY layer, carries out intelligent decision making, detects spectral vacancies and then through processing at the network layer, allocates the optimal channel to the SU as described in Fig. 4. A multi-objective optimization problem that tries to minimize IFP to PUs and maximize the SINR at the SUs is developed. Since a single mathematical model that relates the SINR and IFP at the PUs and SUs with the network throughput is not feasible, a FL based system employing linguistic descriptions of the problem to arrive at an optimal solution is described. This FL optimization process is based on similar work in [20, 21].

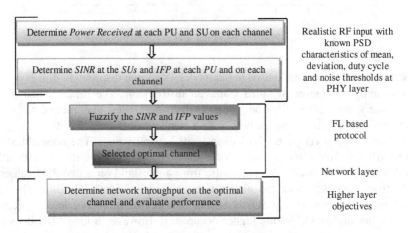

Fig. 4. Operation of the developed model

4 Development of the FL System

4.1 Model Test Setup

The simulation environment is developed in MATLAB using Simulink modules. We develop our test bed basing on usage characteristics derived in Sect. 3 and on the actual RF readings. To achieve the realistic power allocations as determined in the work of [4] the transmit powers of the nodes are constrained to range from −80 to −120 dBm. The scenarios are simulated and observed in timeslots, where the average value of the normalized network throughput is evaluated for the different time slots. The performance of the system in assigning the optimal channel was determined by its efficiency in attaining the highest possible network throughput for about 3000 time slots.

In the fuzzification process, the SINR and IFP values were assigned linguistic descriptions of [None, Low, Medium, High] and correspondingly normalized on the interval [0–1] through the fuzzification process. The decision regarding the selected channel was similarly assigned descriptions of [Channel bad, Channel, Medium, Channel Fine, Best channel]. We divide the spectrum occupancy state into discrete time slots at each of which we run the optimization technique to determine the best possible channel. For comparison, the performance of the FL based system is compared against a technique that would theoretically achieve the highest throughput. The efficiency in attaining this value is evaluated. The average value of the network throughput is evaluated for the different number of time slots.

4.2 Results of the Test Runs

The RF spectrum characteristic as determined from analysis in Sect. 2 was used as the input for the FL protocol in our model. The SU therefore has to opportunistically utilize the spectrum with those statistical characteristics of mean, minimum power levels and DC. Next we study the indoor scenario with $\alpha = 4$ and DC = 0.47 and 0.997. Figure 5 shows the average normalized throughput achieved and the corresponding efficiency of the system in achieving that result is shown in Fig. 6. It is seen that the indoor case achieves higher efficiency for the case of DC = 0.47 than for 0.997. We then study the outdoor scenario with $\alpha = 4$ and DC = 0.233 and 1. Figure 7 shows the average normalized throughput achieved and the corresponding efficiency of the system in achieving that result is shown in Fig. 8. It is seen that the outdoor case achieves higher efficiency for the case of DC = 0.233 than for 1.

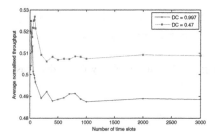
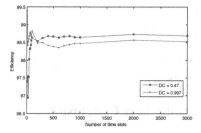

Fig. 5. Average normalized throughput for indoor case

Fig. 6. Average efficiency for indoor case

For both the indoor and outdoor cases, we select DCs that result in a low and high spectrum occupancy so that we can study how the hybrid protocol behaves when it faces such a sparsely and congested spectrum situation. With a high DC (=1) the optimization technique finds it more difficult to achieve an optimal solution due to the high channel occupancy and the difficulty in finding a "best channel" for use from this situation of high spectrum congestion. Since all spectral bands are highly utilized it is difficult to find a band which will "best" solve the MOOP of minimizing IFP and maximizing SINR.

The outdoor case achieves slightly a higher efficiency than the indoor case for low duty cycles although the discrepancy for the outdoor case is larger when the DC varies. The low and high DCs in the Indoor case result in almost the same efficiency (approximately 98.55 %). This could be attributed to the fact that in an indoor case, the signal received by any node suffers the same levels of path loss, fading, attenuation or scattering (i.e. when indoors the signals are of similar characteristics) compared to an outdoor case where the effects of some of these factors may be less or their effect is greatly varied.

We observe that after about 3000 time slots across the bands, the efficiency and throughput achieved by the hybrid protocol converges to a steady state. There is a variation in the result for a low number of time slots as the hybrid protocol has not yet reached a final solution and this cannot be taken as a final optimal solution of the run of the simulation.

When using the hybrid protocol, it generally performs better for low DCs than for high DCs and as the DC increases, the efficiency is lower for the outdoor scenario than the indoor case. Since a low DC means that the spectral usage is low it means that the hybrid protocol can through is optimization process differentiate between usable and unusable spectrum more easily than when the spectrum is highly used and there is no clear distinction between used spectrum and potential usable spectrum. System efficiency is also observed to be high for all scenarios.

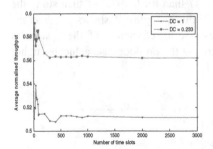

Fig. 7. Average normalized throughput for outdoor case

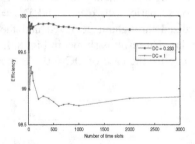

Fig. 8. Average efficiency for outdoor case

5 Results and Conclusion

It is seen that the selection of two variables (SINR and IFP) and describing them with linguistic expressions suffices in solving the optimization problem using the discrete FL based technique and it achieves a global objective of maximizing the network throughput. The hybrid protocol does have the capacity to yield solutions that are optimal in terms of achieving high SINRs and low IFPs. It is also seen that the Fuzzy optimal choice does achieve the performance goal of high network throughput for indoor and outdoor cases with efficiencies of 98–99 %. even when DC = 1, i.e. 100 % spectral occupancy, the efficiency is above 98 % hence FL protocol is an excellent candidate for CR system deployment based on the observed efficiency and expected ease of implementation.

This paper shows that the SINR and IFP parameters have a huge impact on the network throughput and can adequately decide the channel selected by the SU. The variation of the parameters is shown to impact the way the channels are selected by the SU and eventually the goal of maximizing the network throughput. The hybrid protocol achieves 98–99 % efficiency in assigning the channel that attains the highest possible network throughput.

We observe that it possible to select lower layer parameters (SINR and IFP) and achieve a higher layer protocol goal (network throughput). This type of cross layer interaction is feasible with a FL based system where linguistic description for the parameters is sufficient to solve an optimization problem for the CRN. With the desire to show the behavior of the goal-oriented CR device i.e. the SU who aims to utilize the available RF channels and achieve a high network throughput, it is clearly shown that the using linguistic descriptions in the FL based hybrid protocol has a direct impact on the channel selected and eventually the network throughput (high layer protocol functions). The inherent features of a FL design therefore make it possible for the basic knowledge of lower protocol layer (PHY) information using only two core parameters (SINR and IFP) to achieve global CRN system objectives at higher protocol layers (network throughput and channel allocation decision).

As a result the protocol stack is reduced to a hybrid form where only the parameters that directly impact on the desired goal need to be considered and can be described in a common language (linguistically) that reduces the protocol design to one specifically tuned to achieve the desired objective. While it is intended to use few low layer parameters [24] in SINR and IFP, the system can more easily be easily integrated to existing protocols in the IEEE family of 802.11af and 802.22 which can provide source layer inputs at the entire network (system), level making test-bed and proposed practical deployment more feasible.

Acknowledgements. We acknowledge the Millennium Science Initiative (MSI) for the research scholarship in Adaptive Bandwidth Management and equipment used for spectral analysis.

References

1. FCC. ET Docket No. 03-322 Notice of Proposed Rule Making and Order (2003)
2. Akyildiz, I.F., Lee, W.Y., Vuran, M.C., Mohanty, S.: Cognitive radio communications and networks. IEEE Commun. Mag. **46**, 40–48 (2008)
3. Hossain, E., Niyato, D., Han, Z.: Dynamic Spectrum Access and Management in Cognitive Radio Networks, pp. 35, 186, 310. Cambridge University Press, Cambridge (2009)
4. Kagarura, G.M., Okello, D.K., Akol, R.N.: Evaluation of spectrum occupancy: a case for cognitive radio in uganda. In: IEEE 9th International Conference on Mobile Ad-hoc and Sensor Networks (MSN) (2013)
5. Kawadia, V., Kumar, P.R.: A cautionary perspective on cross-layer design. IEEE Wirel. Commun. **12**(1), 3–11 (2005)
6. Baldo, N., Zorzi, M.: Fuzzy logic for cross-layer optimization in cognitive radio networks. IEEE Commun. Mag. **46**, 64–71 (2008)

7. Fangwen, V.M., Schaar, D.: Learning for cross-layer optimization. In: Proceedings of Cognitive Information Processing, Santorini, Greece, pp. 69–74. (2008)
8. Mahajan, R.: Cross layer optimization: system design and simulation methodologies. Masters Thesis. Virginia Polytechnic Institute and State University, USA (2003)
9. Sooriyabandara, M., Quadri, S. (eds.): Adaptive reconfigurable access and generic interfaces for optimization in radio networks. ARAGORN (2008)
10. Kolar, V., Mahonen, P., Petrova, M., Sooriyabandara, M., Riihiarvi, J., Farnham, T.: A case for generic interfaces in cognitive radio networks. In: ICT- Mobile Summit Conference Proceedings (2009)
11. Razzaque, M.A., Dobson, S., Nixon, P.: Cross-layer architectures for autonomic communications. J. Netw. Syst. Manage. 15(1), 13–27 (2006)
12. Wang, J., Korhonen, T., Zhao, Y.: Cross layer optimization for fairness balancing based on adaptively weighted utility functions in OFDMA systems. In: World Academy of Science, Engineering and Technology (2007)
13. Ding, L., Melodia, T., Batalama, S.N., Matyjas, J.D., Medley, M.J.: Cross-layer routing and dynamic spectrum allocation in cognitive radio ad hoc networks. IEEE Trans. Veh. Technol. 10(10) (2010)
14. Bogatinovski, M., Gavrilovska, L.: Overview of cross-layer optimization methodologies for cognitive radio. In: 16th Telecommunications Forum TELFOR, pp. 254–257 (2008)
15. Matinmikko, M., Rauma, T., Mustonen, M., Harjula, I., Sarvanko, H., Mamella, A.: Application of fuzzy logic to cognitive radio systems. IEICE Trans. Commun. E92-B(12), 3572–3580 (2009)
16. Tabakovic, Z., Grgic, S.: Fuzzy logic power control in cognitive radio. In: 16th International Conference on Systems, Signals and Image Processing, pp. 1–5 (2009)
17. Ma, M., Tsang, D.H.K.: Cross-layer throughput optimization in cognitive radio networks with SINR constraints. IJDMB, 2010, 13pp
18. Shi, Y., Kompella, Y.T., Sherali, H.D.: Maximizing capacity in multihop cognitive radio networks under the SINR model. IEEE Trans. Mob. Comput. 10(7), 954–967 (2011)
19. Ejaz, W., Hasan, N.U., Awais, M., Kim, H.S.: Improved local spectrum sensing for cognitive radio networks. EURASIP J. Adv. Signal Process. (2012)
20. Ozhathil, D.G.: A fuzzy Logic based channel allocation scheme for cognitive radio networks. Masters thesis, Makerere University, College of Engineering, Design, Art and Technology (Unpublished) (2014)
21. Ross, T.J.: Decision making with fuzzy information. In: Fuzzy Logic with Engineering Applications. pp. 320–323. Wiley, New York (2004)
22. Mueck, M., Nokia, R.C., Piipponen, A., Kalliojarvi, K., Dimitrakopoulos, G., Tsagkaris, K., Demestichas, P., Casadevall, F., Perez-Romero, J., Sallent, O., Baldini, G., et al.: ETSI reconfigurable radio systems: status and future directions on software defined radio and cognitive radio standards. Commun. Mag. IEEE, vol. 48, no. 9, pp. 78–86 (2010)
23. Cordeiro, C., Challapali, K., Birru, D.: IEEE 802. 22: an introduction to the first wireless standard based on cognitive radios. Networks 1(1), 38–47 (2006)
24. Song, Y., Xie, J.: On the Spectrum Handoff for Cognitive Radio Ad Hoc Networks without Common Control. Spectr. [arXiv] (2011)

Green Communications: Large vs Small Cell Deployment

Dorothy Okello$^{(\boxtimes)}$, Moses Niyonshuti, Moureen Nampijja Lukoye,
and Edwin Mugume

Department of Electrical and Computer Engineering, College of Engineering,
Design, Art and Technology (CEDAT), Makerere University, Kampala, Uganda
{dkokello,mniyonshuti,mlnampijja}@cedat.mak.ac.ug,
edwin.mugume@gmail.com

Abstract. A consistent issue of concern in the design of future mobile cellular systems is the energy consumption of the radio access network. This paper quantifies the amount of energy savings that can be obtained due to deployment of small cells in an area given a user density for that area. It also compares the cost increase that arises due to the deployment of small cells with the gains that are realized. A high-data rate Long Term Evolution (LTE) network in a developing country context is considered in this paper.

Keywords: Long term evolution · Energy consumption gain · Energy consumption ratio

1 Introduction

The issue of energy consumption in cellular networks has attracted significant attention in both industry and academia over the last few years. This is due to the explosive growth in traffic demand. The volume of transmitted data increases approximately by a factor of 10 every five years, which corresponds to an increase of the associated energy consumption by approximately 16 to 20 %. This has led to the increased capital expenditure and operational costs such as electricity cost. In cellular networks each base station can require up to 2.7 kW of electrical power which can lead to an energy consumption of tens of MW per annum for wide area networks. Energy consumption analysis shows that between 50 % and 80 % of the total energy in a wireless network is consumed in the base stations [1–3].

Operators are looking for economical and sustainable solutions to reduce their operational expenditure most especially the cost of energy and also check the associated greenhouse gas (CO_2) emissions. Several techniques can be used to reduce network energy consumption such as improved radio base station equipment design, energy-efficient cooling systems or avoiding cooling by using remote radio units [4–7]. This paper compares energy savings that can be obtained by deployment of small cells. The deployment of small cells is generally accepted as a good strategy for increasing network throughput in a way that is both cost and energy efficient [2, 8–10]. The contribution of this paper is assessing the gains for small cell size deployment in a developing country context with a comparison of deployments in rural and in urban

© Institute for Computer Sciences, Social Informatics and Telecommunications Engineering 2015
A. Nungu et al. (Eds.): AFRICOMM 2014, LNICST 147, pp. 93–100, 2015.
DOI: 10.1007/978-3-319-16886-9_10

areas. This paper is organized as follows. First the system model used in the simulation is analyzed, followed by the results obtained in the simulation and the observations and conclusions as per the results obtained.

2 System Model

2.1 Case Study

This paper studies the energy savings that accrue from deployment of small cells in rural and urban areas. One area of two square kilometers each was considered for a rural and an urban deployment. The areas considered were Kampala, Central Uganda, for the urban area and Kisoro, South Western Uganda, for the rural area. The average number of users to be served in that area for a given cell radius was determined. Population estimates were based on Uganda Bureau of Statistics (UBOS) 2012 estimates which give a population density of 9,574 and 362 people per square kilometer respectively for Kampala and Kisoro.

To obtain the average number of subscribers in the two regions, we assumed that mobile subscriber population is distributed in accordance with the population distribution per country. We further assume that the subscribers are uniformly distributed across the network. Using a 2013 estimate for mobile subscribers nationwide of about 16 million subscribers, and assuming an operator with a 52 % market share, we obtained the average number of subscribers for the operator at 4,136 and 164 respectively for the urban and rural areas under consideration for this study.

The number of LTE e-NodeBs that cover the area for the varying cell radius was calculated for the different inter e-NodeB distances. Hexagonal cellular cell deployment was considered in the selected areas. The radius of a cell-site denoted by R is fully adjustable with an inter-site distance of $1.5\,R$ for a hexagonal geometry. Base stations (e-NodeBs) are configured with three sector antennas, with directions of 0, 120, and 240 degrees. The area to be served, $A_{network}$, is defined with N cells each of area, A_{cell}, radius, R_{cell}, and average cell transmission power per sector, P_{cell} [2]:

$$A_{network} = NA_{cell} = \frac{3NR^2\sqrt{3}}{8} \tag{1}$$

$$P_{network} = P_{cell} \times N \tag{2}$$

To determine the best deployment cell size, the energy efficiency performances of large cells and small cells is evaluated by measuring the energy efficiency performances achieved for various cell sizes and antenna heights while maintaining the quality of service (for a given cell coverage and average cell capacity) under a cell transmission power constraint. The energy efficiency metrics used in this paper are the Energy Consumption Ratio (ECR) and the Energy Consumption Gain (ECG). For example, after comparing the Energy Consumption Ratio (ECR) for each cell size, a suitable system deployment option can be found in terms of the cell size. Similar calculations are performed for the Energy Consumption Gain (ECG) across the network.

2.2 Power Model

A base station consists of multiple transceivers (TRXs), each of which serves one transmit antenna element. A TRX comprises a power amplifier, a radio frequency small-signal TRX module, a baseband engine including a receiver (uplink) and transmitter (downlink) section, a DC-DC power supply, an active cooling system, and an AC-DC unit (mains supply) for connection to the electrical power grid. The following power model was used while carrying out these simulations [3]:

$$P_{IN} = \left\{ \begin{array}{ll} N_{TRX} * P_0 + \Delta * P_{OUT}, & 0 < P_{OUT} \leq P_{max} \\ N_{TRX} * P_{sleep}, & P_{OUT} = 0 \end{array} \right\} \tag{3}$$

where P_{OUT} is output power, P_{sleep} is sleep mode power consumption, N_{TRX} is the number of transmit chains, P_0 is the power consumption at the minimum non-zero output power, Δ is the slope of the load-dependent power consumption, and P_{max} is the output power at maximum load [3, 11]. It should be noted that for this project, sleep mode capability is not investigated. The power savings that are quantified are due to deployment of small size cells.

2.3 Energy Metrics

The total system wide energy includes embodied energy as well as operational energy for services delivery. The operational energy is a function of the radio access architecture (cell size, base station antenna height, antenna radiation pattern, distance of the transmitting and receiving antennas, interference, multipath fading, shadowing, radio resource management, user density, user mobility, traffic scenarios etc.). Although the embodied energy is a critical part in the energy performance evaluation, we do not consider it in this paper. This is because embodied or manufacturing energy is relatively much smaller than operational energy in radio base stations that may have a 10-year or longer lifetime [12].

The energy metrics that are used in this paper include the Energy Consumption Ratio (ECR) which represents the energy per delivered information bit [2]:

$$ECR = \frac{E}{M} \tag{4}$$

where E is the energy required to deliver M bits over time T. The other parameter is the Energy Consumption Gain (ECG). This is the ratio of the power of a radio access network (RAN) for large cell deployment to small cell deployment for a given period of time:

$$ECG = \frac{P(RANLARGE) * t}{P(RANSMALL) * t} \tag{5}$$

3 Results and Discussion

Results obtained for this paper are based on the Vienna LTE network simulator that was developed in Matlab [13]. System parameters and simulation assumptions are chosen to comply with known LTE standards. Some of the main parameters used in the simulation are shown in Table 1, where the same transmitter and receiver heights are assumed for the urban and rural settings. The cost of the different cell sizes was computed based on a flexi e-NodeB that supports up to 250 active users.

Table 1. Simulation parameters.

Parameter	Value
Frequency	2 GHz
Bandwidth	5 MHz
Propagation model	COST 231 HATA
Transmitter height	20 m
Receiver height	1.5 m

3.1 Network Performance for Large Cell Versus Small Cell Deployment

The first measure of interest is the gain in energy consumption in promoting small cell deployment. Figure 1 presents the total power consumed for varying cell sizes in the rural and urban areas. It is observed that the power consumed decreases as cell size reduces down to a radius of about 350 m for the urban and 1,000 m for the rural area. In this case, the numbers of users supported per small cell are 460 and 84 respectively for the urban and the rural area considered in this paper.

For cell radii smaller than the 350 m or 1,000 m above, it is observed that the total power consumed increases. This is because deploying small cell sizes increases the number of base stations required to support a given user density. While the individual base stations in small cell sizes transmit at lower power values due to reduced number of users, the total fixed power from all the base stations contributes to the overall total power consumed in a network.

Performance of the large cell versus small cell deployment is also considered in terms of two energy metrics, namely, the Energy Consumption Gain (ECG) and the Energy Consumption Ratio (ECR). Good performance is marked by values much greater than 1 for the ECG and by low values for the ECR.

Figure 2 reveals that the urban area has a wider cell size range across which reduced cell sizes are expected to yield a significant improvement in power utilization ($ECG > 1$) between large versus small cell deployment. Therefore small cells are more efficient to deploy in the urban areas as compared to rural areas. However, the ECG benefit for urban areas must take into consideration the higher energy consumption ratio (ECR) as observed in Fig. 3.

ECR for the urban area increases at a higher rate than that for a rural area due to larger subscriber density. This is because for any given cell size, there are more users to be supported in the urban area compared to the rural area. A key assumption being

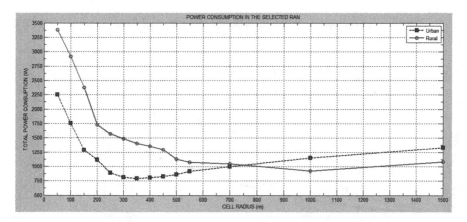

Fig. 1. Total power consumption versus cell radius

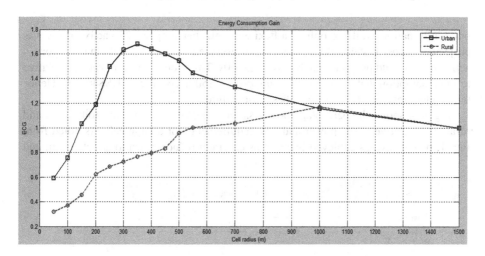

Fig. 2. Energy consumption gain versus cell radius in urban and rural area

made in this paper is that there will be an equal number of active users in each of the small cells as the sizes as reduced. However, in a practical network, not all base stations will have active users neither will all bases stations have the same number of users [14]. Furthermore, the distribution of users in urban and rural areas may greatly differ even while it is generally expected that the number of active users will increase with cell size. Further work is therefore needed to analyse small cell deployment taking into account active user distribution in a developing country context.

3.2 Cost-Benefit Analysis of Large Versus Small Cell Deployment

Since the number of base stations increases as the number of small cells deployed increases, it is important to assess the cost benefit of deploying small cells. Based on

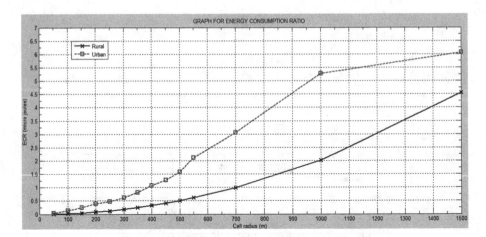

Fig. 3. Energy consumption ratio versus cell radius in urban and rural area

price information available online, a flexi e-nodeB that supports 250 active users was projected to cost US$40,000. It was further assumed that an e-nodeB that supports s active users would proportionately cost US$160s. This would give a lower cost relative to the assumption that e-nodeBs that support 0 – 250 users all cost US$40,000. Hence the results presented here are of a best-case nature.

Figure 4 shows the percentage power savings and cost increase for both urban and rural areas relative to the power and cost requirements for a large cell. As noted from Fig. 1, power savings achieved increase as cell radii reduce down to about 350 m and

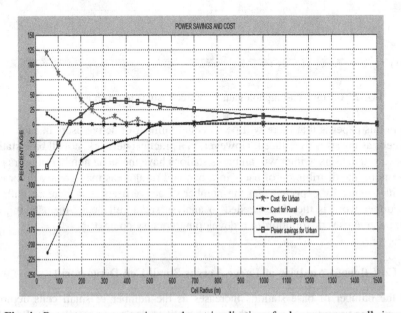

Fig. 4. Percentage power savings and cost implications for large versus small sizes

1,000 m respectively for an urban and a rural area. This means a much smaller size ($\approx$ 350 m) can be accommodated in the urban areas before the total fixed power of the base stations becomes a significant factor in the network energy consumption.

However, the opportunity for reduced cell sizes in the urban area results in noticeable cost increases from cell radii of about 500 m (supporting 828 users). The cost increase for the rural area is not as significant due to the lower user density (33 users supported for 500 m cell radii) relative to the urban setting. Consequently, assuming a proportionate cost of base station versus number of users, lower costs are required per base station in a rural area relative to an urban area. This also means that the cell sizes in rural areas could be increased to match ECR_{rural} to acceptable values of ECR_{urban}. For example, if the ECR_{urban} at 500 m is deemed acceptable, this would correspond to an ECR_{rural} for cell radius of 850 m that support 82 users resulting in fewer base stations required for a given rural area.

The cost implications for small cell deployment as depicted in Fig. 4 calls for the need to optimize a function of the desired small cell sizes, the energy consumption, and financial costs associated with the cell sizes. With an affordability index of 37.3 % [15], network deployment in Uganda needs to be cognizant of reducing service delivery costs. It should be noted that the analysis has only considered the capital costs for the base stations, and not their ongoing operational costs which do increase with the number of base stations deployed.

4 Conclusion

In this paper, the effect of reducing the cell size was investigated in an LTE wireless network. Two energy metrics were considered to analyse the network performance, that is, the Energy Consumption Ratio and the Energy Consumption Gain. Given the context of Uganda as a developing country, it was also important to assess the cost benefit of large cell versus small cell deployment. The results presented show that energy consumption savings are indeed achieved with smaller cell sizes. Furthermore, the ECG results show that it is more efficient to deploy smaller cells in the urban areas than in the rural areas. However, the energy consumption gains are governed by some constraints. For instance, the energy gains are lost for cell radii smaller than 300 m for urban deployment. We show that network design for green communications needs to optimize a function of the desired small cell sizes, the energy consumption, and financial costs associated with the cell sizes.

References

1. Hasan, Z., Boostanimehr, H., Bhargava, V.K.: Green cellular networks: a survey, some research issues and challenges. IEEE. Commun. Surv. Tutorials 13(4), 524–540 (2011)
2. Badic, B., O'Farrell, T., Loskot, P., He, J.: Energy efficient radio access architectures for green radio: large versus small cell size deployment. In: 70th IEEE Vehicular Technology Conference Fall, pp. 1–5. (2009)

3. Mugume, E., Prawatmuang, W., So, D.K.C.: Cooperative spectrum sensing for green cognitive femtocell network. In: 24th IEEE International Symposium on Personal Indoor and Mobile Radio Communications (PIMRC), pp. 2368–2372. IEEE (2013)
4. Rinaldi, R., Veca, G.M.: The hydrogen for base stations. In: 29th International Telecommunications Energy Conference (INTELEC), pp. 288–292. IEEE (2007)
5. Hodes, M.: Energy and power conversion: a telecommunication hardware vendors perspective. Power Electronics Industry Group (2007)
6. Chabarek, J., Sommers, J., Barford, P., Estan, C., Tsiang, D., Wright, S.: Power awareness in network design and routing. In 27th IEEE Conference on Computer Communications (INFOCOM). IEEE (2008)
7. Marsan, M.A., Chiaraviglio, L., Ciullo, D., Meo, M.: Optimal energy savings in cellular access networks. In: IEEE First International Workshop on Green Communications (GreenComm). IEEE (2009)
8. Sappidi, R., Mosharrafdehkordi, S., Rosenberg, C., Mitran, P.: Planning for small cells in a cellular network: Why it is worth it. In: 2014 IEEE Wireless Communications and Networking Conference (WCNC), pp. 2307–2312 (2014)
9. Li, C., Zhang, J., Letaief, K.B.: Energy efficiency analysis of small cell networks. In: 2013 IEEE International Conference on Communications (ICC), pp. 4404–4408. IEEE (2013)
10. Abbas, N., Dawy, Z., Hajj, H., Sharafeddine, S.: Energy-throughput tradeoffs in cellular/wifi heterogeneous networks with traffic splitting. In: 2014 IEEE Wireless Communications and Networking Conference (WCNC), pp. 2324–2329. IEEE (2014)
11. Auer, G., Giannini, V., Desset, C., Godor, I., Skillermark, P., Olsson, M., Imran, M.A., Sabella, D., Gonzalez, M.J., Blume, O., Fehske, A.: How much energy is needed to run a wireless network? IEEE Wireless Commun. Mag. 18(5), 40–49 (2011)
12. McLaughlin, S., Grant, P.M., Thompson, J.S., Haas, H., Laurenson, D.I., Khrallah, C., Hou, Y., Wang, R.: Techniques for improving cellular radio base station energy efficiency. IEEE Wireless. Commun. Mag. 18(5), 10–17 (2011)
13. Christian Mehlführer, C., Ikuno, J.C., Šimko, M., Schwarz, S., Wrulich, M., Rupp, M.: The vienna lte simulators–enabling reproducibility in wireless communications research. EURASIP J. Adv. Signal. Process. (2011)
14. Li, C., Zhang, J., Letaief, K.B.: Energy efficiency analysis of small cell networks. In: IEEE International Conference on Communications (ICC), pp. 4404–4408. IEEE (2013)
15. Alliance for Affordable Internet. The Affordability report (2013)

Health

Adoption and Use of Mobile Phones for Maternal Healthcare Service Delivery

Gorretti Byomire[1](✉) and Gilbert Maiga[2]

[1] Department of Business Computing, Makerere University Business School,
Kampala, Uganda
bgorretti@gmail.com
[2] Department of Information Technology, Makerere University,
Kampala, Uganda
gmaiga@cis.mak.ac.ug

Abstract. Use of mobile phones has the potential to transform maternal healthcare delivery in Uganda, with associated benefits of educating women on pregnancy, monitoring maternal, child progress and post-delivery support. Despite the benefits, user adoption of mobile phone technology for maternal healthcare remains low. There is a lack of understanding of the factors that affect the use of mobile phones in maternal healthcare practice. This paper reports on a study that aimed to determine factors deemed important for the adoption and use of mobile phone technology by healthcare professionals. The study used a questionnaire based field study to determine these factors. The study was carried out with the healthcare professionals working in the maternal sections in selected Health Centers in Wakiso district in Uganda. The results of the study indicate that perceived ease of use, perceived usefulness, social influence, facilitating conditions, perceived value, workflow practices are important factors for the adoption and use of mobile phones in maternal healthcare practice.

Keywords: Mobile phone · Technology adoption · Mobile phone adoption and usage · Maternal healthcare

1 Introduction

Maternal health care consists of methods and procedures designed to reduce the deaths and related health complications associated with pregnancy, focusing on antenatal and postnatal care [1]. One of the millennium development goals (MDGs) is to improve maternal health with the target of reducing maternal mortality by three-quarters between 1990 and 2015 [2]. Pregnant women face some level of maternal risk with 40 % experiencing delivery complications, 15 % requiring obstetric care to manage life threatening complications to both mother and infant [3]. While most Ugandan women (94 %) attend at least one antenatal care (ANC) visit with a skilled provider, fewer women deliver in health facilities (41 %) or have a skilled birth attendant at delivery (42 %) [4].

Mobile phones are used to keep in touch with family members and conducting business [5]. Majority of the Ugandan households have access to at least one mobile

© Institute for Computer Sciences, Social Informatics and Telecommunications Engineering 2015
A. Nungu et al. (Eds.): AFRICOMM 2014, LNICST 147, pp. 103–114, 2015.
DOI: 10.1007/978-3-319-16886-9_11

phone [6]. The rapidly growing presence of mobile phones in sub-Saharan Africa offers a paradigm shift and a unique opportunity in the provision of maternal health services [7]. The diffusion of mobile phones creates opportunities to significantly contribute to achieving MDGs thereby lowering the maternal mortality ratio. Pregnant women miss crucial antenatal checkups due to ignorance of healthcare and the forgetfulness of medical appointments which problem can be rectified using the SMS functionality on mobile phones [8].

2 Mobile Phones and Maternal Healthcare

2.1 Maternal Healthcare

Maternal health care (MTH) is a reliable measure of developmental achievements of any country and depicts the risk of maternal death relative to the number of live births [9]. According to [8] inadequate care during pregnancy affects both women and their babies. The death or illness of a woman of reproductive age has clear implications for a country's productive capacity, labour supply, and economic well-being, and also translates into substantial economic loss and social hardship for her family [2]. For every woman who dies as a result of pregnancy or childbirth, a further 20 women suffer serious or chronic health consequences which can have severe physical, psychological, social and economic repercussions for both the woman and her family [1]. Poor maternal health and health care not only affects women's survival but has serious implications for the survival of their newborns as well [10]. Children whose mothers die or are disabled in childbearing have vastly diminished prospects of leading a productive life [11]. Motherless children especially girls are less likely to have access to education and health care resources as they grow up [12].

2.2 The Role of Mobile Phones in Maternal Healthcare Practice

The explosion of cell phone use in developing countries has led to the growth of mobile health (mHealth) programs that connect health workers to the information they need at their point of care so they can more effectively serve their clients [17]. mHealth technology can stimulate health education and awareness where messages are delivered to subscribers' phones using messages tailored to personal needs [18]. mobile devices can advance progress on maternal healthcare in some of the most remote and resource-poor environments as nearly 85 % of the world's population is now covered by one or more commercial wireless signals [19].

Mobile phones are an effective tool for improving pre-natal and post- natal care in Indonesia [13]. An intervention known as the "wired mothers" aimed at reducing maternal and neonatal morbidity by using mobile phones was done by the Ministry of Health and Social Welfare Zanzibar, Tanzania, [14]. The wired mothers are linked to primary healthcare units in case of acute and non-acute problems [14]. Nurse midwives in Ghana under the Mobile Technology for Community Health (MOTecH) project have used mobile phones to consult and communicate with their peers, supervisors and other medical colleagues on complex maternal health cases [13]. Mobile phones have helped patients to communicate with their health-care providers which saved travel time and resulted in quicker more efficient delivery of health services. Health Child is Community Based Organization operating in Jinja, Uganda aims toed at improving accessibility to health and other services for prevention of child and maternal morbidity and mortality complemented by Information and Communication technology. Health Child is implemented a project to enhance uptake of antenatal, postnatal, Prevention of Mother To Child Transmission (PMTCT) and child health services by utilizing SMS messages for community awareness raising and mobilization of pregnant mothers to access Maternal Child Healthcare (MCH) services at 7 government health centers [15]. Applab Uganda Project operates a Health Tips application, educating users on sexual and reproductive health. Applab, an initiative of the Grameen Foundation have been working since September 2007 to establish the physical, human, and technological infrastructure needed to support the initiative. The pilot phase ended in 2009 and has since been rolled-out nationally [16].

2.3 Issues for the Use of Mobile Phones for Maternal Healthcare

A number of challenges, constrain the adoption of mobile phones for maternal healthcare in Uganda. These include: cultural factors, technophobia by health workers, shared phone access and ownership, literacy and translation to local languages and access divides. Developed countries are known to take their technological innovations into developing countries without the consideration of cultural impacts [20]. Culture plays a role in the adoption or non-adoption of information technology [21]. Designers need to understand and be aware of the cultural priorities and the value system of users [22]. In Uganda, many health workers are not used to using mobile technologies for healthcare due to lack of training and sensitisation. Most districts have no reliable power which makes the charging of mobile devices quite difficult. The acceptability of mHealth is a big challenge as most Ugandans prefer face to face discussion with medical practitioners [23]. Nurses and patients also share phones with family members so there are times when the mobile phone is not available. Sharing mobile phones with non- Health Service staff risks the leak of patient data. Furthermore, nurses are unsatisfied with using personal phones for professional purposes [24]. Most of the targeted communities for mHealth projects based on SMS for information dissemination are often not literate in any language. Most of the participants cannot read either English or their local languages [24]. Despite the pervasiveness of mobile phones, not everyone has a phone, and the most disadvantaged populations will likely be the ones excluded from these health communication interventions, leading to a form of double exclusion [25]. Access divides to mobile technology means that critical health information is not communicated to disadvantaged populations of the developing countries. In low- and middle-income countries, up to 74 % of married women do not have a mobile phone as their spouses do not allow it, and 64 % do own phones as it makes their husbands "suspicious" [26].

3 The Methodology

3.1 Conceptual Framework for the Study

The conceptual model presented here extends the Mobile Phone Adoption and Usage model by Van Biljon and Kotze (2008). The model has both determining factors and the mediating factors. The determining factors are basic constructs that influence mobile phone usage and consist of social influence (SI) that encompasses human nature influence (HNI), cultural influence (CI), facilitating conditions (FC), perceived ease of use (PEOU), perceived usefulness (PU) and behavioural intention to use (BI). Mediating factors influence the determining factors. Mediating factors may inhibit the adoption of mobile phones. Demographic, socio-economic and personal factors are important aspects for technology adoption and use. Figure 1.

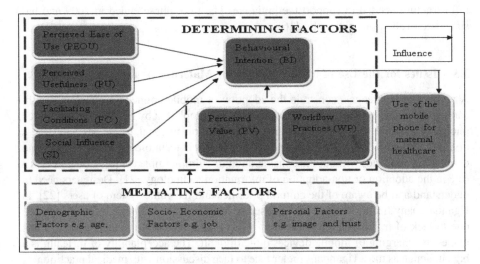

Fig. 1. Theoretical Model for Adoption of Mobile Phones in Maternal Healthcare (Extension of The Mobile Phone Adoption Model by Van Biljon And Kotze (2008).

In this study, five key constructs of the Mobile Phone Adoption and Usage model by [22] were used to determine factors deemed necessary for the adoption of mobile phones in maternal healthcare by medical healthcare professionals. The constructs used were perceived ease of use (PEOU), perceived usefulness (POU), facilitating conditions (FC), social influence (SI) and behavioural intention to use (BI). While measuring physicians' understanding of online systems use, physicians' behaviour, their workflow practices, and their perceptions regarding the value of specific information systems were found to be more significant [27]. Therefore this study introduces two new concepts of Workflow Practices and Perceived Value to understand the adoption of mobile technology in healthcare.

3.2   The Field Study

To determine the factors for successful adoption and usage of mobile phones in maternal healthcare in Uganda, a field study was used to collect data. Data was collected through semi- structured close ended and open ended questionnaires which were administered to healthcare professionals working in the maternal sections at selected Health Centre V's, Health Centre IV's and Health Centre III's in Wakiso district. Uganda's health sector is organized at four levels of health service delivery as follows HC I is a community based and promotive Health Centre at a village level serving a population of 1000 people [28]. HC II is a Health Centre found at a parish level serving a population of 5000 people responsible for providing preventive, promotive, outpatient curative health services and out reach care. HC III is found at sub county level serving a population of 20,000 and offers preventive, promotive, out-patient curative, maternity, inpatient health services and laboratory services. HC IV is a Health Centre found at county level serving a population of 100,000 people and it offers promotive, out-patient curative, maternity, in-patient health services, and Emergency surgery, Blood transfusion and laboratory services. HC V is a Health Center found at the district level. It is a district hospital serving an approximate population of 500,000 people.

The data collected was then categorized, quantified, coded and analysed using statistical package for social sciences (SPSS). Results from the survey elicited the factors for successful adoption of mobile phones for maternal healthcare service delivery and answered the research objective. Records from the Wakiso District Health Officer as of 2013 indicated that there were 157 individuals in the district who are concerned with the delivery of maternal health services. The study applied Krejcie & Morgan's 1970 formula for estimating the sample size in Eq. 1. The sample size addressed issues of precision and confidence. It was a function of the confidence interval of (± 5 %), a confidence level of 95 % and the population size.

$$SS = \frac{Z^2 * (X) * (1 - X)}{C^2} \tag{1}$$

Where: S = Sample Size; Z = Z Value (e.g. 1.96 for 95 % confidence interval); X = Percentage picking a choice, expressed as decimal (0.5 used for sample size needed); C = Confidence interval, expressed as decimal (0.05) $\pm$ 5 used for sample size needed. The above formula helps to determine the required sample regardless of the size of the population. Cochran's 1977 correction formula was used to calculate the final (new) sample size (SS) according to Eq. 2 as follows:

$$n = \frac{SS}{1 + (SS - 1)/N} \tag{2}$$

$$n = \frac{384}{1 + (384 - 1)/157} = 157 \tag{3}$$

4 Results

The results from the analysis of the data collected during the survey are presented in this section. Out of a total of 150 medical professionals working in the maternal sections that were given questionnaires, 126 respondents returned validly filled questionnaires showing a response rate of 80 %. The data was classified into usable categories, coded and arranged in the appropriate themes of perceived ease of use (PEOU), perceived usefulness (PU), facilitating conditions (FC), social influence (SI), perceived value (PV), workflow practices (WP) and behavioural intention to use (BI). The findings as presented in the following sections. The descriptive statistics are presented as bar graphs showing levels of agreement stated as strongly agree (SA), agree (A), not sure (NS), disagree (D), and strongly disagree (SD).

4.1 Perceived Ease of Use (PEOU)

Data was collected on respondents' view on whether PEOU contributes to successful adoption and use of mobile phones for maternal healthcare.

Figure 2 indicates that PEOU of the mobile phone is important for healthcare workers intention's to adopt it in practice. This is illustrated by their level of agreement with the following parameters used to measure PEOU namely: easy to learn, easy to operate, not difficult to understand and flexible to interact with as shown in Fig. 2.

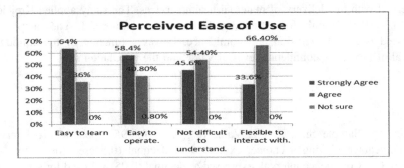

Fig. 2. Perceived Ease of Use

4.2 Perceived Usefulness (PU)

Data was collected on respondents' view on whether PU contributes to successful adoption and use of mobile phones for maternal healthcare.

Figure 3 shows that PU of the mobile phone is important for healthcare workers intention's to adopt it in practice. This is illustrated by their level of agreement with the following parameters used to measure PU namely: improves disease diagnosis, enhances effectiveness in patient care, increases my productivity and accomplishes tasks more quickly as shown in Fig. 3.

Fig. 3. Perceived Usefulness

4.3 Social Influence (SI)

Data was collected on respondents' view on whether SI contributes to successful adoption and use of mobile phones for maternal healthcare.

Figure 4 indicates that SI of the mobile phone is important for healthcare workers intention's to adopt it in practice. This is illustrated by their level of agreement with the following parameters used to measure SI namely: the proportion of health workers using the mobile phone for maternal healthcare practice is very high, fellow healthcare professionals who use the mobile phone for maternal healthcare practice have more prestige than I do, Important and Influential professionals suggest that I use the mobile phone for maternal healthcare practice as shown in Fig. 4.

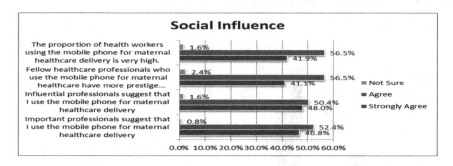

Fig. 4. Social Influence

4.4 Facilitating Conditions (FC)

Data was collected on respondents' view on whether FC contributes to successful adoption and use of mobile phones for maternal healthcare.

Figure 5 indicates that FC of the mobile phone is important for healthcare workers intention's to adopt it in practice. This is illustrated by their level of agreement with the following parameters used to measure FC namely: I have the necessary resources, I have the necessary knowledge and skills, it is compatible with the other systems that I use and user support available when I get a problem as shown in Fig. 5.

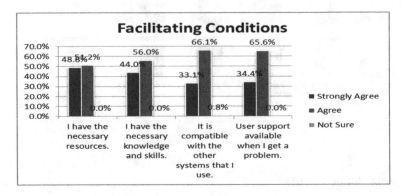

Fig. 5. Facilitating Conditions

4.5 Perceived Value (PV)

Data was collected on respondents' view on whether PV contributes to successful adoption and use of mobile phones for maternal healthcare.

Figure 6 indicates that PV of the mobile phone is important for healthcare workers intention's to adopt it in practice. This is illustrated by their level of agreement with the following parameters used to measure PV namely: saving costs for patients and health care providers, reducing the time and effort of health care professionals and additional monetary benefits/rewards are given as shown in Fig. 6.

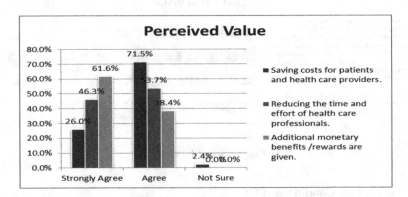

Fig. 6. Perceived Value

4.6 Workflow Practices (WP)

Data was collected on respondents' view on whether WP contributes to successful adoption and use of mobile phones for maternal healthcare.

Figure 7 indicates that WP of the mobile phone is an important consideration for healthcare workers intention's to adopt it in practice. This is illustrated by their level of agreement with the following parameters used to measure WP namely: it fits easily my daily work practices, it decreases on time I spend on routine job tasks and it facilitates convenient doctor to patient collaboration as shown in Fig. 7.

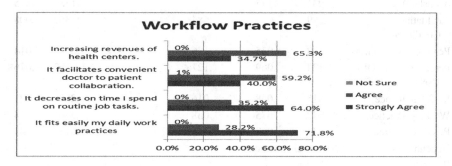

Fig. 7. Workflow Practices

4.7 Behavioural Intention (BI)

Data was collected on respondents' view on whether BI contributes to successful adoption and use of mobile phones for maternal healthcare.

Figure 8 indicates that BI of the mobile phone is important for healthcare workers to adopt it in practice. This is illustrated by their level of agreement with the following parameters used to measure BI namely: there is praise and recognition for work done, there are promotional opportunities and there is free training on the use of mobile phone as shown in Fig. 8.

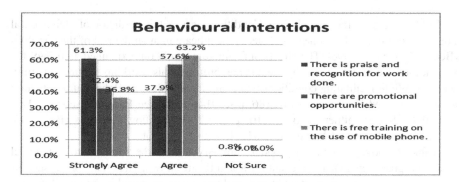

Fig. 8. Behavioural Intention

4.8 Results of Regression Analysis

A regression model was generated to determine the degree to which PEOU, PU, FC, SI, PV, WP and BI can explain the adoption of mobile phones for maternal healthcare. Table 1 shows the regression model while Table 2 presents the model summary.

Table 1. Regression Model

Model	Unstandardized Coefficients		Standardized Coefficients	t	Sig.
	B	Std. Error	Beta		
(Constant)	.031	.195		.158	.875
Facilitating Conditions	.589	.070	.584	8.357	.000
Perceived Usefulness	.188	.075	.186	2.491	.014
Perceived Ease Of Use	.124	.069	.127	1.792	.076
Social Influence	.015	.068	.016	.227	.821
Working Practices	.042	.075	.038	.564	.574
Perceived Value	.041	.067	.041	.613	.541

Dependent Variable: Behavioural Intentions

R	.718
R Square	.516
Adjusted R Square	.490
F Statistic	20.249
Sig.	.000

Table 2. Model Summary

Model	R	R Square	Adjusted R Square	Std. Error of the Estimate
1	.718[a]	.516	.490	.42690

[a]Predictors: (Constant), Workflow practices, Social Influence, Perceived Usefulness, Facilitating Conditions, Perceived Value, Perceived Ease of Use

Table 1 reveals that Facilitating Conditions is a better predictor of Behavioural Intention to use mobile phones for maternal healthcare than all the rest of the variables (Beta = .584, Sig. < .000). The effects of facilitating conditions explained 49.0 % of the variance of usage intentions by healthcare professionals working in the maternity sections. While facilitating conditions had a significant effect on Behavioural intention to use, Perceived Usefulness (B = .186, p < .014), Perceived Ease of Use (B = .127, p < .076), Social Influence (B = .016, p < .821), Workflow Practices (B = .038, p < .574) and Perceived Value (B = .041, p < .541) did not.

Table 2 above presents the model summary and at the footnote to the model summary, predictors that are relevant for R and R^2 are shown. The predictors of success factors for mobile phone adoption in maternal healthcare proposed in the model include Workflow practices, Social Influence, Perceived Usefulness, Facilitating Conditions, Perceived Value and Perceived Ease of Use. The multiple correlation coefficient R which is square root of R Square shows how strongly the multiple independent variables relate to the one dependent variable. R varies from 0 to 1, in Table 2 above, R = 0.718 which implies that there is a strong relationship between the multiple independent variables and the dependent variable.

5 Discussion and Conclusions

The use of the mobile phone for maternal healthcare faces complexities such as technophobia on the side of the health workers, shared phone access and ownership, literacy and translation to local languages and access divides which need to be addressed before the mobile phone can be used for maternal healthcare. Developing countries' environments are different from those of developed countries and the need therefore remains to identify factors responsible for successful adoption of mobile phones for maternal healthcare in developing countries.

The results of the study point to the fact that the respective variables had scores of above 50 % in agreement. This implies that over 50 % of the respondents agreed that the above constructs with their respective variables are contributing factors for successful adoption of mobile phones in maternal healthcare in Uganda. The adoption of the mobile phone in maternal healthcare increases revenues of health centers, saves costs for patients and health care providers, facilitates doctor to patient collaboration, easily fits in daily work practices for and decreases on time for routine job tasks and reduces the time and effort of health care professionals. The study also shows that adoption of mobile phones in maternal healthcare is simplified if they are easy to learn and use, easy to operate, not difficult to understand and flexible to interact with. The attitude towards the use of the mobile phone for maternal healthcare is shaped by fellow healthcare professionals who use mobile phone for healthcare and have more prestige than they do. They are also more likely to adopt and use Mobile phones for healthcare if they are given monetary benefits, praise and recognition for work done and promotional opportunities.

References

1. Ministry of Health and Social Welfare Tanzania (MHSWT): A Performance Audit on the Monitoring, Evaluations and Budget Allocation for Maternal Health Care Activities in Tanzania (2011)
2. Nanda, G., Switlick, K., & Lule, E.: Accelerating progress towards achieving the MDG to improve maternal health: A collection of promising approaches. Health Nutrition and Population, the World Bank Discussion Paper (2005)
3. WHO (World Health Organization): The World Health Report 2000 Health Systems: Improving performance. World Health Organization, Geneva (2000)
4. Global Health Initiative: Uganda. A Strategy for accelerating reductions in Maternal and Neonatal Mortality. US Mission Uganda Interagency Health team (2011)
5. Nyamba, S.Y., Mlozi, R.S.: Factors influencing the use of mobile phones in communicating agricultural information: a case of Kilolo district, Iringa, Tanzania. Int. J. Inf. Commun. Technol. Res. 2(7), 2223–4985 (2012)
6. Intermedia: Mobile money in Uganda. Use, Barriers and Opportunities. The financial Inclusion Tracker Surveys Project (2012)
7. Oyeyemi, S.O.: The use of cell phone for maternal health: The Abiye Project. Thesis, Faculty of Health Sciences, Department of Clinical Medicine, University of Tromso, Sweden (2012)

8. Ssemaluulu, P., Muma, W., Mwase, M., Katongole, P.: Maternal monitoring: lowering child mortality by use of ICTs. Special topics in Computing and ICT research strengthening the role of ICT in development. Int. J. Comput. ICT Res. **4**, 202–218 (2010)

9. World Health Organization: Make Every Mother and Child Count (2005)

10. Lawn, J.E., Cousens, S., Zupan, J.: Neonatal survival 1: 4 million neonatal deaths: when? where? why? Lancet **365**(9462), 891–900 (2005)

11. World Bank: Safe motherhood and the World Bank: Lessons from 10 years of experience. World Bank, Washington (1999)

12. Panos, L.: Birth Rights: New Approaches to Safe Motherhood. Panos and the London School of Tropical Hygiene and Medicine, London (2001)

13. Mechael, P.N.: MOTecH: MHealth Ethnography Report. Dodowa Health Research Center for the Grameen Foundation, Washington, DC (2009)

14. Lund, S.: Mobile Phones can Save Lives, pp. 18–19. Profile / Global Health, University of Copenhagen, Copenhagen (2009)

15. Walakira, B.A., Nalweyiso. B.: Mobile Phones giving modern solutions for Child and Maternal Health (MCH) in Uganda. A Case of Health Child. Jinja District, Uganda (2011)

16. Nchise, A.C., Boateng, R., Shu, I., Mbarika, V.: Mobile phones in health care in Uganda: the applab study. Electron. J. Inf. Syst. Developing Countries **52**(2), 1–15 (2012)

17. Earth Institute. : Barriers and gaps affecting mHealth in low and middle income countries: A policy white paper. Washington, DC: mHealth Alliance (2010)

18. Gurman, A.T., Rubin, E.S., Roess, A.A.: Effectiveness of mHealth behavior change communication interventions in developing countries: a systematic review of the literature. J. Health Commun.: Int. Perspect. **17**(1), 82–104 (2012)

19. UNESCO.: Report of the Broadband Commission Digital Development to the United Nations Secretary-General (2010)

20. Lynch, T., Szorenyi, N., Lodhia, S.: Adoption of Information technologies in Fiji: Issues in the study of cultural influences on Information technology Acceptance. IT for Developing countries and indigenous people (2002)

21. Hill, C., Loch, K., Straub, D.W., El-Sheshai, K.: A qualitative assessment of Arab culture and information technology transfer. J. Global Inf. Manage. **6**(3), 29–38 (1998)

22. Van Biljon, J.A., Kotze, P.: Cultural factors in a Mobile Phone Adoption and usage Model. J. Univ. Comput. Sci. **14**(16), 2650–2679 (2008)

23. Kagumire, R.: How Uganda's health care problems can end with a phone. The Independent (2009)

24. MOTECH, Mobile Technology for Community Health in Ghana.: What it is and what Grameen Foundation has learned so far. Grameen Foundation, Washington, DC, USA (2011)

25. De Tolly, K., Benjamin, P.: Mobile phones: opening new channels for health communication. In: Obregon, R., Waisbord, S., Handbook of global health communication. Wiley-Blackwell, West Sussex, UK (2012)

26. GSMA mWomen Programme: Striving and surviving: Exploring the lives of women at the base of the pyramid. GSMA mWomen, London (2012)

27. Furukwa, M.F., Ketcham, J.D., Rimsza, M.E.: Physician practice revenues and use of Information Technology in patient care. Med. Care **45**(2), 168–176 (2007)

28. HURINET-U: The state of Regional Hospitals in Uganda; Economic, Social and Cultural Rights projects with Democracy Governance Facility (DFG) Uganda and DIAKONI (2012)

A Model of e-Health Acceptance
and Usage in Uganda: The Perspective
of Online Social Networks

Edward Miiro[1] and Gilbert Maiga[2(✉)]

[1] Department of Business Computing,
Makerere University Business School, Kampala, Uganda
emiiro@mubs.ac.ug
[2] Department of Information Technology,
Makerere University, Kampala, Uganda
gmaiga@cit.mak.ac.ug

Abstract. Online social networks are transforming e-government service delivery across the World. Whereas they have been utilized to enhance delivery of other e-government services, their usage in health care in the developing country context still faces a lot of challenges. These include lack of policies, limited knowledge of what motivates user acceptance and usage of social networks for e-Health and lack of trust in the information shared in these networks. In the past decade, many acceptance models have been developed to explain user acceptance of e-government technology. However, none has been developed to utilize the mighty power of online social networks in a developing country context. In a bid to close this gap, this paper presents the results of a study that develops a Social Networked Model for improved e-Health service acceptance and usage in Uganda. Requirements for the model elicited in a field study are used to extend the generic E-government Acceptance Model which emphasizes Social Network factors for e-Health Acceptance and usage. The extended model has dimensions of Social support, Social awareness, Social attractiveness and Social influence. The Social Networked Model is generic and can be used by other transitioning countries.

Keywords: E-government · e-Health acceptance · Social networks · Social networked model · E-government Acceptance Model

1 Introduction

The advent of online social networks is transforming the way government services are delivered to the citizens. On the other hand, it is changing the way people connect with each other and how information is shared and distributed. Initiated by the private sector with telecommunication companies offering Internet services, banks deploying ATMs, companies developing websites, many governments are embracing ICT to deliver their services to the natives through a technology commonly known as e-government. E-Health which refers to the application of ICTs particularly the Internet for improving access to healthcare services [14] is one of the key e-Government practices embraced

© Institute for Computer Sciences, Social Informatics and Telecommunications Engineering 2015
A. Nungu et al. (Eds.): AFRICOMM 2014, LNICST 147, pp. 115–126, 2015.
DOI: 10.1007/978-3-319-16886-9_12

by the government of Uganda. The renown key importance for e-health have been improved access to health information, enabling patients to be more active participants in the treatment process which leads to better medical outcomes [7]. It also has the potential to revolutionalise the way healthcare is delivered as it can reach into areas such as rural areas and in wars where traditional healthcare is difficult [15]. In many developed countries, online social networks have been used as platforms to increase the acceptance and usage of e-Government services. A study by [13] discloses that there is an increasing desire to use online social networks for e-Government services across the world. Kes-Erkul and Erkul [10] lament that online social networks have the capacity to change the relationship between the Internet and its users, and can change power structures and increase the opportunity for users to engage in greater community participation. Osimo [18] adds that social networks have opened up tremendous new possibilities of engaging the public in government work in very different ways. This has come with change in people expectation of how the government should deliver to them especially the millennium generation of social networked citizens who wish government agencies should interact with them in the same way that commercial companies interact with them through various social network sites [20]. The increasing number of Ugandans on key social network channels such as Face book, Tweeter, LinkedIn, YouTube makes it a tremendously valuable e-Health tool. With mobile Internet access becoming cheaper, a growing number of Ugandans are able to use phones and other internet-enabled devices to access social networks, news sites, and other websites at a reasonable cost. For example, a mobile internet package through MTN Uganda, the country's leading telecom company, can cost Shs500 for 20 MB of data. Free access to Face book is also available to MTN and Orange mobile network subscribers. It is noted that these powerful social network tools despite enhancing acceptance and usage of e-Government services in the developed countries, they have not been used to enhance the same in Uganda. To address this issue we extended the E-Government Acceptance Model (EGAM) proposed by [19] to examine Social Network users' intention towards using their social networks for e-Health. It is based on the Technology Acceptance Model by [5] and in addition to TAM's Perceived Ease of Use and Perceived Usefulness; EGAM adds three more important constructs of Top leadership involvement, government policy and regulation and perceived strength of control. Many scholars have come up to support Sahu's constructs including [1] who emphasized the importance of involving management and users in Information technology implementation activities. Although Government policy and regulation together with top leadership involvement are key to acceptance, much has to be done from the user perspective within their social circles. It is on this basis that the study explored social network constructs of social communication, social influence, social awareness, social support and social attractiveness as having a major role to play in improving e-Health acceptance and usage.

2 Online Social Networks

Online Social Networks are defined as web-based services that allow individuals to construct a public or semi-public profile within a bounded system, articulate a list of other users within whom they share a connection, and be able to view and traverse their list of connections and those made by others within their system [3]. They are online platforms where users create virtual networks with likeminded people analogous to social networks in real life [9]. They are characterized by creation of a public profile within a defined system, ability to connect with others, user-generated content and are part of a larger category of technologies known as Web 2.0 [3]. The most common social networking sites include Face book, WhatsApp, Twitter, YouTube, Google+ and LinkedIn. In the recent years, these social networks have become some of the most popular destinations for online traffic. According to [10] social networks have the capacity to change the relationship between the Internet and its users, and can change power structures and increase the opportunity for users to engage in greater community participation thus powerful tools for e-health acceptance.

3 e-Health

According to [21], e-Government consists of various fast moving fields, e-health being a very specific one of them. It refers to the application of ICTs particularly internet for improving the healthcare services [14]. Shiferaw and Zolfo [7] urges that e-health is an emerging field in the intersection of medical informatics, clinical practice, public health, and business, referring to health services and information delivered through the Internet and related technologies. According to World Health Organization (WHO) E-health is the leveraging of the ICT to connect provider and patients and governments; to educate and inform healthcare professionals, managers and consumers; to stimulate innovation in care delivery and health system management; and to improve our healthcare system [16]. Issues of health service provision are central to any discussion of development and has picked a lot of interest amongst many governments of developing countries. This has come with a change in how people expect their governments to deliver its services to them as regards health. There are a number of benefits associated to e-health and among others are the following; E-health provides improved access to health information which enables patients to be more active participants in the treatment process leading to better medical outcomes [7]. E-Health has the potential to revolutionize the way healthcare is delivered as it can reach into areas such as rural areas and in wars where traditional healthcare is difficult [15]. Shiferaw and Zolfo [7] also laments that the adoption of e-health in developing countries is appropriate for addressing the problems that exist which include; high mortality and morbidity rates, high population and poor communication infrastructures. Health is information-intensive, generating huge volumes of data every day. It is estimated that up to 30 % of the total health budget is spent handling information, collecting it, looking for it and storing it. It is therefore imperative that information is managed in the most effective way possible in order to ensure a high quality, safe service all provided by e-Health. Despite the multi-disciplinary benefits offered by using e-health, it is evident that this technology has not picked up to its potential in many developing countries. This study sought to establish the factors important to utilize the wide spread online social networks in the delivery of e-Health services.

3.1   e-Health Adoption in Uganda

e-Health Adoption is the intention to use e-Health services. There are a number of health information systems running in the country including; the Health Management Information System and Integrated Diseases Surveillance and Response System (IDSR) and the Vital Registration-Management Information System (VSR-MIS). The Health Management Information System (HMIS) of the MoH is also in place and has evolved for now over 15 years and it encompasses data from all levels of the health system: the village or grass roots health unit, parish, sub-county, HSD, district, and national level. Data are captured using a hybrid of paper forms, registers, and tally sheets at the health unit level. The kind of data collected is primarily patient data and mortality but also includes health care facilities, staffing, drug supplies, family planning, and population. In 2004, the Ugandan government formulated the e-government strategy and set up numerous ICT projects in various sectors to facilitate e-governance [17]. This platform brought hopes of increased transparency of government activities, enabling government departments to share public data and enhance interdepartmental coordination thus reducing costs and generally work efficiency [8]. Despite all these investments with regard to the health sector, the adoption process is still very limited with a number of challenges. Therefore there is a need to analyse these challenges and in the context of this study, see how social networks can be of help.

3.2   Challenges to e-Health Adoption

The challenges to Adoption of e-Health as an e-government system in Uganda are numerous. Most of them arise as a result of multidimensionality and complexity of these e-government initiatives which result into massive failure of most of these projects [6]. Notable among others is non-adoption. Whereas e-government adoption has increased for most countries, it remains constrained by low adoption rates in economically and technologically transitioning countries [12]. Another challenge points to limited ICT and network infrastructure. With the wide digital divide gap, the government is not able to deploy appropriate and acceptable ICT infrastructure for e-Health initiatives [14]. The poor attitude, resistance and fear of change is yet another challenge to e-Health adoption. With the wide spread unemployment levels in the country, there is a lot of resistance from public service employees to the digital hospital. Ndou [14] adds that technology has created two groups of people i.e. the digital natives and the non digital natives. There is always a challenge of making the non-digital natives cope up with the latest technology for fear of change because in the world over, technology has replaced manpower especially the unskilled labor and this has been the greatest fear for employees [14]. Policy issues also pause a big challenge to e-Health adoption. Unlike in the developed world, many underdeveloped countries don't have strong laws enacted by the governments to facilitate the use of ICT and E-health adoption in particular. According to [11] E-Government can only be achieved when the legal laws on adoption of digital technology are strengthened.

Finally, the un-affordability of ICT services also puts a big challenge to the adoption of e-Health. Access to ICT services in the developing countries is majorly left to the individual efforts of the nationals. These equipments come with varying degrees of expenditure leaving the majority poor nationals with no alternative other than non-adoption.

3.3   The Role of Adoption Models Applicable to e-Health

E-Health as an e-government service, is built on the generic e-government infrastructure. Therefore, addressing e-Health adoption requires a discussion of the different e-government adoption models. Many models have been put up by different researchers to help understand e-government acceptance/adoption. The e-government adoption models presented and compared are the Cultural based E-Government Adoption Model [2] the E-governance Acceptance Model [19], the Conceptual adoption model for e-government [4], the citizen based Model for E-Government Adoption [1] and the Unified Theory of Acceptance and Use of Technology (UTAUT) [22]. These models were compared on the basis of of the different social network measures and are presented in Table 1.

Table 1. A generic view of e-government adoption measures

Measures (factors)	Cultural model	EGAM	Conceptual model	Citizen model	UTAUT
Ease of use	✓	✓	✓	✓	✓
Usefulness	✓	✓	✓	✓	✓
Privacy and Trust	X	✓	✓	✓	✓
Setting up ICT infrastructure	X	X	✓	✓	X
Government involvement	✓	✓	✓	X	X
Culture	✓	X	✓	X	✓
Social influence	X	X	X	X	✓
Social communication	X	X	X	X	X
Social attractiveness	X	X	X	X	X
Social support	X	X	X	X	X
Social awareness	X	X	X	X	X

Table 1 above shows that four out of the five models compared, do not consider social network factors. With the exception of UTAUT which also only considers social influence, all the models are silent about social support, social communication, social attractiveness and social awareness which are very important for people to use their social networks for e-Health in the context of this study.

The E-government Acceptance Model (EGAM) proposed by [19] is used in this study. It is based on the Technology Acceptance Model by [5] and in addition to TAM's Perceived Ease of Use and Perceived Usefulness; EGAM adds three more important constructs of Top leadership involvement, government policy and regulation and perceived strength of control. Many scholars have come up to support Sahu's constructs including [1] who emphasized the importance of involving management and users in Information technology implementation activities. Although Government policy and regulation together with top leadership involvement are key to acceptance, much has to be done from the user perspective within their social circles. It is on this basis that the study explored social network constructs of social communication, social influence, social awareness, social support and social attractiveness as having a major role to play in improving e-Health acceptance and usage.

4 The Methodology

4.1 Field Study

The study sought to identify the factors that are important for people to use their social networks for e-Health and later were used to design the Social networked Model. The study made use of a Questionnaire that was issued out to Online social network users in this case IT/IS graduate students in the three selected Universities of Makerere University (FCIT), Kampala International University (SIT&C) and Nkumba University (IT&S). The questionnaire was pretested with 18 respondents. Out of a total of 317 (three hundred and seventeen) respondents who were given the questionnaires, 278 (two hundred and seventy eight) returned valid filled questionnaires showing a response rate of 87.6 %. The data collected was then categorized, quantified, coded and arranged in themes with respect to the objectives of the study using frequency tables and bar charts. Data analysis was done using statistical package for social sciences (SPSS).

4.2 Results of the Field Study

4.2.1 Barriers to Using Online Social Networks for e-Health

The study sought to identify the barriers to using the respondents' social networks for e-Health. The proposed barriers were lack of awareness from trusted friends, lack of role models using social networks for health care, complexity of e-Health systems, lack of friends support, limited social communication, unattractiveness of e-Health tools, fear to share personal health information with friends and lack of user protective/ confidentiality policies. The responses are presented in Fig. 1.

Findings from the Fig. 1 reveal that 68 % of the respondends agreed that lack of awareness from their trusted friends hindered them from using their social networks for eHealth, 3.2 % of the respondents were not sure while 28.8 % disagreed. Furthermore 57.1 % of the respondents agreed that lack of role models using social networks for eHealth contributed to their not using their social networks for eHealth, 10.8 % of these were not sure while 32.1 % disagreed. To note, 53.3 % of the respondents agreed that the complexity of using eHealth systems through their social networks was a reason for them not to use the same for eHealth, 10.4 % of these were not sure while 36.3 % disagreed. 52.9 % agreed that lack of friends support was a reason not to use their social networks for eHealth, 14.7 % were not sure while 32.4 % disagreed. 41.4 % sighted lack of social communication as barrier against using their social networks for eHealth, 4.7 % were not sure while 53.9 % disagreed. In addition, 64.7 % of the respondents agreed that the unattractiveness of eHealth tools was a reason not to use their social networks for eHealth, 16.2 % of these were not sure while 19.1 % disagreed. 66.9 % of

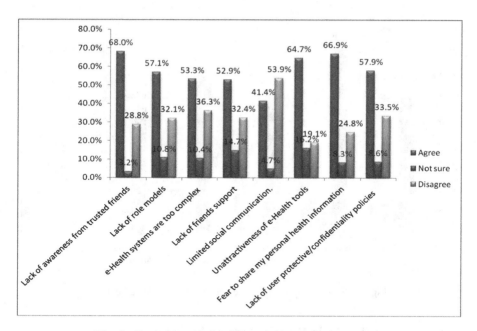

Fig. 1. Barriers to using online social networks for e-health

the respondents agreed that fear to share their personal health information over social networks was a reason not to use their social networks for eHealth, 8.3 % were not sure while 24.8 disgreed. 57.9 % of the respondents agreed that lack of user protective policies hindered them from using their social networks for eHealth, 8.6 % of them were not sure while 33.5 % disagreed.

4.2.2 Factors Important to Use Social Networks for e-Health

This study investigated the factors that the respondents consider important to use their social networks for e-Health. These factors included Social support, Social Influence, Social Communication, Social Awareness and Social Attractiveness. The results on the different factors are presented in the Fig. 2.

Findings show that 65.5 % of the respondents agreed that the availability of social support would make them use their social networks for e-Health, 9.7 % of these were not sure while 24.8 % disagreed. On the other hand, 82.2 % of the respondents treasured social influence as an important factor to use their social networks for e-Healh, 1.8 % were not sure while 15.5 % disagreed. When asked whether social communication contributed to their use of social networks for e-Health, 61.5 % agreed, 4.7 % of these were not sure while 33.8 % disagreed. Findings also revealed that 73.4 % agreed with social awareness for them to use their social networks for e-Health, 6.5 % were not sure while 20.1 % disagreed. In the same line, 56.9 % of the respondents agreed that social attractiveness was important to use their social networks for e-Health, 5.4 % of these were not sure while 37.8 % disagreed.

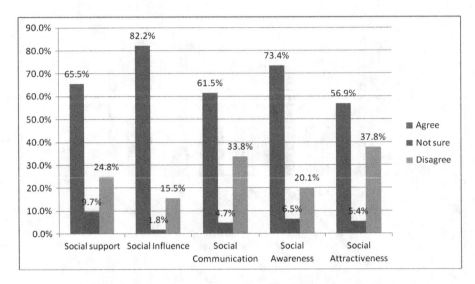

Fig. 2. Factors important to use social networks for e-health

5 Regression Analysis Results for the Social Networked Model

Regression analysis was used to explain the relationship between the dependent variables and the independent variables as listed in the Table 2 below;

Table 2. Relationship between the dependent and the independent variables

Dependent variable	Independent variable
Perceived Usefulness	Social influence, Social awareness, Social communication
Perceived Ease of Use	Social support
Behavioral Intention to use	Social attractiveness
Attitude towards using	Top leadership involvement, Perceived strength of control
Perceived strength of control	Government policy and regulation

To explain perceived usefulness, multiple regression analysis was performed with perceived usefulness as the dependent variable and (social influence, social awareness and social communication) as independent variables. The extended EGAM explained up to 45.9 % of variance in perceived usefulness. Evidence from regression shows that out of the three variables, two were found to exert a significant influence on perceived usefulness. This is because their respective p-values were less than the level of significance ($p < 0.05$) and according to the results, these variables included: Social influence ($p = .000$) and Social Awareness ($p = .030$). This suggests that holding other factors constant perceived usefulness in the context of this study is dependent on only these two variables, the third variable (Social communication) playing a negligible role at (p = .138). The factors determining perceived usefulness were social influence (B = 1.218, p = .000) and Social awareness (B = .607, p = .030). Social communication was not significant at the .05 level in the model.

To explain attitude towards using e-Health, multiple regression analysis was performed with attitude towards using e-Health as the dependent variable and (top leadership involvement, perceived strength of control) as independent variables. The extended EGAM explained up to 20.9 % of variance in attitude towards using e-Health. Although both the independent variables were found to be significant in influencing the dependent variable, Perceived strength of control had the most significant influence with a significance level (p = .000) and its counterpart (Top leadership involvement) having a significance level (p = .014).

To explain Perceived ease of use, regression was performed between perceived ease of use (dependent variable) and social support (independent variable). The extended EGAM explained up to 68.3 % of variance in perceived ease of use. The results from the regression show that the independent variable (Social support) was positively related with the dependent variable (Perceived ease of use). Specifically, its coefficient was 0.827 which implies the existence of a positively linear relationship with the dependent variable. This variable was found to be significant in influencing the dependent variable with a significance level (p = .000).

To explain behavioral intention to use, regression was performed between behavioral intention to use (dependent variable) and social attractiveness (independent variable). The extended EGAM explained up to 31.3 % of variance in behavioral intention to use. Results from regression in show that the independent variable (Social attractiveness) was positively related with the dependent variable (Behavioral Intention to use). Specifically, its coefficient was 0.559 which implies the existence of a positively linear relationship with the dependent variable. This variable was found to be significant in influencing the dependent variable with p value = .000.

To explain Perceived strength of control, regression was performed between Perceived strength of control (dependent variable) and Government policy and regulation (independent variable). The extended EGAM explained up to 1.4 % of variance in Perceived strength.

6 Presentation of the Social Networked Model

Results from regression analysis presented above revealed that Social influence and Social awareness have a significant impact on perceived usefulness with p values = .000 and .030 respectively. Social support was found to impact perceived ease of use with p = .000. Top leadership involvement and perceived strength of control were found to exert a significant impact on attitude towards using social networks for e-health with p values = .014 and .000 respectively. In the same line, social attractiveness significantly influences behavioral intention to use social networks for e-Health with p value = .000. Figure 3 presents a summary of these findings and the Social Networked Model.

The understanding of the factors important to use online social networks for e-Health in Uganda is important if we are to improve the Acceptance and usage of these critical services. This study examined the applicability of the extended EGAM model

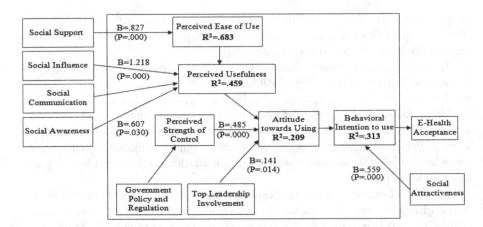

Fig. 3. Results of the regression analysis (significant relationships at p < .05)

using social network based factors for e-Health Acceptance that significantly influenced perceived usefulness, perceived ease of use, attitude towards using and behavioral intention to use.

The results show that the factors that have significant and strong influence on perceived usefulness are Social influence and Social awareness. This means that if the citizens are to take e-Health as a useful technology, they must get influence from their friends in the network. In the same line, citizens must be made aware of the usefulness of using their social networks for e-Health if Acceptance and usage is to be increased.

Those with significant and strong influence on attitude towards using e-Health are Perceived strength of control and Top leadership involvement. This implies that if citizens are to use their social networks for e-Health, they must be sure of controlling their user accounts hence giving them a positive attitude towards this technology and consequently, acceptance and usage. In addition, top leaders must be involved in the use of these social networks for e-Health hence changing the attitudes of the citizens towards accepting and using e-Health.

The results also depict that social support has a strong and significant influence on perceived ease of use. One of the barriers to using online social networks for e-Health was identified as the complexity of e-Health systems. If the citizens are to use their social networks for e-Health, the support from friends in the network is very important.

Furthermore, Social attractiveness was found to have a strong influence on behavioral intention to use. This means that e-Health applications must be designed with attractive features that will keep enticing the users just like the case with their social networking sites.

7   Conclusion and Future Work

The model presented in this study outlines the factors important to use online social networks for e-Health as social support, social awareness, social influence and social attractiveness. These factors are used to extend the E-government Acceptance Model [19]. Theoretically, the model provides the basis for using social networks to improve the Acceptance and usage of e-Health services in Uganda. The model contributes to e-Health Adoption literature with a bias towards the factors important in using online social networks for e-Health. The social networked model developed in this work is generic and can reliably be applicable in other transitioning countries with a similar context like Uganda. A regression analysis provided support for relating the Social network factors (social support, social awareness, social influence and social attractiveness) to the existing EGAM constructs of perceived usefulness, perceived ease of use, attitude and behavioral intention. Whereas EGAM has been successfully used to predict general e-government Acceptance, this model provides support for using EGAM as a theory to predict e-Health Acceptance bearing in mind the social network element. Future studies should be geared towards implementing and validating this model.

References

1. Al-Adawi, Z., Yousafzai, S., Pallister, J.: Conceptual model of citizen adoption of e-government. In: The Second International Conference on Innovations in Information Technology (IIT'05) (2005)
2. Al-Hujra, O., Al-dalahmeh, M., Aloudat, A.: The role of national culture on citizen adoption of eGovernment services: an empirical study. Electron. J. e-Gov. 9(2), 93–106 (2011). www.ejeg.com
3. Boyd, D.M., Ellison, N.B.: Social network sites: definition, history and scholarship. J. Comput. Mediated. Commu. 13, 210–230 (2008)
4. Bwalya, K.J., Healy, M.: Harnessing e-government adoption in the SADC region: a conceptual underpinning. Electron. J. e-Gov. 8(1), 23–32 (2010). www.ejeg.com
5. Davis, F.D., Bagozzi, R.P., Warshaw, P.R.: User acceptance of computer technology: a comparison of two theoretical models. Manage. Sci. 35(8), 982–1003 (1989)
6. Eilu, E.: A Systematic Approach to Designing and Implementing E-Government Systems in the Developing World. Makerere University, Buganda (2009)
7. Shiferaw, F., Zolfo, M.: The role of information communication technology (ICT) towards universal health coverage: the first steps of a telemedicine project in Ethiopia. Glob Health Action (2012)
8. Huawei: E-government in Uganda (2010). http://www.huawei.com/publications/view.do?id=6091&acid=113928. Accessed 10 Aug 2013
9. Kaplan, A.M., Haenlein, M.: Users of the world, unite! the challenges and opportunities of social media. Bus. Horiz. 53, 59–68 (2010)
10. Kes-Erkul, A., Erkul, R.: Web 2.0 in the process of e-participation: the Case of Organizing for America and the Obama Administration, National Center for Digital Government Working Paper Series, 9(1), pp. 1–19 October 2009, (2009)
11. Lau, E.: Challenges for e-government Developement. Organisation for Economic Co-Operation and Development (OECD e-government Project). http://unpan1.un.org/intradoc/groups/public/documents/UN/UNPAN012241.pdf) (2003)
12. Maiga, G., Asianzu, L.: Adoption of E-tax Services in Uganda: The Perspective of the Technology Acceptance Model. College of Computing and Informatics Technology, Makerere University (2012)
13. Mossberger, K., Wu, Y.: Civic engagement and local E-Government: social networking comes of age. University of Illinois at Chicago. Institute for Policy and Civic Engagement, Chicago (2012)

14. Ndou, V.D.: E-Government for developing countries: opportunities and challenges. The Electronic Journal on Information Systems in Developing Countries (2004)
15. Zanifa, O., Lupiana, D., Mtenzi, F., Bing W.: Analysis of the challenges affecting e-healthcare adoption in developing countries: a case of tanzania. Int. J. Inf. Stud. 2(1) (2010)
16. Oh, H., Rizo, C., Enkin, M., Jadad, A.: What is eHealth?: a systematic review of published definitions. World Hospital Health Serv. 41(1) (2005)
17. Ornager, S., Verma, N.: E-Government Toolkit for Developing Countries. UNESCO, New Delhi (2005)
18. Osimo, D.: Web 2.0 in Government: Why and How?. European Commission Joint Research Center, Institute for Prospective Technological Studies (2008)
19. Sahu, G.P., Gupta, M.P., Sahoo, T.: Towards a model of e-government acceptance. In: Proceedings of the 2nd International Conference on e-Governance, ICEG (2004)
20. Tapscott, D.: Grown Up Digital: How the Net Generation is Changing Your World. McGraw Hill, New York (2009)
21. Trauner Verlag: E-taxation: state and perspectives, series informatics. http://www.ocg.at/egov/files/. vol. 21, pp. 195–206 (2007). Accessed 20 Dec 2013
22. Venkatesh, V., Morris, M., Davis, G., Davis, F.: User acceptance of information technology: toward a unified view. MIS Q. 27(3), 425–478 (2003)

Field Testing a Drug Management Application at Ugandan Health Facilities

Julianne Sansa Otim[1(✉)], Celestino Obua[2], Grace Kamulegeya[1],
Alex Mwotil[1], and Perez Matsiko[3]

[1] College of Computing and Information Sciences, Makerere University,
P.O. Box 7062, Kampala, Uganda
{sansa, gkamulegeya, amwotil}@cit.ac.ug
[2] College of Health Sciences, Makerere University, P.O. Box 7072
Kampala, Uganda
cobua@chs.mak.ac.ug
[3] Uganda Christian University, P.O. Box 04, Mukono, Uganda
pmatsiko@ucu.ac.ug

Abstract. A Drug Management Application (DMA) provides health care facilities with a tool to enhance drug inventory and drug orders. The objective of conducting the field tests was to evaluate attitudes, effective use and effects of the DMA during a time-limited trial at carefully selected rural health centers. At the end of the field-tests, rural health workers reported several benefits experienced through using the DMA including: (i) it is a time-saving approach for ordering drugs; (ii) it allows feedback from the drugs distribution center; (iii) it is cost-effective since transport costs are eliminated; (iv) it facilitates effective inventory management; (v) it presents an opportunity to monitor and stay within the drugs budget of the health facility. This contributes to the implementation of rational drug management and use of medicines.

Keywords: e-health · Drug application · Field-tests · Rural internet connectivity

1 Introduction

The World Health Organisation's policy for rational use of Drugs states that "Patients should receive medication appropriate to their clinical needs, in doses that meet their own individual requirement, for an adequate period of time and at the lowest cost to them and their community [1]." Implementing this policy is still complex especially in low income countries evidenced by the following global drug management challenges:

- 1.7 billion people have inadequate or no access to life-saving medicines;
- Antiretroviral therapy is available to less than 10 % of those in need;
- 1 million die from malaria, 2 million from TB and 3 million from AIDS yearly
- 30–50 % of health care budgets are used for drugs in resource poor countries.

In Uganda, two key drug management challenges exist, namely: (i) the drug supply chain is not optimized since some essential drugs are not available at the health facilities at certain times when they are needed. In addition medicines expire at the Medical Stores

© Institute for Computer Sciences, Social Informatics and Telecommunications Engineering 2015
A. Nungu et al. (Eds.): AFRICOMM 2014, LNICST 147, pp. 127–133, 2015.
DOI: 10.1007/978-3-319-16886-9_13

as well as the health facilities and the process of ordering drugs is time-consuming; (ii) The existing Drug Management System is paper-based e.g. the essential drug lists used by health facilities as well as the clinical or treatment guidelines referred to during prescription are all paper-based. This makes drug reactions hard to follow-up and increases the health workers work-load during manual routines.

To address some of the aforementioned challenges a Drug Management Application (DMA) was developed within the AGLARBRI framework [2, 3]. The DMA provides health care facilities with a tool to enhance drug inventory and drug orders.

The inventory function allows a health care facility to manage its drug inventory. Current stocks of all medicines can be edited either to indicate a reduction or an increase of such medicine. Also, the current availability in the inventory of each drug can be checked using the DMA application.

The order function allows the health care facility to manage its drug orders. The requesting procedure is taken care of in the application by simple user interface. This makes the ordering process easier and helps in avoiding loss of information between the health facility and the drug distribution center. New orders can be created and previous orders are listed whose details are viewable on simply clicking on them.

2   Research Objective

The scientific objective of conducting the field tests was to evaluate attitudes, effective use and effects of the DMA during a time-limited trial of this application at carefully selected rural health centers. The Joint Medical Stores (JMS) and two health facilities participated in the field tests. The two health centers are Bishop Ceasar Asili Hospital – Kasana, Luwero, (which is under the Uganda Catholic Medical Bureau) and Mawundo Health Center which is a member of Family Life Education Programme in Jinja, Uganda (and is under the Uganda Protestant Medical Bureau). Both health facilities receive drugs and other medical supplies from the JMS. The DMA field tests were made possible with seed funding from SPIDER [4].

3   Related Work

e-Health is the use of available electronic/digital technologies, systems and methods to facilitate health service delivery that include records, information, supply chain management, referral and counter-referrals, tele-consultations, and tele-conferencing amongst others. The Government of Uganda in 2012 started a 5 year project to enhance e-Health in Uganda. The project is being executed jointly by the Ministry of Health (MoH) and the Uganda Communications Commission (UCC) working with local beneficiaries in the districts, such as Regional Referral Hospitals, District Hospitals and Health Centre IVs. The establishment consists of; a Resource Centre at the MoH headquarters, computer centres at the beneficiary facilities, Local Area Network (LAN), Fibre-optic network, telemedicine equipment, Solar Power equipment, National Grid connection as well as relevant software. Expected output will include virtual linkage to the MoH resource centre by district health headquarters and other hospitals providing accessibility to the MoH portal, e-CMEs, Online Medical Journals, e-libraries and e-consultations. This will ease communication, harmonise referrals, and improve patient care and consultations by well informed health workers [6]. Therefore, the DMA, being an application of e-Health in the supply chain management, complements the government e-health initiative in rural health facilities.

4   Methodology

4.1   Research Approach

In this project, we started out using a similar strategy as the one developed in the Tanzania ICT4RD program [5] and generally used in the AGLARBRI framework. The approach to implement the strategy includes:

1. Identification and invitation of rural communities (RCs) to participate in the DMA field-tests and coach them in the formulation of their drug management automation development plan.
2. Training health center staff in general computer skills and effective use of the DMA.
3. Purchasing and configuring the computer hardware to run the DMA.
4. Creating simple designs of the RC local area network and internet connectivity options.
5. Providing interconnectivity to the DMA server.
6. Monitoring and supporting the use of the DMA.

4.2   DMA Technology Description

The DMA is a web-based client-server application that is database centric. The technical specifications of the DMA are explained below:

4.2.1   Client Side

- The clients access the application through web browsers such as Google Chrome and Firefox on any operating system.
- Each Client has a specific server URL from which inventory and order management can be done.

4.2.2   Server End

- The server runs Ubuntu 12.04 operating system with minimal specifications of 2 GB RAM, 500 GB Hard Drive and a reliable internet connection.
- The database is developed in CouchDB, a document-oriented and open source database. It contains details such as the facilities, drugs, orders and reports all stored as documents.
- Documents are presented to the client's web browser as html pages using Javascript.

4.2.3   The DMA Client-Server Process

The DMA client-server process is such that:

- The client facility visits a provided custom URL (server web address).
- From the page displayed by visiting the above URL, the client can perform functions such as managing the inventory and making orders. Inventory management activities include manual modification of stock provided new values and automatic updates as provided by a packaging order received from JMS.
- On making an order, the administrator at JMS will review it depending on the availability of drugs in their stock. The administrator does this by also visiting an administrator page of the DMA application.
- After clearing the order, a delivery notice with the packaging is sent to the client.
- The client then reviews the delivery with the packaged drugs.
- If the delivery and the packaging match, a report is generated and sent to the administrator. The client can then commit the packaging to the database and the inventory is automatically updated.

4.2.4   Internet Connectivity

During the field tests, the server was deployed at Joint Medical Stores, while both Bishop Caeser Asili Hospital and Mawundo Health Center run client PCs. JMS has a well established Local Area Network (LAN) with Internet connectivity. There was neither LAN nor internet connectivity at both health facilities. Therefore, while the staff were being trained, a simple LAN was designed for each of the health facilities. A LAN facilitates smart connectivity of computers to the Internet. Internet connectivity was required since the DMA is a web-based application.

The simple LAN design is shown in Fig. 1. This figure shows that the recommended Internet connectivity option is using a fiber optic cable to National Backbone Infrastructure (NBI) or Research and Education Network for Uganda Network (RE-NUNet) which would give the most reliable and cost-effective access to the DMA server. This requires laying last-mile fiber optic cable from the health facility to the nearest termination/distribution point for NBI or RENUNet institution or research organization. Another form of connectivity is using wireless although this option

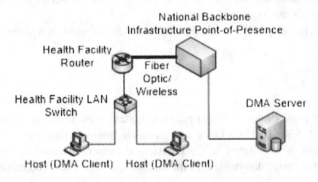

Fig. 1. Physical Local Area Network (LAN) design for the health facilities

presents several challenges in terms of maintenance and reliability as well as line of sight issues considering the rural nature of these health facilities.

The designed LANs were not actually implemented due to budgetary constraints, however, Internet connectivity to the PC supporting the DMA application was provided via a GSM modem. Negotiations are still underway to interconnect these health facilities through the public fiber owned by the government of Uganda and managed by the National IT Authority.

5 Results

The results of the field tests show that rural areas in low income countries present a genuine need for the Internet and its applications although they hardly have any Internet Infrastructure. A significant interest in the Internet was raised among the participating communities by demonstrating how the DMA (an internet based application) simplified an otherwise tedious and repetitive task.

This approach ensures that Community Based Networks that will eventually emerge; are sustainable by establishing local community goodwill (through the promotion of local ownership, local communication needs identification and services provisioning). Furthermore, there will be technical committee mentorship, raising of ICT awareness and capacity building, evolution of methods that support application of ICT in supply chains, universal access business models and technical solutions to cater for the lack of infrastructure.

We anticipated that the DMA would improve the quality of basic public health care services by providing timely access to drugs, reduction in drug theft and diversion within the supply chain and improving on drug budgeting within health centers. Both JMS and the rural health facilities acknowledged experiencing this benefit by articulating the following during the information sharing seminar held at the end of the field-tests period:

For JMS, health care services and drug supply chain are improved since the DMA keeps historical data about each health center drug consumption (by keeping all the previous history of orders) for a given time period. This data, if analyzed, can support planning to avoid current supply chain challenges like stock-outs and expiry of drugs in the JMS stores. In addition the DMA offers an online ordering option. This alternative is more convenient than the currently hand delivered orders. This manual procedure leads to people sitting for long hours waiting for their orders to be processed which in turn can be very frustrating.

For the rural health facilities the DMA application has the following benefits as feedback got from the representatives of these facilities in the seminar.

- It is a time-saving approach of drug ordering since it is a short procedure, which can be done from any internet connected computer. This is because, there is a real-time view of the current drug stock levels using the DMA system thus making the ordering process as simple as creating an order for what is currently not in stock or under stocked.

- Allows the timely feedback from the JMS (indicating at which stage the drug order has reached: viewed, packed, dispatched) to be received in real-time by the health center.
- It is cost-effective since transport costs related to drug ordering and dispatch are reduced. This is because, only one trip from each rural health centre is made for picking the physical package from JMS unlike in the manual process where more than one trip is normally made before a physical package is picked.
- DMA facilitates effective stock control and inventory management by the supply and health centre store manager so as to avoid stock-outs or over-stocking.
- Presents the opportunity to monitor and stay within the drugs budget of the health facility as only drugs that are needed will be ordered since there is a real-time view of the updated store stock levels in DMA.

6   Conclusions

Through the field tests, the DMA benefits (mentioned Sect. 5) have been experienced by the two rural health centres and workers. This contributes to the implementation of rational drug management and use of medicines. Due to the short duration of the pilot deployment of the DMA at JMS and two rural health centres, the following have been specifically achieved:

  i. Interest has been raised among the rural health facilities and Joint Medical Store about the usefulness of the DMA in ordering and drug supply chain specifically, and Internet applications in general.
 ii. The need to connect rural health facilities generally to the National Broadband Infrastructure has been raised high on the agenda of the Research and Education Network of Uganda and the National IT Authority of Uganda.

Further work includes:

  i. Supporting rural communities to establish their local area networks.
 ii. Supporting rural communities to interconnect to each other and to the national broadband infrastructure.
iii. Interfacing the DMA with the JMS enterprise resource planning application.
 iv. Interfacing the DMA with the Finance, administration and pharmacy of the health facilities for better monitoring of stock and drug costs.
  v. Designing and field-testing a new DMA version that include interactive, data analysis and learning tools.

Acknowledgments. The authors are grateful to: the Swedish Program for ICT in Developing Regions (SPIDER) for funding the field-tests. AGLARBRI partners especially Prof. Bjorn Pehrson, Dr. Amos Nungu, Prof. Lars L Gustafsson, Joseph Ngenzi for the research partnership and support. The Joint Medical Stores, Bishop Caeser Asili Hospital, Family Life Education Programme and Mawundo Health Center for accepting to participate in the field tests.

References

1. World Health Organization: The selection of essential drugs: report of a WHO expert committee. Technical report series no 615. World Health Organisation Press, Geneva (1977)
2. Ngarambe, D., Nungu, A., Sansa-Otim, J., Masinde, M., Kariuki, E., Kyalo, V., Pehrson, B.: African great lakes rural broadband research infrastructure. In: IST-Africa Conference, Dar es Salaam, May 2012
3. Sosa, M., Cabarkapa, D., Fiallos, A., Skinner, A., Rahmonov, I., Kechkhoshvili, M., Talaganov, G.: African great lakes rural broadband research infrastructure: networks, services and applications. January 2012. Documentation at HYPERLINK http://csd.xen.ssvl.kth.se/csdlive/content/aglarbri
4. Ngarambe, D., Pehrson, B.: e-Health Services in the rural African Great Lakes Region, project proposal to SPIDER, August 2011
5. Tanzania ICT for Rural Development Program. www.ict4rd.ne.tz
6. e-Health: The Uganda Situation. www.itu.int

IoT, Cloud Computing and TVWS

Spectrum Resource-as-a-Service: Cloud Architecture Framework for Dynamic Spectrum Request Response Networks

Luzango Pangani Mfupe[1,2(✉)], Litsietsi Montsi[1],
and Fisseha Mekuria[1]

[1] Meraka Institute Council for Scientific and Indutrial Research (CSIR),
P.O. Box 395, Pretoria 0001, South Africa
{Lmfupe,Lmontsi,Fmekuria}@csir.co.za
[2] Department of Electrical Engineering, Tshwane University of Technology
(TUT), Private Bag X680, Pretoria 0001, South Africa

Abstract. Cloud computing has a potential to solve scalability issue in dynamic spectrum request response (DSR[2]) wireless networking. Radio frequency (RF) spectrum is a pervasive resource whose optimal utilisation requires efficient management techniques to allow a sustainable growth of innovative wireless communication technologies. Multi-tenancy cloud hosting architectures are considered to be prime enabler to a concept of spectrum resource-as-a-service (SRaaS) for DSR[2] networks. Such architectures allows a single instance of software application to be delivered as a service to multiple users (tenants) requesting different services from different or same locations as opposed to running multiple instances of same software applications to each tenant. This chapter discusses a proposed conceptual framework for managing RF spectrum resources in dynamic spectrum request response wireless networks.

1 Introduction

Cloud computing presents organisations with necessary resources required for deployment of pervasive network infrastructures [1]. Such infrastructures may include wireless networks that utilises dynamic spectrum sharing techniques assisted by spatial-temporal spectrum geo-location databases (GLSDs). It was noted in [2][1] that due to a large number of players (tenants) involved; successful implementation of spectrum resource as a service (SRaaS) concept would require a multi-tenancy cloud-hosted infrastructure platform [2]. This would enable a single instance of software application to be delivered as a service to multiple tenants requesting different services as opposed to running multiple instances of same software applications to each tenant [3]. The concept of managing radio frequency (RF) spectrum resources as a service in a dynamic spectrum sharing environment has been discussed before. A white spaces identification system (WSI) model that would be made possible through deployment of a wide area network of sensors in a geographical area and time of interest is proposed

---

[1] Parts of this chapter appeared in WCMCS 2013, October 4–6, Hammamet, Tunisia. This version presents a more refined SRaaS concept.

© Institute for Computer Sciences, Social Informatics and Telecommunications Engineering 2015
A. Nungu et al. (Eds.): AFRICOMM 2014, LNICST 147, pp. 137–143, 2015.
DOI: 10.1007/978-3-319-16886-9_14

in [4]. As a hosted service, such network of sensors could provide information about available spectrum opportunities to the white space devices [4]. This chapter contributes a refined concept of a cloud-based SRaaS architecture to efficiently manage radio spectrum resources in an even larger geographical areas transcending across provincial and national borders. The reminder of the chapter is arranged as follows: Sect. 2 discusses related work; In Sect. 3 Multi-tenancy SRaaS framework is briefly introduced. Section 4 discusses a framework for SRaaS workflow and business logic. Section 5 presents a case study and Sect. 6 concludes this chapter.

1.1 Database Assisted Geologically-Based Dynamic Spectrum Resource Allocation

Radio frequency (RF) spectrum is considered to be a scarce resource for the national information and communications and technology (ICT) infrastructure. This scarcity is attributable to the inefficient spectrum management approaches by national regulatory authorities. Whereby, RF spectrum is statically allocated on the service-by-service or band-by-band basis. Such inefficient allocations leave swaths of locally unused RF spectrum on spatial-temporal dimensions. This unused RF spectrum is referred to as White Spaces (WS). WS spectrum can be dynamically requested and allocated on a secondary basis to provide useful wireless telecommunications services such as broadband connectivity to under-served areas. However, such usefulness of WS spectrum can only be exploited provided that existing or primary licensed services such as TV broadcasting stations are protected from potential harmful interference as a result secondary usage. GLSD systems are currently a preferable practical means to provide such protection to incumbent users [5]. Such systems vary in computational complexity and size of required area to performing their operation (i.e., local, provincial, national, or international). The extra-size and computational burden makes a reasonable argument for utilising cloud computing. To speed-up the response process the database system could be based on the NoSQL design [6, 7]. Figure 1 describes a conceptual high-level framework of Africa-wide GLSDs. Each regional grouping is treated with an instance of a GLSD within which country-specific instances of GLSDs are found. The system could be hosted in the cluster-based centers for high performance computing (CHPCs) infrastructure.

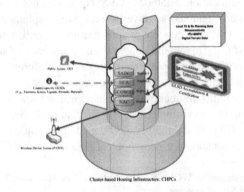

Fig. 1. Conceptual high-level cloud hosting framework for Africa-wide GLSDs

2   Related Work

Significant body of research work has been directed towards the DSR^2 networking domain. Similarly the concept of cloud computing and its related architectures are receiving a lot of research focus and exploration. However, there is a lack of research attention and consensus on the scope and need for defining possible service provisioning architectures combining the two domains necessary to unlock the potential services of DSR^2. We hereby briefly highlight related work across the select relevant domains.

2.1   Pervasive Dynamic Demand Response Database Platforms

In [8] a pervasive dynamic demand response (D^{2}R) cloud computing platform for managing power utility grid is discussed. It is argued that such a platform is important as human operators are ill-equipped analyze and optimally utilize large chunks of data that are constantly flowing due to the dynamic nature of a smart grid network. In [9] a design of a two-chambered (bicameral) GLSD for dynamic spectrum management is introduced; chamber 1 is designated for spectrum trading with a guarantee of quality of service (QoS) to users based on their demand. Chamber 2 is designated for spectrum commons that are not guaranteed QoS. This approach proposes a system of Europe-wide interconnected GLSDs. Even though potential services have been highlighted, there still no detailed discussion on how interested stakeholders could access the platform to render or access such services. Similarly, in [10] a proposal for a cloud model and concept prototype for a pervasive cognitive radio networks is discussed. This medium access (MAC) layer model is based on spectrum sensors assisted by a database. They argue that such a model could enable seamless Internet connectivity in metro areas.

3   Multi-tenancy SRaaS Framework

This Section discusses characterisation of core service delivery cloud planes within the cloud-computing paradigm. The cloud planes are exposed to the relevant tenants (stakeholders) in the form of application programming interfaces (APIs) in the application and services layer:

(1) *The local spectrum cloud (LSC):* This is the service plane at a provincial level for provisioning of radio spectrum resources on demand to wireless devices.
(2) *The intermediate spectrum cloud (ISC):* This is the service plane at a national level for disseminating regulatory directives as well as monitoring and enforcing of the radio spectrum resource policy, planning and usage.
(3) *The higher spectrum cloud (HSC):* This is the service plane for cross-border monitoring and enforcing.

The aforementioned service delivery cloud planes should be mapped to the design of SRaaS architecture to provide access to provincial, national and global instances of GLSD. It is envisaged that the global instances should cater for the spectrum overlap services along the boundaries of nations. A national instance should carter for spectrum services nationally as a federate of provincial instances. The provincial instance should cater for the local DSR^2 based networks.

Table 1. Attributes for SRaaS provisioning

Tenant	API	DB schema	Protocol, Language	Service Accessed/ or Rendered
Regulatory authority	LSC ISC HSC	Shared-DB, different schema	PAWS JSON-RPC	Regulatory Enforcement, Monitoring
Security provider	LSC ISC HSC	Shared-DB, logical table	TLS	Security
DB admin	LSC ISC	Shared-DB, different schema	PAWS JSON-RPC IP, HTTP	Channel allocation Certification, Registration
DSR^2 Devices	LSC ISC	Shared-DB, schema	PAWS JSON-RPC IP, HTTP	DB discovery Connectivity
WISP	LSC	Shared DB, Different schema	IP	Connectivity
General public	LSC	Shared-DB, logical table	IP, HTTP	Data transfer

3.1   Attributes for SRaaS Provisioning

It is noteworthy that for cloud services to be effectively rendered to, and be accessible by various stakeholders a number of key attributes need to be in place:

Tenants: These are actors with a varying degree of rights to the GLSD. For example the national regulatory authorities have highest rights than other stakeholders. The national regulator can change the spectrum policy and regulations, can approve database administrators, can add or remove licensed users as well as technical parameters of towers, and can coordinate the harmonisation of cross-border spectrum usage.

APIs: These are primarily the gateway to the actual cloud services. APIs are exposed to the relevant tenants via the web.

Database Schema: Databases lie at the heart of the SRaaS architecture. There are a number of database architectures that can be implemented in the multi-tenancy architecture. These include shared database and shared schema, shared database but different schema and isolated databases for each tenant. The aforementioned architectures have their limitations in the SRaaS eco-system particularly, during cases of tenant data recovery after failure. However, innovative techniques such as chunk folding of logical tables can be utilised [11].

Protocol and Language: These are basically the vehicles that can be used by the stakeholder to transport or convey data of desired service over the cloud.

Services: Depending on the environment, tenants can be services renderers, service consumers or both. These attributes are summarised in Table 1.

4   SRaaS Workflow and Business Logic Framework

A typical workflow and business logic architectural framework for SRaaS is depicted in Fig. 2. Service Oriented architecture (SOA) is specifically for the delivery of SRaaS services to different types of devices. Depending on the parameters such as device geographical location, quality of service (QoS), or bandwidth requirements; a relevant interference avoidance method is invoked to guarantee maximum protection of primary users as well as among secondary devices. Additionally, different levels of tenants such as security provider, billing provider, regulator, and GLSD administrator and wireless service providers are all catered for in a synchronized manner.

Fig. 2. High-level SRaaS workflow and business logic framework

5   Case Study: Distributed Smart Meters Scenario

25001 hypothetical tenants are spatially distributed across South Africa according to irregular small areas known as mesoframes [12]. The tenants have observed mean distance of 7 km and nearest neighbor index (NNI) of 1.254. The tenants are assumed to be smart meters that are dynamically sending requests to the South Africa instance of GLSD to be allocated white space spectrum via an API for protocol to access whites space database (PAWS). The requested spectrum is to be used by tenants to fulfill various service tasks such as scheduled meter readings, remote software updates, power grid quality notification messages, or newly devices registration to the grid management system. The polling times are assumed to be discreet in nature. The GLSD is hosted at the CHPC; the API for PAWS can be accessed at the following URL http://whitespaces. meraka.csir.co.za/PawsService. Figure 3(a) depicts locations around South Africa where smart meters made their dynamic white space spectrum requests. Figure 3(b) depicts a snapshot of the GLSD response of estimated spatially available white space spectrum that can be used by the smart meters.

 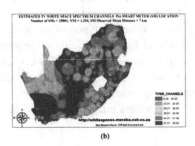

(a)   (b)

Fig. 3. (a) A spatial distribution of 25001 hypothetical smart meters in South Africa. The smart meters are assumed to be sending dynamic requests for white space spectrum resources from the GLSD (b). Snapshot of estimated spatially available spectrum resources returned as a response from the GLSD to the requesting smart meters. The dynamic interaction between smart meters and the GLSD is performed through PAWS service API.

6   Conclusion

This chapter has presented a proposed concept of spectrum resource as a service (SRaaS) architectural framework for geo-location spectrum databases (GLSDs). Currently, national spectrum regulators across the world prefer GLSDs as practical enabler to dynamic spectrum request response (DSR^2) wireless broadband networks. DSR^2 wireless devices utilises spectrum-sharing techniques to opportunistically access unused spectrum (this spectrum is commonly referred to as white space) in a particular geographical area and time of use. A practical example is found in the frequency planning table for terrestrial broadcasting TV where spectrum resource is divided into channels, and in any given geographical area not all channels have TV transmitters within the range, such spectrum resources can be exploited on a secondary basis. The proposed cloud-based SRaaS concept could particularly be useful as the adoption of policy to allow dynamic spectrum sharing techniques could potentially cause a proliferation of DSR^2 devices and pervasive network services that would require efficient management.

Acknowledgments.   The authors wish to thankfully acknowledge the CSIR and TUT for their continuous financial and material support.

References

1. Bellavista, P.: Pervasive computing at scale: challenges and research directions. IEEE Sens. **58**, 639–642 (2011)

2. Mfupe, L.P., Montsi, L, Mekuria, F.: Spectrum databases-as-a service for broadband innovation and efficient spectrum utilization. In: Cognitive Radio and Opportunistic TVWS Broadband Wireless Networks for Sustainable Broadband Provision in Emerging Economies, International Conference on Cloud Computing and Multimedia (ICCCM' 2013) (2013)
3. Saleh, E., Shabaani, N and Meinel, C.: A framework for migrating traditional web applications into multi-tennant SaaS. In: The second International Conference on Advanced Communications and Computation (INFOCOMP 2012), pp. 100–104 (2012)
4. Weiss, M., Delaere, S., Lehr, W.: Sensing as a service: an exploration into practical implementation of DSA. In: IEEE New Frontiers in Dynamic Spectrum Access Networks (DySPAN 2010), pp. 1–8 (2010)
5. Mfupe, L., Montsi, L., Mekuria, F., Mzyece, M.: Geo-location White Space Spectrum Databases: Review of Models and Design of a Dynamic Spectrum Access Coexistence Planner and Manager. In: Mishra, A.K., Johnson, D.L. (eds.) White Space Communication. Signals and Communication Technology, pp. 153–194. Springer, Heidelberg (2015)
6. Shvachko, B., Kuang, H., Radia, S.: Sensing as a service: the hadoop distributed file system. In: IEEE Mass Storage Systems and Technologies (MSST 2010), pp. 1–10 (2010)
7. Escriva, R., Wong, B., Sirer, E.: Hyperdex: a distributed searchable key-value store. ACM SIGCOMM Comput. Commun. Rev. **42**, 25–36 (2012)
8. Simmhan, Y., Amman, S., Kumbhare, A., Rongyang L., Stvens, S., Qunzhi Z., Prassana, V.: Cloud-based software platform for big data analytics in smart grids. IEEE J. Comput. Sci. Eng. **15**, 38–47 (2013)
9. Mwangoka, J., Marquese, P., Rodriguese, J.: Exploiting TV white spaces in Europe: the COGEU approach. In: IEEE New Frontier in Dynamic Spectrum Access Networks (DySPAN 2011), pp. 608–612 (2011)
10. Wu, S., Chao, H., Ko, C., Mo, S., Jiang, C., Li, T., Cheng, C., Liang, C.: A cloud model and concept prototype for cognitive radio networks. J. IEEE Wireless Commun. **19**, 49–58 (2012)
11. Aulbach, S., Grust, T., Jacobs, D., Kemper, A., Rittinger, J.: Multi-tenant databases for software as a service: schema-mapping techniques. In: International Conference on Management of Data (SIGMOD 2008), pp.1195–1206 (2008)
12. Naudé, A., Badenhorst, W., Zietsman, L., Van Huyssteen, E., Maritz, J.: Geospatial Analysis Platform – Version 2: Technical overview of the mesoframe methodology and South African Geospatial Analysis Platform. CSIR Report number: CSIR/BE/PSS/IR/2007/0104/B (2007)

Addressing Privacy in Cloud Computing Environment

Mangqoba V. Shabalala[✉], Paul Tarwireyi, and Matthew O. Adigun

Department of Computer Science, University of Zululand,
Private Bag X1001, Kwadlangezwa 3886, South Africa
{mvshabalala,ptarwireyi}@gmail.com,
adigunm@unizulu.ac.za

Abstract. Cloud computing is growing in popularity due to its ability to offer dynamically scalable resources provisioned as services regardless of user or location device. However, moving data to the cloud means that the control of the data is more on the hands of the cloud provider rather than the data owner. This to a certain extent means that cloud users are skeptical about losing their privacy when moving data to environments they do not control. From this stems the need for the means to allow the data owner to monitor what is happening to her/ his data. This paper presents a framework that could assist in efforts to address privacy issues in the cloud. A proof of concept prototype implementation is presented to validate the framework. Evaluations are then carried out to test the utility and applicability of the proposed solution.

Keywords: Cloud computing · Security · Privacy · Trust · Confidentiality · Integrity · Accountability · Availability · Compliance

1 Introduction

Cloud computing has become the most enticing technology of today due to its ability to offer dynamically scalable resources provisioned as services over the internet. Cloud computing provides services that are cost effective, flexible and easy to use. However, despite all these advantages, security and data privacy concerns are slowing the adoption of the cloud.

According to a report from the Institute for Health Technology Transformation, almost 20 percent of healthcare organizations have suffered a security breach, some 804 breaches have occurred with more than 500 patient records between 2009 and 2013 [1]. Improper disclosure of private information such as financial or health information could result in discrimination, loss of business and much more harm. Privacy is one of the major challenges that have not received much attention in the cloud, yet it is one of the factors that slow down adoption of the cloud [2].

Privacy is a fundamental right that encompasses the right to be left alone. It entails the protection and appropriate use of the personal information, and the meeting of expectations of the client about its use. For organizations, privacy entails the application of laws, policies, standards and principles such Fair Information Practice Principles (FIPPs) which represent widely-accepted concepts concerning fair information practice in an electronic world.

© Institute for Computer Sciences, Social Informatics and Telecommunications Engineering 2015
A. Nungu et al. (Eds.): AFRICOMM 2014, LNICST 147, pp. 144–153, 2015.
DOI: 10.1007/978-3-319-16886-9_15

Any information stored in the cloud eventually ends up on a physical machine owned by a particular company or person located in a specific country, and it subjected to the laws of that country where the physical machine is located. Therefore, the location of information in the cloud has significant effects on the privacy and confidentiality protections of information and on the privacy obligations of those who process or store the information [3]. For example, any data stored in U.S is subjected to U.S patriotic act. This act allows the Federal Bureau of Investigation (FBI) to access any business record that is stored on the service provider's data center given based on the court order, so the cloud users' privacy can't be protected [4].

Only few acts and regulations in the USA, with the exception to the new Health Information Technology for Economic and Clinical Health Act (HITECH) and Health Insurance Portability and Accountability Act (HIPAA) include the role of a Service Provider. This implies that if there is a violation of data privacy compliance, it's not the service provider which will face the violation of the rule of law [3].

As a way of preserving data from unauthorized disclosure a comprehensive data protection system has been established in Europe through what is known as a European data protection directive (95/46/EC), which tries to enforce limited data collection and concerted redistribution [5].

The Organization for Economic Co-operation and Development (OECD) privacy principle mandates several principles such as limited collection of data, the authorization to collect data with informed consent from the individual whose data is being collected for processing. It also seeks to give the data owner the right to correction and deletion of the collected data as well as the right to demand the proper security safeguards for the collected data [6].

Many countries have adopted data protection laws that follow the European Union model the OECD model or the Asia-Pacific Economic Cooperation (APEC) model. Under these laws the data controller or owner remains responsible for the collection and processing of private data, even when third parties process the data. The data controller is required to ensure that any third party processing data on its behalf takes adequate technical and organizational security measures to safeguard the data [7].

Since Outsourcing data does not absolve the data collector and the data subject from their legal liabilities to comprehend what happens to the data in the cloud and which security measures are deployed to preserve its state of confidentiality [8].

Therefore, there is a need for a solution that will enable the cloud customers to retrace in detail what happens to their data and who has access to it and what levels of security and privacy are applied to it, where it is stored.

2 A Comparison of Various Data Protection Laws Based upon Fair Information Practice Principles

A ground breaking resolution was reached by authorities from fifty countries which gathered in Madrid in 2009 and was dubbed Madrid Resolution [9]. The Madrid resolution is a universal principle for the protecting personal data and privacy [9]. It defines a set of rules and principles that governs and ascertains uniform protection of privacy with regard to storing and processing personal identifiable information internationally in accordance with the applicable privacy protection regulations. FIPPs are important because they provide the underlying policy for many national laws addressing privacy and data protection matters. The core principles of privacy addressed by these principles are:

Notice/Transparency/Awareness- ensures no secrete data collection, it stresses that the data collector must provide the consumers with clear and conspicuous notice of their information practices before any information is collected.

Consent/Choice – data collectors should give individuals a choice as to how they wished their information to be used, this includes the secondary usage of data beyond the reason it was initially collected for.

Access - allows individuals reasonable access to review the information that has been collected about them and ensure that it's accurate and up to date.

Information Protection - requires organizations to take reasonable steps to protect the security, quality and integrity of the personal information they collect.

Integrity/Security - Information collectors must ensure that there are proper security safeguard put in place to protect the collected data, this safeguard may include, but not limited to encrypting the collected data before storage and close monitoring of personnel who access this information.

Enforcement - holds organizations accountable for complying with FIPPs.

Whereas the Generally Accepted Privacy Principles (GAPP) framework was developed from a business perspective to protect the privacy of personal information it is therefore used by certified public accountants (CPAs) in the United States and chartered accountants (CAs) in Canada, both in industry and in public practice, to guide and assist the organizations they serve in implementing privacy programs that addresses privacy risks and obligations, and business opportunities.

Unlike GAPP, the Asia-Pacific Economic Cooperation (APEC) was established in 1989 to further enhance economic growth and prosperity for the region and to strengthen the Asia-Pacific community. The APEC Privacy Framework is aimed at encouraging the development of appropriate information privacy protections and that will ensure the free flow of information in the Asia Pacific region.

HIPAA on the other hand regulates the management, collection, storing and distribution of health information records on clinics, hospitals, doctor's offices and even on insurance companies to mitigate the risk of privacy violation which may result from it [10].

Payment Card Industry (PCI) Data Security Standards (DSS) is a comprehensive standard for enhancing the information security controls surrounding payment card transactions. It also helps to alleviate the risk of associated credit card information fraud by putting policies in place which stipulates that the cardholder data should be protected during storing or when transmitted [10]. Every Cloud Service Provider (CSP) should adhere to these privacy regulations, the discussed privacy regulations have much in common, they all adhere to the principles of the Fair Information Practice Principles and Directive (95/46/EC).

CSP are required by the law to sign the non-disclosure agreements with its customers, this agreement must reflect the customer's needs for data protection and operational details that will be continuously reviewed. CSP making use of third party resources services to store and process data is required to select and monitor that outsourced third party provider is in compliance with the privacy laws of the country where the data originates.

A CSP is required by the industry best practice to publish on their portals/websites the third party service reports as well as their internal audit reports. Upon the implementation of the cloud computing technology the CSP is required to secure its components with security measures that are relevant to particular industry standards such as COBIT and ISO207001 and document such information security baselines such that they can be used for auditing purposes. It is also required to segregate the data of each tenant from the other data subjects and it must be encrypted upon storage.

The differing privacy laws create a dilemma for cloud customers and security professionals making it even more difficult for them to keep track of them all and comply with them. Furthermore, it is expensive to comply with restrictive privacy laws and similarly, if privacy is not ensured valuable marketing data may be lost to other business rivals.

3 Related Work

Kandukuri et al. [11], highlights the importance of using SLAs to secure the trust of the cloud customers. The author proposes that these SLAs must describe the security measures put in place by the CSP to maintain security to make it client compliant. IBM [12] develop a fully homomorphic encryption scheme which enables the processing of encrypted data without compromising the encryption.

However, this approach leads to high computational and size overhead, since the ciphers in ciphertext are larger than plain texts hence computation overhead and decrease computational performance.

Cryptographic techniques are generally used by cloud computing service providers to solve security related problems. Whoever, cryptanalysis advances day by day and they can easily render a well-known cryptographic algorithm insecure when a flaw is discovered in the algorithm. This flaw is used by the perpetrators to turn what used to be a strong encryption into a weak encryption or, no encryption at all [13].

Oliveira et al. [14], propose architecture that automatically generates and protect evidence in what concerns personal data transfer in the cloud computing environment. In order to demonstrate compliance with privacy regulation as far as international data transfer laws are concerned.

Lindell et al. [15], discuss the secure computational algorithms which have been used to perform computation on an untrusted server, the author highlights that these algorithms enable the cloud users to use insecure cloud infrastructure to compute without revealing the exact input for the computation. This is achieved by implementing the Yaos protocol discussed in [16] which provides basic techniques to perform such computation without revealing the actual expression.

Mulero et al. [17], Analyzed current privacy protection solutions and highlighted the problems that solutions presents. The work of Wang et al. [18] uses the privacy preserving audit protocol. It allows auditors to audit consumers' data without having knowledge of the data contents. The author also proposes batch audit public protocol through the use of multiple algorithms to achieve different goals. This was extended by making privacy as service in the work of Itani et al. [19], the author uses the tamper-proof capabilities of cryptographic coprocessors to secure the storage and processing of confidential data of the cloud users in the cloud computing environment. However, according to Abadi [20] resorting to trusted third parties may not be always practical, as it typically results in deployment difficulties, communication overhead, and other additional costs which makes the process even more expensive.

Mowbray and Pearson et al. [21, 22], the authors propose a Client-Based Privacy Manager; this manager helps users to remotely manage the privacy of their data in the cloud. Privacy manager provides the obfuscation feature which allows for data obfuscated to the degree specified by the data owner, obfuscation is a form of data encryption which requires no decryption key to reverse.

Most researchers have used various approaches to tackle issue of data privacy however most of their efforts so far have focused on providing data privacy monitoring mechanism from the context of cloud providers which may not really provide adequate private data security. Our work on the other hand considers the user control aspect which is mostly responsible for building trust between the cloud customer and cloud service provider.

This work is builds upon [21, 22] and to compensate for its drawbacks the informative event and access logs was employed. The core advantages of Informative event and access logs is that (1) enable user to retrace in details what happened to his data, (2) where they are stored and (3) who accesses them and (4) help them understand an choose the security safeguards applied to protect it.

4 Proposed Framework

From the review of literature, the following design criteria have been identified and taken into consideration while designing the framework presented in Fig. 1 which enables the cloud customers to retrace in detail what happens to their data and who has access to it. These design criteria include:

A. **Automate and Manage data Collection, Reporting and Alerting:** The proposed framework must automatically identify important privacy violating events and alerts appropriate individuals. A detection mechanism is therefore mandatory should any in-compliance be detected.

B. **User driven definition of events and specifications:** The framework must be able to dynamically define and provide specifications of the conditions that will trigger alerts.

C. **Limit data access to authorized users:** The framework should prevent unauthorized users from accessing confidential data. The framework must also protect its customers from insider threats by keeping track of what their administrators are doing.

D. **Encrypts data in transit and at rest-** The solution should apply advanced encryption algorithms such as AES 128-bit or AES 256-bit encryption since they are efficient in both software and hardware and they are the current approved standards for strong encryption.

From the design criteria outlined above and how they are achieved has led to what components should privacy monitoring framework entail in order to addressing the issues of privacy monitoring in the cloud computing environments. Therefore, the Privacy Monitoring Framework consists of five major component, informative events and access logs analyzer, access right delegator, personae, preference setting and Alerting component. One main component of this framework is information events and access logs analyzer component which retrieves specific logs using user preference parameters/filters for analysis and forensic investigation. If an actionable event is identified, appropriate individual is notified.

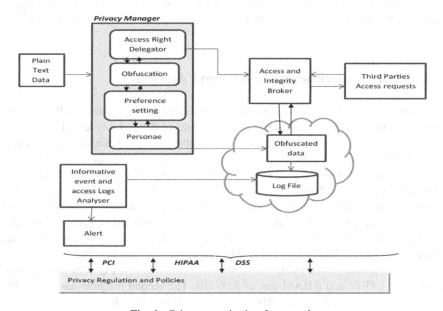

Fig. 1. Privacy monitoring framework

The access right delegator enables the cloud customer to regulate who can have access to outsourced data and who cannot. While the personae feature enables users to choose the manner in which they would like to interact with the cloud agent, by enabling the user to act anonymously, partially or fully disclose his identity. This helps to protect the identity of the user if he wishes to operate on anonymity ground with the system. Sudoname is used instead of user personal identity in case the user chose to act anonymously in order to protect his/her identity. The user's choice of persona provides a simple interface to a possibly complex set of data use preferences communicated to the service provider via the preference feature, and may also determine which data items are to be obfuscated.

Preference setting component on the other hand creates and applies simple filters using complex regular expression driven filters that pick out the customer entries of interest, since on many level logs files can contain towering amounts of uninteresting, hard to decipher events, burying more useful information [23]. This component enables the cloud customer to explicitly configure the system according to his personal preferences. To spare the user from privacy technical jargons and to save time pre-configured settings are already in place for the user to choose from. P3P and PRIME have also followed the same approach [24]. The preferences then form the policy and this resultant policy is together sent to the cloud with the personally identifiable information obfuscated with the degree that the customer deems appropriate.

The alert component is responsible for alerting the user of the useful actionable critical events. An event record is only regarded as actionable if and only if the event record indicates a strong likelihood of malicious activity, personal data revealing. Critical events always lead to an immediate alert and responsive investigation by the administrator. All these components communicate amongst each other by exchanging messages, since monitoring is a complex task which cannot be achieved by a single component.

5   Usability Experimental Results and Analysis

An electronic health record system prototype was developed to test the feasibility of our proposed framework. This section presents the results of the usability test of portions of a design prototype, derived from using the System Usability Scale (SUS); SUS is a simple ten-item scale giving a global view of subjective assessments of usability.

Participants were given a chance to interact with the system being evaluated, without thinking about their experience for a long time the respondents were asked to record their immediate response to the questionnaires provided for as required by the SU. The participants in this study were generally students from different faculties within the university, with a range of technology skills (Amateur, intermediate and expert users). Two Intel (R) Core (TM) machines that support the virtualization technology machines were used, one of the machines has i3 CPU with a processing speed of 2.13 GHZ and a RAM size of 4.00 GB. The second machine has as i5 CPU with a processing speed of 320 GHZ and RAM size of 3.00 GB.

The application installed on top of the cloud middleware in order to provide an API for customers, a web monitoring service which can be accessed using a standardized communication protocol was developed and exposed using Netbeans 7.1.1. The web monitoring services monitors the operation carried out on the outsourced data by system users, this web monitoring service was deployed in three machines that were used when interacting with the system.

A statistical analysis was carried out using SPSS version 18. To calculate the SUS score, we used Brooke [25] method. The obtained average SUS score from all 60 participants is 80. A SUS score above a 68 is considered above average and anything below 68 is below average. The score of 80 that the system obtained indicates that users are likely to be recommending the system to a friend. An 80 SUS score is interpreted as a grade of a B. SUS scores have a range of 0 to 100.

To evaluate user-control participants were asked to rate the ease of performing the different user centric tasks. They were asked to use a scale of 1 to 5, in order to establish if the system allow the participants to, (1) control how their medical records are handled, (2) control who has access to their medical information, (3) Be able to examine and update personal data.

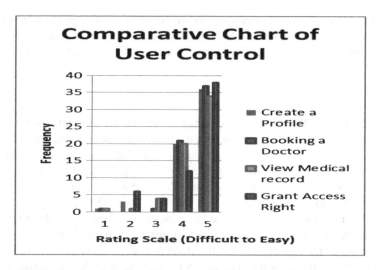

Fig. 2. Comparative chat of frequency distribution scale for user control

Figure 2 illustrates the comparative frequency distribution scale of ease of understanding and, as evident above the majority of participants understand the main service model of the prototype as expected. These results indicate that the prototype worked very well, but that there was room for improvement, with the creation of a profile with the standard deviation of 0.87, booking a doctor the standard deviation of 0.70 and medical record the standard deviation of 0.83 as well as grants of access right the standard deviation of 0.99 respectively.

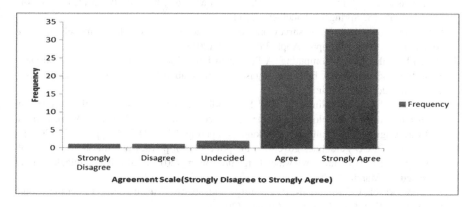

Fig. 3. Ease of use

To evaluate Ease of Use participants were asked to rate the ease of using the services with a rating scale from 1 to 5 with 1 being "Strongly Disagree", 3 = Undecided, 5 = Strongly Agree. The average ease of use rating was 4.43 (SD = 0. 79), which represents a rating of "very easy". A frequency count of the ratings is shown in Fig. 3, and it can be seen that the most common ratings were 4 or 5.These are important finding that indicates that the main service model of the prototype is understandable and easy to use by the targeted end users. The results of the study showed that the proposed framework perform well in terms of ease of use and user control.

6 Conclusion

The shared nature of the cloud storage infrastructure and the fact that when the data is stored in the cloud, the control of the data is more on the hands of the cloud provider rather than the data owner is of a great challenge that continues to hinder cloud computing from successfully reaching its successful capability. If not monitored closely, public cloud services can place sensitive data at risk, jeopardizing enterprise data privacy just as much as they do to end users' privacy. Data privacy has become increasingly critical in recent years due to an increase in high profile breaches. In an effort to tackle this challenge, researchers have discussed on building many data privacy frameworks and algorithms from the cloud providers' context. This work adds to these efforts by proposing a data privacy monitoring framework that enables the data owner to stay in control over their data, thereby providing the required transparency to comprehend how personal data is handled in the cloud.

References

1. Pearson, J., Logan, C., Reis, D., Taveras, L., Koerner, D.: Answers to Healthcare Leaders' Cloud Questions (2014)
2. Allison, D.S., Capretz, M.A.: Furthering the growth of cloud computing by providing privacy as a service. In: Kranzlmüller, D., Toja, A.M. (eds.) ICT-GLOW 2011. LNCS, vol. 6868, pp. 64–78. Springer, Heidelberg (2011)
3. Subashini, S., Kavitha, V.: A survey on security issues in service delivery models of cloud computing. J. Netw. Comput. Appl. **34**(1), 1–11 (2011)
4. Hogan Lovells.: Cloud Computing: A Primer on Legal Issues, Including Privacy and Data Security Concerns (2010). https://www.cisco.com/web/about/doing_business/legal/privacy_compliance/docs/CloudPrimer.pdf
5. Lenk, A., Klems, M., Nimis, J., Tai, S., Sandholm, T.: What's inside the cloud? An architectural map of the cloud landscape. In: Proceedings of the 2009 ICSE Workshop on Software Engineering Challenges of Cloud Computing, CLOUD 2009. pp. 23–31 (2009)
6. Regard, H,: OECD guidelines governing the protection of privacy and transborder flows of personal data (2013). http://www.oecd.org/sti/ieconomy/2013-oecd-privacy-guidelines.pdf. Accessed 20 March 2014
7. Reed, A., Rezek, C., Simmonds, P.: Security Guidance for Critical Areas of Focus in Cloud Computing V3.0. Cloud Security Alliance (2011)
8. Glott, R., Husmann, E., Sadeghi, A.-R., Schunter, M.: Trustworthy clouds underpinning the future internet. In: Domingue, J., et al. (eds.) Future Internet Assembly. LNCS, vol. 6656, pp. 209–221. Springer, Heidelberg (2011)
9. Lovrek, I., Lovric, T., Lucic, D.: Regulatory aspects of cloud computing. In: 2012 20th International Conference on Software Telecommunications and Computer Networks (SoftCOM), pp. 1–7. IEEE (2012)

10. Ngugi, B., Dardick, G.: Security and Privacy Assurance in Advancing Technologies, 30 November 2010
11. Kandukuri, B.R., Patturi, V.R., Rakshit, A.: Cloud security issues. In: 2009 IEEE International Conference on Services Computing, pp. 517–520 (2009)
12. Prince, B.: IBM Discovers Encryption Scheme That Could Improve Cloud Security, Spam Filtering. http://www.eweek.com/c/a/Security/IBM-Uncovers-Encryption-Scheme-That-Could-Improve-Cloud-Security-Spam-Filtering-135413/
13. Grobauer, B., Walloschek, T., Stöcker, E.: Understanding cloud computing vulnerabilities. IEEE Secur. Priv. **9**, 50–57 (2011)
14. De Oliveira, A.S., Sendor, J., Garaga, A., Jenatton, K.: Monitoring personal data transfers in the cloud. In: Proceedings of the International Conference on Cloud Computing Technology and Science, CloudCom, pp. 347–354 (2013)
15. Lindell, Y., Pinkas, B.: An efficient protocol for secure two-party computation in the presence of malicious adversaries. J. Cryptol. **28**, 312–350 (2014)
16. Yao, A.C.: Protocols for secure computations. In: 23rd Annual Symposium on Foundations of Computer Science, Sfcs 1982 (1982)
17. Muntés-Mulero, V., Nin, J.: Privacy and anonymization for very large datasets. In: Proceeding of the 18th ACM Conference on Information and Knowledge Management - CIKM 2009, p. 2117 (2009)
18. Wang, C., Chow, S.S.M., Wang, Q., Ren, K., Lou, W.: Privacy-preserving public auditing for secure cloud storage. IEEE Trans. Comput. **62**, 362–375 (2013)
19. Itani, W., Kayssi, A., Chehab, A.: Privacy as a service: privacy-aware data storage and processing in cloud computing architectures. In: 8th IEEE International Symposium on Dependable, Autonomic and Secure Computing, DASC 2009, pp. 711–716 (2009)
20. Abadi, M.: Trusted computing, trusted third parties, and verified communications. In: Deswarte, Y., Cuppens, F., Jajodia, S., Wang, L. (eds.) Future Internet Assembly. IFIP, vol. 147, pp. 291–308. Springer, Heidelberg (2004)
21. Pearson, S., Shen, Y., Mowbray, M.: A privacy manager for cloud computing. In: Jaatun, M. G., Zhao, G., Rong, C. (eds.) Cloud Computing. LNCS, vol. 5931, pp. 90–106. Springer, Heidelberg (2009)
22. Mowbray, M., Pearson, S., Shen, Y.: Enhancing privacy in cloud computing via policy-based obfuscation. J. Supercomput. **61**, 267–291 (2012)
23. Anderson, C.L., Agarwal, R.: Practicing safe computing: a multimethod empirical examination of home computer user security behavioral intentions. MIS Q. **34**, 613–615 (2010)
24. Mather, T., Kumaraswamy, S., Latif, S.: Cloud Security and Privacy. O'Reilly, Sebastopol (2009)
25. Brooke, J.: SUS-A quick and dirty usability scale. Usability Eval. Ind. **189**, 194 (1996)

Energy Efficient Data Caching in Wireless Sensor Networks: A Case of Precision Agriculture

Kizito Patrick Musaazi, Tonny Bulega, and Stephen Mutaawe Lubega(⊠)

Department of Networks, School of Computing and Informatics Technology,
Makerere University, Kampala, Uganda
{patrickmusazi,smutaawe}@yahoo.co.uk, tbulega@gmail.com

Abstract. Implementation of information and control technologies is essential for application areas such as precision agriculture, where Wireless Sensor Networks are deployed. In wireless sensor networks (WSNs), data is collected from the source nodes and routed to the sink. And from the sink, this data is sent to the internet. Energy conservation is paramount during the communication phase in order to prolong the lifetime of the sensor nodes. The main method deployed to conserve energy consists of switching off the nodes transceiver when not transmitting nor receiving packets.

In this project, we introduce a Data Caching Algorithm (DCAL) that optimises the sleep/wake up periods of wireless sensor nodes to achieve low energy consumption and latency. The algorithm was used to analyse data in order to avoid situations of continuously transmitting the same information from the source node to the sink. This approach exploits the duty cycling scheme and operating on top of Media Access Control (MAC). We implement a Data Caching Algorithm (DCAL) in MIXIM (Mixed simulator for wireless and mobile networks using OMNET++ simulation engine) running on OMNET++ (Objective Modular Network Testbed in C++) simulator where different network sizes and simulation times were varied. We compared the performance of our algorithm with Data gathering MAC (DMAC) and Sensor-MAC (SMAC) and results showed that DCAL scheme significantly performs better in energy conservation and achieved a better latency than the DMAC protocol. Further still the DCAL approach performed extremely well in large, random networks.

Keywords: Data caching · Data Caching Algorithm (DCAL) · Precision agriculture

1 Introduction

Implementation of information and control technologies is essential for application areas such as precision agriculture, where Wireless Sensor Networks are deployed [1]. Wireless sensor networks consist of a large number of battery operated low

© Institute for Computer Sciences, Social Informatics and Telecommunications Engineering 2015
A. Nungu et al. (Eds.): AFRICOMM 2014, LNICST 147, pp. 154–163, 2015.
DOI: 10.1007/978-3-319-16886-9_16

power tiny devices, deployed in a geographical area in order to monitor the physical phenomenon of an environment [2]. These low powered devices find applications in dynamic and hard to reach environments (such as war zone areas, national parks, precision agriculture) thus making it hard to recharge or replace their power sources. A typical sensor node is an integration of basically four major components that include: wireless communication subsystem for transmission of data, sensing subsystem for data collection, processing subsystem for local data processing and a power source that provides the energy needed to perform its tasks [3]. Sources of energy wastage in wireless sensor networks have been identified in literature and these include: collisions of packets where a node receives more than one packet simultaneously from different sources. This phenomenon will consequently cause a retransmission of packets which then consumes another chunk of the sensors energy. Secondly, MAC protocols are characterized with the idle listening state that enables a node to determine a free (idle) channel for data transmission. Overhearing is another source of energy wastage where nodes receive packets destined to other nodes [4]. This is due to the fact that these nodes will turn on their radios to receive data which is intended for other destinations. When the sending and receiving nodes are not synchronized, the packets will be transmitted to a destination which is not ready to receive any data and such occurrence is referred to as over-emitting. In other words, the sending node radio will be active until the receiving node accepts data. These factors can be addressed by designing an energy efficient protocol and deploying a duty cycling scheme. Basic protocols use a fixed duty cycle and some others implement adaptive duty cycle in which they adapt to changes in traffic over time and place [3]. Recent research has proven that the wireless communication subsystem consumes more energy when transmitting data between nodes than sensing and processing units. Similarly the idle state of the radio consumes more or less the same energy as in transmit or receive states [4]. Therefore the demand for prolonging the lifetime of battery operated sensors calls for energy efficient protocols.

1.1 Precision Agriculture

Precision Agriculture is a farming technology aimed at periodically collecting, analysing, and managing information obtained from farms in the essence of achieving optimal profitability, environmental protection and sustainability. Precision Agriculture involves monitoring temperature, moisture content of the soil, crop development, fertilizer application, pesticide control application etc. Additionally, this farming technology forms a basis for possible Decision Support System (DSS) used to distribute inputs according to the need of a particular sub field [1].

1.2 Problem Statement

It is always a challenging task to design an optimal protocol that can address the applications requirements in terms of throughput, low latency and prolonged lifetime of sensor nodes. Often sending same sensed data values to the sink is a common practice in sensing applications and protocols [4,5]. Recent research has proven that the wireless communication subsystem consumes more energy when transmitting data between nodes than sensing and processing units. Similarly the idle state of the radio consumes more or less the same energy as in transmit or receive states [3]. In precision agriculture where periodic data is sent to the sink, there is need to conserve transmission energy which is wasted when nodes send duplicate sensed data [5]. Since transmission energy drains the sensor battery [4], by introducing data caching in wireless sensor networks this energy can be conserved. The design of this solution can be tailored towards agricultural applications where data is periodically collected and relayed to a sink node.

Therefore in this paper, we designed DCAL with a data caching functionality aimed at optimizing sleep/wake up periods of wireless sensor nodes to achieve low energy consumption and latency. The rest of the paper is organized as follows: Sect. 2 discusses related work, while Sect. 3 describes the methodology used. Section 4 discusses the results and analysis, and finally Sect. 5 contains the conclusion and future work.

2   Related Work

Energy conservation of wireless sensor networks has taken centre stage in recent years and the study in this field is enhanced by the influx of applications implemented on the sensor technology platform. Most research has mainly focused on prolonging the networks lifetime and this section will highlight the contributions on duty cycling schemes done in literature. Work done in duty cycling scheme has been selected mainly because it is closely related to the project being undertaken. In [6] Qi Han, Sharad Mehrotra, and Nalini Venkatasubramanian proposed adaptive data collection mechanisms for sensor environments. This mainly concentrated at minimizing energy consumption and quality of data transmitted to sink node. In their study they considered different sensor models with an aim at developing a quality aware data collection mechanism. The protocol used the basic radio modes that included active, listening and sleep states. Their main idea was to reduce the time the sensor node is in active or listening mode when not transmitting data to sink node. In [7] Gang Lu, Bhaskar Krishnamachari, and Cauligi S. Raghavendra proposed a DMAC protocol, an energy efficient and low latency MAC that was designed and optimized for data gathering trees in wireless sensor networks. Their protocol exploited the staggered active/sleep schedule to solve the problem of data forwarding interruption that was identified in the S-MAC. Additionally they utilised a data prediction scheme which dynamically adjusts the duty cycle in case nodes on the same level of the routing tree and sharing a parent have data to send to the sink in the same slot. In all this research, they didn't consider same sensed data in transit from the source node to the sink.

Rahman and Hussain [5] proposed a few ways of improving energy efficient data routing protocol in WSNs for continuous monitoring applications. The proposed improvements focused on data negotiation, development of data exchange expectance and data vanishing. From their experimental evaluation, results revealed that data negotiation between sensors and Base Stations was improved and active sensors could adjust their sensing frequency to avoid unnecessary sensing. Furthermore, the improvement was able conserve energy. Data evaluation in this case was at the application level and the temperature ranges were categorized into low, normal and high and were using patterns to predict temperature sensing [5].

2.1 Research Gap

Most of the research done in wireless sensor networks has concentrated mainly on achieving long sleeping periods of these sensor nodes as a technique of minimizing energy consumption. Nodes that are not transmitting data should remain sleeping or turn off their radios. However the studies done in wireless sensor networks have not optimized the sleeping periods of these nodes. This refers to a situation where the same data is subsequently acquired and transmitted unnecessarily to the sink node. They have mainly focused on scheduling sleep/wakeup periods of the nodes. Secondly, research done on data caching has mainly focused on reducing the delay in accessing data by employing clusters or coordinator nodes. However, such protocols have not considered the energy consumption as a result of transmission of data between clusters.

3 Methodology

In this section, we mention the methods and tools that were used to achieve the objectives of this project.

3.1 Simulation Setup

Simulations in this study were carried out using OMNET++ simulator. OMNET++ is a discrete event object oriented Simulator architecture based on Eclipse platform equipped with functionality of creating and configuring models, performing batch executions and analysing simulation results [8]. This simulator can be used for protocol modelling, modelling of wired and wireless networks, modelling of queuing networks and evaluating of performance aspects. The random deployment approach will depict the scalability of the DCAL algorithm especially in large network situations where the positioning of the nodes is not a known priori. In all simulations, we adopted the shortest path routing approach that forms dynamic routing tree of nodes. In all network sizes, the simulations were ran for 200 s in MIXIM operating on OMNET++ simulator platform and the results were averaged over 5 runs.

3.2 Performance Parameters

Performance parameters that were used include;

- Energy consumption
  Energy consumption is the energy consumed during the transmission of a packet from source node to the sink. A lower value of energy consumption indicates a better performance of the protocol.
- Mean latency
  Mean latency was computed as;

$$Mean\ Latency = \frac{(Maximum\ latency + Minimum\ latency)}{2} \quad (1)$$

where Maximum latency was the maximum time a packet took to move from the node (source) to the sink (destination) while Minimum latency was the minimum time a packet took to move from the node to the sink. A lower value of latency indicates a better performance of the protocol.

3.3 Sensor Node

In this project, we present the sensor node specifications that were used.

Table 1. TMote Sky sensor node specifications [9]

Sensor specifications	Value
Radio	CC2420
Outdoor range	50/100 m
Data rate	250 Kbps
Sleep power	60 μW sleep
Receiving power (RX)	63 mW receive
Transmit power (TX)	57 mW Wmit
Start up time	1 ms setup

From Table 1, Texas instrument chip CC2420 is a 2.4 GHz IEEE 802.15.4 compliant transceiver with low power consumption (RX: 63 mW and TX: 57 mW) was used, found suitable for low power WSN applications, consequently making it an ideal choice for this project. Additionally, in this study, we were looking at temperature sensing domain which catered for by this sensor.

3.4 DCAL Algorithm

DCAL algorithm, is an energy efficient caching protocol which designed based on the staggered tree approach for collecting data in wireless sensor networks. Data is collected from the sensor nodes and periodically transmitted to the sink. If the data is different from that cached locally, the source node drops the previously stored information and consequently updates its memory with the newly acquired data. This phenomenon of dropping the packets in this research has been termed as "wisely dropped packets". The algorithm was designed based on the following assumptions;

(i) The transmission range of a node does not go beyond the borders of the most immediate neighbour (in most cases it is the brother node).
(ii) A homogeneous network of sensors sensing the same data type, temperature was used.

3.4.1   Pseudo Code

Implementation of DCAL is based on the following pseudo code as illustrated in Table 2.

Table 2. Pseudo code for Data Caching Algorithm

```
Pseudo Code for Data Caching Algorithm
Sense data
Wake up to send data
Require: Generated packet with temperature value
Begin if
        If temperature value is same as previously generated, wisely drop packet
        Record scalar number of packets wisely dropped
    else
                Begin if
                There exists a temperature value in the cache memory
                Replace the existing temperature value with a new one.
                else
                Store new temperature value in the cache memory
                end if
        Forward packet
        Record scalar number of packets forwarded
end if
Forward data to the next hop
Wait for backoff period
                Begin if
                If backoff period expires
                Sleep.
                else
                Wait to receive any packet for transmission
                end if
```

With the DCAL algorithm, source node in its sleeping state will concurrently sense and capture data from the environment in which it is deployed. The processor will evaluate the captured data and ascertain whether it is different from that previously cached or it is the same value. Intuitively, if the data is different from the cached value, the source node will wake up and transmit the data to its parent. Otherwise the newly sensed data will not be forwarded to the sink thus saving the energy that would be wasted in transmitting the same information to the sink node. As a result, the energy saved is reflected in the results analysis section thus a relatively good performance of the protocol.

4   Results and Analysis

In this section, we present the results out of the simulations which were carried out using OMNET++ simulator. Results for DCAL were obtained using two values of n which were n = 2 and n = 4. n is a value which is meant to regulate the rate at which the temperature changes. This means that n controls the similarity or difference in temperature values. For n = 2, it implies that;

$$temperature\ change\ rate = \frac{2}{10} \tag{2}$$

Two out of ten temperature values will be the same. Similarly, for n = 4, is implies that four out of ten temperature values will be the same. The same applies to n = 10. The simulation results are represented in the figures.

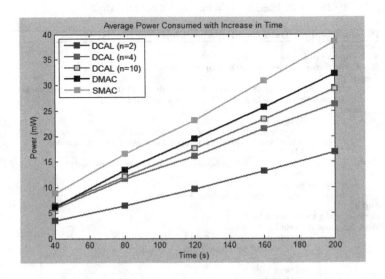

Fig. 1. Average power consumption with increase in time

As illustrated in Fig. 1, generally the average power consumption increased with increase in time. SMAC consumed more energy as compared to DMAC and DCAL. This was as a result of DCALs ability to drop some of the packets before transmission and SMACs synchronous wakeup of all nodes and sending of data at the same time. Initially, DMAC and DCAL (n = 4) had very closely related power consumption values. This indicated that with even fewer nodes, the margin of power consumption between both protocols is small. At 200 s, DCAL conserved up to 58.8 % of the energy. This is a good performance of the protocol with respect to network growth. SMACs power consumption was maintained at a higher value as compared to that of DMAC and DCAL. DCAL (n = 4) conserved up to 19.4 % of energy at 200 nodes.

As illustrated in Fig. 2, generally, average power consumption was maintained with increase in number of node. Results indicate that DMAC consumed almost twice the energy used by DCAL in transmitting packets. This is as a result of DCALs ability to wisely drop packets after confirming that they do exist in the cache memory. At 60 nodes, there is a sharp increase in power consumption for DMAC. On the other hand, at 60 nodes, DCALs power consumption gradually

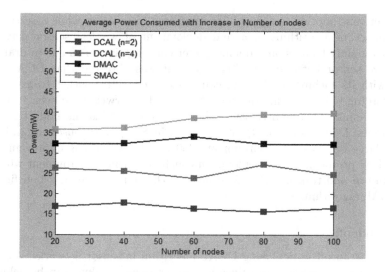

Fig. 2. Average power consumption with increase in number of nodes

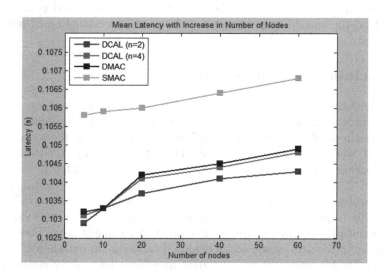

Fig. 3. Mean latency with increase in number of nodes

decreases. In response increase in network, it was observed that DCAL consumes relatively less energy. Latency plays a key role in evaluating the performance of the protocol as sensor nodes send data to the sink. Normally, sensor networks are characterized collisions and retransmissions especially as nodes increase. This is due to the fact that sensor nodes have a limited computing power. From Fig. 3, it was observed that the mean latency values for DMAC are relatively higher than that of DCAL. At 60 nodes, DMACs mean latency had increased by 0.0006 s. This implied that DCAL is a better performing protocol than DMAC.

Power consumption is a very important area to focus on while assessing the performance of algorithms in actual deployment of wireless sensor networks. Research mainly focuses on reducing power consumption so as not to drain the small size sensor batteries. In this regard, it was observed that DCAL algorithm with its caching mechanism can greatly reduce on packet transmissions by discarding redundant information that would otherwise have been transmitted to the sink. This greatly saved the battery energy as the node transmits less packets. DCAL was able to record up to 58.8 % power conservation, in relatively large deployment environment (200 nodes). With this improvement in the DMAC protocol, sensor deployments such as sensing environment which at times record and transmit the same data to the sink, can greatly benefit from the DCAL algorithm.

4.1 Tradeoff

There is a tradeoff in deploying DCAL algorithm in sensor networks. As much as lower power consumption values and lower latency values can be achieved, the DCAL protocol exploits the data caching as a mechanism which creates a computation overhead. This implies that there is an increased computation overhead on the small size processor for the nodes, in evaluation of sent and received data.

5   Conclusion and Future Work

In this research we presented the results for DCAL algorithm, an energy efficient caching protocol which designed based on the staggered tree approach for collecting data in wireless sensor networks. Data is collected from the sensor nodes and periodically transmitted to the sink. The algorithm adopted the staggered tree approach in order to achieve low energy consumption and low latency. Furthermore, DCAL utilises the staggered wakeup/sleep schedule operating on top of MAC protocol and is able to dynamically adapt to changes in traffic conditions. This helps in allowing a continuous flow of traffic on a multihop path and carry out pre-duty cycle adjustments based on volume of data. These facets are suitable for wireless sensor nodes deployed randomly in untethered environment. The DCAL algorithm was designed to achieve low energy consumption by eliminating transmission of unnecessary information from the source nodes to the sink. In our OMNET++ simulation, the results showed that the DCAL algorithm achieved lower energy consumption levels in different nodal densities than DMAC and SMAC protocols. Further still our algorithm achieved lower latency levels than DMAC protocol.

In our future work, we aim at deploying the DCAL algorithm in mobile wireless sensor networks and study the impact of our algorithm in such environments. The future work will focus on deploying DCAL algorithm in environments where nodes have 3-dimensional mobility. Further research should also focus on deploying DCAL algorithm in other wireless sensor network domains such as smart meters, agriculture and smart cities.

References

1. Sahota, H., Kumar, R., Kamal, A., Huang, J.: An energy-efficient wireless sensor network for precision agriculture. Wirel. Commun. Mob. Comput. **11**, 1628–1645 (2013)
2. Anastasi, G., Conti, M., Di Francesco, M., Passarella, A.: Energy conservation in wireless sensor networks: a survey. Ad Hoc Netw. **7**, 537–568 (2009)
3. Mihaylov, M., Borgne, Y., Tuyls, K.: Distributed cooperation in wireless sensor networks. In: Proceedings of the 23rd Belgium-Netherlands Conference on Artificial Intelligence, pp. 141–142 (2011)
4. Anastasi, G., Conti, M., Francesco, M., Passarella, A.: An adaptive and low-latency power management protocol for wireless sensor networks. In: Proceedings of the 4th ACM International Workshop, pp. 67–74 (2006)
5. Rahman, M., Hussain, S.: Effective caching in wireless sensor network. In: Advanced Information Networking and Applications Workshops, vol. 1, pp. 43–47 (2007)
6. Ye, W., Heideman, J., Estrin, D.: Medium access control with coordinated adaptive sleeping for wireless sensor networks. J. IEEE/ACM Trans. Netw. (TON) Arch. **12**, 493–506 (2004)
7. Lu, G., Raghavendra, S.: An adaptive energy-efficient and low-latency MAC for data gathering in wireless sensor networks. In: Proceedings of the 18th International Parallel and Distributed Processing Symposium (IPDPS 2004), pp. 863–875 (2004)
8. Yu, F.: A survey of wireless sensor network simulation tools. Washington University in Saint Louis, vol. 4, pp. 9–16, August 2008
9. Xue, Y., Sung Lee, H., Yang, M., Kumarawadu, P., Ghenniwa, H.H., WeimingShen, H.: Performance evaluation of NS-2 simulator for wireless sensor networks. In: IEEE International Conference on ElectroInformation Technology, pp. 955–957 (2008)

A Survey of TV White Space Measurements

Timothy X. Brown[1,2]([✉]), Ermanno Pietrosemoli[3], Marco Zennaro[3],
Antoine Bagula[4], Hope Mauwa[4], and Sindiso M. Nleya[5]

[1] Interdisciplinary Telecommunications Program,
University of Colorado, Boulder, USA
timxb@colorado.edu
[2] Department of ICT, Carnegie Mellon University, Kigali, Rwanda
timxb@andrew.cmu.edu
[3] ICT4D Laboratory, International Centre for Theoretical Physics, Trieste, Italy
{ermanno,mzennaro}@ictp.it
[4] ISAT Lab, Department of CS, University of the Western Cape,
Bellville, South Africa
bbagula@uwc.ac.za, 3364810@myuwc.ac.za
[5] CS Department, National University of Science and Technology, Bulawayo,
Zimbabwe
sindiso1.nleya@nust.ac.zw

Abstract. Unused spectrum in the television band (so-called TV white space) has the potential to provide new spectrum for access to information and communication services in developing countries. This claim has been subject to a variety of measurement studies. The purpose of this paper is to survey these studies to better characterize the spectrum that is provided by TV white space. We discuss some of the challenges to such studies and characterize the available TV white space spectrum in terms of the total volume that is available.

1 Introduction

The growing demand for wireless data transmission drives the search for alternatives to the current spectrum management schemes. In the long term, the only viable solution seems to be dynamic spectrum access once the technical details for its implementation are solved. In the near term, the use of currently vacant spectrum allocated to TV broadcast (so-called TV white spaces) can alleviate the spectrum crunch while opening the path for dynamic spectrum access. Several measurements campaigns have shown that the TV broadcasting spectrum is mostly unused in sparsely populated areas, especially in developing countries, as there is not enough return on investment for broadcasters to provide many simultaneous TV channels. For the same reasons, these are precisely the areas in which Internet access is frequently lacking.

TV White Spaces (TVWS) technology can take advantage of the improved propagation capabilities of these frequencies to provide affordable Internet access in rural areas. White spaces are also present in densely populated areas as a consequence of the transition from analog to digital TV, and these can be harnessed

© Institute for Computer Sciences, Social Informatics and Telecommunications Engineering 2015
A. Nungu et al. (Eds.): AFRICOMM 2014, LNICST 147, pp. 164–172, 2015.
DOI: 10.1007/978-3-319-16886-9_17

for wireless Internet access as well as other wireless communication services. The lower frequencies as compared with the ones used for WiFi (which in some places is becoming too crowded), are less attenuated by walls and offer an interesting alternative also for indoor Internet access, as well as for multimedia distribution. Finally, for machine to machine applications and the "Internet of Things" paradigm TVWS technology has significant advantages both for developed and developing economies.

A quest towards understanding the potential of TVWS has been initiated by way of experimental measurement campaigns that objectively strive to establish the nature and extent of spectrum usage and the resulting TVWS availability. These measurements vary based on factors such as their definition of occupied or not occupied, where they are made (e.g. outdoor vs. indoor) or the granularity of their occupancy metric. Though there is variation in the measurement techniques used and the precise occupancy metrics, these campaigns clearly assist to ascertain spectrum utilization and qualitatively understand current usage patterns. From the spectrum utilization or usage patterns it is feasible to ascertain the quantity of available white space spectrum. Furthermore, these measurements, since spectrum usage varies in time and space, provide a good opportunity to validate TVWS spectrum and channel models. These models provide a better understanding of current and projected spectrum usage that will allow devices to adaptively make more effective dynamic spectrum access decisions.

It is imperative that long term occupancy measurement campaigns and related analysis studies be carried out so as to ensure that government bodies, research and development agencies, and other interested parties target the real and evolving spectrum situation. However, in spite of the numerous active occupancy measurements in different parts of the world, there has been no comprehensive effort to date to analyze the different efforts that are scattered across the literature. Such efforts we believe should form the basis of informing better and more realistic spectrum occupancy expectations. As a step in this direction, the purpose of this paper is to survey spectrum occupancy measurement campaigns described in the literature.

We first discuss the basic measurement considerations from an occupancy perspective in Sect. 2. This is followed by a summary of survey outcomes in Sect. 3 which we subsequently discuss in Sect. 4. We conclude with Sect. 5.

2 Measurement Considerations

To measure the available TVWS, there are two approaches. The first is to use a device to physically scan the airwaves to detect the presence of TV signals (the detector approach). The alternative is to use a database of known transmitters (the database approach). In either approach, the gathered information must be interpreted to define what is meant by "available" white space spectrum.

2.1 The Detector Approach

The detector approach uses the combination of a measurement device and a measurement plan. The measurement device can be a general-purpose power detector such as a spectrum analyser or a detector specific to the type of signal. The ability to detect a signal depends on the characteristics of the detector. The sensitivity of the detector determines how weak the signal can be and still get detected. There are fundamental limits to how weak a signal is detectable according to the noise floor, which depends on the measurement bandwidth, interfering signals present and detector noise figure. Higher quality detectors have lower noise figure and are thus able to discern weaker signals from noise. Signal specific filters and signal processing improve detection sensitivity.

The antenna configuration also plays a role. Higher gain antennas increase sensitivity but are more focused in a narrower set of directions. The cable and connector losses between the antenna and the detector can also decrease detection performance. Setting detection thresholds in terms of field strength can remove some of this dependence on the antenna configuration. Even using field strength, it is still true that antennas mounted higher above the ground see less clutter and signal blockage than lower mounted antennas.

The measurement plan considers location, frequency, and time. For instance a device could move through a region seeking a specific TV signal. Or, it could seek out which TV signals are present across spectrum at a fixed location. Or, it might track the presence of a specific TV signal over time.

The primary challenge with the detector approach is the presence of detection errors where the detector either fails to detect the presence of a TV signal or gives false detections when no TV signal is present. The latter can be caused by noise and other signals. Or, atmospheric conditions can enable TV signals to be detected 100's of kilometers from their normal coverage area. A particular challenge comes once a white space is identified and then used by a secondary user. Subsequent measurements may see this as an occupied band and no longer identify it as white space. Because of these challenges, spectrum regulators advocate the database approach.

2.2   The Database Approach

This approach consists of accessing a database of known transmitters and their operational characteristics such as location, antenna parameters (radiation pattern, height above the ground), transmit power, times of operation and so on. From this database, topographic data, and potentially other data such as demographic data are used to predict what frequencies are available at different locations and times. Here the correct identification of the presence of a TV signal at a given location depends on the fidelity of the database information and the propagation model used to predict signal coverage. The primary challenge with the database approach is to find accurate information since in most countries spectrum usage information can be stored in many formats, electronic and paper, and the regulator has not collected these into a useful centralized database that is publicly available. Even when available, the approach is also computationally intensive if assessing a large region.

2.3   Characterizing Available Spectrum

There is a larger problem for both methods. Both methods focus on the *transmitted* primary signals. However, white space users must avoid interfering with the primary *receivers*. For example, an indoor detector antenna can fail to sense a TV signal that is nevertheless visible to a roof mounted receiving antenna, consequently allowing transmission in a channel that would cause interference to the incumbent. Conversely, a TV signal may be present and detected, but the intended secondary use is for a low-power indoor application that will not affect reception of stronger TV signals in other homes.

So, the results of both methods must be interpreted to yield a measure of the available white space spectrum. A detection threshold must be set. Measured (or calculated in the case of the database approach) primary transmitter signal strengths must be below this threshold value to declare a white space. Higher threshold values yield more white space while lower threshold values yield less. Generally, the threshold depends on the characterisitics of the primary service as well as the characteristics of the secondary user. For a lower power secondary service the threshold can be higher and vice versa.

Another concern is the frequency characteristics of the primary receiver and secondary transmitter. A primary receiver that does not have sharp front-end filters or a secondary transmitter that spills into adjacent bands will require large guard bands on each side of the detected primary transmitters. Larger guard bands mean that less bandwidth will be available for white space users.

Given the detection threshold and the guardband, the measurement data can yield what frequencies are available at what locations and when. Availability can be considered in two ways, at the channel level and at the band level [5]. The former is associated with measurement of individual channels, either with the same or with different channel width and possibly spread over several different frequency bands to determine the fraction of these channels that are available. The latter strives for a measurement of a frequency band, specified by start and stop frequency, with a step width (or frequency resolution) that is usually smaller than the channel spacing, to determine the degree of occupancy over the whole band.

Measurements at either the channel or band level result in successive variable size blocks alternating between white space and primary user spectrum. A key metric to characterize the white space spectrum is the total white space bandwidth that is available at a given location. Broadband access favours a large block of spectrum more than many smaller blocks. So, another metric is the largest white space block size. The frequency distribution of the white space spectrum, whether mostly at lower frequencies or more at higher frequencies is also another characteristic. In this paper we focus on the total white space bandwidth that is available.

3   Paper Survey Results

This review paper focused on studies of white spaces in the UHF television broadcasting frequencies from 470 MHz to 862 MHz. Most studies considered

Table 1. Total white spaces found by different studies in MHz

| | Type | Location | No guard bands | | | Guard bands | | | |
			Urban	Urban indoor	Rural	Urban	Rural	Year published
1.	Database	UK	≈150			≈30		2009 [13]
2.	Database	Europe	176					2011 [15]
3.	Database	Europe	≈125			30		2012 [9]
4.	Database	India	≈112					2014 [12]
5.	Detector	India	194		217			2013 [7]
6.	Detector	China	112		40			2012 [17]
7.	Detector	China	≈232					2013 [16]
8.	Detector	Hong Kong	≈168	≈235				2013 [18]
9.	Detector	Philippines	304					2012 [14]
10.	Detector	South Africa	≈307					2013 [2]
11.	Detector	Uganda	≈208					2013 [6]
12.	Detector	Vietnam	≈141					2011 [1]
13.	Detector	Italy	48	304				2014 [3]
14.	Detector	Romania	168		262			2014 [10]

a subset of this band in accordance with the local allocation of spectrum to the UHF TV band. The results obtained from these studies through the use of both geo-location databases and direct measurement via a detector are presented in Table 1. All of the results are outdoor measurements, except where noted otherwise.

From the table, it is easy to see that there is a need to specify a number of factors under which a spectrum measurement attempt is made to give a clear picture of the actual TV white space available and its potential for use. How much TV white space is detected depends on these factors. For example, one needs to specify whether an attempt is made in an urban place or rural, outdoor or indoor, or whether guard bands are considered or not. The use of a particular frequency spectrum by wireless devices is affected by how contiguous it. Consequently, it is also important to mention how much of the white space is contiguous to highlight its potential for use by white space devices. The results and some of the factors are discussed in detail in the next section.

4 Discussion

The studies from different countries reviewed in this paper have revealed that a significant amount of TV white space spectrum is available in the UHF band for utilization by secondary users; from 30 MHz to several 100 MHz. The actual results differ from each other because every country is autonomous regarding local frequency allocation and is also bound by local regulatory bodies [4]. However, observations from these studies have shown that the typical total volume found is largely affected by a number of factors discussed here.

4.1   Conservative Settings vs. Relaxed Settings

Studies have shown that when conservative settings as mandated by the US regulator, FCC are used, the amount of TV white space found is reduced. For example, Yin *et al.* [17] found no TV white spaces in all the locations they did their studies in China when they used a sensing sensitivity threshold of −114 dBm. However, relying on the analog terrestrial television (ATT) database as ground-truth data for the ATT channel occupancy situation in Beijing, setting the sensitivity threshold to −97 dBm was enough to find white space ATT channels in indoor scenarios. Small variations in threshold values have also a very big impact on the amount of TV white spaces found. Lopez-Benitez *et al.* [8] reported that small variation in threshold value as low as 5 dBm or less, could change the spectrum occupancy observed from 100 % to 0 %. McHenry *et al.* [11] were able through careful measurements to determine detection thresholds that provided few missed detections with false alarm rates in the 20 % to 60 % range. These observations show that the signal detection threshold value is a critical parameter in deciding how much white space is detected. It highlights the importance of using an adequate criterion to select the decision threshold [8].

4.2   Indoor vs. Outdoor

Another important observation noted from the studies is the difference in the amount of white space between indoor and outdoor scenarios. There is more white space in indoor scenarios than outdoor scenarios. For example, the study in Hong Kong [18] found that there were more indoor white spaces than outdoor white spaces which they associated with signal attenuation due to the blocking effects of walls. The blocking effect of walls was also found significative in [3], where it is reported that channels found occupied at the rooftop were almost always free in the basement thereby increasing the amount of white space available.

4.3   Rural vs. Urban

Almost all the studies except one found that rural areas had more white spaces than urban areas, which is attributed to the greater number of TV broadcasting stations in urban areas with respect to rural areas. Kumar *et al.* [7] associated more white space spectrum in rural areas with the continuous fluctuation of TV signals as we move away from urban areas where TV transmitters are located to more remote rural areas. There is a sharp contrast between the findings by Yin *et al.* in [17] versus the rest of the studies. They found more white spaces in urban areas than in rural areas. They did their study during the digital transition period in China, and they attributed their contrasting result to the lenghty transition time of the migration process from analogue terrestrial television (ATT) to digital terrestrial television (DTT), resulting in concurrent broadcasting of ATT and DTT in rural areas. All in all, the exact number and frequency composition of TVWS vary from location to location and is determined by the spatial arrangement of TV transmitters and their nationwide frequency allocation planning [13].

4.4   Guard Bands and Spectrum Distribution

While almost all of the studies found more than 100 MHz of spectrum including urban areas and developed countries. It is unlikely that all of this spectrum will be made available for TVWS. For instance, guard bands are required to avoid adjacent channel interference between TVWS users and primary TV transmitters. Newer digital TV receivers are more tolerant to adjacent channel signals than older analog TV receivers. This is one benefit of the digital TV transition. Even so, a single unused TV channel surrounded by adjacent channels actively used by TV transmitters will have bandwidth removed on both sides and leave little or no useful bandwidth.

For bigger blocks of two or more contigious unused channels, the amount of spectrum available will depend on the size of the guard band. For instance, if the guard band is a full channel (meaning more than two contigious unused channels are needed in order to have any TVWS bandwidth), then the available spectrum is reduced dramatically. In two studies shown in the table, the available specrum goes from more than 125 MHz with no guard bands to approximately 30 MHz with one-channel guard bands averaged across several cities. Most cities with one-channel guard bands have many 10's of MHz of TVWS spectrum with one-channel guard bands while some cases, such as central London, would have none. However, these are a worst case scenario of an urban area in the UK and Europe. We would expect that in other areas more spectrum would be available.

The size of the guardband depends on the transmit power of the TVWS transmitter. Low power devices such as sensors or indoor devices may be able to operate with a smaller guard band and more available bandwidth. For instance, if the guard band was reduced to half a channel, the amount of free bandwidth would increase from 30 MHz to about 80 MHz. This 50 MHz that is unused by high-power TVWS and TV transmitters could be useful for many low-power applications.

4.5   Regional Variations

Very few studies have focused on studying regional variations. Out of the thirty plus studies analyzed, only one dealt with regional variations. Van de Beek et al. [15] studied the availability of TV white space in some European countries, and when compared with the US, they found that their results show that at an average location in a representative European region, about 56 % of the spectrum is unused by TV networks, compared to the 79 % in the USA. They concluded that their results confirm quantitatively the often-stated expectation that there are fewer white spaces available in Europe compared to the United States of America. In general, developed regions have less white spaces than developing regions largely due to the differences in the number of TV broadcasting stations. Even in urban areas, the average amount of TVWS spectrum in developing countries is about 200 MHz.

5   Conclusion

From the papers analyzed, we can conclude that there is a great potential for leveraging white space frequencies to provide badly needed two way telecommunication services in rural areas, especially in developing countries where white spaces are abundant and telecommunications infrastructure is lacking. In developed countries, indoor white spaces can better be harnessed for low-power wireless sensor applications like electrical power meters and for indoor content distribution to address congestion in the 2.4 and 5 GHz unlicensed bands. A combination of database consultation and spectrum sensing could provide a more accurate assesment of channel occupancy, leading to a more efficient spectrum usage while protecting incumbents from interference. The establishment of the power level threshold to decide spectrum occupancy is very critical, and further studies are warranted to refine its choice. Other occupancy detection methods relying not in the power but on the statiscal properties of the incumbent signals could prove useful in the future as the required signal processing becomes more affordable.

References

1. Bao, V.N.Q., Thuan, T.D., Quy, N.T., Trung, L.M.: Vietnam spectrum occupancy measurements and analysis for cognitive radio applications. In: 2011 International Conference on Advanced Technologies for Communications (ATC), pp. 135–143. IEEE (2011)
2. Barnes, S.D., Jansen van Vuuren, P.A., Maharaj, B.T.: Spectrum occupancy investigation: measurements in South Africa. Measurement **46**(9), 3098–3112 (2013)
3. Bedogni, L., Di Felice, M., Malabocchia, F., Bononi, L., Spa, T.I.: Indoor communication over TV gray spaces based on spectrum measurements. In: Proceedings of IEEE Wireless Communication and Networking Conference (WCNC) (2014)
4. Elshafie, H., Fisal, N., Abbas, M., Hassan, WA., Mohamad, H., Ramli, N., Zubair, S.: A survey of cognitive radio and TV white spaces in Malaysia. Trans. Emerg. Telecommun. Technol. (2014)
5. Harrold, T., Cepeda, R., Beach, M.: Long-term measurements of spectrum occupancy characteristics. In: IEEE Symposium on New Frontiers in Dynamic Spectrum Access Networks (DySPAN), pp. 83–89. IEEE (2011)
6. Kagarura, G.M., Okello, D.K., Akol, R.N.: Evaluation of spectrum occupancy: a case for cognitive radio in Uganda. In: IEEE Ninth International Conference on Mobile Ad-hoc and Sensor Networks (MSN), pp. 167–174. IEEE, December 2013
7. Kumar, P., Rakheja, N., Sarswat, A., Varshney, H., Bhatia, P., Goli, S.R., Sharma, M.: White space detection and spectrum characterization in urban and rural India. In: IEEE 14th International Symposium and Workshops on World of Wireless, Mobile and Multimedia Networks (WoWMoM), pp. 1–6. IEEE, June 2013
8. Lopez-Benitez, M., Casadevall, F.: Spectrum usage in cognitive radio networks: from field measurements to empirical models. IEICE Trans. Commun. **97**(2), 242–250 (2014)
9. Makris, D., Gardikis, G., Kourtis, A.: Quantifying tv white space capacity: a geolocation-based approach. IEEE Commun. Mag. **50**(9), 145 (2012)

10. Martian, A.: Evaluation of spectrum occupancy in urban and rural environments of Romania. Revue Roumaine Des SCiences Techniques: Serie Electrotechnique et Energetique **59**(1), 87–96 (2014)
11. McHenry, M., Seadman, K., Lofquist, M.: Determination of detection thresholds to allow safe operation of television band 'white space' devices. In: 3rd IEEE Symposium on New Frontiers in Dynamic Spectrum Access Networks (DySpAN), vol. 3, no. 1, pp. 144–155. IEEE, October 2008
12. Naik, G., Singhal, S., Kumar, A., Karandikar, A.: Quantitative assessment of TV white space in India. In: 2014 Twentieth National Conference on Communications (NCC), pp. 1–6. IEEE, February 2014
13. Nekovee, M.: Quantifying the TV white spaces spectrum opportunity for cognitive radio access. In: Mehmood, R., Cerqueira, E., Piesiewicz, R., Chlamtac, I. (eds.) EuropeComm 2009. LNICST, vol. 16, pp. 46–57. Springer, Heidelberg (2009)
14. Pintor, A.L.C., To, M.R.S., Salenga, J.S., Geslani, G.M., Agpawa, D.P., Cabatuan, M.K.: Spectrum survey of VHF and UHF bands in the Philippines. In: 2012 IEEE Region 10 Conference on TENCON 2012, pp. 1–6. November 2012
15. Van de Beek, J., Riihijarvi, J., Achtzehn, A., Mahonen, P.: UHF white space in Europea quantitative study into the potential of the 470790 MHz band. In: 2011 IEEE Symposium on New Frontiers in Dynamic Spectrum Access Networks (DySPAN), pp. 1–9. IEEE, May 2011
16. Xue, J., Feng, Z., Chen, K.: Beijing spectrum survey for cognitive radio applications. In: 2013 IEEE 78th on Vehicular Technology Conference (VTC Fall), pp. 1–5. IEEE, September 2013
17. Yin, L., Wu, K., Yin, S., Li, J., Li, S., Ni, L.M.: Digital dividend capacity in China: a developing country's case study. In: 2012 IEEE International Symposium on Dynamic Spectrum Access Networks (DYSPAN), pp. 121–130. IEEE, October 2012
18. Ying, X., Zhang, J., Yan, L., Zhang, G., Chen, M., Chandra, R.: Exploring indoor white spaces in metropolises. In: Proceedings of the 19th Annual International Conference on Mobile Computing and Networking, pp. 255–266. ACM, September 2013

ICT4D Applications

ICT4Governance in East Africa

Varyanne Sika[1(⊠)] and Nanjira Sambuli[2]

[1] Institute for Development Studies,
iHub Research, University of Nairobi, Nairobi, Kenya
varyanne88@gmail.com
[2] iHub Research, Nairobi, Kenya

Abstract. There is growing interest and increasing investment in the role of Information and Communication Technologies (ICTs) in governance across Africa, however, empirical evidence on the use of ICTs in governance in East Africa remains scanty. The ICT for Governance study in East Africa is a study investigating how ICTs are being used in four specific areas of governance (i) access to information, (ii) public service delivery, (iii) tracking corruption and (iv) civic participation. This study seeks to identify, describe and analyze situations in which ICTs have and can be used to successfully facilitate or how they have hindered, two way interaction between government and citizens in Kenya, Uganda and Tanzania. This extended abstract discusses the theoretical frameworks and methodology used in this study.

Keywords: e-Governance · Governance · Civic participation · ICT and Governance · ICT4D

1 Introduction

The increasing growth and general prevalence of Information and Communication Technologies (ICTs) in Africa is as a result of various contributing factors. One of the most dominant reasons for governments encouraging the growth of ICTs is for the stimulation of economic growth, and more broadly, social and economic development [1]. The massive support and encouragement of ICT adoption in Africa by governments usually in collaboration with bilateral donor organizations, and the private sector has contributed to an ICT revolution in Africa. ICT is now widely accepted to be a powerful tool with which to combat many of the challenges that African countries struggle with. One of the major challenges faced by African countries is governance. Exploring ways to deal with the poor governance that has plagued many African countries is a fundamental aspect of solving other social and economic challenges.

Information and Communication Technologies (ICTs) are changing how both social and economic structures operate and interact within themselves and outside themselves. In influencing stimulation of positive social and economic changes, ICTs are also changing the ways in which local, regional and national government authorities communicate within themselves, with each other and with the citizens [2]. ICT being a newly prevalent phenomenon, is under researched [3] but this has not slowed down the application of ICTs in various area of governance. ihub Research[1], as part of the

---

[1] iHub Research, the research arm of iHub, focuses on technology and its uses in East Africa.

© Institute for Computer Sciences, Social Informatics and Telecommunications Engineering 2015
A. Nungu et al. (Eds.): AFRICOMM 2014, LNICST 147, pp. 175–179, 2015.
DOI: 10.1007/978-3-319-16886-9_18

ICT4Democracy East Africa network[2] is undertaking a study to assess how ICT tools are being used for and in various aspects of governance in Kenya, Uganda and Tanzania. This study looks beyond e-governance and examines other channels of ICT use in governance. The following are the questions this study seeks to answer;

i. Which ICT tools are in use for governance in the three East African countries in these areas; access to information, public service delivery, tracking corruption and civic participation?
ii. In which ways are ICT tools used in the four areas identified?
iii. What successes and challenges exist in the use of these tools?

2 Concepts and Theoretical Frameworks

A universal definition of the concept of e-governance does not exist. This study is therefore reliant on a combination of two definitions of e-governance. The first definition is that e-governance is the use of technology (and ICTs) to enhance access to and deliver efficiently, government information and services [4]. The second definition is that e-governance involves relationships between governments and customers (including citizens, businesses, and other governments or government agencies) using electronic means [5].

This study is framed within the first and the third approaches of Garson's [6] four proposed theoretical frameworks on ICT use in governance. The first framework is of ICT use in decentralization and democratization and the third theoretical framework emphasizes a continuous two-way interaction between ICTs and the organizational and institutional environment [7]. The second and fourth approaches proposed by Garson which are excluded in framing this study are; the dystopian approach which underlines technology's limitations and contradictions, and the approach in which e-governance is placed within the theories of globalization.

This study is also framed within the proposition of the interdependence of actors in governance [8] in which Government, Civil Society and the Private Sector (and citizens) are the interdependent actors in governance. These actors are influenced and interact with traditions, technology, history and culture throughout the governance process.

Finally, this study adopts a general framework for understanding interaction in governance based on Yildiz's [7] general evaluation of the theory and practice of e-government and e-governance. This framework outlines interactions in e-governance as being; Government-to-Government, Government-to-Citizen, Government-to-Civil Society, and Citizen-to-Citizen. This study has gone ahead to add on to the four interactions, Civil Society-to-Citizen, Civil Society-to-Government, Citizen-to-Government and Citizen-to-Civil Society. These are interactions possible in the use of ICT tools for governance (Fig. 1).

---

[2] The ICT4Democracy in East Africa network is *"premised on the recognition that ICT enhances communication and the right to freedom of expression as well as the right to seek, receive and impart information."*

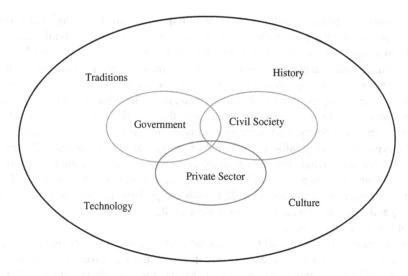

Fig. 1. Interdependence of actors in governance. (Source [8])

3 Methodology

This study is a qualitative audit of the existing ICT tools in governance in Kenya, Uganda and Tanzania. The study also uses both primary and secondary data.

This study is being conducted in specific towns and cities in Kenya, Uganda and Tanzania based on the presence of ICT4Democracy East Africa partners in the towns as explained below.

i. In Kenya, the study focuses on Nairobi and Nakuru. These selections are based on the prominence of ICT initiatives in the areas. Nairobi, as the ICT hub in the East African region was a natural fit for the study. Nakuru, on the other hand, is the first town in Kenya to get free wi-fi therefore enabling citizens to have access to unrestricted internet connectivity. This move was aimed at enhancing ICT in ensuring better public service delivery and simplifying public participation in governance through social media.

ii. In Uganda, the study focuses on Kampala, the capital city, and in Apac, a peri-urban town which is also a post conflict area. Kampala, being the capital city, has prominence of ICT use and infrastructure. Apac, on the other hand, is one of the towns in which there exists heavy use of ICT tools for governance as we discovered in our exploratory study.

iii. In Tanzania, the study focuses on Dar-es-Salaam and in Mwanza. Both cities have a high presence of organizations and projects whose central theme is ICT for Development, within and outside of the ICT4Democracy East Africa network.

Starting with an exploratory study, data collection through crowdsourcing[3] was carried out on social media and online spaces such as Twitter, Facebook and the ICT4Democracy East Africa Network which iHub Research is a part of, 18 ICT tools were identified and categorized based on the governance actor responsible for their implementation, that is, Government, Civil Society, and Citizens or the Private sector. This was done for all the three East African countries. These tools were further categorized according to their primary functions, that is, (i) access to information, (ii) public service delivery, (iii) tracking corruption and (iv) civic participation.

The exploratory study informs collection of primary data from the three Countries. Data collection will include key informant interviews from two government institutions from each country implementing ICT tools for governance, interviews with five Civil Society Organizations implementing ICT tools or projects for governance in each country, and interviews with three developers of ICT tools used for governance in each of the three countries.

Focus group discussions will be conducted with at least eight participants in each group in two selected towns in each of the three countries to investigate challenges, successes and user experience considerations that went into the design of the ICT tools identified in the exploratory study.

4 Data Analysis

This study will use content analysis to answer the research questions as well as quasi-statistics for data such as ICT tools used in the four areas of Governance discussed in the introduction section of this extended abstract. Content analysis will be used in particular to understand data collected from Civil Society Organizations, Government Institutions, Developers of ICT tools and the focus group discussions. The broader thematic focus areas will be on successes, challenges in implementation, motivation for using the ICT tools, de-motivation against using the ICT tools.

Findings from this study will be disseminated to the East African governments, Civil Societies, developers and citizens interested and working in governance. Recommendations based on the findings will be drawn and shared with relevant stakeholders in ICT for Governance in the region. In addition, an interactive map will be built using the Ushahidi platform to map the different ICT tools that were discovered in this study together with brief descriptions about each ICT tool.

References

1. Schuppan, T.: E-government in developing countries: Experiences from Sub-Saharan Africa. Gov. Inf. Q. **26**, 118–127 (2009)
2. Misuraca, G.C.: E-Governance in Africa: From Theory to Action. Africa World Press, Inc & International Development Research Center (IDRC), Ottawa (2007)

[3] Crowdsourcing is the process of getting information, funding or work done, online, from a crowd of people.

3. Waema, T., Ofwona, E.A.: Local Governance and ICTs in Africa: Case Studies and Guidelines for Implementation and Evaluation. Pambazuka Press, Cape Town (2011)
4. Brown, M.M., Brudney, J.L.: achieving advanced electronic government services: An examination of obstacles and implications from an international perspective. In: Paper presented and the Public Management Research Conference, Bloomington (2001)
5. Means, G., Schneider, D.: Meta-Capitalism: The e-business revolution and the design of 21st Century Companies and Markets. Wiley, New York (2000)
6. Garson, G.D.: Information systems, politics and government: leading theoretical perspectives. In: Garson, G.D. (ed.) Handbook of Public Information Systems, pp. 591–605. Marcel Dekker Inc, New York (1999)
7. Yildiz, M.: E-government research : Reviewing the literature, limitations and ways forward. Gov. Inf. Q. **24**, 646–665 (2007)
8. Graham, J., Amos, B., Plumptre, T.: Principles for Good Governance in the 21st Century. Institute on Governance, Ottawa (2003)

Computer Education and Training: Human Capacity Building for e-Government in Malawi

Patrick Albert Chikumba[✉] and Martin Msendema

Department of Computing and Information Technology,
University of Malawi-the Polytechnic, Private Bag 303, Blantyre 3, Malawi
patrick_chikumba@yahoo.com, mmsendema@poly.ac.mw

Abstract. Electronic governance has been hailed as a way to improve service delivery and responsiveness to citizens through two-way interaction, which results in the long run and generating greater public confidence in government. Apart from citizens, government interacts with business community and government nationally and internationally. The Government of Malawi has put several initiatives in area of ICT such as developing e-bill and national ICT policy, introducing Computer Studies in secondary schools, introducing computer courses in tertiary education institutions, establishing e-Government department, and currently, it is building e-government infrastructure. Some government departments and ministries are using computerised systems to support the public services. Therefore this paper discusses contribution of computer education and/or training being conducted in various training institutions in Malawi to human capacity which is one of factors that influence the successful implementation of e-government. An e-government toolkit for Malawi emphasizes continuously the development of human capital through education, lifelong education, and tax incentives to companies investing in worker training as a mission critical component of any successful, long-term e-government project.

Keywords: Computer education · e-Government · e-Government infrastructure · Human capital

1 Introduction

Government of Malawi has put several initiatives in area of Information and Communication Technology (ICT) such as developing e-bill and national ICT policy, introducing computer studies in secondary schools, introducing computer courses in tertiary education institutions, establishing a full e-Government department and currently, it is building e-government infrastructure. Some government departments and ministries are using computerised systems to support public services. An e-government toolkit for Malawi emphasizes continuously the development of human capital through education, lifelong education, and tax incentives to companies investing in worker training as a mission critical component of any successful, long-term e-government project.

Even at World Summit on Information Society in Tunis in 2005, The State President of Malawi, late Dr Bingu wa Muthalika, highlighted some importance of ICTs in socio-economic development. For example, (a) a nation-wide fibre-optic broadband network

© Institute for Computer Sciences, Social Informatics and Telecommunications Engineering 2015
A. Nungu et al. (Eds.): AFRICOMM 2014, LNICST 147, pp. 180–188, 2015.
DOI: 10.1007/978-3-319-16886-9_19

is under development; (b) a government wide area network is also being developed as a communication backbone for e-government; (c) Malawi recognizes that ICTs in education is a very important strategy to build sustainable ICT human resource capacity and increase people's literacy levels through e-learning; (d) the government of Malawi has started adopting the e-education curriculum at secondary and tertiary levels of education to enhance ICT knowledge and competence of youth; and (e) ICTs are also being utilized to enhance administration and management of the education institutions.

The national ICT policy focuses in areas of human resource in ICT sector. The Government of Malawi is drafting an e-bill which emphasises issues of e-government services. Public administrators have to take initiatives to encourage and facilitate the use of ICTs for the purposes of improving public services rendered to users, particularly, by setting up websites and electronic communication means.

With widespread adoption of ICT usage in public service delivery throughout the world, African countries, like Malawi, have vowed not to be left behind. An e-government policy is being developed as part of the Malawi ICT. An adoption of robust e-government depends on the strategy employed to implement it. The e-government requires human capital. People involved in the e-government require ICT skills and experiences that can be obtained through computer education and training.

The e-government in Malawi has stakeholders such as ICT experts for supporting the system and citizens who access e-government services. For these stakeholders to perform their duties, they need computing skills and knowledge that can be obtained through computer education and training. Therefore this paper discusses contribution of Computer Education and Training to human capacity which is one of the factors that influence the successful implementation of e-government.

2   e-Government, Human Capacity and Computer Literacy

The digital revolution has allowed government organizations to store, analyse and retrieve information effectively and efficiently [2]. There is an increasing amount of attention on electronic government (e-government) [3]. Governments are beginning to embrace e-government [1] and information technology has slowly but consistently permeated government organizations and institutions at all levels [2].

The e-Government is affecting the public sector through an ever-growing and pervasive use of ICTs [8]. It is believed that the e-government provides a good platform for government and its citizens to exchange information; provide and access services respectively in efficient and effective way. Different authors [1, 2, 4–6] have defined the e-government in various ways but all definitions focus on the online provision of information and delivery of services through the Internet.

Electronic governance has been hailed as a way to improve service delivery and responsiveness to citizens through two-way interaction, which results in the long run and generating greater public confidence in government [4]. Depending on type of interactions, there are various types of e-government relationship namely government to business (G2B) and business to government (B2G), government to citizen (G2C) and citizen to government (C2G), and government to government (G2G) nationally and internationally [6, 7].

As shown in Table 1, maturity of interactions is in several stages [1, 4, 7]. The Layne and Lee (2001) model provides four stages of maturity [1, 7] such as catalogue; transaction; vertical integration; and horizontal integration. Watson and Mundy (2001) take a more political view than Layne and Lee and identify three phases of e-government growth and relate them to democracy [7]. Hiller and Belanger (2001) model is similar to the work done by Watson and Mundy (2001) and identify five stages of e-government growth.

Table 1. Four stages of e-government maturity

Stage	Descriptions
Catalogue	Information is posted statically on a website for viewing and possibly for retrieval.
Transaction	Users can exchange information at the website and complete transactions.
Vertical Integration	Users can go to a website that spans a number of departments across a unit of government so that new businesses might be able to register electronically.
Horizontal Integration	Users can complete transactions that span levels of government so that a local government might be able to host a portal to help citizens or businesses complete transactions with state or federal agencies.

With reference to Table 2, there are a number of factors that place barriers to the development, acceptance, and use of electronic services and may stem from different areas [8]. These include legislative, administrative, technological, user-culture and social barriers. In order to increase implementation plan efficiency, it is important to have a strategy for promoting e-government which must include provisions for over-coming these barriers.

Table 2. Barriers to the development, acceptance, and use of electronic services

Barrier	Descriptions
Legislative barriers	Related to the existence of appropriate laws, regulations and directives that allow or facilitate the deployment of electronic services
Administrative barriers	Related to lack of appropriate business models, justification of costs, availability and allocation of skilled personnel, and the need for structural reforms
Technological barriers	Associated with the availability of suitable tools, standards, and infrastructure to develop, deploy, and use electronic services
User-culture barriers	Which are set by the user groups' culture or profile
Social barriers	Impediments related to stakeholders' social status, such as fear of job loss or status degradation; established power structures, and contact networks may also view these developments as a threat

Stakeholders affect the successful development of e-government. There are several categories of e-service stakeholders which include managers, domain experts, IT staff, help desk workers, administrators, and end-users (see Table 3). All stakeholders identified above require necessary knowledge and skills, particularly computing, for them to perform their duties in e-services. Therefore, it is important for any government to invest on human capital.

Table 3. Stakeholders of e-Service

Stakeholders	Responsibilities
Managers	Organize and supervise public services and making decisions about implementation of new services or alteration of existing ones
Domain Experts	Possess and provide the necessary background knowledge for designing and implementing public services, including laws, processes, directives and prerequisites
IT staff	Provide the necessary technological knowledge for the development of an electronic public service and maintain the e-service
Help desk workers	Support e–service end-users, helping them to familiarize themselves with the environment of the e-service scope with possible problems that may occur
Administrators	Manage user accounts and ensure data integrity (such as back up functions) and system security
End-users	Mainly citizens or enterprises that make use of the service

People are the main actors in every society. Therefore human capital is critical factor for success of any organisation or society. The human capital is broadly defined to include the knowledge, skills, attitudes and capacities of individuals as well as the social and cultural endowments of the collective, including capacity for discovery, invention, innovation and resourcefulness [11]. The human capital simply means people.

The human capital is the stock of competencies, knowledge, social and personality attributes embodied in the ability to perform labour so as to produce economic value. Many theories explicitly connect investment in human capital development to education. The role of human capital in economic development, productivity growth, and innovation has frequently been cited as a justification for government subsidies for education and job skills training. The human capital increases through education and experience [10]. It is vitally important for an organization's success [9].

On the other hand human capacity is the ability of individuals to perform functions, solve problems, and set and achieve objectives in a sustainable manner. Through a process called human capacity development, abilities are obtained, strengthened, adapted and maintained over time. Human capacity development is developing the will, skills, capabilities, and systems to enable people.

In modern technical financial analysis, "balanced growth" is critical which refers to the goal of equal growth of both aggregate human capabilities and physical assets that produce goods and services. People are assets whose value can be enhanced through investment whose goal is to maximize value while managing risk. It is believed that as the value of people increases, so does the performance capacity of the organization, and therefore its value to clients and other stakeholders. Organization's human capital policies must be aligned to support organization's mission, vision for the future, core values, goals and objectives, and strategies by which the organization has defined its direction and its expectations for itself and its people. Therefore people involved in e-Government services need computing knowledge and skills.

Computer is developing rapidly and becomes the essential tool for life in current society. According to [14] increasing attention is given to computer literacy because today's society is becoming more and more dependent on new technology. How to obtain the information, complete the work and improve the living through computer skills are becoming the essential ability for the human being for living [13]. People with less access to technology are at a disadvantage as compared to those with more access when it comes to seeking higher levels of civic participation [14]. It is believed that having the basic knowledge of a computer and its functionalities are the essential computer literacy for the modern people.

It is important to reduce the digital divide with specific focus on demanded public services by the groups with low access because people who have low computer literacy and limited access to the Internet are unable to access online services. The low level of computer literacy is a critical challenge for developing e-government [12]. While e-government can also improve services to citizens through other channels, the inability to provide online services to all citizens can hold back e-government programmes [12].

Computer literacy has been a subject of educational research for recent years. According to different definitions [14], the computer literacy includes (a) the ability to use a computer and its software; (b) an understanding of the concepts, terminology and operations that relate to general computer use; (c) the essential knowledge needed to function independently with a computer; (d) the ability to use applications rather than to program; (e) the comfort level someone has with using computer programs and other applications that are associated with computers; and (f) the ability to use computers at an adequate level for creation, communication and collaboration in a literate society.

Literature shows that many education institutions, particularly those offering tertiary education, have introduced computer literacy courses to their students with various objectives. For example, [15] points out that computer literacy skills are taught because they (a) lay the foundations for developing a critical understanding of the information age; (b) help students make effective use of computers, both in classroom and workplace settings; (c) shape a proactive view regarding the role of computers in everyday life; (d) assist those who are 'technophobic' to overcome fears of increasing computerisation of government and social support agencies; (e) create a solid skills base among students so that they can collectively pursue more creative uses of computers in the syllabus; (f) extend the personal enjoyment gained through keeping in touch by regular email use, for example, or in finding satisfying search engine results; and (g) provide 'realia' for terms that relate to hardware, software, the Internet, and the many different uses and phenomena that have arisen from online culture.

3 Methodology

This was the desk research and the data was gathered from the Internet and reports. Participatory observations and some few interviews were used to gather some data. Both authors in this paper participate in computer education and training at university level and also some colleges. They also work with e-Government department as training consultants. Semi-structured interviews were conducted with some e-Government ICT staff on the different roles exist in the system. Some interviews were conducted randomly with ordinary Malawian citizens on the computer literacy and training.

4 e-Government in Malawi

Government of Malawi has several initiatives going on in order to provide a good environment for electronic government services. One of the initiatives is to develop websites for ministries and departments so that citizens can have access to important information from their government.

Currently, e-government project is underway in Malawi. The Government of Malawi is setting up necessary infrastructure for implementation of e-government. In terms of human capital, it is establishing e-government technical team and it already has a department that is responsible for all ICT activities in the entire government. It also has an ICT institution which trains civil servants and general public in computing. In past years, it has established Government Wide Area Network (GWAN) with an aim of connecting all government offices across the country.

Different government departments and ministries have websites to disseminate information to citizens and general public. The Malawi Government has its own official website (www.malawi.gov.mw) which provides information about The Office of President and Cabinet, ministries, publications, speeches, parliament, cabinet list, and also webmail. In total, there are seventeen ministries and among them some have grown in terms of online information publication (see Table 4).

Table 4. Availability of websites of ministries as in august 2014

No	Ministry of	Comment
1	Finance and Economic Development	http://www.finance.gov.mw
2	Foreign Affairs and International Cooperation	http://www.foreignaffairs.gov.mw
3	Labour	No website
4	Health	No website
5	Gender, Children, Disability & Social Welfare	http://www.gender.gov.mw
6	Justice and Constitutional Affairs	http://www.justice.gov.mw
7	Agriculture, Irrigation & Water Development	http://www.moafsmw.org
8	Transport & Public Works	http://www.motpwh.gov.mw
9	Trade & Industry	http://www.trade.gov.mw
10	Lands, Housing and Urban Development	http://www.lands.gov.mw
11	Natural Resources, Energy & Mining	http://www.mines.gov.mw
12	Education, Science & Technology	No website
13	Defence	No website
14	Youth, Sports Development and Culture	No website
15	Information, Tourism & Civic Education	No website
16	Local Government & Rural Development	No website
17	Home Affairs & Internal Security	No website

From Table 4 above, it has been shown that out of seventeen ministries, nine ministries (representing 52.9 %) have domains and websites. It has been observed that most of websites were developed by institutions or organisations outside the government and information on the website is not updated frequently except the main website (www.malawi.gov.mw) is under the custody of e-Government Department and is updated frequently. A question can rise: *Does the Malawi government not have its own skilled IT staff that can develop and update the ministerial websites?* The answer can be 'NO'. The Malawi Government has well established IT structure down to the district level. The ministries, district councils, town councils, municipalities and city councils have established positions of ICT officers.

Even private sector is playing its part to enhance computer network infrastructure. For example, Malawi Telecommunication Limited (MTL) and Electricity Supply Commission of Malawi (ESCOM) have constructed fibre links across the country. This has improved tremendously the Internet connectivity to Malawian individuals, companies and organisations.

5 Computer Education and Training in Malawi

Education system in Malawi follows 8-4-4 pattern comprising primary (8 years), secondary (4 years) and tertiary (minimum of 3 years). The Government of Malawi (GoM) through the Ministry of Education (MoE) in partnerships with British Council, SchoolNet Malawi and other stakeholders, introduced Computer Studies as an optional subject at senior secondary level (Forms 3 and 4). Successful completion of the final two years of secondary education (senior cycles) qualifies eligible students to sit for Malawi School Certificate of Education (MSCE) examinations managed by Malawi National Examinations Board (MANEB) and Computer Studies is one of the subjects. According to examination results of academic years of 2010, 2011 and 2012, students opting to write Computer Studies were very few and even numbers dropped in terms of percentages as shown in Table 5.

Table 5. Students wrote computer studies at MSCE in the last 3 Years

Year	Total Students	Students wrote Computer Studies	Percentage
2010	97,543	3,811	3.91 %
2011	120,806	3,904	3.23 %
2012	122,701	3,400	2.77 %

At the degree level, there are courses that are targeting computing. University of Malawi introduced programmes such as BSc in Information Technology, BSc in Management Information Systems, BSc in Computer Sciences, BSc in Mathematical Sciences Education (Computing), BEd in Business Studies and Computing, MSc in Informatics, Master of Public Health (Health Informatics), and MPhil in Applied Sciences (Information Technology). At Mzuzu University (another public university) has BSc in Information and Communication Technology, BSc in Library and

Information Sciences, BSc in Information Theory, Coding and Cryptography and PhD in Information Theory, Coding and Cryptography. Apart from these two public universities, the government opened another public university of Science and Technology which has also degree and master programmes in computing. The Government of Malawi has an ICT training institution under e-Government department which also produces degree graduands in Business Information Technology in conjunction with University of Greenwich.

All these programmes produce graduands in every year but the numbers are not encouraging for instance in 2014 University of Malawi produced between 120 and 140 first degree graduands and Mzuzu University produced about 49 first degree graduands. These graduates are needed, not only in government services but also in private sector. Most graduates prefer to work in private companies/organisations because of better packages than government departments.

Apart from degrees, some government and private colleges offer computing courses at certificate, diploma and advanced diploma levels with international examination bodies such as City and Guilds, ABMA, IMIS, AMITY and ACP. One of the advantages of these courses is that anyone can pursue them and this gives chance to a good number of students to have basic computing knowledge and skills.

In the education system, there is an introduction of computer and its operations almost to students joining tertiary education regardless of which course they pursue. For instance, at universities, students go through computer training in their first year. Even some private secondary schools introduce computing to their students. This development seems to assist to have a nation which is computer literate.

The issue now is that how many citizens have access to such computer training. Very few individuals have the access particularly those staying in towns and cities. According to 2008 national population and housing census, the large population is in rural areas in Malawi which is about 85 % [16]. This population is underprivileged in terms of computer literacy and access to computer education and training. But it is this population needed or targeted for e-Government services. It is believed that this rural population should be given enough attention in human capacity building for e-Government.

There are a number of initiatives that Malawi government is doing to provide the ICT access to rural Malawians. For instance, through Malawi Communications and Regulatory Authority (MACRA), and in partnerships with International Telecommunication Union (ITU), local and business communities the government of Malawi established a pilot network of public access ICT facilities called Multipurpose Community Telecenters in rural areas with the aim of addressing the digital divide by providing universal access to basic ICT services in reasonable walking distances [17].

6 Conclusion

It has been observed that computer education and training contribute a lot in human capital for e-Government in Malawi in all levels of managers, domain experts, IT staff, help desk workers, administrators and end users. What is needed is to increase the access to these trainings to the rural population where majority is. It is necessary to come up with a good strategy of introducing computer training places in rural areas.

One way is to use already existing infrastructure of telecenters to offer computer training as some have already started.

References

1. Holden, S.H., Norris, D.F., Fletcher, P.D.: Electronic government at the local level: progress to date and future issues. Public Perform. Manage. Rev. 26(4), 325–344 (2003). http://www.jstor.org/stable/3381110
2. Bretschneider, S.: Information technology, e-government, and institutional change. Public Adm. Rev. 63(6), 738–741 (2003). http://www.jstor.org/stable/3542469
3. Norris, D.F., Moon, M.J.: Advancing e-government at the grassroots: tortoise or hare? Public Adm. Rev. 65(1), 64–75 (2005). http://www.jstor.org/stable/3542582
4. West, D.M.: E-government and the transformation of service delivery and citizen attitudes. Public Adm. Rev. 64(1), 15–27 (2004). http://www.jstor.org/stable/3542623
5. Kim, S., Layne, K.: Making the connection: e-government and public administration education. J. Public Aff. Educ. 7(4), 229–240 (2001). http://www.jstor.org/stable/40215538
6. Ghayur, A.: Towards good governance: developing an e-government. Pakistan Dev. Rev. 45(4), 1011–1025 (2006). Papers and Proceedings PARTS I and II Twenty-second Annual General Meeting and Conference of the Pakistan Society of Development Economists Lahore, December 19–22, 2006 (Winter 2006), pp. 1011-1025 [Online] http://www.jstor.org/stable/41260665 (2006)
7. Reddick, C.G.: Empirical models of e government growth in local governments. e Service Journal 3(2), 59–84 (2004). http://www.jstor.org/stable/10.2979/ESJ.2004.3.2.59
8. Vassilakis, C., Lepouras, G., Fraser, J., Haston, S., Georgiadis, P.: Barriers to electronic service development. e-Serv. J. 4(1), 41–63 (2005). http://www.jstor.org/stable/10.2979/ESJ.2005.4.1.41
9. Crook, T.R., Todd, S.Y., Combs, J.G., Woehr, D.J., Ketchen, D.J.: Does human capital matter? a meta-analysis of the relationship between human capital and firm performance. J. Appl. Psychol. 96(3), 443–456 (2011)
10. Sullivan, A., Sheffrin, S.M.: Economics: Principles in action, p. 5. Pearson Prentice Hall, Upper Saddle River (2003). ISBN 0-13-063085-3
11. Šlaus, I., Jacobs, G.: Human capital and sustainability. Sustain. 2011(3), 97–154 (2011). http://www.mdpi.com/journal/sustainability10.3390/su3010097
12. Janenova, S.: E-Government in Kazakhstan: Challenges For A Transitional Country. http://www.nispa.org/files/conferences/2010/papers/201004220915450.janenovasaltanat.pdf
13. Hsiao, H.-C., Lin, Y.-C.: Factors Affecting Computer Literacy of College Students in Taiwan. http://conference.nie.edu.sg/paper/Converted%20Pdf/ab00369.pdf
14. Lingard, R., Madison, R., Melara, G.: Assessing the effectiveness of computer literacy courses. In: Proceedings of the 2002 American Society for Engineering Education Annual Conference & Exposition. American Society for Engineering Education (2002)
15. Corbel, C., Gruba, P.: Teaching computer literacy. National Centre for English Language Teaching and Research, Sydney (2004)
16. National Statistical Office (NSO): 2008 Population and Housing Census. National Statistical Office, Malawi (2008)
17. Chikumba, P.A.: Utilization of ICTs in multipurpose community telecentres in rural malawi. In: Popescu-Zeletin, R., Rai, I.A., Jonas, K., Villafiorita, A. (eds.) AFRICOM 2010. LNICST, vol. 64, pp. 93–101. Springer, Heidelberg (2011)

Implications of Institutional Client-Server Geographic Information System: A Case of Mzuzu Agriculture Development Division

Daniel Nkosi[1] and Patrick Albert Chikumba[2(✉)]

[1] MSc in Informatics (Student), Department of Computer Sciences,
University of Malawi, P.O. Box 280, Zomba, Malawi
danielnkosi@gmail.com
[2] Department of Computing and Information Technology,
University of Malawi-The Polytechnic, Private Bag 303, Blantyre 3, Malawi
patrick_chikumba@yahoo.com

Abstract. Stand alone GIS applications at Mzuzu ADD make it difficult if not impossible for the top management to access data and make decisions accordingly. The applications make it difficult for members of staff to share spatial information and further more there is duplication of work and inconsistency in the spatial data collected by the ministry. The current setup influences what is termed as the institutional challenge. This situation arises due to GIS experts not being able to communicate effectively to the decision makers. This is as a result of the absence of the link or availability of the GIS applications and its data to the decision makers. Institutional challenge is one of the many challenges facing in the adoption of GIS usage. As a way of eliminating or reducing the stated problems above, this study proposes client-server GIS application. One such application can be a Spatial Data Infrastructure at an institutional level. The aim of this research was to identify implications that can arise in introducing an institutional GIS client-server application over stand-alone GIS applications.

Keywords: GIS · Standalone GIS · Mzuzu ADD · Client-server GIS · Spatial data infrastructure · GIS application

1 Introduction

Knowledge of where something happen matters in people and in organizations [2, 7]. Decision systems, expert systems and intelligent systems when integrated with domain specific knowledge help in making informed decisions and representing a model of the world [4]. An information system that can ably present places on earth and give information about them is Geographic Information System (GIS) [4]. Application of GIS by people and organizations can either be on day-to-day basis or for strategic purposes [12]. General GIS application areas include Government and public services, business and service planning, logistics and transportation, and socio-economical and environmental modeling [12].

Agriculture as a business sector is well suited for the application of GIS [15]. The sector is natural resource based which requires the movement, distribution, and utilization

© Institute for Computer Sciences, Social Informatics and Telecommunications Engineering 2015
A. Nungu et al. (Eds.): AFRICOMM 2014, LNICST 147, pp. 189–197, 2015.
DOI: 10.1007/978-3-319-16886-9_20

of large quantities of products, goods, and services [15]. It is increasingly required to record details of its business operations from the field to the marketplace. Economists, agronomists, community planners and farmers use GIS to research and device practices that will enable sustainability of food production and ensure the survival of human race.

When compared to other business sectors worldwide GIS user community in production agriculture is rather small [16]. There is a lack of formal opportunities to share applications and innovations of GIS specifically in agriculture. The following are some of reasons why GIS technology has not been fully adopted [9]; (1) inadequacy of digital data; (2) contrasting file formats; (3) expensive GIS hardware and software; and (4) institutional impediments.

This research is intended to look at challenges of using GIS at Mzuzu Agriculture Development Division (ADD) when data is made available centrally. Mzuzu ADD is a government entity that offers agricultural related services to the general public. As such, GIS application at Mzuzu ADD can be looked at partly as being applied in the government/public service and partly in socio-economical/environmental modeling.

GIS is used in two of the technical departments at Mzuzu ADD but its use in agricultural related activities is yet to be recognized by many. Lee et al. [11] believe that obstacles to the extended use of GIS in Agriculture can be partially removed by employing client-server model. These days the emerging way of information exchange via network is web technology on the Internet and Intranet [11]. The web-oriented model can contribute to the remote operation of GIS applications, with which users can communicate interactively.

Stand alone GIS applications at Mzuzu ADD make it difficult if not impossible for the top management to access data stored in them and make decisions accordingly. The applications make it difficult for members of staff to share spatial information. Furthermore, there is duplication of work and inconsistency in the spatial data collected by the division.

The current setup influences what is termed as the institutional challenge. This situation arises due to GIS experts not being able to communicate effectively to the decision makers. This is as a result of the absence of the link or unavailability of the GIS applications and their data to the decision makers. Institutional challenge is one of many challenges in the adoption of GIS [9, 17]. As a way of eliminating or reducing the stated problems above, this study proposes client-server GIS application. One such application as proposed by this study is Geonetwork, implemented at an institutional level. When Geonetwork is part of a Spatial Data Infrastructure, in a community-oriented GIS application, it helps in addressing problems that are associated with data, technology and institution [16].

Creating a community-oriented GIS application serves as a vehicle to integrate a wide range of disparate information sources held in various formats by various departments. Rybaczuk [16] points out that though system integration may seem to be a mundane task for most developed countries, they are still finding it a challenge to have access to integrated information system. Further, a community-oriented GIS application improves communication between departments and within them by facilitating information flows [16].

The aim of this paper is to highlight implications that can arise in introducing an institutional GIS client-server application over stand-alone GIS applications. Internally improved ICT can potentially enhance and strengthen an organizational infrastructure by increasing the efficiency of information sharing between departments and staff [5]. Client-server application will be an improved ICT system for Mzuzu ADD as far as GIS usage is concerned.

Setting up an institutional GIS client-server application is a step towards setting up a national spatial data infrastructure. The national spatial data infrastructure will support efforts of e-government project which the Malawi government is currently implementing. As Aalders & Moellering [1] put it, Spatial Data Infrastructure (SDI) promotes interaction in the spatial community among information providers and users. Examples of spatial data infrastructures are the US National Spatial Data Infrastructure (NSDI) and the System Grid Project ESG [3]. NSDI provides a platform for data sharing. ESG with grid computing is used in climate modeling research. Global Spatial Data Infrastructure (GSDI) links the national SDIs to share and reuse the available datasets for all users worldwide.

Wisse [18] observes that currently there are many developments of geospatial data infrastructure and not many studies have been conducted on the same. With this in mind studying implications of GIS client-server application will add to the literature of geospatial data infrastructure.

2 Client-Server Geographic Information Systems

Geographic Information System (GIS) is looked at as a computer system that has the capability of assembling, storing, manipulating and displaying data referenced by geographic coordinates [10, 14]. GIS organizes geographic data that a person reading a map can select data necessary for a specific task. Its ability to combine datasets in many ways makes it useful to nearly every field.

GIS has greatly advanced. Initially in the 1960s cartographers wanted to adopt computer techniques in map-making and today GIS is a versatile toolkit [16]. The GIS toolkit has evolved largely by innovations created in one application of GIS being shared and built upon in subsequent applications [16]. Thus, GIS users, by sharing their innovations and applications formally and informally, were very important to the development of GIS tools available today. Sharing applications and innovations among users remains an important aspect of GIS both within and across disciplines and business sectors [16]. This study promotes the sharing of spatial data through the use of the client-server application.

Before the 1970s GIS was mainly for programmers who interacted with the technology through a command line [12]. In the 1970s and 1980s the high demand of GIS use influenced the development of interfaces for interacting with the application [12] and GIS application was unique in the sense of the data it held and operated on.

Longley et al. [12] state that increase in the interest of GIS usage was mainly due to the coming of graphical user interface (GUI), customization capabilities and high level programming languages. GUI made it easy for users to interact with the application.

High level programming languages facilitated the creation of GIS software tailored for specific organization.

Depending on organization needs, different organizations use different types of GIS application. The coming of web service with client-server technology has made it possible to link geographically distributed GIS application to form one GIS application with many functionalities [12].

GIS technology can be accessed over a standalone computer where all the hardware, software, data and people required to use the technology are centrally located [12]. With the advancement of the Internet and Intranet, distributed GIS has become of much importance than centralized GIS [12, 13]. Centralized computing encourages much of individualism which can only encourage confusion as people will define terms in ways they can only understand. This can further lead to data redundancies and worst of resources due to duplicated efforts.

Stand alone computing is cheaper than client server computing in sense that it just requires one computer with required application. Client-server computing, on the other hand, requires a computer network with access to a server. Despite client server computing being expensive it is advantageous in that it promotes sharing of information and thus reducing redundancies in data collected by an organization. For this study a Local Area Network is already installed at Mzuzu ADD with required servers.

In GIS applications, a client-server model is achieved through the use of web services. Web service is a developer-oriented software component that can be accessed and integrated by application developers through standard application program interfaces (APIs). When GIS applications are used with web services they become web GIS. Web GIS provides an open and distributed architecture for disseminating geospatial data and web processing tools on the Internet. This enables organizations to distribute maps and tools without time and costs restrictions.

Web GIS architecture has two components: client and server. Client is where users interact with spatial data and analysis tools. GIS programs display different forms of outputs based on user commands, tools and tasks that have been triggered by the client-side.

The web GIS server is further categorized into four components: web server, application server, map server and data server. The web server responds to HTTP requests that are made by the browser on the client-side. Examples of a web server can be Apache and Jetty.

In this study the Geoserver is used as a web server. As open source software it implies that the software is readily available and there is no cost implications associated with it. One of the limiting factors developing countries face in the use of the GIS applications is the costs that come with the application [9].

3   Methodology

This study takes an experimental approach. Janssens & Kramer [8] attest that an experimental approach is advantageous compared to other empirical approaches in that: (1) lab environment offers control to factors like social networks, beliefs and health which might otherwise have bias to the results of the study; (2) Experiment offers insights into decisions that can be made within a short time span; and (3) Participants interact with a prototyped application directly, which elicits behavior that differs from hypothetical survey questions. The advantages of experimental approach justify its application in this study. This study qualifies to be a framed field experiment because it has been conducted in a natural setting of the people, computers and network infrastructure [6] that make up the Mzuzu ADD as the environment in which implications of GIS as a client-server application was studied.

The semi-structured interviews were conducted twice, prior to the set up of the prototype and then after users had interacted with the prototype. The first interviews gathered information on current practices and challenges members of staff are facing which resulted in building the requirements specification of the prototype. The second interviews gathered general user feedback, limitation, challenges pertaining to the installed client-server GIS application. After the demonstration participants were interviewed for their feedback on the proposed GIS.

Most data was collected through the evaluation of a client-server GIS prototype whose spatial data was collected from the technical departments at Mzuzu ADD. The GIS prototype was demonstrated to staff members of technical departments and supporting departments. It was performed by applying the DECIDE framework [19]. The demonstration focused mainly on accessibility and sharing of spatial data between offices and departments at Mzuzu ADD.

4   Client-Server GIS at Mzuzu ADD

In this study the Geonetwork is purposively selected and implemented as a client-server GIS solution for two reasons: (1) to facilitate local data sharing in form word, excel and portable documents files (2) to facilitate sharing of spatial data locally as one way to motivate staff members to use GIS applications. The Geonetwork server has been centrally installed on the Dell Edge server computer, in the IT office at Mzuzu ADD. When spatial data is uploaded, the application allows users to interactively interact with it. The uploaded data is overlaid over a global map. Users can zoom in/out, pan, adjust opacity and print the map by selecting the desired area of interest.

Apart from directly uploading spatial data and documents, data can be harvested to the application. Data harvesting is when a Geonetwork is configured to obtain data from Geoserver, another Geonetwork node or a spatially enabled DBMS. A Geoserver can be on the same computer as the Geonetwork it can also be on a remote computer. The Geonetwork used in this study comes embedded with Geoserver. This means that installing Geonetwork on the Dell Edge server computer automatically installs Geoserver on it.

In order to harvest data from another Geonetwork node, Geoserver or a DBMS one must have credentials and Universal Resource Locator (URL) address to access these resources. Data harvesting on a Geonetwork can be configured to periodically check for updates from the data sources. This is to ensure that changes made from the sources are periodically reflected on the harvesting Geonetwork node.

As a catalogue before uploading or harvesting data, Geonetwork requires users to clearly describe what is to be uploaded/shared. The information about data to be uploaded is called metadata. Among other things, metadata requires users to give the following information about the data being uploaded name, date of creation, owner of data, brief description stating what the data is about. The information provided helps in searching data and also for users to see the relevance of the data.

A user can only log in if the user exists in the Geonetwork. When creating a user, a role must be specified for the user and a group to which the user belongs. Roles of the user are: (1) Editor - create, import, and edit metadata records within its own group; (2) Registered User - view metadata records that they have access right to; (3) Content Reviewer - create, import, and edit metadata records within its own group; (4) User Administrator - create, import, and edit metadata records, transfer ownership, and user management for its own group; and (5) Geonetwork Administrator - super user having unlimited access to the application.

In this study all departments of Mzuzu ADD are created as groups (see Fig. 1). Thus the 10 groups are Crops, Extension, Land Resources, Veterinary, Finance, Planning, Human Resources, Office of Superintendent, Workshop, and Building. This study revealed that data authorization at departmental level and outside a department does not necessarily require authorization from head of department. To this effect all users were configured with a role of Content Reviewer.

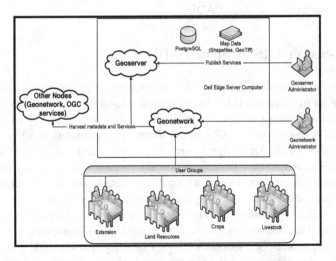

Fig. 1. Institutional client-server GIS prototype at Mzuzu ADD

The user configured as a Geonetwork Administrator harvests data from Geoserver, other Geonetwork and geospatial enabled database. Harvesting can be configured to check for changes or new data periodically. In this study harvesting is only from one source, the Geoserver.

All users, except a user with the role of registered user, in web browser from a client can upload data to Geonetwork. The following can be uploaded: word documents, Excel documents, and PDF. When data has been uploaded it is assigned the privileges which are on group basis and include downloading, viewing data in an interactive map, and editing data. Viewing data in an interactive map enables users to overlay data from different sources.

The access privileges assigned to data ensures that data is available to a particular desired group of users. In addition to user credentials, data access privileges are a control of who has access to a particular data.

5 Implication of Institutional Client-Server GIS Application

Implementation of a client-server GIS application requires a workforce that has at least basic skills in computer usage and that is willing to share data. When sharing data adequate information about the data need to be provided for people viewing the data to quickly see the relevance of the data. With a client-server GIS application like Geonetwork, the workforces that exist in the technical departments (Land Resources, Crops, Extension and Livestock) suffice in availing spatial and non-spatial data for sharing across Mzuzu ADD despite the need for further training on the capabilities of a computer and in GIS. However, the application requires an administrator.

The administrator must be knowledgeable in database management, networking and general system management which involves user management, local integration of the Geonetwork with locally available desktop GIS application and spatial enable database. The administrator must be resourceful in identifying remote Geonetwork nodes and databases to have a rich resource of spatial data available for the institution. The organizational policies and structure are not affected in any way at the inception of a client-server GIS application, in fact they are reinforced.

A user of a client-server GIS application like Geonetwork can be configured as an editor, registered user, content reviewer, user administrator, Geonetwork administrator. A user administrator can be the head of the department as in case of Mzuzu ADD. The head of the department can appoint personnel within the department to publish departmental data (content reviewer) or departmental members who can just view the data available in the Geonetwork. The departmental data can be configured to allow other departments to view, download or edit it by the content reviewer.

Client-server GIS application has the following technological implications for an institutional; centralized data storage, reliable network, installation of desktop GIS application, and linking to other spatial data providers. The client-server GIS application must be implemented with a centralized repository which should be readily available for access, i.e., it should be on a computer that should be on all the time. Computers that can stand up time several hours are computers with high processing power, like server computers. These computers should also allow multi user concurrent access.

If implemented on an intermittent local area network, users are de-motivated to use the application. Spatial data is usually a couple of mega bytes in size, which requires a fast network connection to be downloaded or viewed. To use the downloaded spatial data users must have desktop GIS installed on their computers. Desktop GIS application range from viewers like ArcView, which enable users to view the data they have downloaded to complete GIS applications like QGIS which enables users to edit, analyze and model the spatial data which has been downloaded.

For the institutional client-server GIS application to be useful it needs to have plenty of spatial data available to its users. The data can be provided by the users themselves but also the application can be configured to harvest data from remote computers. At Mzuzu ADD, there is a large amount of spatial data from the technical departments. Geonetwork can be configured to get data from other Geonetwork nodes and spatial enabled databases.

Couple of challenges associated with Geonetwork is identified. Firstly, Geonetwork provides a platform for data sharing through harvesting, uploading and downloading of data, but the harvested data cannot be directly downloaded and used in another GIS application. Secondly, Geonetwork being the cataloguing software, users use metadata templates to describe resources they have uploaded, these metadata are long. Thirdly, in this study, coupling the possibilities of Geonetwork and user competency in computers was not an easy fit. For most participants when on computer, they are writing an important document on Microsoft word thus leaving no room to try out possibilities of new applications.

When data has been harvested and made available to users, the data cannot be downloaded in shape files for use with other GIS software. A map in the harvested data can only be viewed in an interactive map in Geonetwork or downloaded and be viewed in Google map on a computer or the map can be printed as PDF and used in a report. The maximum file size that can be uploaded is 50 Mb, yet geospatial data, especially raster data tend to be more than 50 Mb which resulted in failure to upload some files into client-server GIS application at Mzuzu ADD.

When uploading data, Geonetwork has a choice of templates from which users can choose for filling the metadata. Most templates have many fields that are required to be filled. This proved to be a challenge in this study. Respondents wished if only there were asked to give a name and brief description of the data uploaded. Neither the manual nor the help from the application fully describes what each template is for and how different it is from the others. Users have to make an intelligent guess on their use.

In this study it was found that most respondents are not competent enough in operating computers. Most research participants had QGIS installed on their computers. This was done at one point when the department of Land Resources organized a one week GIS workshop for all departments. From this study, none of the trainees used QGIS after the training. Most respondents felt they are too busy to start experimenting on new application.

After implementing Geonetwork, users were trained on how to access it, upload and download data from it. Although research participants were trained how to upload and download data from Geonetwork, the results show that few changes was made on upload of data in three weeks of observation. Geonetwork did not give provision to monitor who has logged in and what activities they have been doing whilst logged in. The only way to notice user activity was when data was uploaded.

6   Conclusion

The aim of this research was to identify implications that can arise in introducing an institutional GIS client-server application over stand-alone GIS applications. Internally improved ICT can potentially enhance and strengthen an organizational infrastructure by increasing the efficiency of information sharing between departments and staff.

It was believed that client-server application would be an improved ICT system for Mzuzu ADD as far as GIS usage is concerned and it was proved true. But still there is a good number of issues that should considered when implementing the institutional client-server GIS at a particular institution or organisation like Mzuzu ADD. Some of the considerations include computing skills, user training, software, hardware, network infrastructure, data standards and integration, data accessibility and so on.

Implementation of a client-server GIS application requires a workforce that has at least basic skills in computer usage and that is willing to share data. When sharing data adequate information about the data need to be provided for people viewing the data to quickly see the relevance of the data.

References

1. Aalders, H., Moellering, H.: Spatial data infrastructure. In: Proceedings of the 20th International Cartographic Conference, pp. 2234–2244, Beijing, China (2001). http://www.gdmc.nl/publications/2001/Spatial_data_infrasructure.pdf. Accessed 23 August 2012
2. Roy, A. et al.: Arc India News ESRI India Magazine 1(3) (2007) www.esriindia.com
3. Deng, M., Di, L.: Building an online learning and research environment to enhance use of geospatial data. Int. J. Spat. Data Infrastruct. Res. 4, 77–95 (2009)
4. Eldrandaly, K.: Expert Systems Research Trends. Nova Science Publishers, New York (2007)
5. Fine, A.H.: Evaluating the Impact of information technology. Innovation Network, INC (2003). www.innonet.org
6. Harrison, G.W., List, J.A.: Field experiments. J. Econ. Lit. 42(4), 1009–1055 (2004)
7. Jankowski, P., Nyerges, T.: Geographic Information Systems for Group Decision Making. Taylor and Francis Group, London (2001)
8. Janssens, W., Kramer, B.: The social dilemma of microinsurance A framed field experiment on free-riding and coordination in microcredit groups (2012)
9. Jha, M.K., Chowdary, V.M.: Challenges of using remote sensing and GIS in developing nations. Hydrogeol. J. 15(1), 197–200 (2006)
10. Jones, M.: Mobile Interaction Design. Wiley, Chichester (2006)
11. Lee, B.-L., Kim, Y.-C., Yun, J.-I.: Web interface for GIS in agriculture. Paper by the Asian federation for information technology in agriculture, pp. 107–111. (1998)
12. Longley, P.A., et al.: Geographical Information Systems and Science, 2nd edn. Wiley, New York (2005)
13. Mathew, D.: Information Technology and public health management of disasters—a model for south asian countries. Prehospital Disaster Med. 20(1), 54–60 (2004)
14. Nelson, M.R., et al.: Applications of geographic information systems and geostatistics in plant disease epidemiology and management. Plant Dis. 83(4), 308–319 (1999)
15. Pierce, F.J., Clay, D.: GIS Application in Agriculture. Taylor & Francis Group, Boca Raton (2007)
16. Rybaczuk, K.Y.: GIS as an aid to environmental management and community participation in the Negril Watershed, Jamaica. Comput. Environ. Urban Syst. 25(2), 141–165 (2001)
17. Tanser, F.C., le Sueur, D.: The application of geographical information systems to important public health problems in Africa. International journal of health geographics 1, 4 (2002)
18. Wisse, E.: Earth Observation Acceptance by GIS Users. Vrije Universiteit Amsterdam, Amsterdam (2006)
19. Sharp, H., Preece, J., Rogers, Y.: Interaction Design: Beyond Human Computer Interaction, 2nd edn. Wiley, Chichester (2007)

Electricity Theft in Kampala and Potential ICT Solutions

Ruth Mbabazi Mutebi[1], Julianne Sansa Otim[1(✉)],
Richard Okou[1], and Ben Sebitosi[2]

[1] Makerere University, Kampala, Uganda
{rmbabazi,sansa}@cit.ac.ug, richardokou@yahoo.com
[2] StellenBosch University, Stellenbosch, South Africa
sebitosi@sun.ac.za

Abstract. Electricity theft is the main source of non-technical losses in electricity distribution utilities. This paper presents data from an ongoing research to study the causes of electricity theft in Kampala, Uganda and people's response to the efforts being made to reduce it. Our study reveals that electricity theft in Kampala is largely due to economic reasons and corruption within the utility company. It confirms that people perceive electricity theft as the utility's problem and are not willing to report electric theft suspects. We propose ICT technologies to encourage consumer participation in reducing electricity theft.

Keywords: Energy · Electricity distribution · Electricity theft · Non-technical losses · ICT · Mobile applications · Consumer participation

1 Introduction

Electricity distribution utility companies world over are grappling with electricity theft [1–6]. Due to electricity theft, utilities are losing an estimated $25 billion annually [2], with some being driven to bankruptcy [1, 3]. Electricity theft makes it difficult for the utilities to plan for the grid leading to power black outs [2]. The unavailability and irregularity of power caused by an unstable grid slows down the economy because industries and businesses cannot operate profitably [7, 8], and in some cases, public services like transportation, telecommunication and health cannot function normally. In addition, innocent lives are lost due to fires and electrocution brought about by unprotected illegal connections and unprofessional electrical terminations [9, 10].

Electricity theft is complex problem that requires thorough study [1, 11]. In this paper we present our findings on a study of electricity theft in Kampala, Uganda and make some recommendations. The rest of this paper is organized as follows: in Sect. 2 we briefly highlight the problem and efforts towards reducing it. Section 3 mentions related work, while Sect. 4 explains the study approach. In Sect. 5 we present the findings of the research which we briefly discuss in Sect. 6. Section 7 contains the recommendations and we conclude in Sect. 8.

© Institute for Computer Sciences, Social Informatics and Telecommunications Engineering 2015
A. Nungu et al. (Eds.): AFRICOMM 2014, LNICST 147, pp. 198–206, 2015.
DOI: 10.1007/978-3-319-16886-9_21

2 Problem Definition

Theft of electricity in Uganda is a problem resulting into losses of $30 million annually for UMEME Ltd, the main electricity distribution utility [12]. The utility company launched a campaign against electricity theft, starting with installation of prepaid meters [13] and aerial bundle conductors in 2011, and media campaigns in 2013 to 2014. The media campaigns through radio, television and billboards, lasting for six months to one year, encouraging people to desist from stealing electricity and to report suspects. The installation of prepaid meters and aerial bundled conductors will go on until 2018 [14]. Additionally, efforts are being made to tighten the laws against electricity theft [15]. Given the complex nature of the factors that lead to electricity theft, Smith [1] recommends that before any action is taken against electricity theft it is crucial that the problem be understood and a multi-disciplinary approach taken. This research was undertaken to understand the reasons why Kampala residents engage in electricity theft and therefore design additional approaches to curb it.

3 Related Work

Previous work has been done to identify factors that lead to electricity theft, focusing on one or two factors at a time. Smith [1] related electricity theft to governance and corruption and found that electricity theft is a major problem in countries with weak structures and poor governance. Steadman [3] considered the connection between electricity theft, economic factors and crime. Her work reveals that demand for electricity stays the same regardless of the price and that electricity theft is higher when the cost of living is high than when it is low. Mimmi et al. [16] studied the socio-economic factors that lead to theft in the peri-urban slum dwellers of Brazil. They find that the quality of power supply and feelings of being discriminated against by the utility, lack of access to electricity connections, home businesses and poor energy efficiency practices all contribute to electricity theft. Winther [6] looked at the relational nature of the problem and found that people were forced to comply to payment of electricity bills due to fear of social pressure rather than technology and formal law. Faisal and Ahmed [5] carried out an economic investigation of electricity theft and concluded that people only steal electricity if the perceived benefits are more than the risks.

4 Methodology

We conducted a descriptive research to understand electricity theft from the consumers' perspectives. Random stratified sampling was used to ensure that we capture a representative sample of domestic and commercial consumers. Industrial consumers where not willing to participate so they were left out. Electricity theft is a sensitive issue and we feared that respondents would become suspicious thinking we are spies from the utility company. Consequently, we feared that asking respondents whether or not they had participated in electricity theft would make them defensive. Therefore we reasoned that since the reasons that would make someone consider stealing electricity are the same reasons that would cause someone to actually do it, we interviewed respondents as potential electricity thieves, regardless of whether they had done it before or not. We also asked respondents to report actual cases of electricity theft bearing in mind that these could be their own cases. Fortunately we were able to get some respondents who where open enough to admit that they had done it. The main data collection tool was a survey questionnaire that had a mixture of open ended and closed question. For an entire population of 331,337 consumers in Kampala, we used a margin of error of 5 %, a confidence interval of 95 %, and a response distribution of 50 %, the sample size was 384 [17]. Here we present results from 167 respondents.

Of the167 consumers that participated in the research, 60 % where domestic consumers while 40 % were commercial. Among the domestic consumers, 61 % had prepaid meters, and 31 % had ordinary meters while the commercial consumers had an equal number of prepaid and ordinary meters. 61 % of the respondents were male while were 39 % female.

5   Findings

We presented respondents with some of the reasons for electricity theft based on literature, asking them to tick all the reasons they find applicable. Figure 1 shows their responses. The Y-axis shows the percentage of respondents who ticked a particular reason. The significant reasons from left to right on the X- axis, are lack of money, high electricity tariffs, corruption within the utility, weak laws against electricity theft. Other reasons included ignorance, arrogance and the opinion that the previous utility had more affordable electricity.

The respondents were presented some attitudes of people while they are using illegal electricity and we asked which one they agreed with, ticking all applicable. The responses presented in Fig. 2 with the Y-axis representing the percentage and X-axis the attitudes. 50 % selected "why should I pay if I can avoid it", "Some people do it and

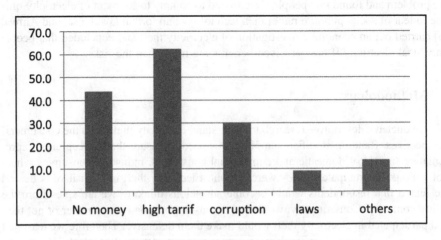

Fig. 1. Motivations for electricity theft

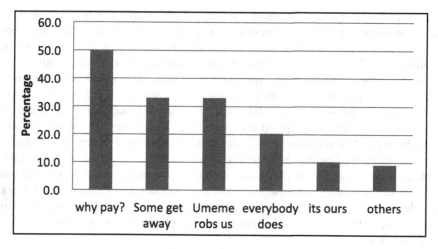

Fig. 2. Attitudes that encourage electricity theft

get away with it" and "UMEME robs us so we should rob them too" each had 33 %.
20 % agreed with "Everybody is doing it" and 10 % "it is our electricity why pay?"
while 9 % had other responses.

We asked respondents who bears the cost for stolen electricity. 40 % respondents
think that the cost is only borne by the utility, 28 % by paying consumers and 22 %
think the cost is shared by the utility and the consumers. These results are represented
in Fig. 3A.

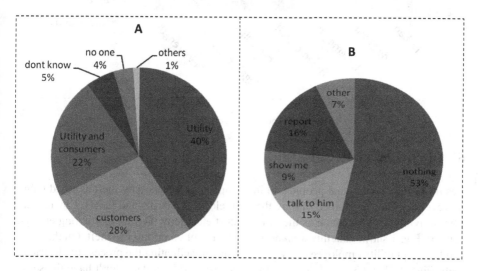

Fig. 3. A shows the responses to who bears the cost of electricity and 3B has the reactions in
case of knowledge of electricity theft.

Like earlier mentioned, we wanted to know how effective the utility's efforts to encourage the public to report cases of theft were. Therefore we asked them what they would do in case they saw their neighbor stealing electricity. 53.4 % said they would do nothing, 16.2 % they would report to the authorities, 14.4 % would talk to the person taking the illegal electricity advising them to stop, 9.0 % would ask to be shown how to do the same and 7.2 % other reactions. These are shown in Fig. 3B.

Lastly, on a scale of 0–5 where; 0 is totally disagree, 5 is totally agree, we asked the respondents how much they agreed with statements concerning their attitude towards electricity theft, their relationship with the utility and the legal system as pertains to electricity theft. We find that 59 % totally agree that illegal use of electricity is a bad habit. 54 % totally agree that utility staff are major contributor to electricity theft and 51 % are sure the utility's campaign against theft will not compel them report illegal use. Much as 42 % are aware of the legal consequences of illegal use, 46 % totally disagree that the law is strong enough to prevent people from stealing electricity. These are shown in Fig. 4.

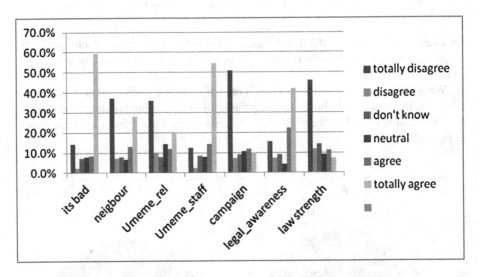

Fig. 4. Responses to general attitudes.

6 Discussion of Results

Results in Fig. 4 show that people within Kampala view electricity theft as a bad habit, however that they are forced into by the high electricity tariffs and the ever increasing cost of living (Fig. 1). Much as the laws against electricity theft are not strong enough (Fig. 4), Fig. 1 shows that this weakness is not a major contributor to theft. On the other hand, corrupt utility employees play a major role in facilitating the process of electricity theft (Figs. 1, 2 and 3). Additionally, Fig. 3 shows that Ugandans don't have the sense of entitlement to electricity as was the case in South Africa [18], and just as trust in the authority's fairness has been found to be a great factor in tax compliance [19, 20], it is also a factor here albeit to a small degree.

Quantification of the cost of electricity theft to both the consumers and the utility is critical for electricity theft reduction. This estimation requires accurate calculation of technical and non technical losses and then a clear identification of all the sources of electricity theft. A report on a study of energy losses [21] placed the 2009 technical losses at 15.1 % and thus concluded that the non technical loss for 2010 which had a total loss of 30 % was 14.9 %. As of September 2014, total energy losses were at 21.6 % from 24.3 % in 2013 [22]. Preliminary findings suggest that in 2012, a 1 % loss cost the country 12 billion Uganda shillings [23]. This study is still ongoing and more definitive results on the economic impact of o electricity theft will be published in a subsequent report.

Whereas the cost of electricity theft is borne by both the utility and consumers [11], the consumers tend to perceive it as only the utility's problem as evidenced by their unwillingness to report theft. Those who were not willing to report thought it was none of their business, or feared the wrath of the neighbors, or did not want to affect their relationships. Others simply wondered what they would stand to benefit from reporting.

7 Proposed System

The utility company is making progress in fighting electricity theft, however more could be achieved if consumers where more involved. Indeed Winther [6] and Faisal and Jamil [5] advocate that a bottom-up approach that relies on the public to curb the problem is needed. Since this research has revealed that consumers are reluctant to report theft, we recommend the following interventions that hopefully might result into increased consumer participation:

(i) **Communicating the Cost of electricity theft to consumers:** In order to generate public interest in electricity theft we recommend that the cost of theft to consumers be made explicit. Studies have shown that display of consumption information on home display units of smart metering consumers, results into efficient energy use [17]. We hope that if the predicted increase in tariffs based on prevailing levels of theft is communicated via SMS or as part of phone application, consumers will see the need to report theft.

(ii) **Applications for collecting theft tips:** Utility companies need applications to effectively collect and manage electricity theft tips. These could take the form of a web and smart phone applications. These applications will provide consumers with a template of the necessary information required.

(iii) **Applications for evaluating and managing electricity theft tip information:** Electricity tips will generate a huge amount of data that would need to be stored and managed by a database. Additionally, tips are prone to being inaccurate and the utilities usually have no way of selecting which tip is true or false. There is a need for an intelligent decision support system that supports the utility in deciding which tips to follow up on. This will reduce wastage of resources on inaccurate tips.

For the aforementioned interventions to be achieved a system for electricity theft monitoring is needed. We propose a system to proactively engage consumers in reporting electricity theft by:

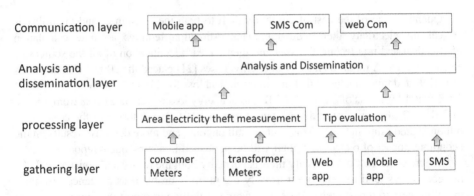

Fig. 5. High-level architecture of proposed system

- Communicating to consumers the electricity lost through electricity theft in their locality and its cost implication in terms of tariff increase.
- Providing user friendly platforms for consumers to report electricity theft, corruption by utility employees, and other performance issues like power black outs.
- Monitoring the trend of electricity theft, number of tips, the accuracy and usefulness of tips, and quality power supplied.

The system shown in Fig. 5, has a four layer architecture that consists of :

1. Information gathering layer: This has the field equipment for measuring electricity consumption at both consumer premises and transformer. It also has consumer applications for reporting electricity theft suspects, utility electricity theft related corruption, electricity supply complaints.
2. Information processing layer: process information from the meters and tips. It is at this layer that electricity theft is measured and the accuracy of tips provided is ascertained.
3. Information analysis and dissemination layer: It combines all the information, analyses and generates reports. In addition it customizes messages for communication on the three platforms; smart phone application, website and SMS.
4. Communication layer: this layer is ensures that there is feedback to consumers by ensuring that communication is passed on by SMS, on the website and the smart phone application.

8   Conclusion

Understanding what causes electricity theft is very crucial if a lasting solution is to be got. In this paper we have studied electricity theft in Kampala, Uganda and have found that electricity theft in Kampala is largely due to economic reasons and corruption within the utility company. We have also highlighted some of the utility's efforts and discussed public response to them. We find that, people consider electricity theft as the utility's problem and are not willing to co-operate. To increase the public's involvement in curbing electricity theft, we propose a system and provide it's high-level architecture. The proposed system is based on making the cost of electricity theft explicit to the consumers, improving transparency between utility and consumer, provision of user friendly platforms of communication and ensuring the tips provide accurate information. An in-depth study of the utility efforts is still ongoing; the findings will be used to improve upon the proposed system.

Acknowledgements. The researchers are grateful for the funding provided by the Makerere University-SIDA Bi-Lateral partnership 2010–2014, through the Gender Main steaming directorate.

References

1. Smith, T.B.: Electricity theft: a comparative analysis. Energy Policy **32**, 2067–2076 (2004)
2. Depuru, S.S., Wang, L., Devabhaktuni, V.: Electricity theft: overview, issues, prevention and a smart meter based approach to control theft. Energy Policy **39**, 1007–1015 (2011)
3. Steadman, K.U.: Electricity Theft in Jamaica. State University of New York, Binghamton (2009)
4. Gulati, M., Rao, M.: Corruption in the electricity sector: a pervasive scourge. In: Campos, J., Pradhan, S. (eds.) The Many Faces of Corruption: Tracking Vulnerabilities at the Sector Level, pp. 114–157. The World Bank, Washington, DC (2007)
5. Faisal, J., Ahmad, E.: An Economic Investigation of Corruption and Electricity Theft Islamabad (2013)
6. Winther, T.: Electricity theft as a relational issue: a comparative look at Zanzibar, Tanzania, and the Sunderban Islands. India. Energy Sustain. Dev. **16**, 111–119 (2012)
7. Golden, M., Min, B.: Theft and Loss of Electricity in an Indian State (2012)
8. Han, G., Luo, W.: A Novel Technique for Preventing Current Method, 5–7 (2010)
9. Blumenthal, R.: A retrospective descriptive study of electrocution deaths in Gauteng, South Africa: 2001–2004. Burns **35**, 888–894 (2009)
10. Taylor, A.J., McGwin, G., Brissie, R.M., Rue, L.W., Davis, G.G.: Death during theft from electric utilities. Am. J. Forensic Med. Pathol. Off. **24**, 173–176 (2003)
11. Steadman, K.U.: Essay on Electricity Theft. State University of New York, Binghamton (2011)
12. Ssekika, E.: Uganda loses Shs 76bn annually to power theft: The Observer, Kampala, Uganda (2013). http://observer.ug
13. Kasita, I.: UMEME starts pre-paid power billing. The New Vision, Kampala (2011). http://www.newvision.co.ug
14. LADU, I.M.: Umeme to install 16,000 pre-paid meters. Daily Monitor, Kampala (2014). http://www.monitor.co.ug
15. Muneza, S.: Umeme Seeks Help To Cut Electricity Theft. The Red pepper, Kampala, Uganda (2014). http://www.redpepper.co.ug
16. Mimmi, L.M., Ecer, S.: An econometric study of illegal electricity connections in the urban favelas of Belo Horizonte. Brazil Energy Policy **38**, 5081–5097 (2010)
17. Sample size calculator. http://www.surveysystem.com/sscalc.html
18. Johnson, R.W.: Not so close to their hearts: an investigation into the non-payment of rents, rates and service charges in South Africa's towns and cities. Johannesburg (1999)

19. Kastlunger, B., Lozza, E., Kirchler, E., Schabmann, A.: Powerful authorities and trusting citizens: the Slippery Slope Framework and tax compliance in Italy. J. Econ. Psychol. **34**, 36–45 (2013)
20. Wahl, I., Kastlunger, B., Kirchler, E.: Trust in authorities and power to enforce tax compliance: an empirical analysis of the ' Slippery Slope Framework. Law Policy **32**, 383–406 (2010)
21. P. B. A. (PTY) L. (PB) : Umeme distribution loss study, Kampala, Uganda (2013)
22. Businge, J.: Umeme, DFCU Fortunes. The Independent, Kampala (2014)
23. Wesonga, N.: Umeme in Bid to Reduce Power Distribution Losses. Daily Monitor, Kampala (2012)

Access to Information

Availability and Use of ICT in Rural Areas: The Case of Bunda District in Tanzania

Amos Nungu[✉]

Computer Studies Department, Dar Es Salaam Institute of Technology,
P.O.Box 2958, Dar Es Salaam, Tanzania
amosnungu@dit.ac.tz

Abstract. The Millennium Development Goals (MDGs) have been streamlined into policy and strategy frameworks of most Countries, Tanzania included. At national level, most countries has made good progress on several MDGs targets. Tanzania is considered to be off-track with regard to the eradication of extreme poverty and hunger which is MDG one. Thus, it has embarked on the MDGs Acceleration Framework (MAF) initiatives to develop a nationally owned MDGs acceleration action plan to speed up progress towards a specific MDG target that is otherwise unlikely to be met by 2015.

This study was carried out with two broad aims: mapping availability and use of ICT in rural areas; and ICTs impact on, and contribution to peoples life. The primary focus of the study was to develop a better understanding related to availability, access and the usage extent, challenges, and the impact of ICTs and associated infrastructure and services in rural areas. To achieve its objective, the study used literature review and field survey through questionnaires, interviews and focus group discussions. The results of the study indicates that primary school is the highest level of education, agriculture was the main economic activity, more than half of respondents have an income per month below 30 USD, majority use mobile phones as a communication tool, and public gatherings are the most effective communication means. ICT services on the livelihood was reported to bring positive changes at various levels in the society.

Keywords: Rural areas · ICT4D · Livelihood · Agriculture

1 Introduction

Tanzania is one of 189 countries which endorsed the Millennium Development Goals (MDGs) in September 2000 [1]. Most countries mainstreamed the MDGs into all policy and strategy frameworks. At national level Tanzania has made good progress on several MDGs targets including those related to primary education, gender equality, child mortality, HIV prevalence and access to drinking water and sanitation in urban areas. It is however considered to be off-track with regard to the eradication of extreme poverty and hunger which is MDG number one [2].

© Institute for Computer Sciences, Social Informatics and Telecommunications Engineering 2015
A. Nungu et al. (Eds.): AFRICOMM 2014, LNICST 147, pp. 209–218, 2015.
DOI: 10.1007/978-3-319-16886-9_22

Tanzanias slow progress in reducing extreme poverty and hunger very much relates to the low income of the poor especially in rural areas.

Agriculture in Tanzania is dominated by small-scale farmers with about 70 % of farming depending on the hand hoe. Given its role in supporting the rural poor and in reducing malnutrition, agriculture has the greatest potential of relieving the poor from extreme poverty and hunger. The sectors slow-moving growth is a result of a combination of many factors. These include poor infrastructure to support agriculture, inadequate extension services, a low level of technology of production, low value addition, lack of appropriate financing mechanisms for agriculture, an unreliable market, unfair and uncompetitive farm gate prices, and environmental degradation.

With about 80 % of the poor living in rural areas [3], promoting agricultural productivity and income generating opportunities in these areas is a priority. National strategies and policies such as MKUKUTA II [4] and KILIMO KWANZA [5] are the primary vehicle to take forward the implementation of the relevant interventions.

The paper is divided into five sections: The second section is providing the background information, objectives and motivation for the study. Methodology used in this study is covered in the third section while fourth section is about research findings and analysis, reporting on the current situation on the ground, demographic and general information, available ICT Infrastructure, ICT access and usage, available services, Impact of ICT on peoples life, and application of ICT in Agriculture. The Last section is about conclusions and recommendations for this study.

2   Background Information

The background information provided include the information about Bunda District, the MDG acceletaion framework, and the objective of the study.

2.1   Bunda District

Bunda District is among the six councils in Mara region. The District has an area of about 3,080 Km^2, of which water occupies an area of 200 km^2 and land is 2,888 km^2. For the land resources, about 480 km^2 is within the Serengeti national park and the rest is agricultural land, grazing land, settlements and forests. The population size in Bunda District is estimated to be 335,061, of which 150,461 or 48.4 % and 172,820 or 51.6 % are male and female respectively [3].

The economy of the Bunda district is mainly depending on three sectors, namely agriculture, fishery and livestock. Other important sectors for the economy are business and tourism on a small scale. Agriculture is one of the economic bases and provides food, employment and income. Agriculture, livestock and fisheries employs more than 81 % of the total residents and other sectors employ about 19 %. It was reported in the Poverty Human Development Report 2005 [6] that about 67.7 % of the district population was below the national basic needs poverty line.

2.2 MDG Acceleration Framework (MAF)

In 2011 Tanzania embarked on the Milleniun Development Goals Acceleration Framework (MAF) [7]. The MAF initiatives helps governments to develop a nationally owned MDGs acceleration action plan to speed up progress towards a specific MDG target that is otherwise unlikely to be met by 2015 [10]. The Tanzania MAF identifies challenges and bottlenecks specifically on 'hunger and poverty (MDG 1), with hunger and nutrition as priority. MAF was piloted in rural districts of Bukoba (Kagera region) and Bunda (Mara region) to leverage on the previous project "Access To Information" (ATI) [8] by the UNDP and SNV (Netherlands Development Organisation), which focused on the localization of MDGs by improving information demand and supply in local governance.

The UNDP has funded MAF activities in 2012 as a follow-up to the ATI funding of 2008. The MAF process has created Agricultural Information Resource Centers (AIRCs), equipping them with various ICT resources to facilitate easy access and dissemination of information. In Bunda District, there are four established AIRCs located in: Bunda town, Kibara ward, Kisorya ward and Mgeta ward. These centers are equipped with a computer, a Printer, a TV, and a DVD player. Bulk SMS services have been introduced by MAF in the four AIRCs where the extension officer (AIRC Manager) is using this service to send out information to beneficiaries. There is no impact report yet as this service is still new.

The Kibara, Kisorya, and Mgeta AIRCs use modem from Vodacom mobile operator for Internet connectivity. Also, both Centers are housed in the Ward (government) office building. The Center Manager is the ward extension officer who is also using the center as his/her office. The Bunda town AIRC is located in the same office as the *Third Millennium Peace Initiative Foundation (a local NGO)*, who are the local implementing partners of MAF project. This AIRC is operated by TMPI themselves.

2.3 Objective of the Study

This study was designed with two broad aims: (1)mapping availability and use of ICT in rural areas; and (2) ICT's impact on and contribution to peoples' life. Hence, the primary focus of the research was to develop a better understanding related to availability, access and usage extent, challenges, and the impact of ICTs and associated infrastructure and services in rural areas. Within the first broad aim of mapping availability and the use of ICT in rural areas, the following research questions were asked:

1. What kind of ICTs is used and/or available in these rural areas?
2. What ICT infrastructure exists and/or is used at the community level?
3. Which ICTs are mostly used in these rural areas and why?
4. How are ICTs used in general and specifically for agriculture service delivery and other closely related sectors such as education and health?
5. How are different groups using ICTs in these rural areas?

6. What strategies are in place to enhance the effective use of ICT in rural communities?
7. What are the problems and challenges when accessing and using ICTs?

For the purposes of this study, ICTs are defined as technologies that facilitate communication and the capturing, processing, storing and transmission of information by electronic means. This definition encompasses the full range of ICTs including radio, television, telephones (fixed and mobile), computers and the Internet.

3   Methodology

Findings from this survey are based on data collected through semi-structured close ended and open ended questionnaires which were administered to respondents in the field. There are also in-depth qualitative data based on Focus Group Discussions (FGDs) with different groups of respondents. Both quantitative information and qualitative information were thus collected and the analysis takes into account the interplay of data from the multiple sources.

The study area was Bunda district where a total of 77 respondents were selected for interview and focus group discussion. Out of the 77 respondents, the questionnaire was administered to 56 villagers. The remaining are the District officers, and ward level officers Respondents were selected using purposive sampling, targeting those involved (farmers or officers) in the MAF project. The data collected was then categorized, quantified, coded and analysed using statistical package for social sciences (SPSS).

4   Findings and Analysis

4.1   Current Situation

The following was observed when studying the current situation.

Management Information Systems. Based on the information gathered from officers at the District Council, there is plenty of Management Information Systems (MIS) for upward communication from the district to the Ministries. Data is either sent via email or using a USB stick. These systems relate to financial management, human resource management, and revenue or tax collection. The various Management Information Systems reported to exist at the District Council include:

1. IFMS Integrated Financial Management System with connectivity to the national central server.
2. iTax Integrated Tax management System. It is a revenue collection system for the district.
3. PlanRep Planning and Reporting tool for Local Government Authority.

4. LGMD Local Government Monitoring Database: used to capture data from all sectors to be used in PlanRep.
5. LGHRIS Local Government Human Resource Information System.
6. HCMIS Human Capital Management Information System, also known as Rawson.
7. LRMIS Land Rent Management Information System.
8. TOMSHA Tanzania's Output Monitoring System for non-medical HIV and AIDS interventions.

Demographic and General Information. Figure 1, 2 and 3 are responses related to age-range of respondents, education level, main economic activities, and their average income per month (Tshs).

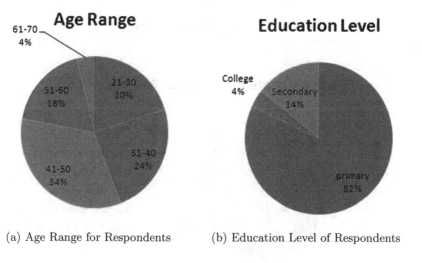

(a) Age Range for Respondents   (b) Education Level of Respondents

Fig. 1. Age and Education Level of Respondents

4.2   Available ICT Infrastructure

Though not reliable, it was noted that electricity is available in all the surveyed areas. Also, out of the current five mobile services providers (Airtel, Vodacom, Tigo, Zantel, and TTCL) in Tanzania, only TTCL is not available in those areas. Note that TTCL is the incumbet telecommunication company in Tanzania that was responsible for landline connections, it does provide mobile services nowdays.
Other ICT initiatives are:

ICT for Rural Development (ICT4RD) is a research and development project that has created a communication infrastructure (connectivity) between Bunda and Serengeti District (http://www.ict4rd.ne.tz). ICT4RD has a network

Main Economic Activities

■ Business   ■ Agriculture

■ Agriculture and Livestock ■ Agriculture and Trade

■ Employee

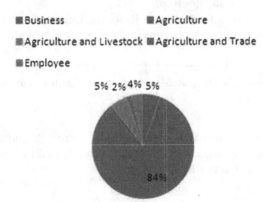

Fig. 2. Main Economic Activities

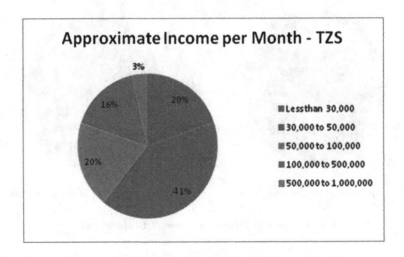

Fig. 3. Approximate Income per Month in TZS

operating Center (NOC) hosted at Bunda Tanesco plant with a server that is hosting local mail within the network [9].

Mazingira Community Radio, also known as "Mazingira FM" is operating from Nyamswa village, broadcasting societal issues as well as awareness information on HIV and AIDS. The actual coverage now is reported as 80 km radius, covering as far as Bunda district, Serengeti district, Tarime district, Butiama district, Musoma town, and Busega district. The radio is currently operating 4 hours a day due to power issues at the transmitter.

4.3   Access and Usage

Through the Focus Group Discussions, it was noted that public gatherings are the most effective communication means. These include meetings or rallies by the Member of Parliament, meetings convened by the District Commissioner, Monthly meetings by extension officers; Market; and cinema van using a generator. It was further noted that MAF has been providing basic training related to farming, poultry and fishery. Farmers visit the center to meet the extension officer, while students visit the Center to discover new information/research topics. Other stakeholders visit the Center to watch TV (news) in the evenings.

Figure 4 is a summary of the responses to the questionnaire on *"what various kinds of ICT tools they use to access and disseminate information in their daily lives"*. It is noted that Computers and "land line" phone are not used at all. Both could be explained by the level of education and income in the area.

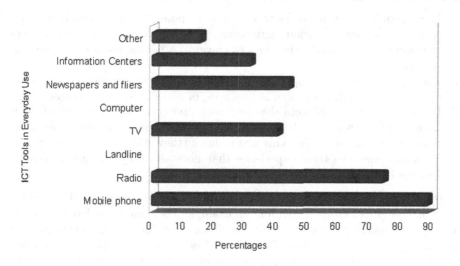

Fig. 4. ICT in Daily Use

4.4   Available Services

Since the AIRCs are still new, it was observed that available services are not yet well defined, communicated to beneficiaries, or experienced by the intended recipients.

Through the Focus Group Discussions, it was noted that AIRCs offer basic training related to agriculture and livestock keeping. Awareness campaigns are also among the services offered by the Center through the use of DVDs, banners, and other training materials. Since these Centers are also used as offices for the ward extension officer, other services offered at these Centers are normal services offered by the extension services officer.

4.5 Impact of ICT on People's Life

Another broad aim was to determine the impact of ICT services on the lives of the people at grass-roots level. Within this broad aim the following research questions were formulated:

"*Do you think access to ICTs (mobile phone, TV, newspaper, etc.) enhance your livelihood? For what purpose do you usually use ICTs tools (Mobile Phone, TV, Radio etc.)? How have ICTs mostly contributed to improving your living standards? Are ICT tools used to increase empowerment and voice of the rural poor in decisions that affect their lives? Which tools play a major role in increasing the empowerment and voice of the rural area?*"

The analysis in this part is a synthesis of quantitative data, observations, and qualitative data, gathered from the literature, questionnaires, and the focus group meetings. The impact can be grouped as follows:

Education: It was noted in various focus group discussions that

1. Local people are using ICTs to access or respond to services such as those related to higher education institutions (make applications, or access selection results). Previously, they had to travel to a nearby town with access to Internet.
2. Local people are changing ways of living after getting exposure from TVs, e.g. they are building modern houses now, or observe hygiene practises.
3. It was also noted in Mugeta that they saw a program on TV where a farmer from Manyara was able to harvest 30 bags of maize from one acre using modern farming practises. This was a shock (they still do not believe it) for them compared to their experience that normally they can get 2 bags or 15 bags if you really follow modern farming.

Agriculture: It was noted that through ICT, they are able to check and compare market prices easily. Providing an example, they made a reference to this year (2013) where they were able to establish that the cotton price provided by the "Tanzania Cotton Board" was very low compared to the world market price. Another impact is the introduction of Sunflow farming; educating and sensitization to farmers on the use of fertilizer, manure and other farm inputs after destroying the land during previous farming practices. The analysis indicates that more that 69 % of the respondents believe that the introduction of the AIRC improved their livelihood.

4.6 Challenges /Problems and Gaps in Using ICTs

When responding to the question on *challenges encountered in daily life while using ICT*, the analysis indicates that cost associated with running the mobile phone is very high. The summary provided in Fig. 5 indicate that more than 76 % indicate that high costs relate to buying credit for making phone calls as well as paying to charge (power) the mobile phones. Further, more than 14 % have indicated electricity as a challenge since they can not charge their phones at home.

Other challenges as came up during the discussions are as follows:

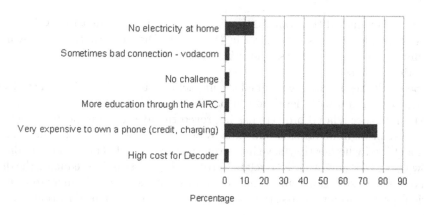

Fig. 5. ICT Challenges encountered

Policies. It has been noted that various Information Management Systems exist at the district level, usually implemented in a top down approach. Inherent challenges in this approach include the fact that the systems does not take into account the local environment, but only have a one way information flow - from district to higher authorities. One cited example was for the LGMD system where the District is supposed to send forms to VEO to fill-in before the district officers can key-in this information into the LGMD system. However, there is no budget specific for production of the forms or facilitating the data collection process.

Infrastructure. Due to lack of ict infrastructure, availability or access of the MAF or other related ICT services to all beneficiaries is not possible. Another challenge was the reliability and accessibility of electricity from national power grid. Yet another challenge noted was lack of general infrastructures such as good roads for transporting crop yields from production/field to processing/market places.

Culture. The extension officer reported a resistance to change mindset from some of the farmers, especially in adopting new ways of doing things. Some farmers are doing their farming by culture.

Poverty. It was reported that some farmers would like to adapt the modern ways of farming, but they can't afford to implement the new methodologies such as buying fertilizer. In addition to that, farmers might not follow farming advice due to a lack of capital/resources, inability to carry compost manure to the site, etc. Deforestation for charcoal was also reported as an attribute of poverty since to some, the activity is not by choice but lack of alternatives.

5   Conclusions and Recommendations

The study examined the availability, access, usage and the impact of ICT on the lives of people at grass-roots level in the Bunda District. Firstly, the research examined the extent of access and utilization of services and in particular examined the main issues.

Secondly, the research examined the impact of other ICT services on the lives of people at grass-roots level and in particular the issues such as whether the MAF and other related projects has improved the lives of rural people, whether they have brought about environmental awareness and sustainable resource management, and whether they have improved their livelihood. The research findings show that MAF and other ICT related projects have assisted in reducing the digital divide, assisted communications for rural villagers, helped farmers to receive agricultural information, assisted NGOs, and finally assisted in education-related issues.

Acknowledgments. This work was partialy supported by ESRF (MAF Project - http://www.esrftz.org/) and WiMEA-ICT Project.

References

1. United Nations - Millennium Declaration, New York
2. Accelerating Progress Towards the MDGs: Country Action Plan 2010–2015, Final Tanzania Country Report
3. National Bureau of Statistics, 2012 Population and Housing Census: Population Distribution by Administrative Areas
4. National Strategy for Growth and Reduction of Poverty II (NSGRP II), Ministry of Finance and Economic Affairs, Dar es Salaam
5. Kilimo Kwanza, Green Revolution, Dar es Salaam
6. Poverty and Human Development Report 2005, Mkuki na Nyota Publishers, Dar es Salaam
7. http://www.undg.org/content/achieving_the_mdgs/mdg_acceleration_framework
8. Milanzi, M.C., Mwisomba, S.T.: Report on Information Demand and Supply in Local Governance in Tanzania: The Case Study Of Bukoba, Bunda, Morogoro, Uyui Districts (2008)
9. Nungu, A.: Towards Sustainable Broadband Communication in Under-served Ar-eas A Case Study from Tanzania, KTH (2011)
10. Millennium Development Goals Acceleration Framework (MAF) Project-Bunda - Baseline Survey (2012)

Building an Argument for Internet Expansion in Dwesa - an Under-Serviced Rural Community in South Africa

Sifiso Dlamini[1,2(✉)], Moshe T. Masonta[1,3], and David L. Johnson[1]

[1] Council for Scientific and Industrial Research (CSIR) – Meraka,
P.O. Box 395, Pretoria 0001, South Africa
sifiso.benerd.dlamini@gmail.com,
{mmasonta,djohnson}@csir.co.za
[2] Department of Industrial Sociology and Labour Studies,
University of Pretoria, Pretoria, South Africa
[3] Department of Electrical Engineering, Tshwane University of Technology,
Pretoria, South Africa

Abstract. The purpose of this paper is to present research findings that investigate the extent of Internet usage as well as options for extending the current reach of the wireless network in Dwesa, a rural area in South Africa's Eastern Cape Province. A mix of methodologies, encompassing ethnographic and quantitative approaches, is used to study the need to expand connectivity in Dwesa and the social impact of providing Internet connection to this rural area. Our findings confirm the need to connect more areas of the Dwesa community - particularly active ICT champions and households of some stakeholders who are willing to use their homes as a central hub for other community members. We also suggest the option of running parallel network links to connect two broadband islands that exist in SLL in order to provide improved redundancy in the network, should one of the satellite links fail. The network will be expanded using wireless mesh technology. In addition, we also propose to make use of TV white space technology – wireless communication making use of unused portions of the TV spectrum – for one of the parallel links connecting the broadband islands.

Keywords: Eastern Cape · Dwesa · Internet · Rural communities · Television white spaces · Siyakhula Living Lab · South Africa

1 Introduction

Lack of sufficient fixed-line telecommunication infrastructure in rural areas, especially in developing regions such as Africa, makes wireless connectivity the only effective and affordable solution for broadband access. In the past decade, mobile penetration in Africa has been growing with an average rate of 6 % per year compared to 3.7 % in developed regions. In contrast, fixed-broadband penetration has been growing at less than 1 % in Africa compared to 27.2 % in developed regions between 2008 and 2013 [1]. Despite the growing number of global mobile subscribers - reported to be at around

© Institute for Computer Sciences, Social Informatics and Telecommunications Engineering 2015
A. Nungu et al. (Eds.): AFRICOMM 2014, LNICST 147, pp. 219–228, 2015.
DOI: 10.1007/978-3-319-16886-9_23

7 billion users [2] - the number of rural users with access to broadband Internet remain low; in 2013 16 % of the population in Africa had broadband access compared to over 75 % in Europe and 61 % in the Americas [1].

Providing broadband access or Information and Communication Technology (ICT) infrastructure to deeply marginalized rural communities remain a challenge to most governments in developing regions [3]. This is due to a complex mix of lack of technical skills (know-how), low economic activity, poor education level and a cultural disconnect with Western thinking embedded within technology and business models for Internet service provision [4]. Access to computers and Internet access in education can have a profound positive effect on the quality of education provided for a learner when coupled with sufficient computer literacy training for teachers and learners. With the current low Internet penetration rate in rural areas of South Africa and Africa, rural schools lack the ability to provide communities with access to the same quality of education experienced by their urban counterparts [5]. The Dwesa community and the Siyakhula Living Lab (SLL), studied in this paper is one successful case study of incorporating Internet access, computer labs and ICT skills development for educators and the wider community of Dwesa to improve the quality of their education and increase the level of economic activity in the area.

Purpose of the Research. The purpose of this research study was to investigate expansion of the SLL community network to other community centres (schools and clinics) and households, using alternative solutions such as the television white space (TVWS) and Wi-Fi mesh technology. The study also investigated the effects of providing Internet access to rural communities like Dwesa.

Research Methodology. A mix method approach was used in this research incorporating an ethnographic style of research, qualitative research and technical analysis. This combination of these complementary research methods resulted in a more holistic multi-disciplinary analysis of the community.

Incorporating the Ethnographic Style. The research team spent a week in Dwesa communicating with various stakeholders in the SLL project and the fact that we stayed in the community, we were in a better chance to understand the daily experiences of the people living in this community. Staying in the community enabled us to glance to some socio-economic factors shaping the lives of the Dwesa citizens and this was also helpful for analysis.

Qualitative Approach. During the research we conducted a series of interviews with various stakeholders including principals and teachers from schools, community health care workers, students attending the computer training course, and executive committee members.

Paper Outline. The remainder of this paper is arranged as follows. Section 2 briefly presents introduction of the Siyakhula Living Lab (SLL), Sect. 3 present our findings from the interviews conducted with selected community members in Dwesa community. Section 4 presents a proposed SLL community network expansion and potential benefits to the community. Section 5 analyses the societal dynamics of rural wireless networks. Section 6 concludes the paper.

2 The Siyakhula Living Lab Community Network

Siyakhula Living Lab (SLL) project is an initiation by people from the University of Fort Hare (UFH) and Rhodes University (RU) which are both situated in the Eastern cape province and both these are steering the project and are engaging with multiple governmental and industrial stakeholders in order to provide sustainable Internet access by involving the local community in the process as much as possible [6]. The notion of community engage aims at involving the community members so that the knowledge and technical knowhow of the project can be passed to the community as they will be driving the process in a long run [7]. The universities have been conducting the project in cooperation with local chiefs and communities from the beginning to instil the notion of taking ownership of the project.

The approach used in this project puts the community as the central point of project direction as the main beneficiaries of the project. For example, the committee composed of active community members have common meetings where they decide who is going to be in charge for a certain part of the maintenance, and when and where should the training take place.

The SLL project is run in the Dwesa region of Mbashe municipality close to the Wild Coast Dwesa-Cwebe Nature reserve and this project is run with full participation of the community and the beneficiaries are the people within the jurisdictions of the Mbashe municipality. Most of the community members own mobile (smart) phones, and only few of the community members own laptops (especially the working class such as teachers and principals). The people of Dwesa subsist on government grants, some crops they grow, livestock and seafood when they can access it [6].

The SLL project is organized along the lines of the emerging Research Development and Innovation processes (RDI) Living Lab methodology of which the underlying principle is co-creation of solutions with empowered users. It demonstrates in a practical manner how marginalized rural communities that are difficult to access can be joined with the greater South African, African and global communities for the economic, social and cultural benefit of all (more information about SLL can be accessed from: www.siyakhulall.org).

3 Findings from Dwesa Community Interviews

As already alluded in the introductory section, the research was driven by three main questions, this section is meant to present findings to answer the three research questions.

3.1 Needs Assessment for Network Expansion

The study found out that there is a great need for providing Internet connection in this community and this finding is based on the responses from different stakeholders which including principals and teachers from schools, and some community members engaged including the executive committee members. Our general finding of the need to connect rural community was informed by the perception that of the schools that were already connected on the Internet, there has been extensive use of the Internet. According to the information we got from teachers and principals in the connected schools, students use the Internet for searching for past question papers, getting information for science expo projects and other educational related material. This finding shows that connecting rural schools on the Internet provides the students with the opportunity to get useful educational content on the Internet and ultimately improving the level of education for the rural schools. The advantage of connecting new schools is that it will increase the impact of the SLL project as a whole as more people in the community especially students, will have access to information through the Internet. The disadvantage is that most of the schools at Dwesa do not have computer labs; if these schools are connected it may create an expectation that the SLL project will also buy computers and build computer labs for these schools.

We also found out that connecting schools also needs to be preceded by a vigorous computer literacy and ethical Internet use program and connecting students to the Internet creates additional strain on already limited resources to carry out these programs. The consequences of not running these programs was demonstrated at one school that had an open Wi-Fi access point that was used to download large amounts of music, videos and pornography – reaching the very small aperture terminal (VSAT) of 3 gigabyte cap for the month within the first few days. Although this could be avoided with improved access control – it is better to guide students towards positive use of the Internet rather and teach them to be responsible Internet citizens than have a heavy handed dictatorial approach.

3.2 Connecting Other Schools, Clinics and Households

Our finding revealed that in connected schools students were benefiting from the Internet provided, and therefore the students in the schools which are not connected were not benefiting. This therefore means that by expanding the connection to the non-connected schools will also provide the opportunity of ICT benefits to these students and as a result creating a strong ICT platform for improving the quality of education in Dwesa.

Our finding did not only point to the need for connecting schools only, but we also found a big need to connect the clinics and other community members who were willing to use their homes as a central point for community members who want to use the Internet. When we asked the clinic personnel if their scope of work or that of their colleagues requires the use of Internet they all responded by saying there is a very serious need for clinics to be provided with Internet connection as this will help them with their work in various ways. For example the anonymous nurse at Gwadu clinic mentioned that they deal with statistics and ART treatments, therefore if they can be connected to the Internet and be provided with ICT resources like computers, then their work will be made easier. Another senior nurse at Msendo clinic also mentioned that patients sometimes come with sicknesses which they as nurses do not understand; therefore if they have access to the Internet they can "Google" the symptoms and even get knowledge on possible treatment. These clinic personnel also mentioned that they need to keep reporting the statistics to Department of Health, and since they do not have computers they have to do the work manually and submit the hard copy to the department.

If clinics can be connected there will be lots of efficiency in administrative work and record keeping. For these clinics, using ICT services and getting connected on the Internet may help the community health care workers track the records of patient's clinic attendance and medication provided to these patients. For example if a patient decides to go to another clinic, the nurse on that particular clinic may refer to the database and see what medication was last given to that particular patient. There is a very serious need to connect the clinics on the Internet.

It also came out in the interviews that in other occasions the community health workers go out door to door in order to inform the community about services. There is also the use of notes which are pasted in public areas to send the message across the community. One of the nurses also mentioned the fact that public gatherings like funerals and weddings are also used to pass messages to the community. If clinics and community members can be connected, the connection may also be used to communicate messages to different parts of the community through emails and other electronic means of passing messages.

When we asked the community health care workers about who else needs to be connected to the Internet in the Dwesa community, one community health worker said there is a need to connect the community members especially metric students.

Our findings also pointed to the need to connect community members and chiefs. However, this may be a task which will cause societal division and questions around how were the selection criteria for determining which community member should be connected. In our understanding of Dwesa as a traditional community led by a chiefs, connecting the chiefs will be the easiest way to get around the questions of how the selection criteria was decided upon. In terms of connecting other community members; only the households of executive committee members will be connected, however the requirement is for the executive committee member to allow his/her house to become a central point for community members who want to access the Internet.

3.3   The Social Impact of Providing Internet Connection to Rural Dwesa

There was no empirical evidence of social impact which was noted during this study, however, since social impact is a gradual process and observed over a period of time; there is anticipated change which is hoped to be seen with the continuous use of the Internet connectivity in Dwesa. For a community like Dwesa specifically, the anticipated social impacts are the building of an ICT information society and helping students develop 21st century skills.

Traditionally, information society is known to be a society where information flow is done through economic, cultural and political activities and these are often regarded as agents of social change. The anticipated social impact for Dwesa community is the use of ICT platform to leverage the social agents of information flow in the community.

For Dwesa, which is characterised by scarcity of resources; 21st century skills are essential for the students in this community. 21st Century skills are regarded as essential competency areas such as collaboration, digital literacy, critical thinking, and problem-solving, skills which are believed to be acquired at school. Having students with 21st century skills is another anticipated social change for the Dwesa community.

4 Proposed Network Expansion and Solutions for Dwesa Community

The existing SLL network is built based on the premise that the local communities will be responsible for the safety and use of the equipment, and that the schools would become centres that provide access to computers and the Internet [8]. However, over the past few years (especially after the year 2010) the Dwesa community is being electrified and the majority, if not all, of the members have access to the electricity grid. Furthermore, the Dwesa area has many clinics which serve the community on daily basis. Thanks to the computer literacy training offered to the community by the SLL, most of the community members (teachers, nurses and students) are computer literate and have email addresses. Therefore, the possibility of expanding the SLL network beyond the schools (to the clinics and some community leaders) seems to be realistic.

4.1 Proposed Network Expansion

The proposed network extension solution that has the potential to address the current needs in SLL and the community at large is shown in Fig. 1. A redundant link to the existing Wi-Max network is created by connecting Badi and Ngwane School. Firstly, the longest link (about 10 km), between these two schools will be created on the ultra high frequency (UHF) band especially that the WiBack supports experimental communications at 760 to 780 MHz frequency. This UHF is currently being used for television (TV) broadcasting. There have been several studies which found that the TV band is not adequately used [9–12], and hence there are initiatives to utilize portions of this unused TV band for providing broadband connectivity in rural areas [13–15]. These unused TV spectrum band is commonly known as TV white spaces or TVWS. WiBack, which stands for wireless backhaul, is a Fraunhofer Fokus technology used to provide carrier-grade service over a larger areas using low-cost wireless technology [16].

Secondly, another redundant link (to the existing Wi-Max) between Badi and Ngwane will be created on a 5 GHZ band via Mevana school's Principal, Nqabara School and then to Ngwane School. This link will allow a performance study on multi-hop links. The choice for 5 GHz band is mainly because it is comparatively cleaner and has lower signal interference when compared to the 2.4 GHz band. In addition to providing home Internet to the Principal (because of his commitment to the SLL project), the principle's home plays an important point as a repeater to link the SLL executive chairperson as well as Gwadu clinic because he is located on a high site.

Nqabara School is already connected to the existing network and also has a 2.4 GHz radio installed (in addition to the Wi-Max node). The WiBack link will be used as a redundant link to the nearby Nqabara clinic will also be connected through the 2.4 GHz Wi-Fi. The proposed expansion will not only allow the trialling of WiBack technology, but will also create opportunity for lots of interesting research, for instance

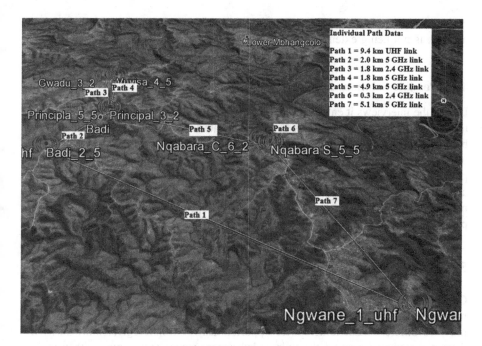

Fig. 1. Aerial view of the proposed SLL network expansion

we can study the performance of white space over 10 km, compare this with the existing WiMax and multi-hop 5 GHz. Another possibility from this proposed link is that we can add a routing rule that switches the Badi cluster to Ngwane's VSAT when the 3 Gigabyte cap is reached at Badi VSAT. Furthermore, these three installations (to the schools) do not come with any requirement from extra computers or local champions within SLL as would be the case if few schools were connected. Link profiles for the proposed WiBack network is provided in the following subsection.

4.2 Local Cloud for Community Data Storage

The study found that the majority of community members use their mobile phones to take photos but often have no way of storing these images on a computer and do not upload them to any central storage service. The community members often end up with a revolving set of best photos on their phones by deleting some photos to make room for new ones. In another interview with a data capturer (Clerk) at Ngwane school, it was found that she uses a laptop to capture the data in the school, but does not have any other means to save the data as a back-up, thus if something happens to her laptop, the entire school dataset will be lost. Providing a local cloud storage service in the community would add a large amount of value to current broadband island concept in SLL. This can be used both to back up content from people's mobile phones and laptops as well as share content freely within the local community. Backup from the local cloud to global cloud service located on the Internet could occur during periods when the network is not being extensively used such as the early hours of the morning.

4.3   Possible Solutions and Benefits for Connecting Clinics

During the interviews it emerged that the community health workers at the clinics have to use their personal cell phones to communicate to the doctor. If these clinics can be connected it would be very easy to communicate to the doctors without having to use airtime from their personal cell phones. One possible solution is to install a VoIP phone that makes use of the existing SLL wireless networks and a dial out service such as Google voice or Skype out to connect to the doctors and hospitals – a set of fixed numbers can be pre-programmed into the VoIP phone to avoid abuse of the service for personal use by clinic staff.

5   Societal Dynamics of Rural Community Networks

Connecting a rural community like Dwesa to the Internet, provides the community members with the advantage of being part of the global connected community and provides different stakeholders with opportunities for technological know-how. But there are dynamics around the unintended consequences that comes with using the Internet and the most important factor is the societal acceptance of the use of technology. Providing Internet connection to rural communities may bring unintended consequences which may shape societal attitude towards the use of technology in these communities.

During our interview with Babalwa Dudumashe known as Babes she mentioned that there were cases in the community where students were demon possessed and when the follow-up was made on the matter it was realized that these students subscribed to an Internet site where they interact with evil spirits and these spirits possessed their lives. Dwesa is a traditional and spiritual community and the Internet could be associated with negative influences in the community causing a backlash against its expansion. Connecting rural communities into the Internet brings about the need to educate these people about the ethical and responsible way of using the Internet. The consequences of not running these programs was demonstrated at one school that had an open WiFi access point that was used to download large amounts of music, videos and pornography – reaching the VSAT 3 GB cap for the month within the first few days. Although this could be avoided with improved access control – it is better to guide students and community members towards positive use of the Internet rather and teach them to be responsible Internet citizens than have a heavy handed dictatorial approach.

In conclusion, it is crucial to connect rural communities on the internet since this is one way of increasing literacy level in a community and providing a platform which has the potentiality to improve the level of education in the rural schools. However, the use of internet can bring unintended consequences like students using the internet for pornography and other unlawful exercises.

6 Conclusion

This paper presents key research findings and possible solutions for expanding SLL community network and services in Dwesa, Eastern Cape Province in South Africa. Connecting schools on the low-cost bandwidth has the potential to provide students in marginalized rural areas with an opportunity to incorporate ICT in their daily learning activities and ultimately improving the level of ICT know-how and the quality of education. However, there is a need to expand the network to community members and other community centres like the clinics. If the clinics are connected this will make the local health system work efficiently as patient information can be made electronically and easily accessible. The use of TVWS technology to expand the SLL network promises to connect more community centres and households despite the geographical setup (such as sparsely populated and mountainous topology) of Dwesa community. Future work includes the actual implementation and testing of TVWS connectivity using the Wi-Back technology.

References

1. International Telecommunications Union: The world in 2013: ICT facts and figures, ITU Telecommunications Development Bureau, Geneva, Switzerland (2013)
2. Ericson: 5G radio access: research and version, June 2013. http://www.ericsson.com/res/docs/whitepapers/wp-5g.pdf. Accessed 08 March 2014
3. Olwal, T., Masonta, M.T., Mfupe, L., Mzyece, M.: Broadband ICT policies in Southern Africa: initiatives and dynamic spectrum regulation. In: IST Africa Conference and Exhibition, Nairobi, Kenya (2013)
4. Kapuire, G.K., Winschiers-Theophilus, H., Chivuno-Kuria, S., Bidwell, N.J., Blake, E.: A revolution in ICT, the last hope for African rural communities' technology appropriation. In: 4th International Development Informatics Association Conference Exploring Success and Failure in Development Informatics: Innovations, Research and Practice, Cape Town, South Africa (2010)
5. Herselman, M.: ICT in rural areas in South Africa: various case studies. Information Science InSITE - Where Parallels Intersect, pp. 945–955 (2003)
6. Dugmore, H.: The Siyakhula Living Lab: an important step forward for South Africa and Africa. Communications & Marketing Division, Rhodes University (2012)
7. Gumbo, S., Thinyane, H., Thinyane, M., Terzoli, A., Hansen, S.: Living lab methodology as an approach to innocation in ICT4D: The Siyakhula Living Lab experience. Dar es Salaam, Tanzania (2012)
8. Dalvit, L., Siebörger, I., Thinyane, H.: The expansion of the Siyakhula Living Lab: a holistic perspective. In: Popescu-Zeletin, R., Jonas, K., Rai, I.A., Glitho, R., Villafiorita, A. (eds.) AFRICOMM 2011. LNICST, vol. 92, pp. 228–238. Springer, Heidelberg (2012)
9. Lysko, A.A., Masonta, M.T., Johnson, D., Venter, H.: FSL based estimation of white space availability in UHF TV bands in Bergvliet, South Africa. In: SATNAC (2012)
10. Patrick, G.: Radio spectrum occupancy in South Africa. EngineerIT Mag., 26–30 (2006)
11. TENET: The Cape Town TV White Spaces trial, September 2013. http://www.tenet.ac.za/tvws. Accessed 14 March 2014

12. Masonta, M.T., Johnson, D., Mzyece, M.: The white space opportunity in Southern Africa: measurements with meraka cognitive radio platform. In: Popescu-Zeletin, R., Jonas, K., Rai, I.A., Glitho, R., Villafiorita, A. (eds.) AFRICOMM 2011. LNICST, vol. 92, pp. 64–73. Springer, Heidelberg (2012)
13. Masonta, M.T., Kliks, A., Mzyece, M.: Framework for TV white space spectrum access in Southern African Development Community (SADC). United Kingdom, London (2013)
14. FCC: Unlicensed operation in the TV broadcast band. Fed. Reg. Rules Regul. **77**(96), 29256–29247 (2012)
15. Fitch, M., Nekovee, M., Kawade, S., Briggs, K., Mackenzie, R.: Wireless services provision in TV white space with cognitive radio technology: a telecom operator's perspective and experience. IEEE Commun. Mag. **49**(3), 64–73 (2011)
16. Fraunhofer Fokus: WiBack: Introducing Fraunhofer's wireless backhaul technology, March 2014. http://net4dc.fokus.fraunhofer.de/content/dam/net4dc/en/documents/140307_Whitepaper_Introducing_WiBACK.pdf. Accessed 03 July 2014

A Comparison of Four End-User Devices as Thin Clients for Public Access to the Internet in Poor Communities

Kevin Duff, Ingrid Siebörger[✉], and Alfredo Terzoli

Department of Computer Science, Rhodes University,
P.O. Box 94, Grahamstown 6140, South Africa
slottler@gmail.com, {i.sieborger,a.terzoli}@ru.ac.za

Abstract. In poor areas, where ICT infrastructure is being deployed with developmental aims, there is a need to provide appropriate, sustainable technologies that meet the needs of the local community. Current trends for ICT interventions favour the use of mobile user equipment, such as tablets and cellphones, but we think that they are inappropriate to allow production as opposed to mainly consumption of digital content, at least for the foreseeable future. Thus our objective is to reduce the cost of deployment of traditional communal Internet Access Points using PCs. In this paper we compare four candidate computers to be used as thin clients in such settings, according to seven different categories. Our study identifies the strengths, weaknesses and problems of each device, and concludes with recommendations for anybody wishing to deploy such devices as Linux Terminal Server Project (LTSP) thin clients in a public Internet Access Point.

Keywords: Thin client computing · ICT4D · Public access centres · LTSP

1 Introduction

Development of the poor segments of society is seen as a priority in South Africa; information and knowledge are key strategic resources for social and economic development. Information Communication Technologies (ICTs) are seen as important tools in any development, assisting in enabling change through economic development [1]. Policy makers in South Africa are concerned with bridging the digital divide [2] that exists between high socio-economic areas and low socio-economic ones in the country [3]. Organizations such as the CSIR [3] and other academic institutions, such as the universities in South Africa (Rhodes, Fort Hare [1, 4], University of the Western

A. Terzoli—This work was undertaken in the Distributed Multimedia CoE at Rhodes University, with financial support from Telkom SA, Tellabs, Genband, Easttel, Bright Ideas 39, THRIP and NRF SA (TP13070820716). The authors acknowledge that opinions, findings and conclusions or recommendations expressed here are those of the authors and that none of the above mentioned sponsors accept liability whatsoever in this regard.

© Institute for Computer Sciences, Social Informatics and Telecommunications Engineering 2015
A. Nungu et al. (Eds.): AFRICOMM 2014, LNICST 147, pp. 229–238, 2015.
DOI: 10.1007/978-3-319-16886-9_24

Cape [5]) have been investigating sustainable methods of bridging the digital divide between rich and poor communities of South Africa.

However, many development projects using ICTs in the developing world mimic projects in the developed world. Researchers have found that this approach to development is not necessarily appropriate in the contexts of developing nations and argue that development projects need to thoroughly investigate their contexts in order to make decisions about appropriate technologies [6]. It can be argued that the investigation and use of appropriate technologies that are grounded in the local context and support the needs of the local communities is key to the success of ICT-based developmental projects in developing nations [6].

In the context of South Africa, where the Siyakhula Living Lab (SLL) is located [4], communities are faced with socio-economic challenges associated with poverty and poor infrastructural development. In South Africa the penetration of telecommunications infrastructure is low, with an estimated 5 % fixed-line teledensity in some rural regions of South Africa [7]. In addition, these regions tend to suffer from a limited road network, limited access to government services, inadequate education and health care facilities, a lack of connections to the national electricity grid, and poor or vandalized telecommunication infrastructure in some areas [6, 8].

In the Dwesa region, the primary site where the SLL is located, local schools act as technology access centres for community members. Not only are community members and schools unable to afford computer and telecommunication facilities, but the region also suffers from inadequate and erratic grid electricity supply. In order to make the facilities economically sustainable and easier to maintain for the limited staff and students providing support for the dispersed facilities, we employed thin client computer labs. Specifically, we use Edubuntu Linux [9] which incorporates the Linux Terminal Server Project (LTSP) [10]. Thin client computer facilities offer a number of advantages, such as a longer service life, reduced power consumption (depending on the hardware chosen), easier configuration management, improved security, reduced space requirements and are less susceptible to theft (as thin clients are useless without the server) [11]. Furthermore, the use of thin client computers provides users with a desktop experience that allows them to not only be consumers of information (such as that afforded by mobile handsets like tablet PCs or smart phones) but also producers of information; contributing to actively taking part in the digital networked society.

In this paper we compare and contrast four different thin client computer architectures for use with LTSP servers in providing ubiquitous access to previously disadvantaged users in South Africa. The paper consists of four sections which: describe the hardware of the four thin client architectures; compare, contrast; discuss findings; and finally conclude with recommendations.

2   Description of Hardware Devices

The hardware devices evaluated in our survey are: a generic x86 box (Proline Nanoware), an HP t510 thin client, a Raspberry Pi model B, and the APC 8750. For brevity, we refer to these devices respectively as the Nanoware, HP, Pi and APC.

The reasons for selection of these specific devices for this study were as follows: The Nanoware was chosen as it has similar specifications to the generic recycled computers which are often used in LTSP labs, and thus provides a useful baseline for comparison. The HP provides an interesting comparison, as it is a purpose-made commercial thin client. The Raspberry Pi was investigated because it was the lowest-cost single-board computer that we could find, with the the potential to function as a thin-client. Costing marginally more, the APC was tested as an alternative to the Pi, as it potentially offers several advantages over the Pi.

Table 1 summarises the specifications of the respective devices. The remainder of this section describes first the architecture of the server platform, then describes each of the thin clients.

Table 1. Summarised specifications for thin client hardware devices

	Nanoware	HP t510	Raspberry Pi	APC 8750
Processor	1.6 GHz Intel Atom 230	1 GHz, 2 core VIA Eden X2	700 MHz ARM 1176JZF-S	800 MHz VIA ARM Processor
Memory	1024 MB RAM, 200G HDD	2 GB RAM, 1 GB Flash	512 MB RAM, SD card socket	512 MB RAM, 2 GB Flash
Graphics	VGA output, up to max 1680 × 1050	DVI-I & DVI-D, incl DVI-I to VGA adapter	RCA, HDMI, DSI. max 1920 × 1080	HDMI and VGA. Resolution up to 720p
Input/ output	6x USB, audio, PS/2 mouse/kbd	4x USB, audio, PS/2 mouse/kbd	2x USB, single audio in/out port	4x USB, audio in/out
Network	10/100 Ethernet	Gigabit Ethernet, 802.11a/b/g/n	10/100 Ethernet	10/100 Ethernet
Price	R 2127.82	R 3768.12	US $35	US $49
Power	65 W at AC 220 V	65 W at 19 V DC	3.5 W at 5 V	4 W–14 W, 9–12 V
Dimensions	282 × 282 × 95 mm	58 × 215 × 219 mm	85 × 56 mm	170 × 85 mm

2.1 Edubuntu Server Platform

The hardware requirements for an Edubuntu server are modest: Indeed, our experiments [14] show that a quad-core server with 4 GB of RAM can support up to 14 thin-clients running Firefox, or 12 running OpenOffice.org Writer. Furthermore, our results confirm that LTSP thin client computing (using the applications tested) is a memory-bounded problem more than a processor-bounded problem.

In order to test several versions of Edubuntu with multiple thin-client devices, Oracle Virtualbox [17] was chosen to host the servers on virtual machines. The host machine was an Asus N53-SV with a 2 GHz hyper-threaded quad-core Intel i7 processor, 4G RAM, and a Samsung EVO-II SSD, running Ubuntu 13.10.

The Edubuntu server versions used for testing were: 12.04 LTS 32-bit and 64-bit, 13.10 64-bit and 14.04 LTS 32-bit and 64-bit. The virtual servers were configured to run with two processing cores and 2048 MB of RAM.

2.2   Thin Client Devices

Generic x86 Box: Proline Nanoware. Edubuntu LTSP labs are often built using recycled PC computers, which have become too old and slow to support modern applications. We thus include a comparable, old low cost PC in our evaluation, to provide baseline specifications for the purposes of our comparison.

HP t510 Thin Client. Our survey includes one purpose-made commercial thin-client solution: the HP t510 Thin Client [16]. With 2G of RAM and a dual-core processor, the HP far exceeds the basic requirements for an LTSP thin-client.

Raspberry Pi Model B. The Raspberry Pi Model B [12] is a credit-card-sized single-board computer developed in the UK by the Raspberry Pi Foundation with the intention of promoting the teaching of basic computer science in schools.

The BerryTerminal [13] project provides software specifically developed to allow Raspberry Pis to work as LTSP thin clients. BerryTerminal, a stripped-down Debian-based Linux distribution, is the software used for this survey.

APC 8750. The first platform to adopt the compact size of the Neo-ITX form factor, the APC 8750 [15] integrates memory, storage, and a full set of consumer I/O features, providing ample computing power at an affordable price.

The APC costs only marginally more than the Raspberry Pi, but potentially offers several advantages, including: onboard nonvolatile storage, a faster processor, and native VGA support.

3   Comparison of Thin Client Devices

This section evaluates the four devices according to seven criteria: connectivity, power, video, storage & network booting, casing, price, and performance/usability.

3.1   Connectivity

This section explores peripheral connection options and limitations, within the Edubuntu thin-client context, and notes the relevant findings.

USB Ports. Whereas the Raspberry Pi has only two USB ports, the other devices have four or more. The HP and the Nanoware have USB ports on both the front and rear of their casings, for ease of access.

A concern is that the mouse and keyboard could possibly occupy both the USB ports on the Pi, leaving none free for additional devices. However, USB flash drives are not presently supported on BerryTerminal thin clients.

Audio Connectors. All the devices in this survey include standard mini-jack connectors to support audio. However, the Pi has only a single connector (facilitating both input and output) whereas the other devices have discrete inputs and outputs.

Both the HP and the Nanoware have front-panel audio connectors on their casings, for ease of access. The HP includes a small internal speaker.

Mouse and Keyboard. Neither of the ARM-based devices (Pi and APC) have standard PS/2 mouse and keyboard connectors, thus only USB keyboards and mice are supported (unless a PS/2 to USB adapter is used). Conversely, the remaining devices (HP and Nanoware) do have PS/2 connectors, allowing greater flexibility.

3.2   Power Considerations

In this section, we consider the issues associated with powering each of the devices.

Power Consumption. For this comparison, we use the rated consumption figures as supplied by the respective manufacturers. It is clear that the two ARM-based boards require significantly less power than the x86 devices, by a large factor. The Pi uses just 3.5 W, the APC uses slightly more (4–13.5 W), whereas both the HP and the Nanoware have 65 W supplies.

Power Supply. Both x86 devices (HP and Nanoware) are supplied with 220 V AC power supplies. The Nanoware has a standard internal switched-mode supply, whereas the HP has a 19 V laptop-style external supply.

Neither of the ARM boards (Pi and APC) are sold with a power supply included: this must be purchased separately.

The APC requires between 9 and 12 V DC, via one of two DC-in connectors: a standard laptop-style connector, or a four pin Molenx port.

The Pi also has two choices: via MicroUSB, or via pins on the GPIO connector. The MicroUSB port allows Pis to be powered by devices such as active USB hubs.

Power Switches. The HP and Nanoware devices both have standard power switches. Furthermore, both can be configured to power-on automatically after a power failure.

The Pi has no power switch. It starts immediately when it receives power. The APC has an onboard microswitch for power, which must be pressed to start the APC. This is undesirable, as the switch would not be reachable if the APC were inside a casing. It is however possible to connect an external power switch.

3.3   Video Issues

The different video capabilities of devices in this survey are discussed below.

Video Connectors. The Raspberry Pi supports only HDMI and composite video outputs. Thus, in order to use it with a standard VGA or DVI display, a separate adapter is required. HDMI to DVI adapters are cheaper than HDMI to VGA adapters, as the former are passive whereas the latter require active electronics.

The APC has both VGA and HDMI connectors, thus can connect to a standard VGA display without requiring an adapter.

The Nanoware machine has only a VGA connector. The HP has both DVI-I and DVI-D native, with a DVI-I-to VGA adapter included.

Resolution Limitations. Not all of the devices support FHD graphics (1920 × 1080). If a FHD screen is desired, this may be of concern.

Remarkably, the humble Raspberry Pi supports FHD. However, during our testing we discovered that it could only support this resolution via a HDMI to DVI adapter. When we tested with a HDMI to VGA adapter, the Pi ran at a reduced resolution setting, despite the fact that the adapter specifications indicated FHD support.

Regrettably, the APC only supports up to 720p HD graphics (1280 × 720). The Nanoware's integrated graphics controller supports VGA output, up to max 1680 × 1050. The HP t510 unit is able to support FHD.

3.4   Nonvolatile Storage and Network Booting

In theory, an LTSP thin client can operate without any local nonvolatile storage (such as hard drive, flash memory, etc.).

Although both of the x86 clients have nonvolatile storage, it is not used when the machines boot from the network as thin clients. Instead, the operating system is loaded via PXE network booting.

Regrettably, the ARM clients do not support PXE network booting. Instead, the thin-client software must be installed onto each ARM client individually. The APC includes onboard flash storage, onto which a thin-client could be installed.

The Raspberry Pi has no onboard storage. Rather, it requires a standard SD card, onto which a bootable image must be preloaded.

3.5   Casing Considerations

Whereas both x86 devices were supplied in compact desktop boxes, neither the Pi nor the APC include a casing as standard. Separate casings are thus required.

Casing Availability. A standard case is available for the Raspberry Pi, but the case suffers disadvantages within the thin client context. The SD memory card is externally accessible, leading to the risk of theft or tampering. Furthermore, the MicroUSB power cable is exposed and removable, leading to the risk that users will disconnect the Pi in order to use the USB cable for charging cellphones.

The APC conforms to the Neo-ITX is form factor, which is also compatible with Mini-ITX and MicroATX. Regrettably, however, at the time of writing we have been unable to find a domestic supplier for suitable low-cost casings for the APC.

Connector Layout. The Raspberry Pi has connectors all four sides, as well as an SD card socket. This limitation inhibits the construction of a suitable low-cost custom casing, with access to necessary IO connectors.

The APC has a more sensible connector layout. All important connectors are on the back of the board, and a rectangular backpanel is supplied.

3.6   Price Comparison

Although our research context falls within South Africa, we discuss prices both in terms of Rands and US Dollars, as RSA domestic hardware prices tend to fluctuate relative to the US Dollar exchange-rate.

Clearly, either of the x86-based units would cost several times that of an ARM-based unit. Thus the x86 devices are significantly more expensive, unless donated or recycled hardware is available.

The price difference between the Pi and the APC is a mere US$14. But when one considers that the Pi additionally requires an SD memory card and a HDMI-DVI converter (not required by the APC), their total prices are approximately equivalent.

It is important to note that both the Pi and the APC would additionally require power supplies and casings to be purchased, thus adding to the price. We estimate the cost of power supply and casing would add between US$10 and $20 to the total.

3.7   Performance and Usability

Although all the devices in this survey have the potential to operate as efficient thin clients, they did not all perform as well as we anticipated.

Do They Work at All? As expected, the generic x86-based Nanoware worked well as an Edubuntu thin client.

The HP worked well with Edubuntu version 12.04 LTS, but not with Edubuntu 13.10 nor 14.04. The problem was logged as a "longhaul" error. Longhaul is a technology used in certain VIA chipsets to scale the CPU frequency for green computing [18]. At the time of writing, very little information was available regarding this problem. It is likely that the problem will be fixed in future versions of Edubuntu.

The Raspberry Pi worked well after BerryTerminal was installed on the SD card.

Although the APC is capable of running Linux, we were not able to find a BerryTerminal port for the APC, nor suitable alternative software. APC development appears to focus around the Firefox OS. Thus, further development work would be required in order to use the APC with Edubuntu.

Startup Delays. In order to compare the startup performance of each device, we measure the time taken to boot-up each of the different clients. Two metrics are measured: *Boot Delay* (time from power-up until the login screen appears) and *Login Delay* (time from when the user enters a correct password, until the desktop appears) (Table 2).

It is interesting to observe that the Raspberry Pi requires significantly less than half the time required by the x86 machines, to boot to a login screen. But the Pi is loading BerryTerminal from a local SD card, whereas the x86s are loading a different LTSE image via the network. The Boot Delay of the Raspberry Pi will relate to the speed of SD card used, as several different speed classes are available.

Table 2. Bootup and login delay measurements

Device	Boot delay	Login delay
Proline Nanoware	51 s	15 s
HP t510 Thin Client	58 s	15 s
Raspberry Pi Model B	22 s	15 s
APC 8750	–	–

After the initial boot delay, a constant 15 s is required to complete the login and launch the Edubuntu desktop (Login Delay), regardless of which thin client is used.

The APC was not tested, as suitable thin-client software is not available.

User Experience. Once logged-in, all the thin clients tested provided an adequate, useable experience. Applications loaded in a reasonable amount of time, which as expected did not vary significantly depending on the device tested.

An issue was noted with the Pi that was not present with the x86 clients: After login, mouse movement would be jerky, with a noticeable lag, for approximately one minute. Thereafter, the mouse would behave normally.

As a full HD display was used for testing, we noted a degraded experience with the Nanoware, which could not run at full resolution.

The Raspberry Pi (running BerryTerminal) offers a slightly less-rich graphical experience than the x86 clients. It appears that a lower pixel bit-depth is used for efficiency reasons. However, the Pi is entirely usable.

4 Discussion

This section of the paper consolidates our findings, provides recommendations, and looks at future work.

4.1 Numerical Comparison

In order to compare the four devices, we assign each a score out-of-ten for each of the seven categories compared. The score is based on our findings from the previous part of this paper. Each category is assigned an integral weight, chosen according to deemed importance relative to the other categories. The results are summed, and expressed as a percentage of the maximum score (Table 3):

Although the choice of parameters for the comparison was highly subjective, the results of the comparison provide a useful way to quantify our findings.

We note that the generic x86 Nanoware achieves the best score, of 79.44 %. However, the Raspberry Pi is a close-second with a score of 74.44 %.

Table 3. Numerical comparison of thin client devices

	Weight	Nanoware	HP	Pi	APC
Connectivity	2	10	10	6	7
Power	1	9	8	10	8
Video	2	6	10	9	7
Storage	1	10	10	5	7
Casing	3	10	10	5	0
Price	5	10	3	10	10
Performance	4	8	7	9	0
Score		79.44 %	61.67 %	74.44 %	43.89 %

The Nanoware scores 10 for price, as it is assumed to be free. In the absence of free hardware, however, the Pi scores 10 as it is the cheapest single-board computer.

The HP scores 61.67 %, despite having excellent hardware specifications and capabilities, whereas the unusable APC scores only 43.89 %. The APC's score would improve were suitable thin-client software available.

4.2   Observations and Recommendations

With the exception of the APC, all the devices tested were able to function adequately as LTSP thin-clients.

The APC would be good choice, were suitable thin-client software available. Our only reservation would be that the APC does not support full HD graphics.

However, devices based on VIA chipsets which use Longhaul frequency scaling (such as the HP) are not supported at the time of writing by Edubuntu.

x86-based clients are preferrable to ARM-based clients for several reasons, including: they are able to network-boot, they offer better USB support, and they require no local storage.

Conversely, ARM-based clients are lower-priced, consume less energy, boot quicker, and thus provide an elegant thin-client solution.

Although not ideal, we are not presently aware of any other device at a comparable price to the Raspberry Pi, offering thin-client functionality. Presently, the Pi facilitates the most cost-effective method to build labs of LTSP thin-clients, if recycled (free) computers are not available.

5   Conclusion

In this paper, we contrasted and evaluated four different potential thin client hardware devices for use with LTSP in South African Edubuntu School Labs. We compared two x86-based devices with two ARM-based single-board computers according to seven different subdivided categories.

By qualitative and numerical comparisons we determined that, although free recycled x86 computers are preferred, the Raspberry Pi is a capable and cost-effective alternative when deploying low-cost LTSP thin-client laboratories.

Our study identified the strengths, weaknesses and problems of each respective device that we tested, and provided recommendations for anybody wishing to deploy such devices as LTSP thin clients.

References

1. Pade, C., Sieborger, I., Thinyane, H., Dalvit, L.: ICTs and sustainable solutions for the digital divide: practical approaches - development informatics and regional information technologies: theory, practice and the digital divide. IGI Global, 2010, vol. 2, ch. The Siyakhula living lab: a holistic approach to rural development through ICT in rural South Africa
2. Prensky, M.: Digital natives, digital immigrants. On the Horizon 9(5) (2001)

238 K. Duff et al.

3. Conradie, D., Morris, C., Jacobs, S.: Using information and communication technologies (ICTs) for deep rural development in South Africa. Communication **29**(1), 199–217 (2003)
4. Sieborger, I., Terzoli, A.: WiMAX for rural SA: the experience of the Siyakhula Living Lab. In: Southern African Telecommunication Networks and Applications Conference, The Future - a Society Driven by Innovation and Applications, 6–8 September 2010
5. Telkom Centre of Excellence, University of the Western Cape: Centre of Excellence in Internet Computing. http://www.coe.uwc.ac.za/
6. van Reijswoud, V.: Appropriate ICT as a tool to increase effectiveness in ICT4D: theoretical considerations and illustrating cases. Electron J. Inf. Syst. Dev. Countries **38**(9), 1–18 (2009)
7. South African Consulate General: Communications (2003). http://www.southafricanewyork.net/consulate/telecom.htm
8. Palmer, R., Timmermans, H., Fay, D.: From Conflict to Negotiation: Nature-based Development on South Africa's Wild Coast. Human Sciences Research Council, Pretoria (2002)
9. Canonical: Edubuntu (2013). http://www.edubuntu.org/
10. McQuillan, J.: LTSP.org: Linux Terminal Server Project (2013). http://www.ltsp.org/
11. Brinkley, D.: Thin-clients in the classroom: software compatibility and a survey of systems. In: Proceedings of World Conference on E-Learning in Corporate, Government, Healthcare, and Higher Education, pp. 383–390 (2006)
12. Raspberry Pi Foundation: The Raspberry Pi (2014). http://www.raspberrypi.org/
13. BerryTerminal (2014): http://www.berryterminal.com/
14. Sieborger, I., Terzoli, A., Cheryl, H.-W.: LTSP DNS round robin clusters: green technology access enablers for telecommunication services in marginalised communities. In: Southern African Telecommunication Networks and Applications Conference (2011)
15. VIA PC-1 initiative: The APC 8750a (2014). http://apc.io/products/8750a/
16. HP: The HP t510 Thin Client (2104). http://h10010.www1.hp.com/wwpc/pscmisc/vac/us/product_pdfs/HP_t510_021312_Data_Sheet.pdf
17. Oracle Corporation: Oracle VM VirtualBox (2014). https://www.virtualbox.org/
18. LongHaul: In Wikipedia, The Free Encyclopedia, 18 May 2012. http://en.wikipedia.org/w/index.php?title=LongHaul&oldid=493257463

ICT4D Miscellaneous

MalariaScope's User Interface Usability Tests: Results Comparison Between European and African Users

Tiago Devezas[1], Luis Domingos[1], Ana Vasconcelos[1],
Carlos Carreira[1], and Bruno Giesteira[2(✉)]

[1] Fraunhofer-AICOS, Rua Alfredo Allen, 455, 4200-135 Porto, Portugal
{tiago.devezas,luis.domingos,ana.vasconcelos,
carlos.carreira}@fraunhofer.pt
[2] FBAUP, ID+, University of Porto, Av. Rodrigues de Freitas, 265,
4049-021 Porto, Portugal
bgiesteira@fba.up.pt

Abstract. Malaria is one of the most severe public health problems worldwide. It is estimated that 3.3 billion people live in areas at risk of malaria transmission, and in 2010 caused around 655,000 deaths, 91 % of them in the African Region. In this study we assess if the mHealth application "MalariaScope" developed by Fraunhofer Portugal AICOS (FhP AICOS) found to be usable and satisfactory by users from a European country, Portugal, can achieve similar positive results in an African country, Mozambique, which is one of its intended contexts of use. To this end, an academic partner from that African country conducted locally a usability evaluation of the application following the same procedure with participants with similar scientific backgrounds to the Portuguese counterparts. A comparison of the usability metrics of the two evaluations found no significant differences between the Portuguese and Mozambican set of users.

Keywords: ICT4D · HCI4D · Cross-cultural HCI · Usability

1 Introduction

In developed countries, interfaces are usually designed by technology users for similarly experienced people. However, when the target users are from resource-constrained settings, the designers can't rely solely on their intuition and experience, due to the likely mismatches between the frames of reference of the former and the latter [15]. If the users' needs and the context of use are not properly understood, the solution's acceptance might be impaired [7, 10, 16].

Commonly mentioned issues that should be taken into account when designing for developing countries include illiteracy or low literacy (both textual and technological), lack of adequate mental models and understanding of established interaction metaphors, language and dialect barriers, economic constraints, social and cultural differences, ethical issues, and political environments [4–6, 17].

Due to this multitude of potential barriers, some authors stress the difficulty for people living in the developed world to gain an accurate understanding about the lives

© Institute for Computer Sciences, Social Informatics and Telecommunications Engineering 2015
A. Nungu et al. (Eds.): AFRICOMM 2014, LNICST 147, pp. 241–250, 2015.
DOI: 10.1007/978-3-319-16886-9_25

of users from developing countries, even after thorough research [16]. Others question if obtaining the necessary knowledge is even possible [4].

Thus, it doesn't come as a surprise that the importance of partnering with natives from the target culture during the product development process is a recurring theme in the Human-Computer Interaction for Development (HCI4D) literature, a recent subfield of research of the Information and Communication Technologies for Development (ICT4D) area [1].

Local HCI partners, through their deep knowledge of the community and its context, can quickly establish a climate of trust with the users and provide clear feedback to the research team [14, 16]. Such partnerships can help overcome possible reactions towards foreign researchers, such as hostility, skepticism, indifference, or eagerness to please due to differences in perceived status [1, 16]. The process of translating text and audio and developing culturally appropriate graphics can also benefit greatly from this kind of involvement [8].

International partners also need to be involved in the usability testing stage. Russo and Boor [12] so that the tests should be performed earlier, and the results can be incorporated before the product is released. Testing with local users will ensure that the user interface is culturally appropriate, thus enhancing the user experience and increasing its chances of acceptance [13].

This paper presents the results from a comparative study between two usability evaluations of a mobile application, one conducted in Portugal and the other in Mozambique. A solid baseline for comparison was established by following the same procedure in both evaluations. The goal was to investigate if there were significant differences, in terms of usability and subjective satisfaction, between these two countries.

The study was conducted under the umbrella of the ICT4D Competence Center (ICT4DCC), a virtual model through which a team of international experts from the FhP AICOS institute and international partners from scientific institutions and industry collaborate to develop ICT solutions.

Following the recommendations from the ICT4D and HCI4D literature, the usability tests in Mozambique were performed by a local academic partner of the ICT4DCC: the Eduardo Mondlane University Informatics Center (CIUEM).

Section 2 describes the system evaluated in this study. The method followed for this experiment is presented in Sect. 3. Section 4 presents the results from the comparison of the two evaluations regarding the usability metrics considered for this study and the subjective satisfaction with the system. Finally, Sect. 5 discusses the results and presents the conclusions.

2 System Description

The evaluated mobile application, named MalariaScope [11], is a project of the ICT4DCC aiming to allow health technicians without specialized knowledge in malaria diagnosis to easily triage blood samples potentially infected with malaria. The app, which is intended for developing countries where malaria constitutes a serious public health problem, can be installed in any Android smartphone and is used in conjunction with an optical magnification system.

The technician collects and prepares a blood sample from a patient, which he/she then inserts in a slot in the optical system. Then, using the smartphone application, the user can create a new patient in the app or use one of the patients already in the system. The user can then create a new sample for the patient (which corresponds to the actual blood sample placed on the slot) and, using the smartphone camera, capture different views of the physical sample, which will be magnified by the optical device. The captured views can then be sent be sent for remote analysis, where an image detection algorithm is applied to each view and a risk assessment report returned. If the technician is not a malaria expert, the results can be analyzed by one, and the correct clinical course of action undertaken.

The end users are expected to be literate and have knowledge of how to work with blood samples. The system is intended to be used on urban or rural settings under varying network and power connectivity conditions.

3 Method

Two usability evaluations were conducted: one in Portugal and other in Mozambique. They all followed the same methodology: field observations with think aloud method and a series of predefined tasks. Both evaluations took place in the field, in a more natural setting than the controlled environment of a usability lab. In addition to manual data collection methods, video and audio of the users' interaction with the device was recorded.

The same version of the app was evaluated in both countries. This version was a significant improvement from the initial iteration, in which several usability issues were found, and ironed out, after a round of user testing conducted in Portugal. The app's language was English.

Participants were also asked to think out loud while solving a set of tasks with the evaluated system in a predefined order. Each usability evaluation was conducted with six users. Research has shown that six participants can uncover 80 % of the major usability problems within a system [9].

3.1 Experimental Design

A set of nine tasks were selected for representing the most frequent actions a user would have to execute in order to effectively use the application. They also aimed to assess potential issues regarding the navigation flow, the comprehensibility of the different actions and concepts and the adequacy of the information architecture. All the participants were asked to complete the following tasks using the system:

1. Create a patient
2. Edit the patient and add a surname to the name
3. Create a new sample for that patient with a given id, add a view with a picture from the gallery, and analyze it
4. Add three views from the camera: take four pictures, delete the first picture taken, choose to analyze the remaining later

5. Change patient and choose the patient with a given name
6. Open Sample 1
7. Change to Sample 2
8. Analyze a view that has not been analyzed
9. Open the view with the worst results and delete it

A pre-test questionnaire was administered to collect background data. After the test, participants were asked to fill a System Usability Scale (SUS) [3] and a debriefing interview took place to gather the users' opinions.

3.2 Participants

A total of 12 participants, six in Portugal and six in Mozambique, were recruited for the two usability evaluations. None of them had previously interacted with the application.

Regarding the tests conducted in Portugal, the six participants (3 male and 3 female) included health and life sciences researchers and lab technicians. They were selected for having potential similarities with the intended audience in terms of technical and scientific background, including some laboratory work experience. The average participant age was 43 (SD = 8.75), with the minimum age being 31 and the maximum, 52.

Only two of them were experienced with touch-enabled devices. The remaining four used a feature phone daily and only one of them had limited experience with a touch device. In terms of education level, all of them had a Bachelor's degree or higher.

In Mozambique, the six participants recruited (3 male and 3 female) were all university students from the biology and health fields, thus fitting the intended profile. Average participant age was 21.3 (SD = 1). Minimum age was 20 and maximum, 23. Five out of the six participants owned or had previous experience with touch-enabled devices.

3.3 Procedure

The same procedure was followed in the two evaluations. To ensure that all participants received the same information and the same sequence of events was followed, the facilitators used a testing protocol document.

The session started with the facilitator greeting the test subjects and giving them a brief description of the MalariaScope project, its context, and the system. The participants were then asked to sign an informed consent form and permission to record the session. They were asked some background questions (occupation, age, smartphone ownership and touch-device experience) and were given additional information and instructions about the procedure. These included asking them to try and complete the tasks as if the facilitator wasn't present but to ask for help if they felt they were stuck, to think aloud during task execution and to voice any opinions – positive or negative - about the system. Then, the nine tasks were read aloud one at a time in the predefined sequence.

After the last task, a SUS questionnaire was administered and an informal conversation to collect additional comments and opinions took place. Finally, the participants, who were not compensated in any way, were thanked for their contribution before being dismissed.

3.3.1   Equipment

In Portugal, all the six participants used the same device to interact with the application: a "Samsung Galaxy Note II" smartphone (5.5" 1280 × 720 pixel screen). A "Panasonic HDC TM-700" camera, placed on a tripod and pointed at the device's screen, was used for audio and video recording.

All the Mozambican test participants used a "Samsung Galaxy S4" (5" 1980 × 1080 pixel screen). The sessions were recorded using a "Samsung Galaxy Camera".

3.3.2   Test Setting

Tests with the Portuguese users took place on a single day in the premises of the National Health Institute Dr. Ricardo Jorge, in Porto. The tests were conducted in the library room. One facilitator sat left of the participant while the other sat to the right in a facing position where she could gather observational data.

In Mozambique, the sessions were conducted throughout the course of several days in a room at the premises of the Eduardo Mondlane University. One facilitator, sitting at the right of the participants, administered the tests. In addition to the facilitator and the participant, a third person was present in the room to properly record the session, since no tripod was available.

3.3.3   Metrics

The following usability metrics for effectiveness were measured: errors, deviations and assists. An error was considered every time the participant performed an action that did not contribute to task completion. A deviation was measured every time the participant followed a different path from the predefined ideal flow to complete the task. An assist was registered each time the facilitator intervened to aid the participant follow through with the task.

Efficiency metrics, such as time per task, were not considered for this study, because no baseline was established.

The subjective satisfaction was measured through a post-test administration of the SUS. The users' remarks and opinions during and after the test were also collected.

3.3.4   Data Analysis

The video recordings of the six Portuguese users and the six Mozambican participants were coded and analyzed using the "Observer XT" software package, from Noldus. The same coding scheme was used for registering the occurrence of errors, assists, deviations and user comments. All the quantitative and qualitative data of interest was compiled for further analysis.

The data analysis process for the Portuguese and Mozambican evaluations was performed independently by two researchers.

4   Results

4.1   Errors, Deviations and Assists

In order to determine the differences between the two evaluations, an independent two-sample t-test was computed for each metric. The data was found to be normally distributed via a Shapiro-Wilk test. The statistical analysis was performed using the "Microsoft Excel" software package.

As shown in Fig. 1, a total of 50 errors were identified by the two usability evaluations. In the evaluation conducted in Portugal, the six participants committed a total of 24 errors, while the six Mozambican users made 26 errors in total. The t-test shows no significant difference between the two evaluations ($t10 = 0.25$, $p > 0.1$).

In terms of deviations, a total of 10 occurrences were identified in the two evaluations. Of these, 5 were found in Portugal and 5 in Mozambique, as Fig. 1 shows. The difference between the number of deviations is not significant ($t10 = 0$, $p > 0.1$).

A total of 13 assists (shown on Fig. 1) was found, 8 in Portugal and 5 in Mozambique. Again, the difference is not significant ($t10=0.73$, $p>0.1$).

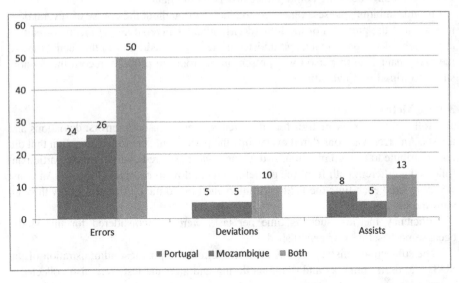

Fig. 1. Total number of errors, deviations and assists found on the Portuguese and Mozambican evaluations

When comparing the number of errors per task, shown in Fig. 2, the tasks with the higher number of errors differed among the Portuguese and Mozambican participants. Task 4 (T4) was the one where Portuguese erred the most (7 errors), while T2 and T5, each with 7 errors, presented the most problems to the Mozambican users. However, no significant differences were found in the number of errors for each task.

When comparing the number of deviations per task for both countries, shown in Fig. 3, t-tests showed that no significant differences between the two samples.

Similarly, a comparison of the number of assists per task (Fig. 4) found no significant differences between Portuguese and Mozambican participants.

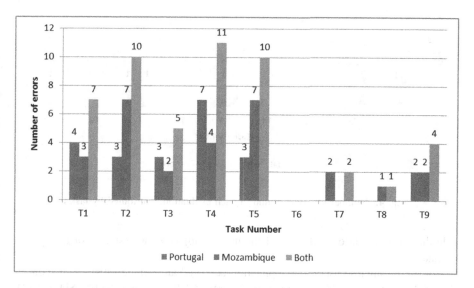

Fig. 2. Number of errors found in each evaluation, distributed by task

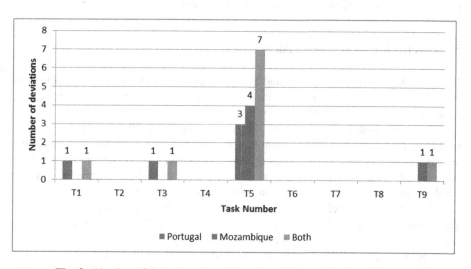

Fig. 3. Number of deviations found in each evaluation, distributed by task

4.2 Satisfaction

The participants' satisfaction with the system was measured by administering a SUS questionnaire at the end of each session. The SUS is a standard industry ten-item Likert

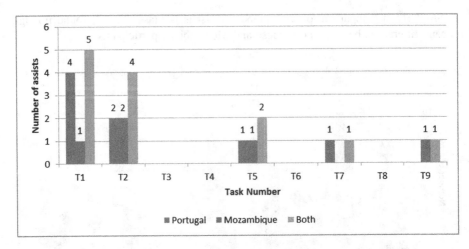

Fig. 4. Number of assists found in each evaluation, distributed by task

scale that provides an overall view of the users' subjective assessments of the system evaluated.

For the Portuguese users, the application achieved an average satisfaction score of 83.75 (SD = 14.38). In Mozambique, the average SUS score was 87.08 (SD = 8.13). A t-test shows no significant difference between the two evaluations ($t10 = 0.49$, $p > 0.1$). In both cases, the scores indicate a very high satisfaction with the system [2].

5 Discussion and Conclusion

In this paper we employed identical test procedures and data analysis methods to compare the results from two usability evaluations of the same mobile application conducted in Portugal and Mozambique.

The results from both evaluations showed no significant differences in the number of errors, deviations and assists identified in each country. Likewise, the subjective satisfaction scores were not significantly different between the two countries and both were equally high. This indicates that the users from these two countries performed similarly and so the second evaluation brought no added benefit.

Thus, the main conclusion is that a mobile application deemed usable and satisfactory by users from a developed country can achieve similar results in a developing region, even without local adaptations.

It is not our goal, by any means, to understate the importance of performing usability tests with local users. In effect, it was only through the evaluation with the Mozambican users that we were able to find that there weren't significant differences and achieve that conclusion.

Regarding the limitations of this study, it can be argued that the evaluated application has a very specific purpose and target audience and thus that the results can't be extrapolated for a broader population. The fact that the application is not image-heavy and has a relatively simple screen flow, thus not raising culturally-sensitive barriers, is also a potential explanation.

Another possible argument is that Mozambique, being a former Portuguese colony, and despite the markedly different socio-economic realities, shares cultural similarities with Portugal and, consequently, a preference for certain user interface and interaction patterns.

However, the results from this study indicate that, when local usability testing is not feasible, and under circumstances such as the mentioned above – a specific purpose and target users, little use of culturally-sensitive elements, and cultural similarities between the countries - a system properly tested, designed and refined in the context of developed country can be deployed in its current state in a developing region and be equally acceptable. They also demonstrate the relevance of the ICT4DCC as a virtual model through which international partners, namely Africans, conduct local iterative usability tests for adequate ICT solutions.

Acknowledgements. We would like to acknowledge the financial support obtained from North Portugal Regional Operational Programme (ON.2 - O Novo Norte), Portuguese National Strategic Reference Framework (NSRF) and the European Regional Development Fund (ERDF) from European Union through the project ICT4DCC (ICT4D Competence Center) NORTE-07-0124-FEDER-000042.

Also, our appreciation to the ICT4D Competence Center's partners, CI-UEM (Informatics Center of University Eduardo Mondlane, Mozambique) and NMMU (Nelson Mandela Metropolitan University, South-Africa) for logistical support and revision process.

References

1. Anokwa, Y., et al.: Stories from the field: reflections on HCI4D experiences. Inf. Technol. Int. Dev. **5**, 4 (2009)
2. Bangor, A., et al.: Determining what individual SUS scores mean: adding an adjective rating scale. J. Usability Stud. **4**(3), 114–123 (2009)
3. Brooke, J.: SUS-A quick and dirty usability scale. Usability Eval. Ind. **189**, 194 (1996)
4. Dray, S., et al.: Indra's Net: HCI in the developing world. Interactions **10**(2), 28–37 (2003)
5. Ho, M., Smyth, T.: Human-computer interaction for development: the past, present, and future. Ldots Int. Dev. (2009)
6. Jensen, K., et al.: NUIs for new worlds: new interaction forms and interfaces for mobile applications in developing countries. In: CHI 2012 Ext. Ldots, pp. 2779–2782 (2012)
7. Lalji, Z., Good, J.: Designing new technologies for illiterate populations: a study in mobile phone interface design. Interact. Comput. **20**(6), 574–586 (2008)
8. Mierzwa, S., et al.: Effective approaches to user-interface design with ACASI in the developing world. Interactions **20**(3), 58–61 (2013)
9. Nielsen, J., Landauer, T.K.: A mathematical model of the finding of usability problems. In: Proceedings of the INTERACT 1993 and CHI 1993 conference on Human factors in computing systems, pp. 206–213 ACM (1993)
10. Poole, E.S.: HCI and mobile health interventions. Transl. Behav. Med. **3**(4), 402–405 (2013)
11. Rosado, L. et al.: Automatic Detection of Malaria Parasites in Thick Blood Smears. 7º Congresso Luso-Moçambicano de Engenharia/IV Congresso Inhambane. Simpósio Nº17, Moçambique (2014)

12. Russo, P., Boor, S.: How fluent is your interface?: designing for international users. In: Proceedings of INTERACT 1993 CHI 1993 Ldots (1993)
13. Shen, S.-T., et al.: Towards culture-centred design. Interact. Comput. **18**(4), 820–852 (2006)
14. Sherwani, J., et al.: Orality-grounded hcid: understanding the oral user. Inf. Technol. Int. Dev. **5**(4), 37 (2009)
15. Smith, A., et al.: A process model for developing usable cross-cultural websites. Interact. Comput. **16**(1), 63–91 (2004)
16. Toyama, K.: Human–computer interaction and global development. Found. Trends Hum.-Comput. Interact. **4**(1), 1–79 (2010)
17. Walsh, T., Vainio, T.: Cross-cultural design for mhealth applications. In: Extended Abstracts of the Third International Workshop on Smart Healthcare Applications, p. 1 (2011)

Validating a Structured ICT for Development Evaluations Approach

Florence Nameere Kivunike[1]([⊠]), Love Ekenberg[1,3], Mats Danielson[1],
and F.F. Tusubira[2]

[1] Department of Computer and Systems Sciences, Stockholm University,
Postbox 7003, 16407 Kista, Stockholm, Sweden
{florence,lovek,mad}@dsv.su.se
[2] Knowledge Consulting Ltd, Kampala, Uganda
fftusu@gmail.com
[3] International Institute of Applied Systems Analysis, IIASA, Vienna, Austria

Abstract. The use of structured evaluation approaches, especially those that
rely on qualitative criteria for the appraisal of the Information and Communications Technology (ICT) contribution to development, is a fairly new occurrence, whose relevance to research and practice is to a large extent unclear. For
this purpose, this paper proposes and applies a multidimensional validation
framework that is based on the validation square framework initially developed
for the evaluation of design methods. It is applied to validate an evaluations
approach developed for appraisal of the ICT contribution to social and economic
development. Based on the proposed validation framework it is established that
despite some skepticism, the structured approach is generally useful for the
evaluation of the ICT contribution to development because (i) its underlying
theoretical basis demonstrates its likelihood to facilitate evaluations of the ICT
contribution to development; (ii) in comparison to the existing approaches, using
the structured evaluation approach will most probably produce results in less
time and less cost; and finally (iii) it is useful in a variety of contexts.

Keywords: ICT for development · ICT4D · ICT projects · Impact evaluation

1 Introduction

Evaluations are generally essential for sound decision-making at various levels from
policy to implementation. For this reason, there have been several attempts at devising
means of evaluating the Information and Communications Technology (ICT) contributions to development. Given the complexities inherent in the interactions between
ICT and society to realize development, majority of the existing evaluation approaches
have been in-depth descriptive exercises. While these provide a rich understanding of
the benefits at micro, or project level, they are resource intensive since they require
more time, and are problematic for evaluations that involve multiple projects.

For this purpose Kivunike et al. [1, 2] propose a structured evaluation approach
based on qualitative criteria comprising outputs, outcomes as well as the contextual
factors that moderated the realisation of ICT benefits from the initiative. While the
outputs are the behavioural changes associated with technology use, outcomes are

A. Nungu et al. (Eds.): AFRICOMM 2014, LNICST 147, pp. 251–260, 2015.
DOI: 10.1007/978-3-319-16886-9_26

concerned with the wider benefits, as well as the costs associated with the outputs, as suggested by, e.g., [3, 4]. It was envisaged that among others this approach streamlined data collection for impact evaluations that cannot satisfactorily be achieved through the in-depth evaluation approaches.

The approach was applied and empirically tested through the evaluations of the ICT contribution to improved healthcare delivery in Uganda, however there is insufficient evidence regarding its validity. Therefore the aim in this paper is to validate a structured evaluation proposed for the evaluation of the ICT contribution to development in general, and specifically applied for to appraise the ICT contribution to improved healthcare delivery in particular. This builds confidence and credibility in terms of rigor and practical usefulness of the approach. As Heeks [5] notes, this analytical approach to validation ensures that the proposed evaluation contributes to the ICT for development body of knowledge as a foundation for future works.

We adapt the "validation square" framework [6, 7] originally developed in the engineering design field. The rationale of its use here is that it was proved useful in validating such research outcomes in general including information systems. However despite some efforts, such as in Eilu and Baguma [8], its use in the information systems field is still limited, so to be reasonably instrumental, it is further specified to ensure relevance in this context. What follows in Sect. 2 is a discussion of the suggested validation framework defining the criteria in more detail. Section 3 presents the methodology, while Sect. 4 provides findings and discussions. Section 5 concludes the paper.

2 The Validation Framework

As underlying principle, the validation square seeks to build confidence in the usefulness of the research outcome with respect to a purpose. Unlike the mainly scientific validations, verifying research outcomes in this context, should also aim at establishing their external relevancy (the practical value) besides internal consistency.

The research outcome should fulfil six requirements on *structural* and *performance validity* from a theoretical as well as a performance perspective [6, 7]. Structural validity evaluates the effectiveness of the process, i.e. whether research outcomes are produced correctly in requirements (1) to (3) below. Performance validity on the other hand seeks to evaluate efficiency, i.e. the production of correct research outcomes in requirements (4) to (6). Validation criteria were defined for each of these requirements to facilitate a more structured, relevant and meaningful validation process in our research context.

(1) *Acceptance of constructs validity:* builds confidence in the individual constructs of the research outcome. Two main validation criteria are proposed, *conceptual clarity* and *credibility*. Conceptual clarity is achieved through the reliance on relevant sources in terms of degree of maturity, the period for which the outcome constructs have been referenced for similar purposes in literature. The other is to demonstrate the level of acceptance and value attached to the research outcome constructs its underlying concepts. Credibility ensures that the constructs measure what they intend to measure; to ascertain that the findings match reality [9].

(2) *Acceptance of the overall research outcome structure:* builds confidence in the way the constructs of the overall research outcome are put together. Two criteria are defined: *internal consistency* and *assumptions validity*. While internal consistency focuses on whether constructs are satisfactorily put together to ensure structural logic; assumptions validity involves the explicit identification of the underlying relevant information (assumptions). In this case three assumptions relevant for the interaction between ICT and development were proposed: relatedness, technology acceptance and multidimensionality.

(3) *Acceptance of the example problems:* validates the appropriateness of the example problems used to verify the usability of the research outcome. It involves establishing the *relevance* and *significance* of the example problems. While relevance seeks to establish the extent by which the example problem is typical of one for which the research outcome could be applied, significance assesses its importance towards the testing of the research outcome.

(4) *Acceptance of the usefulness of the research outcome with respect to the initial purpose for some chosen example problem(s):* seeks to build confidence in the usefulness of the research outcome by ensuring that representative problems are used. This is achieved by determining if an articulated purpose (benefit) has been achieved, like improvement in quality, reduction in cost and/or time, or the production of additional scientific knowledge. Based on the argument developed in Kivunike et al. [10] that use of an artefact determines its benefits; we propose sub-criteria developed and tested in these studies to validate *practical usefulness* in terms of ease of use, usefulness and intention to use (or future use). The second criterion is the *theoretical significance* related to contributing to the body of knowledge.

(5) *Acceptance of the linkage between the achieved usefulness and the research outcome:* seeks to build confidence that the usefulness exhibited through the use of the research outcome actually comes from it. This may be achieved through *comparability* with other similar approaches.

(6) *Acceptance of the usefulness of the research outcome beyond the case studies:* builds confidence in the generality, and adoption of the proposed research outcome to other contexts. It is achieved through induction, basing on the results obtained from steps (1) to (5). The relevant criteria are: *generality* aimed at ascertaining that findings can be applied in a different setting than the one in which they were tested [11]; and *dependability* which relates to reporting the research in detail, to enable future repeatability. For this purpose Shenton [9] notes that the research write-up should consist of the research design and its implementation, the methodology and reflective appraisal of the project (ibid pp. 71–72).

3 Methodology

The validation of the evaluation approach relied on both theoretical and empirical studies. Theoretical validation was achieved through the literature analyses undertaken in prior studies. These specifically assessed the requirements (1), (2) and (6).

The empirical evaluation informed requirements (3), (4) and (5). Table 1 below presents the interview items that addressed requirements (4) and (5).

Table 1 Empirical study interview items

Validation dimension	Criteria	Interview items
(4) Acceptance of the usefulness of the research outcome for some example problems	Practical usefulness (Usefulness)	**HCD1:** Were the proposed criteria appropriate for the evaluation of the ICT contribution to healthcare?
	Practical usefulness (Future use)	**HCD2:** Would you apply the results obtained through this approach to a decision-making context? And for what purpose(s) would you apply the results obtained in this study?
(5) Acceptance of the linkage between the achieved usefulness and the research outcome	Comparability	**HCD3:** How would you compare this approach (more so one that relies on indicators) to others you have used before in evaluating the impact of ICT on social and economic development?

The empirical validation was part of the study that tested the evaluation approach in assessing the ICT contribution to improved healthcare delivery. It involved collecting stakeholder opinions regarding the current and future usefulness of the proposed evaluation criteria. These opinions were sought from people likely to use this approach in reporting or advising subsequent decisions on implementing ICT for healthcare delivery. These included decision-makers and practitioners who guide the use and adoption of ICT in healthcare delivery. These experts first participated in the testing of the evaluation approach by ranked the importance of the proposed criteria [2]. Thus, they were well informed of the evaluation criteria, a prerequisite for the validation study. Data was collected between January – June 2014 through one-on-one interviews, using a semi-structured interview guide comprising items HCD1-HCD3 (Table 1). The use of a semi-structured questionnaire facilitated flexibility and encouraged the interviewees to speak more widely on the usefulness of the evaluation approach. Interviews lasted between 20 to 30 mins and were conducted with eight (8) experts including: two (2) medical practitioners at decision-making level, four (4) officers at the Rural Communications development fund (RCDF), a government Universal services fund program involved in the implementation of ICT4D initiatives for rural development and two (2) private practitioners. The interview sample size was determined by the concept of saturation, i.e. the number of interviewees were deemed sufficient when it was clear that new data did not provide new information regarding the proposed evaluation approach as Mason [12] suggests.

4 Findings and Discussion

Applying the proposed validation framework, this section draws from our prior research and the empirical study to build confidence in the practical relevancy and scientific soundness of the proposed evaluation approach.

4.1 Acceptance of Constructs Validity

4.1.1 Conceptual Clarity

The main evaluation approach constructs; i.e. outputs, outcomes and contextual factors are drawn from well-developed conceptual foundations in information systems and development studies fields. First is Heek and Molla's [13, p. 8] ICT4D value chain model, which argues that an ICT4D initiative progresses from inputs, through outputs to outcomes moderated by the contextual factors. Second is Sen's capability approach [14] drawn from development studies that defines development from a multidimensional perspective as freedom both in terms of the opportunities (outputs) and achievements (outcomes) that enable people live the lives they value.[1] Regarding the degree of maturity as well as the level of acceptance; clearly the research outcome constructs proposed in this study have been extensively accepted and applied for the evaluation of ICT4D initiatives see for example [13, 16–19].

These conceptual frameworks were integrated to cater for their inherent weaknesses in this context. For instance the ICT4D value chain is somewhat simplistic, assuming a linear relationship between ICT and development that is not sufficiently represent the development process [19]. On the other hand as a normative framework, the capability approach is a multi-purpose flexible approach applicable in different contexts. Therefore starting with the ICT4D value chain as a guide, the focus of evaluation i.e. impact is identified and integrated with a development perspective, to realize the conceptual model [1].

4.1.2 Credibility

Various provisions were made to ensure the credibility of the constructs. First, the overall research process which evolved from understanding the research problem domain [20, 21], through the design and development of the evaluation approach [1, 10, 15], to its testing [1, 2, 15]. Secondly, prolonged engagement was achieved through prior consultation of documents and literature [1, 2, 10, 15, 20–22]; and preliminary visits to the study sites [2]. This developed a better understanding of the concepts and operations of the study sites, and built a trust relationship between the researchers and participants. Third, multiple data collection strategies and consultation of multiple sources were applied where appropriate such as in [20, 21]. Fourth participants were asked to voluntarily provide feedback on the study aspects. Finally, the research outcome constructs have also been subjected to various modes of scrutiny such as reviews from journals reviewers, as well as input at conferences and workshops.

---

[1] Detailed discussions of these individual constructs have been undertaken and supported by our prior studies [1, 10, 15].

4.2 Acceptance of the Overall Evaluation Model

4.2.1 Internal Consistency

Clearly presented in [1], the research outcome (evaluation model) constructs, i.e. outputs (opportunities) precede the outcomes, while the contextual factors moderate the interactions, as well as the nature of outputs derived from the ICT characteristics i.e. communication, interactions, transactions etc. This evidently shows a logical flow of the constructs. Furthermore, the fact that this builds on already well-accepted conceptual frameworks also demonstrates the inherent internal consistency.

4.2.2 Assumptions Validity

The first assumption was that rather than aim at attributing impact to a specific initiative, emphasis was placed on the contribution an ICT initiative has had on development in as far as relatedness is concerned [23, p. 273]. This supports the notion that ICT is just one of several interventions that does not cause but only contributes to development. Second, the development of the evaluation model draws from the premise regarding technology acceptance and how this affects the conception of ICT use as initially proposed by Davis [24]. On this basis it has been proven that people's perception of ICT importance affects the intention of ICT use, subsequently determining the actual behaviour to adopt and use the technology. Third, we agree with Sen [14, p. 4] that "assessment of progress has to be done primarily in terms of whether the freedoms that people have [or value] are enhanced". Development is thus highly multidimensional, comprising opportunities i.e., the means that are of instrumental value, as well as intrinsically valuable achievements. Both these are catered for in the evaluation model; the assessment of all constructs is considered a comprehensive account for the ICT contribution to development.

4.3 Acceptance of the Example Problem(s)

4.3.1 Relevance

In as far as relevance is concerned, evaluating the ICT contribution to healthcare delivery is a typical case for which the proposed evaluation approach is applicable since ICT plays a pivotal role in all aspects of human life. Similar approaches in the sense that they seek to establish the ICT benefits to healthcare delivery but apply different techniques do exist see for example, Merrill et al. [25]. Additionally the evaluation demonstrated in Kivunike et al. [2] has the potential of delivering various recommendations, further justifying the relevance of healthcare delivery in the application of the evaluation approach.

4.3.2 Significance

It is also a known fact that the quality of life in as far as health is concerned has a significant influence on other development sectors such as the national economy. This makes healthcare delivery a significant example in demonstrating the use of the proposed evaluation approach to improve its delivery, thus improving people's health, which culminates into national development.

4.4   Acceptance of the Usefulness of the Research Outcome

4.4.1   Practical Usefulness

To assess usefulness of the approach (Item HCD1 in Table 1), all interviewees generally acknowledged the usefulness of the proposed criteria albeit with some reservations. For example some experts noted that "[it] provides a good benchmark for evaluation of the significance of ICT tools in the delivery of healthcare", "adequate", and "a good starting point". However at the same time, the qualitative measures were insufficient and needed to be supplemented with some quantitative measures.. One of the interviewees argued that decision makers might remain more sceptical if presented with data from only qualitative findings, advocating for a more mixed methods approach. The quantitative metrics, when available, should be used, e.g., for providing details of how many patients are attended to in a given day, or how much time a patient waits to receive service. As far as ease of use is concerned, it is clear from the one-point in time appraisal performed in Kivunike et al. [2] that the proposed approach is less resource intensive, presumably permitting a saving of cost and time. Regarding future use (interview item HCD2) experts suggested that the proposed evaluation approach was useful for supporting (evidence based) decision-making at various levels. For instance in terms of: "identifying gaps e.g. skills gaps to improve future planning", "quickly identifying which areas are making the most significant contribution", "showing where more ICT investment should be focused to [..] provide far reaching and cross cutting benefits", and "showing the most viable ICT tools as well as their most viable use".

4.4.2   Theoretical Significance

Of great theoretical significance is the operationalization of Sen's capability approach in terms of dimensions and criteria (outputs and outcomes) for the evaluation of the ICT contribution to development [1, 10]. This is in response to one of the major concerns regarding the usability of the approach [26]. Secondly, drawing from various fields i.e. development studies, information systems and decision analysis this also contributes to advancing research in the interdisciplinary ICT4D research field. Finally the adoption of these various theoretical perspectives is in itself a contribution to the body of knowledge seeking to ground ICT4D research in appropriate theoretical and conceptual frameworks.

4.5   Linkage Between the Achieved Usefulness and the Research Outcome

4.5.1   Comparability

Regarding the usefulness resulting from the application of the evaluation approach (Item HCD3 in Table 1), majority of the experts had never conducted or participated in a similar evaluation. Majority of the evaluations were technical monitoring and evaluation exercises of the day-to-day operations. In comparison with the proposed approach these were prerequisites of evaluations seeking to establish ICT benefits to development. It is thus clear that despite over a decade of implementing ICT to facilitate healthcare delivery, there are still limited efforts in establishing their contribution to development.

This may be attributed to the challenges inherent in the evaluation process, such as the time factor (i.e. when is it appropriate to conduct an impact evaluation), the lack of appropriate methods or the complexities or resource requirements of the existing approaches as discussed above. The flexibility in the proposed approach may address some of these challenges. This is possible because it seeks to establish the contribution ICT makes, an aspect that may be assessed at various implementation stages since it is based on stakeholder perceptions of benefits.

4.6 Acceptance of Usefulness of Research Outcome Beyond the Case Studies

4.6.1 Generality

In as far as generality is concerned, the approach is applicable to various contexts depending on aspects such as the purpose of evaluation, level of analysis and availability of data. More specifically it is applicable in the following scenarios:

1. A comparative assessment of the performance of two or more similar projects on various social and economic outcomes as reported in Kivunike et al. [2].
2. An evaluation of how an initiative or project contributes to one or more development outcomes, similar to the study in Kivunike et al. [1].
3. An ex-ante evaluation of project proposals to establish perceptions of how they will perform on various outcomes and within the different contexts.
4. An evaluation of the influence of contextual factors on the development outputs and outcomes of one or more initiatives. This is achievable in various ways like assessing the contextual factors as one of the criteria categories e.g. in Kivunike et al. [2]. Alternatively explicitly performing an assessment of contextual factors on the outputs and outcomes e.g. project risks assessments see [15].

4.6.2 Dependability

To ensure dependability, each stage of the research process from problem formulation has been documented and disseminated using various channels. For instance the design and development of the evaluation approach is systematically discussed in [1], while its application and testing is availed in [2]. This is sufficient in facilitating the adoption of the evaluation approach in a different context. Lincoln and Guba [27], also point out that credibility and dependability are closely related, and demonstrating one somewhat ensures the other.

5 Conclusions

In this paper, we have set out to validate the appropriateness of applying a structured evaluation approach, one that is based on qualitative indicators to evaluate the ICT contribution to development. A framework that builds on the tenets of the validation square framework facilitates the validation process. From a general perspective, it involves establishing both practical usefulness and theoretical rigour. Based on the validation undertaken, we assert that despite some scepticism, the structured approach is generally useful for the evaluation of the ICT contribution to development because (i) its underlying theoretical basis demonstrates its likelihood to facilitate evaluations of the ICT contribution to development; (ii) in comparison to the existing approaches, using the structured evaluation approach will most probably produce results in less time and less cost; and finally (iii) it is useful in a variety of contexts. Preferably however the approach should be applied in a mixed methods paradigm, which includes as suggested, qualitative as well as quantitative measures, which some experts' advocate for, but are, limited especially when evaluations involve vague and imprecise data. This aspect can be investigated in subsequent studies.

Acknowledgments. This study was funded in part by the Swedish International Development Cooperation Agency (Sida) and Makerere University; the Swedish research council FORMAS, grant 2011-3313-20412-31, and by strategic funds from the Swedish government within ICT – The Next Generation.

References

1. Kivunike, F.N., et al.: Towards an ICT4D Evaluation model based on the Capability Approach. Int. J. Adv. ICT Emerg. Reg. **7**(1), 1–15 (2014)
2. Kivunike, F.N., et al.: A Structured Approach to Evaluating the ICT Contribution to Healthcare Delivery in Uganda. In: Submitted for the 48th Annual Hawaii International Conference on System Sciences. Kauai, Hawaii (2015)
3. Gomez, R., Pather, S.: Pather ICT evaluation: are we asking the right question? Electron. J. Inf. Syst. Developing Countries, EJISDC **50**, 1–14 (2012)
4. Heeks, R.: Do Information and Communication Technologies (ICTs) contribute to development? J. Int. Dev. **22**, 625–640 (2010)
5. Heeks, R.: Theorizing ICT4D research. information technologies and international development. Inf. Technol. Int. Dev. **3**(3), 1–4 (2006)
6. Seepersad, C.C., et al.: The validation square: how does one verify and validate a design method? In: Lewis, K.E., Chen, W., Schmidt, L.C. (eds.) Decision Making in Engineering Design, pp. 303–314. ASME, New York (2006)
7. Pedersen, K., et al.: Validating design methods & research: the validation square. In: 2000 ASME Design Engineering Technical Conferences, Baltimore (2000)
8. Eilu, E., Baguma, R.: Bridging the User Experience Gap in Mobile Phone Voting in Developing Countries. In: 8th Annual International Conference on Computing & ICT Research, ICCIR 12. Kampala, Uganda (2012)
9. Shenton, A.K.: Strategies for ensuring trustworthiness in qualitative Research. Educ. Inf. **22**, 63–75 (2004)
10. Kivunike, F.N., et al.: Developing criteria for the evaluation of the ICT contribution to social and economic development. In: Sixth Annual SIG GlobDev Pre-ICIS Workshop. Milan, Italy (2013)
11. Yin, R.: Case study research: design and methods. In: Bickman, L., Rog, D.J. (eds.) Applied Social Research Methods, vol. 5, 3rd edn, pp. 150–178. Sage Publications, Thousand Oaks (2003)
12. Mason, M.: Sample size and saturation in PhD studies using qualitative interviews. forum: qualitative. Soc. Res. **11**(3), 1 (2010)

13. Heeks, R., Molla, A.: Impact Assessment of ICT—for-Development Projects: A Compendium of Approaches. The Development Informatics Series (2009)
14. Sen, A.: Development as Freedom. Oxford University Press, Oxford (1999)
15. Talantsev, A., et al.: Quantitative scenario-based assessment of contextual factors for ICT4D projects design and implementation in a web based tool. In: Rocha, Á., et al. (eds.) New Perspectives in Information Systems and Technologies, vol. 1, pp. 477–490. Springer, Heidelberg (2014)
16. Hatakka, M., et al.: Back to basics: why (some) ICT4D projects still struggle. In: Proceedings of the 12th International Conference on Social Implications of Computers in Developing Countries. Sunset Jamaica Grande, Jamaica (2013)
17. Ibrahim-Dasuki, S., Abbott, P., Kashefi, A.: The Impact of ICT Investments on Development Using the Capability Approach: The case of the Nigerian Pre-paid Electricity Billing System. Afr. J. Inf. Syst. 4, 30–45 (2012)
18. Oosterlaken, I., den Hoven, J.: Editorial: ICT and the capability approach. Ethics Inf. Technol. 13(2), 65–67 (2011)
19. Gigler, B.-S., Informational Capabilities - The Missing Link for the Impact of ICT on development. World Bank (2011)
20. Kivunike, F.N., et al.: Investigating Universal Access from a Human Development Perspective. In: IADIS International Conference ICT. Society and Human Beings. Algarve, Portugal (2009)
21. Kivunike, F.N., et al.: Perceptions of the role of ICT on quality of life in rural communities in Uganda. Inf. Technol. Dev. 17(1), 61–80 (2011)
22. Kivunike, F.N., et al.: An Interval-based Verbal Numerical Scale for the Elicitation of Vague and Imprecise Information. Group Decision and Negotiation (2014, Submitted)
23. Mayne, J.: Contribution analysis: coming of age? Evaluation 18(3), 270–280 (2012)
24. Davis, F.D.: Perceived usefulness, perceived ease of use, and user acceptance of information technology. MIS Q. 13(3), 319–339 (1989)
25. Merrill, J.A., et al.: A system dynamics evaluation model: implementation of health information exchange for public health reporting. J. Am. Med. Inform. Assoc. 20(e1), e131–e138 (2013)
26. Robeyns, I.: The Capability Approach in Practice. J. Polit. Philos. 14(3), 351–376 (2006)
27. Lincoln, Y.S., Guba, E.G.: Naturalistic Inquiry. Sage Publications Inc., Newbury Park (1985)

Bootstrapping Software Engineering Training in Developing Countries

Return on Experience at the University of Ouagadougou

Tegawendé F. Bissyandé[1,2,3], Jonathan Ouoba[2,4]([✉]), Daouda Ahmat[2,5],
Arthur D. Sawadogo[3], and Zakaria Sawadogo[3]

[1] SnT, University of Luxembourg, Luxembourg, Luxembourg
bissyande@fasolabs.org
[2] FasoLabs Virtual Laboratory, Ouagadougou, Burkina Faso
ext-jonathan.ouoba@vtt.fi
[3] Université de Ouagadougou, Ouagadougou, Burkina Faso
{sawadogoarthur,sawadogo.87}@gmail.com
[4] VTT Technical Research Centre, Espoo, Finland
[5] LaBRI,Université de Bordeaux, Bordeaux, France
daouda.ahmat@labri.fr

Abstract. ICT4D research has the potential of drastically enhancing the daily life of millions of people in developing countries. However, this potential can only be realized if there is enough skilled professionals to transform research ideas into business opportunities. Thus, education in computer sciences is becoming a priority in many countries in Africa, although harsh conditions involving for example limitations in Internet bandwidth and strong academia staff, have negative impact on student motivation and teacher's as well.

We discuss in this paper an experience at the University of Ouagadougou, Burkina Faso, for a software engineering course. We report on the subject and realization of an engaging project for collectively building a toolset for counting source lines of code in projects. This project fulfilled different goals including (1) efficiently providing expertise to students, (2) effectively participating in the open source community, and (3) engaging students in a collaborative work that forces them to acknowledge their potential.

Keywords: ICT4D · Teaching · SLOCCount · Open · Source

1 Introduction

A major limitation to the expansion of ICT4D research and the exploitation of related results in developing countries is the lack of strong curricula in various computer science themes. Thus, locally in these countries, there is still very few skilled people for both the practice and the research on ICT themes. Yet, it is more likely that ICT4D research performed by local teams, with extended

© Institute for Computer Sciences, Social Informatics and Telecommunications Engineering 2015
A. Nungu et al. (Eds.): AFRICOMM 2014, LNICST 147, pp. 261–268, 2015.
DOI: 10.1007/978-3-319-16886-9_27

knowledge on the context, will yield more realistic and applicable results than when performed by foreign researchers in remote labs [6,7].

However, launching computer science studies at the university level in most developing countries is often challenged by the limited access to Internet, the limited budgets for equipments, and the scarcity of academia staff. Thus, there is a very narrow window of opportunity for training students. Starting Fall 2013, a Master of Computer Sciences was set up at the University of Ouagadougou, in Burkina Faso, the first of its kind at this premier university in the country. One main focus of the curricula in this master is software engineering. Software Engineering is a major pillar for ICT4D practice and research as it is the corner stone for software service development. Unfortunately, bootstrapping the training in software engineering is a difficult endeavour that we have chosen to seek right away. Beyond lectures, during which students are taught the paradigms of programming as well the different languages, programming projects are assigned to students to further complete their training through homework practice. At the university of Ouagadougou however, there were a number of difficulties that arised after when proposing software engineering projects to the students at the university of Ouagadougou:

- No student had Internet access at home. At the university premises, Internet bandwith is critically low, with 4 Mb/s shared among about 800 desktop computers (administration + classrooms). This situation makes it difficult for students to engage in rich software development projects where they would require reading documents online or seeking help on blogs such as stackover-flow.com.
- Although students had studied a few programming languages in class, most of them had never read (let alone written) a program in more than 1 programming language.
- For assignments requesting the development of standard projects, students often copy easily existing software, sub-contract their work, or simply rely on other teams to provide ideas and implementations.

We have proposed an original project that consisted on rewriting a new version of the SLOCCount [9] toolset. The requirements for designing the project was that it should be:

- a project that will lead students to look at the code of different programming languages, learning by themselves outside the classrooms
- a project that would help them understand how the value of a software project can evaluated quantitatively
- a project that will increase their confidence by tackling a world-class topic
- a project that builds on existing blocks from the open source community, for a faster bootstrap

The contributions of this paper are as follows:

1. we propose a short return on experience following recommendations made at the previous session of AFRICOMM conference [1]. We expect this experience

can help other curricula in Software Engineering across Internet underserved countries.

2. we discuss a software development project that is of interests for researchers and practitioners beyond the realm of developing countries.

3. finally we propose an enumeration of the lessons learned to realize our endeavour for bootstrapping software development teaching at the university of Ouagadougou.

The remainder of this paper is organized as follows. Section 2 presents the current implementation of SLOCcount, its worldwide use as well as its limitations. Then, we discuss the subject of the project proposed to the students at the university of Ouagadougou. Section 3 then details the lessons that we have learned and continue to learn following this project proposal. We present a few related work in Sect. 4. Finally, we conclude in Sect. 5.

2   SLOCCount^{++}: Counting Source Lines of Code

SLOCcount is a toolset for counting physical source lines of code (SLOC) in a number of programming languages. It can be, and has been, used to measure the SLOC of popular projects such as GNU/Linux distributions.

2.1   Context

SLOCCount is a free software distributed under the General Public License, making it a truely open source software. The tool takes as input the directory containing the source code of a software development project, and automatically detects the programming languages used and measures the associated sloc. An example of SLOCCount output is provided in Fig. 1. We note that the tool also proposes an estimation of the effort required to produce an amount of code based on the COnstructive COst MOdel (COCOMO) [3], which uses solely the number of lines of code.

SLOCCount is a popular toolset in the research and development community. Its author has requested that any usage for research article be acknowledged, and researchers mostly do so in a footnote. A number of researchers however also add it to the bibliographic references, with the link to the website. Instead of scanning hundreds of thousands of research papers to estimate the adoption of SLOCCount, we rely on Google Scholar which compiles bibliographic references. At the time of writing, around 200 published research articles referenced a version of SLOCCount in their bibliography. Consequently, the actual number is much more higher.

2.2   SLOCCount Limitations

Although SLOCCount is largely used, it still presents a number of limitations that have not been addressed after over a decade of existence. David A. Wheeler, himself, confirms that still remain and new support is not added as "it's just that [he] didn't need it for [his] purposes".

```
tegawende@usensa:~$ sloccount Downloads/sloccount-2.26
Creating filelist for sloccount-2.26
Categorizing files.
Finding a working MD5 command....
Found a working MD5 command.
Computing results.


SLOC      Directory       SLOC-by-Language (Sorted)
4409    sloccount-2.26   perl=2851,ansic=610,sh=559,lex=171,ruby=110,
                         haskell=32,cobol=27,php=22,pascal=10,f90=6,
                         fortran=6,cs=5
                         [GPL]


Totals grouped by language (dominant language first):
perl:         2851 (64.66%)
ansic:         610 (13.84%)
sh:            559 (12.68%)
lex:           171 (3.88%)
ruby:          110 (2.49%)
haskell:        32 (0.73%)
cobol:          27 (0.61%)
php:            22 (0.50%)
pascal:         10 (0.23%)
f90:             6 (0.14%)
fortran:         6 (0.14%)
cs:              5 (0.11%)


Licenses:
    4409 (100.00%) GPL


Percentage of Licenses containing selected key phrases:
    4409 (100.00%) GPL


Total Physical Source Lines of Code (SLOC)              = 4,409
Development Effort Estimate, Person-Years (Person-Months) = 0.95 (11.40)
 (Basic COCOMO model, Person-Months = 2.4 * (KSLOC**1.05))
Schedule Estimate, Years (Months)                       = 0.53 (6.30)
 (Basic COCOMO model, Months = 2.5 * (person-months**0.38))
Estimated Average Number of Developers (Effort/Schedule) = 1.81
Total Estimated Cost to Develop                         = $ 128,292
 (average salary = $56,286/year, overhead = 2.40).
SLOCCount, Copyright (C) 2001-2004 David A. Wheeler
SLOCCount is Open Source Software/Free Software, licensed under
the GNU GPL. SLOCCount comes with ABSOLUTELY NO WARRANTY, and you are
welcome to redistribute it under certain conditions as specified by the
GNU GPL license; see the documentation for details.
Please credit this data as
"generated using David A. Wheeler's 'SLOCCount'."
```

Fig. 1. Output of SLOCCount execution on the source code directory of SLOCCount

Limited number of languages: The first limitation lies in the number of programming languages supported. SLOCCount supports as of this day 27 languages which were supposedly the most encountered at the time of implementation. Existing work has however discussed the popularity of languages and their adoption, and showed that new programming languages are increasingly adopted, leading to a large body of software projects written in such languages [2]. Besides, as of today, the Wikipedia online encyclopedy lists over 600 programming languages, far beyond the number of those that SLOCCount can automatically detect and count their lines of code.

Naive Count of physical lines of code: The second limitation of SLOCCount is in its method for counting source lines of code. Indeed, the tool is limited to physical source lines of code, and thus will overestimate source code with long variable names (e.g., as recommended in Java) that lead to write one statement in several lines.

Restricted effort estimation: Finally, to estimate the development effort for the project as well its cost, current version of SLOCCount only proposes the COCOMO model which however has serious competitors.

2.3 The Project: Collaboratively Building SLOCCount^{++}

As a graded project for the software engineering curriculum, we have proposed to fourth year undergrad students to collaboratively build a new version of SLOCCount, that we will refer to as SLOCCount^{++}, and which should address the limitations listed above. In practice, students had to organize themselves into groups of 2 or 3 people that would bid on 20 of the 600 programming languages listed on Wikipedia. In a class of 15 students, we thus assure the coverage of about 300 languages (over ten times the number currently supported by SLOCCount). Students were encouraged to directly build on top of the existing code of SLOCCount, and add options for counting Logical Lines of code (i.e., by statements) instead of physical lines of code, and also for referring to other cost computation models such as COSYSMO and the Putnam model.

The project has already lasted 3 months during which students strived to find code snippets in their different selected languages so as to understand quickly its internals before implementing the source line counter. The final results and reports of the projects are scheduled to be submitted and compiled at the end of August, and all reports and toolsets will be available at http://www.fasolabs.org/projects/sloccount++/.

Although the project is still ongoing, we are already witnessing its impact on students. Finally, we have received preliminary versions of the reports that provide a glance on the final outcome.

3 Lessons Learned

Developing countries represent a particular setting for computer science training in general and software engineering teaching in particular. The homework project on the development of an improved version of SLOCCount has provided many lessons for better designing our curricula to take into account the local specificities. Among the lessons learned, some are about the positive output of the project realization while others relate to the negative points that were highlighted.

Open source is a good stepping stone: Our experience has shown that it is opportune to leverage open source code to train software developers in the context of developing countries. Indeed, in the absence of unlimited Internet access, students cannot discuss on forums and request assistance online. However, they can find answers in existing open source code, which is usually very well docommented.

Working on a real problem builds confidence: In general, students showed enthusiasm while working on the project. Indeed, most of them showed their surprise that such a worldwide popular program, SLOCCount, had issues that they could also participate to resolve. This reality increased their confidence for their own project, and teachers were happy to hear that students are no longer overimpressed by any code, and thus no longer fear to dive into reading the code of complex programs, include the Linux operating system kernel.

Collaborative work is a good incentive: Letting students bid on different languages to participate in the implementation of a common toolset appears to have been very successful. Students could help each other, while still competing on the final completion of the project.

Aiming very high is not a waste of time: Most of the time, we, teachers at the University of Ouagadougou, and I suppose in many developing countries, look down on students and reduce their potential to the limitations of the context. With this project, which promises to deliver a toolset that is needed around the globe, we have noted that aiming extremely high has been very productive.

A long road to go: The imminent success of the project must not however elude different constraints and limitations in the efforts engaged. In particular, the limitation in Internet connectivity remains a huge challenge for software engineering training.

Looking at code is good, but not enough: Forcing students to read software code in different programming languages lead them to "discover" languages that were not part of the curricula. Some students by reading the code of some scripting languages, e.g., Python, have found them interesting and decided to learn them by themselves. However, most students were content in understanding the delimitations of a statement in their attributed language, the associate comment signs, etc. There is thus a need to push students to be more curious, to ensure that this experience is truly beneficial.

4   Related Work

Since the early days of computer science, researchers have called attention to the problems facing computer science education in developing nations [8]. More recently, researchers at African universities have investigated the challenges facing efficacy tools, including animations, for computer science courses in developing countries [5].

The contributions of this paper are in the same spirit of these works. We highlighted the difficulties for software engineering training at the University of Ouagadougou, which are somewhat in line with the findings in Kenyan institutions [4]. Then, we presented our collaborative project as a stimulating project that engages students and gives them confidence while forcing them to practically look into the code and learn differently than in lectures.

5   Conclusion

In this paper, we have discussed a report on experience for software engineering training at the university of Ouagadougou. The objective of this report was to highlight the constraints that curricula in developing countries face due to the digital divide, and to propose an example of steps to design "useful" homeworks for students.

We have provided the subject of the project and discussed its purpose in the curricula of the University of Ouagadougou. We believe that this project could be carried on around different African universities, in a collaborative student taskforce, that will produce a toolset which is useful beyond Africa.

Finally, we present this report as a contribution for better training the future researchers and practitioners for ICT4D. Indeed, ICT4D services are required to be developed locally to be relevant to the need of local consumers, and thus today's students, despite various constraints, must gain reasonable expertise in software development.

References

1. Bissyandé, T.F., Ahmat, D., Ouoba, J., van Stam, G., Klein, J., Le Traon, Y.: Sustainable ICT4D in Africa: where do we go from here? In: Bissyandé, T.F., van Stam, G. (eds.) AFRICOMM 2013, LNICST 135. LNICST, vol. 135, pp. 95–103. Springer, Heidelberg (2014)
2. Bissyandé, T.F., Thung, F., Lo, D., Jiang, L., Réveillère, L.: Popularity, interoperability, and impact of programming languages in 100,000 open source projects. In: Proceedings of the 2013 IEEE 37th Annual Computer Software and Applications Conference, COMPSAC 2013, pp. 303–312 (2013)
3. Boehm, B.: Software Engineering Economics. Prentice-Hall, Englewood Cliffs (1981)
4. ICTWorks. 12 challenges facing computer education in kenyan schools. http://www.ictworks.org/2011/09/12/12-challenges-facing-computer-education-kenyan-schools/
5. Mtebe, J.S., Twaakyondo, H.M.: Are animations effective tools for teaching computer science courses in developing countries? the case of university of dar es salaam. Int. J. Digital Inf. Wirel. Commun. 2(2), 202–207 (2012)

6. Ouoba, J., Bissyandé, T.F.: Leveraging the cultural model for opportunistic networking in sub-saharan Africa. In: Jonas, K., Rai, I.A., Tchuente, M. (eds.) AFRICOMM 2012. LNICST, vol. 119, pp. 163–173. Springer, Heidelberg (2013)
7. Ouoba, J., Bissyandé, T.F.: Sensing in the urban technological deserts-a position paper for smart cities in least developed countries. In: Proceedings of the International Workshop on Web Intelligence and Smart Sensing, IWWISS 2014, September 2014
8. Robertson, E.L.: The problems facing computer science education in developing nations. In: Proceedings of the Fifth SIGCSE Technical Symposium Computer Science Education, SIGCSE 1975, pp. 56–60 (1975)
9. Wheeler, D.A.: SLOCCount. http://www.dwheeler.com/sloccount/

Performance Evaluation of Fingerprint Biometrics Systems for e-Business Access Control

O.A. Esan[1], I.O. Osunmakinde[2(✉)], and S.M. Ngwira[1]

[1] Department of Computer System Engineerining,
Tshwane University of Technology, Soshanguve Campus, Pretoria, South Africa
{esanoa, ngwiraSM}@tut.ac.za
[2] School of Computing, College of Science, Engineering and Technology,
University of South Africa, UNISA, Pretoria, South Africa
osunmio@unisa.ac.za

Abstract. The performance of a fingerprint authentication system in electronic business depends on the accurate analysis of the quality of input fingerprints. This paper investigates distorted and misaligned fingerprints caused by environmental noise such as oil, wrinkles, dry skin, dirt and displacement of the query fingerprint with the database fingerprint template during matching. The noisy, distorted and/ or misaligned fingerprint produced as a 2-D on x-y image, is enhanced and optimized using a new hybrid modified Gabor filter-hierarchal structure check (MGF-HSC) system model based on an MGF integrated with a HSC. Our findings indicate that structural matching is experimentally confirmed as a reliable matching technique in a fingerprint authentication system, as distorted fingerprints can easily be matched, even when the pixel value detected is low, while the rotational and geometrical transformation that affects fingerprint authentication is addressed. The MGF-HSC approach minimizes false fingerprint matching and the dominant effect of distortion and misalignment of fingerprints to an acceptable level. Our approach, which is benchmarked with publicly available methods, deals with 60 % heavy distortions and misaligned fingerprint and exhibits reliable matching performance for promising e-business security work in terms of visual quality, false rejection rate and false acceptance rate.

Keywords: Authentication · e-Business · Distortion · Misalignment · Noise · Security · Biometric · Fingerprint

1 Introduction

An automated technique for recognizing a person based on physiological and behavioral traits is known as a biometrics system. Physiological traits include the face, fingerprint, palm print and iris, which remain permanent throughout an individual's lifetime [1, 2]. Behavioral traits are signature, gait, speech and keystroke, etc., which change over time [1–3].

The advantages of a fingerprint authentication system make the system the most widely used biometric system for various applications for security and access control at

© Institute for Computer Sciences, Social Informatics and Telecommunications Engineering 2015
A. Nungu et al. (Eds.): AFRICOMM 2014, LNICST 147, pp. 269–281, 2015.
DOI: 10.1007/978-3-319-16886-9_28

airports, borders, immigration offices, houses, offices, banks and other places where security needs to be enhanced [2]. In this regard, the problem of securing information emerged, since information needs to be managed [2].

Securing of data has been of paramount importance in both the private and public e-business sectors. E-business is conducted on internet platforms where information security management is critical as input and output. Thus, as the method of maintaining security increases, the threat of security breaching also increases. A Verizon risk team, in collaboration with the united states security service (USSS), conducted a study on security breaches in financial institutions from 2008 to 2010 and came up with a result of approximately nine hundred million (900 million) data breaches [2, 4]. The record of security breaches at financial institutions from 2008 to 2010 is shown in Fig. 1.

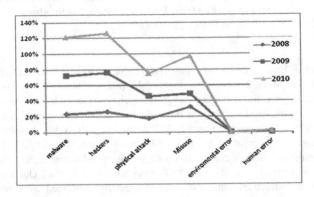

Fig. 1.   Visualization of security breaches in USSS

From Fig. 1 it can be observed that there is a higher incidence of hacking, malware and misuse. This record is not good enough, particularly for financial institutions in e-business. It proves that a traditional authentication system cannot handle the growing number of daily online financial customer transactions across the globe [2]. To counter these threats, advances in biometrics systems have replaced the use of traditional techniques of authentication, since biometrics cannot be lost and forgotten. A biometric system is an automatic technique of identifying a person based on biological and physiological traits [1, 2, 5].

This paper advances the existing bimodal authentication system by addressing the problem of distortion and misalignment in fingerprints to improve the security of access control areas such as financial institutions in e-business. The major contributions of this paper are as follows:

- Performance evaluations of a new biometrics hybrid modified Gabor filter-hierarchical structural check (MGF-HSC) matching system model, which addresses both distorted and misaligned fingerprints for authentication in e-business.
- Analysis of the MGF-HSC on a specific fingerprint noise scenario for ease of implementation.
- Experimental evaluations of biometrics with application to access control areas such as financial systems in e-business using real-life fingerprint images and

benchmarking with publicly available datasets using fingerprint verification competition (FVC) 2000a methods.

The deployment analysis of this approach with application to e-business access control areas, especially in developing countries, is unheard of. The rest of this paper is organized as follows: Sect. 2 presents the theoretical background, which includes related work on the MGF algorithm and HSC algorithm; Sect. 3 presents the fingerprint authentication system model; Sect. 4 critically presents visual inspection and quantitative experimental evaluations of the approach using lightly and heavily distorted fingerprint images, as well as benchmarking our MGF-HSC approach with the artificial neural network (ANN) method. We conclude the paper in Sect. 5.

2 Related Research

There are several fingerprint approaches to access control areas using a fingerprint biometric system. This section presents them as shown in Table 1.

Table 1. Comparison with previous work

Related works	Problem addressed	Method	Result	Limitations
An algorithm for distorted fingerprint matching based on local triangle feature sets [7]	• Problem of non-linear distortion in fingerprint matching.	A novel method using fuzzy feature match (FFM) based on a local triangle feature set to match the deformed fingerprints.	Experimental result confirms that proposed FFM based on the local triangle feature set see more detail in [7]	The drawback of the proposed algorithm is for the overlapping area between the template and input fingerprint should be large.
Fingerprint minutia matching without Global alignment using local structure [8]	• Problem of fingerprint matching based on rotation and translation invariant local structures see more detail in [8]	The approach used a local matching structure and similarity score.	Experimental result shows an improved performance of the proposed method in see more detail in [8].	The approach did not consider the problem of enhancing the distorted fingerprint.
Fingerprint image Enhancement: Algorithm and Performance Evaluation [6]	• Reliably extracting minutiae from an input fingerprint with heavy noise.	Fast fingerprint enhancement algorithm, which can adaptively improve the clarity of ridge and furrow structure see more detail in [6]	Experimental result shows that the algorithm is capable of improving both goodness index and the verification performance.	The approach did not consider the problem of misalignment in the fingerprint
Using MGF & HSC algorithms	• Fingerprint with distortion and misalignments.	Using a MGF algorithm.	Experiments show that our approach obtained good results as shown in Sect. 4 (a)-(b)	It is difficult to find fingerprint orientation in a situation with heavy distortions.

3 Proposed Fingerprint Authentication Using MGF-HSC

The system architecture described in Fig. 2 for a fingerprint biometrics authentication system is divided into two stages, the (i) enrolment phase and (ii) authentication phase.

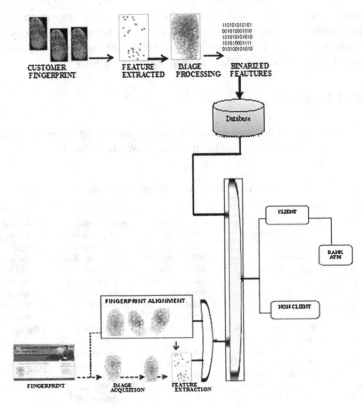

Fig. 2. System Architecture

Fig. 3. Distorted fingerprint with irregular sinusoidal frequency

3.1 The Enrolment Phase

According to the system architecture in Fig. 2, it is at this stage that the fingerprints are rotated in different directions to avoid rotational and directional invariance of the user fingerprint during the authentication stage, as the direction used for the registered user fingerprint on the template of the stored user fingerprint is captured using a fingerprint scanner or fingerprint reader and this is stored together with other relevant information on the user. The enrolment module is sub-divided into:

3.1.1 Image Acquisition Stage

As reflected in Fig. 2, the fingerprint images of users are captured with a fingerprint reader and are saved in a database with other relevant information.

3.1.2 Biometric Feature Extraction Stage

Before feature extraction, the image is passed through image enhancement stages, which include normalization, binarization, segmentation and thinning. After these stages follows feature extraction, represented in Fig. 2, in which the most important features, such as ridges and valleys, are extracted from the fingerprint by subjecting it to image processing and extraction algorithms, as in Algorithm 1.

ALGORITHM 1. COMPUTATION OF RIDGES AND VALLEYS FOR MGF-HSC
INPUT: G = normalized image, block size= $W \times W$ **OUTPUT:** Ridge and Valley
STEP 1: divide G image into $W \times W$ centered (i, j) STEP 2: for each (i, j) STEP 3: compute $l \times w$ STEP 4:   for each block centered (i, j) STEP 5:   compute $\partial_x (i, j)$ and $\partial_y (i, j)$ for each pixel   STEP 6: compute the magnitude $\partial_x (i, j)$ and $\partial_y (i, j)$ at each pixel   STEP 7:   set a local threshold value   STEP 8:   if compute the magnitude $\partial_x (i, j)$ and $\partial_y (i, j) >$ threshold   value, ridge is obtained   STEP 9: else   STEP 10: valley is obtained

In Algorithm 1, the ridges and valleys in minutiae are computed by dividing the image into block-sized centered(i, j), and an oriented window of $w \times l$ is built at each center. The second derivatives and the magnitude of first derivatives are obtained. A local threshold value is set to determine ridge width and valley width: if the magnitude of the first derivative is greater than the threshold, it is a ridge, otherwise it is a valley.

3.2 Authentication Phase

According to the system architecture depicted in Fig. 2, during the authentication module the system requires the user to present his or her fingerprint physically again for the system to confirm whether he/she is who he/she claims to be. This module is preceded by a matching stage.

3.2.1 Matching Stage

At this stage the query fingerprints are compared with the bank fingerprint in the database (template) to determine if the person is who he/she claims to be. This is done by using the matching algorithm and matching score of two minutia pairs of composite features in triplet form to determine if they are identical, as in Algorithm 2.

ALGORITHM 2. COMPOSITE MATCHING OF TWO FINGERPRINT USING HSC
INPUT: ML=Minutiae-list,   Pt=predefined   threshold, M_{ax}=Minutiae-a.x,May=Minutiae-a.y,MM=Matched-minutiae, M_{by}=Minutiae-by,M_{bx}=Minutiae-b.x, NM_a=NORMALIZE(minutiaea.angle) NM_b=NORMALIZE(minutiae-b.angle),X_T=X, tolerance, Y_T=Y-tolerance, T=tolerance, ΘT=ANGLE-TOLERANCE
OUTPUT: TRUE MATCH
STEP 1: MM $\leftarrow 0$ STEP 2:   for each x -source-ML   STEP 3:   for each y target-ML   STEP 4: matches (x, y)MM $\leftarrow$ MM+1   STEP 5:   if MM $\geq$ Pt   STEP 6:   return true   STEP 7:   else   STEP 8: return false   STEP 9:   if $\left(M_{ax} \cdot M_{bx}\right) \leq X_T$ and   STEP 10:   if $\left(M_{ay} \cdot M_{by}\right) \leq Y_T$ and   STEP 11:   if $NM_a - NM_b \leq \theta_T - T$ STEP 12: return true

From Algorithm 2, in matching two fingerprints, the minutiae ML (minutiae-list) is obtained from both the query and template fingerprint on both x and y axes, matches minutiae (x,y) if minutiae matches are greater than or equal to a predefined threshold, otherwise returns false. If the minutia-a,x and minutiae-b.angle are less than or equal to minutiae horizontal tolerance (X_T) and minutiae.a.y with minutiae b.y are less than or equal to vertical minutia tolerance (Y_T) and if Normalized (minutia.a.angle) (NM_a) is minus from Normalized (minutia.b.angle) (NM_b) is less than or equal to tolerance angle minus tolerance, then return true fingerprint else false.

3.3 Analysis of the MGF-HSC for Ease of Implementation

A well-defined fingerprint image has a good sinusoidal frequency shape. A noisy fingerprint image does not have a perfect sinusoidal frequency because the quality of the fingerprint surface is not well-defined [10].

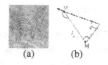

(a)   (b)

Fig. 4. Triangular diagram for the triplet feature extracted

The fingerprint in Fig. 3 can be enhanced to give a clear sinusoidal frequency wave with the following analysis:

First, to compute the orientation estimation of Fig. 3, the gradients in the x and y directions respectively are computed using a Sobel operator.

From the stored template a triangle is drawn at any point on the fingerprint as a

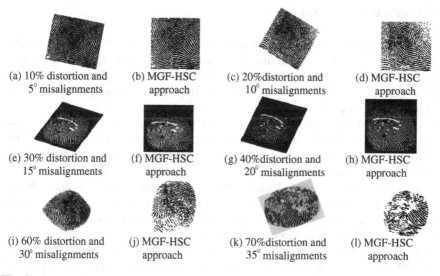

(a) 10% distortion and 5° misalignments

(b) MGF-HSC approach

(c) 20% distortion and 10° misalignments

(d) MGF-HSC approach

(e) 30% distortion and 15° misalignments

(f) MGF-HSC approach

(g) 40% distortion and 20° misalignments

(h) MGF-HSC approach

(i) 60% distortion and 30° misalignments

(j) MGF-HSC approach

(k) 70% distortion and 35° misalignments

(l) MGF-HSC approach

Fig. 5. Images (a), (c), (e), (g), (i), (k) are real-life fingerprints with distortion and misalignment; images (b), (d), (f), (h), (j) and (i) are the enhanced fingerprint using MGF-HSC

reference point, as shown in Fig. 4(a), the triplet parameter features of extracted reference minutiae points.

The extraction of features involves using two minutiae M_i and their neighbor minutia M_j for extracting the composite features. Figure 4(b) gives the definition of a composite feature, which is represented using a triplet form as in [2].

Equations (1-3) as shown in annexure is for parameter rotation (PR) and parameter translation (PT) for (θ, x, y)-component.

Hence, for matching of query minutiae Q and template minutiae P, these two conditions in Eqs. (9),(10) must be met as shown in annexure.

3.4 Scoring and Evaluation Scheme

In this section, the performance of the proposed bimodal biometric is studied through visual inspection as well as quantitatively. During visual inspection, one compares the quality of the pixel value of distorted and misaligned fingerprints with enhanced fingerprint images [9]. The following evaluation models were chosen as quantitative schemes [2, 13, 14]: (i) the false rejection rate (FRR) and (ii) the false acceptance rate (FAR), the schemes in [13], are computed by the following formulas in Eqs. (11),(12) as shown in annexure.

The percentage of system accuracy (SA) is computed by the following formula in Eq. (13) as shown in Annexure. These equations are used as objective evaluation schemes for measuring distorted and misaligned fingerprint enhancement.

4 Experimental Evaluations

One of the objectives of this paper is to apply the theory of our approach in practice by emphasizing applications and carrying out practical work on fingerprints with distortion and alignment using MATLAB, as shown in experiments 6–8 respectively. The fingerprint images are captured with a Futronic fingerprint scanner and the captured fingerprint produces a stream of distortions and misalignments on the x-y axis.

In calculating the percentage of noisy region, the fingerprint image is divided into 3×3 window size; the CN method extracts the ridge endings and bifurcations by examining the local neighbourhood of each ridge pixel,the region with distortion is estimated using a noise detector scheme in (14) as shown in Annexure. The scheme states that: (i) if a pixel x has at least one pixel y among the other eight pixels in the neighbourhood, then x is considered an original pixel and y is deemed similar to pixel x; and (ii) if x does not have at least one similar pixel among its neighbours, it is considered to be distorted as shown in Eq. (14).

However, this work focuses on fingerprint biometrics and enhancing distorted and misaligned fingerprint images. In terms of performance measures, the FAR, FRR and the graph of qualitative performance are shown when evaluating the result of the proposed MGF-HSC approach, as shown in Fig. 6.

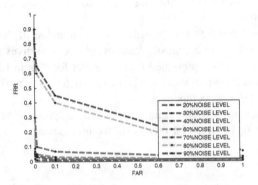

Fig. 6. Plot of FRR/FAR for proposed MGF-HSC model

4.1   Experiment 1: Visual Inspection and Performance of MGF-HSC

The objective here is to observe the performance of the MGF-HSC approach on a real-life distorted and misaligned fingerprint template. However, using the MGF-HSC, we select the parameter of standard deviation σ_x and σ_y for controlling the enhancement result obtained in Fig. 5.

The aim is to demonstrate the performance of our MGF-HSC approach on lightly and heavily distorted and misaligned fingerprint images. In particular Fig. 5(a), (i), and (k) contain 10 % distortion and 5° misalignments, 60 % distortion and 30° misalignments, 70 % distortion and 35° misalignments and 90 % distortion and 40° misalignments respectively. Figure 5(b), (j) and (l) are the fingerprint results obtained after enhancement with the MGF-HSC approach. The performance drops with over 60 % & 30° distortions and misalignments.

4.2   Experiment 2: Quantitative Performance of MGF-HSC Approach

The result in Fig. 6 specifically assesses the graphical performance of our MGF-HSC approach with respect to noise level, ranging from 10 % + 5° to 90 % + 40° (distortions and misalignments).

After comparing the original and distorted fingerprints with the enhanced fingerprints, the graph in Fig. 6 shows various forms of noise and misalignment. One can see that at 70 %, 80 % and 90 % that there is predominant increase in both false rejection and false acceptance rate respectively.

4.3   Experiment 3: Benchmarking Our Approach with Publicly Available Templates and Methods

The aim of benchmarking is to access the qualitative performance of our proposed approach on FVC 2000a DB2 fingerprint database where fingerprint are noticeably different from real-life fingerprint images.

In Fig. 7, the MGF-HSC approach is benchmarked with the ANN. The original fingerprints in Fig. 7(a) and (d) contain distortion. The ANN approach and our MGF-HSC approach were used to enhance and filter the distorted regions. Figure 7(b), (c), (e) and (f) show the result of ANN and our MGF-HSC approach respectively. One can see the result of the MGF-HSC approach in Fig. 7(c) and (f), which show better enhancement compared to the images in Fig. 7(b) and (e).

(a) Original   (b) ANN   (c) MGF-HSC   (d) Original   (e) ANN   (f) MGF-HSC
Image   Method [15]   Approach   Image   Method [15]   Approach

Fig. 7 Images (a) are real-life fingerprints with distortion and misalignment; images (b) and (c) are the enhanced fingerprints

5 Concluding Remarks

We have proposed and demonstrated the use of a fingerprint biometric approach for addressing the issues of security in access control areas, such as in financial business infrastructure. We conducted experiments using the MGF-HSC algorithm to address the issue of distortions and misalignments of fingerprints during authentication. The enhancement of lightly noisy images seemed encouraging in the initial stage, but experimental results on heavily noisy images were discouraging which needs further improvement.

Our findings indicate that the MGF-HSC approach can completely remove noise from a lightly distorted image ranging from 1 % to 60 %, but is limited when the fingerprint is contaminated with heavy noise ranging from 70 % upward, as shown in Fig. 5(b) and (c). In a situation with heavy distortion the fingerprint orientation field is hard to estimate, thus making computation of the ridge width and valley width difficult.

This research has been simulated on financial access control of users, e.g. bank customers, and is strategic method to e-business security. If this technology could be adopted, online financial organizations should be able to (1) authenticate the identities of buyers and sellers on e-business, (2) determine level of authorization assigned to both parties, (3) protects unauthorized altering of information in transaction (4) ensure availability of e-business sections when needed. In future work, the research can be explored further in different forms, including (1) using 3-D fingerprint images for authentication and (2) encrypting fingerprint image to avoid duplicating.

Acknowledgments. The authors acknowledges the financial support of Tshwane University of Technology and resources made available by University of South Africa.

ANNEXURE

Thus, parameter translation (PR) in Eq. (1),

$$PR_{(\phi)} = \begin{cases} PR_{(\phi)} \quad occurs, \quad if \quad \phi_{d1} = \phi_{d2} \\ \\ return \quad failure, \quad if \quad \phi_{d1} \neq \phi_{d2} \end{cases} \quad (1)$$

For x-component in Eq. (2),

$$PR_{(x)} = \begin{cases} PR_{(x)} \quad occurs, \quad if \quad x_1 = x_2 \\ \\ return \quad failure, \quad if \quad x_1 \neq x_2 \end{cases} \quad (2)$$

and for y-component in Eq. (3),

$$PR_{(y)} = \begin{cases} PR_{(y)} \quad occurs, & if \quad y_1 = y_2 \\ \\ return \quad failure, & if \quad y_1 \neq y_2 \end{cases} \tag{3}$$

For parameter distance in Eq. (4) (x, y),

$$m.ax(MP_1 - MP_2) \tag{4}$$

The second distance is in (5), for x-component in Eq. (5),

$$= m.ax(MP_2 - MP_1) \tag{5}$$

Thus, parameter translation (PT) in Eq. (6),

$$PT_{(x)} = \begin{cases} PT_{(x)} \quad occurs, & if \quad x_1 = x_2 \\ \\ return \quad failure, & if \quad x_1 \neq x_2 \end{cases} \tag{6}$$

For the y-component in Eq. (7),

$$PT_{(y)} = \begin{cases} PT_{(y)} \quad occurs, & if \quad y_1 = y_2 \\ \\ return \quad failure, & if \quad y_1 \neq y_2 \end{cases} \tag{7}$$

For the ϕ-component in Eq. (8)

$$PT_{(\phi)} = \begin{cases} PT_{(\phi)} \quad occurs, & if \quad \phi_1 = \phi_2 \\ \\ return \quad failure, & if \quad \phi_1 \neq \phi_2 \end{cases} \tag{8}$$

Condition 1: Matching with a predefined threshold value as in Eq. (9),

$$M_{(m)} = \begin{cases} Q \equiv P, \quad if \quad min \quad utiae \geq threshold \\ \\ return \quad failure \quad otherwise \end{cases} \tag{9}$$

Condition 2: Matching with a specified tolerance value as in Eq. (10),

$$Match_{(Q,P)} = \begin{cases} Q \equiv P, & if \quad \begin{aligned} x &\leq Tolerance \\ y &\leq Tolerance \\ \theta &\leq Tolerance \end{aligned} \\ \\ return \quad failure & otherwise \end{cases} \tag{10}$$

$$FRR = \frac{G}{N} \qquad (11)$$

where G the number of valid users fingerprint who are incorrectly denied access and N is total number of genuine fingerprint tested.

$$FAR = \frac{I}{N} \qquad (12)$$

where I the number of imposters' fingerprints is incorrectly granted and N is the total number of genuine fingerprint tested.

$$SA = \frac{M}{P} \times 100 \qquad (13)$$

where SA is the system accuracy, M is the total number of organized fingerprint image samples and P is the total number of fingerprint samples.

$$x = \begin{cases} x_{ij}^0 & K\{|x-y| \leq D_1\} \geq N_1^{th} \\ x_{ij}^n & else \end{cases} \qquad (14)$$

D_1 is adopted as the maximum depth difference between the similar x and y pixels and is often assumed to be eight pixels in the neighborhood. N_1^{th} is one, as every pixel is assumed to be similar to at least one pixel, and K is the number of y pixels that satisfies Eq. (14) while the distorted pixel is eliminated.

References

1. Senior, A., Bole, R.: Improved fingerprint matching by distortion removal. IEICE trans. Inf. Sys. **E84-D**, 825–831 (2001)
2. Esan, O.A., Ngwira, S.M., Osunmakinde, I.O.: Bimodal biometrics for financial infrastructure security. In: Information Security for South Africa (ISSA), South Africa (2013)
3. Bazen, A.M., Verwaaijen, G.T.B., Gerez, S.H., Veelenturf, L.P.J., van der Zwaag, B.J.: A correlation-based fingerprint verification system. In: proRISC 2000 Workshop on Circuits, System and Sigbal Processing (2000)
4. Team, V.B.R., Service U.S.S.: A Study of Data Breach Investigation Record in Financial Institutions (2010)
5. El-Sisi, A.: Design and implementation biometric access control system using fingerprint for restricted area based on Gabor filter. Int. Arab J. Inf. Technol. **8**(4), 355–363 (2011)
6. Jiang, X., Yau, W.Y.: Fingerprint matching based on local and global structure. In: Proceedings of the 15th International Conference on Pattern Recognition, Barcelona, IEEE (2000)
7. Fons, M., Fons, F., Canto, E.: Design of an embedded Fingerprint Matcher System (2006)
8. Gebroyohanne, T., Kim, D.Y.: Adaptive Noise Reduction Scheme for Salt and Pepper, Computer Engineering, Ajou University, Suwon, South Korea (2008)
9. Hong, L., Wan, Y., Jain, A.: Fingerprint image enhancement: algorithm and performance evaluation. IEEE Trans. Pattern Anal. Mach. Intell. **20**, 777–789 (1998)

10. Yang, J., et al.: Modified Gabor filter designed method for fingerprint image enchacement. Pattern Recogn. Lett. **24**(12), 1805–1817 (2003). Elsevier
11. Uludag, U., Pankanti, S., Jain, A.K.: Fuzzy vault for fingerprints. In: Kanade, T., Jain, A., Ratha, N.K. (eds.) AVBPA 2005. LNCS, vol. 3546, pp. 310–319. Springer, Heidelberg (2005)
12. Xi, K., Hu, J.: Biometric Mobile Template Protection: A Composite Feature -based Fingerprint Fuzzy Vault, School of Computer Science and IT, RMIT University (2003)
13. Awad, A.S., Man, H.: Similar neighbour criterion for impulse noise removal in images. Int. J. Electron. Commun. **64**, 904–915 (2010)
14. Ko, T.: Multimodal biometric identification for large user population using fingerprint, face and iris recognition. In: Proceedings of the 34th Applied Imagery and Pattern Recognition Workshop (AIPR 2005), pp. 144–152 (2005)
15. El-Iskandarani, M.A., Abdul-Kader, H.M.: Biometric authentication system Using fingerprints based on Self-Organizing Map Neural Network Classifier. Alexandra Engineering Journal **44**, 731–743 (2005)

A Framework for Measuring the Value of Enterprise Architecture in South African Telecommunications Organizations

Comfort Fiki Lukhele[1], Ernest Ketcha Ngassam[2],
and Isaac Osunmakinde[2(✉)]

[1] Department of Informatics, Tshwane University of Technology,
Pretoria, South Africa
lukhelecf@yahoo.com
[2] School of Computing, University of South Africa, Pretoria 0001, South Africa
eketcha@gmail.com, osunmio@unisa.ac.za

Abstract. Enterprise Architecture (EA) has gained popularity as an enabler for rapid organizational change with regard to controlling, optimizing and complexity management. It is thus regarded as organizations' blueprint for adaptability, change, evolution and therefore growth. However, its mere deployment would not necessarily yield favorable results; instead, results may vary from one organization to another. This necessitates investigations on organizations' readiness prior to the deployment of EA as well as appropriate mechanisms for monitoring its value during deployment and its impact post-deployment. We hereby, propose a framework for measuring the value of EA in organizations with focus on the telecommunication industry within South Africa. It is shown from case studies that the framework could help organizations not only to make an informed decision on whether to deploy EA or not, but also to constantly monitor its benefits (if any) during its deployment and beyond.

Keywords: Enterprise architecture · Business value · Measurement · Metrics · Framework

1 Introduction

Enterprise Architecture (EA) is a strategic and logical planning process that translates an organization's business vision and strategy into descriptive standards, processes and frameworks [1]. It is extensively used by business and IT managers to guide their organization's design, implementation, and use of IT [2]. As such, the process of its development and implementation within an organization necessitates a mutual effort from stakeholders. In effect, stakeholders should not exclusively focus on technology and/or infrastructure alone, but on EA itself. Of particular importance is on how EA can be designed to fit existing and changing business needs by taking people and processes into consideration.

The rapid evolution of the telecommunication industry has seen many telecom companies move away from relying only on providing basic telephony services as their main sources of revenue. Many of them have moved into newer sources of revenues,

© Institute for Computer Sciences, Social Informatics and Telecommunications Engineering 2015
A. Nungu et al. (Eds.): AFRICOMM 2014, LNICST 147, pp. 282–292, 2015.
DOI: 10.1007/978-3-319-16886-9_29

like providing services such as audio, video, data and Next Generation Networks not only to consumers but also to corporate organizations. Together with the introduction of many entrants, the industry has become highly competitive. Many of these organizations are confronted with having to regularly review their business strategies in order to retain significance and competitiveness [13]. Therefore, change management has become of utmost importance. Since these changes do not only talk to operational issues like technology and processes, telecom companies are also facing a challenge of finding suitable approaches and methods that will address change management at an enterprise-wide level.

In order to maintain their presence in the economic landscape, remain competitive and improve on the quality of their offerings, serious organizations need to take cognizance of markets/industries evolution as well as consumers' dynamics. Business change is the process of transitioning an organization from one state to another. It often entails business process reengineering which is an approach to change management [3]. Predictable business change occurs because organizations want to improve their performance, efficiency and effectiveness to counter competition and to respond to market change [4]. However organizations should also adapt to unpredictable changes that may occur sporadically. This implies that whether organizations are ready or not, change is always inevitable, more especially in the ICT industry. The adoption of EA by organization become curtail in the sense that it has the ability to help organization in their planning for transitioning from their current state (as-is) to a desired future state (to-be) [5].

This work focuses on how EA as a tool that addresses telecoms' challenges, needs and competitive advantages could be of value to the organization. To this end, in order to rely on tangible effects of EA to organizations, we propose a framework that forms the basis for measuring the value of EA at organization-wide. This contribution would enable telecom companies to rely on tangible metrics to support change.

The remainder of this paper is structured as follow: Sect. 2 briefly explore the benefit of EA for telecoms as well as its deployment challenges. In Sect. 3 findings from case studies are used to suggest how value can be measured in organization with regard to any EA deployment as well as the derivation of associated metrics. The foregoing forms the basis for description of our suggested framework in Sect. 4. A conclusion and further direction to this work are presented in Sect. 5.

2 Enterprise Architecture in Telecoms

With the maturity of technologies such as mobile and broadband, the telecommunication industry is regarded as a key role player for the advancement of social and economic development in developing countries. In fact, telecommunication services have been globally recognized as an essential input to quality of education, healthcare, e-government and economic advantages and opportunities [6]. For the past decade, the industry has been marked by rapid evolution, necessitating that telecommunication companies keep abreast with changes in order to preserve significance and competitiveness. As a result, many telecom companies have found it necessary to significantly invest on the latest technologies, IT infrastructure and products so as to be considered as effective service providers [7]. Often, the value of these investments needs to be justified by presenting returns. Return on Investment (ROI) is not only realized by selling products and services, it also emanates from cost savings as a result of an organization's processes and operational performance efficiencies.

In order to exploit operational performance and organizational processes, a number of telecommunications companies have identified and adopted some industry standards and frameworks such as: Information Technology Infrastructure Library (ITIL^{TM}), Control Objectives for Information and related Technology (CoBIT^{TM}), Telecom Applications Map (TAM), Shared Information/Data Model (SID) and the Enhanced Telecom Operations Map (eTOM) [8]. However, these frameworks appear too specialized and present some limitations briefly summarized in Table 1 below.

Table 1. Limitation of EA related frameworks often used by telecoms

Framework	Limitations
CoBIT	Mainly governance-centric
ITIL	Mainly technical-infrastructure centric
eTOM	Only process centric within the organization
TAM	Mainly telecoms' applications-centric
SID	Mostly terminology-centric

These frameworks address various domains of EA as suggested by The TOGAF (The Open Group Architecture Framework). However their adoption at enterprise level would appear complex not only because of their number but also because of the level of training and knowledge required for their integration and standardization. We rely on these frameworks to suggest a more generic and simplistic approach to measuring EA value with focus on the deployment of a new product/service.

Enterprise Architecture is intended to address challenges from technical to business needs in the organization that deploys it. It consists of descriptive representations (models) that are relevant for describing various aspects of the enterprise so that it can address management's requirements (quality) and maintained over a period of time (change) [9]. EA is a complete expression of the enterprise; a master plan for collaboration between aspects of business planning[1], business operations[2], business automationy[3], and enabling technological infrastructurey[4] [10]. The need to establish an EA process can be derived from the dynamics and complexity of the enterprise itself. Market developments, changes in business sectors, organizational adaptation, mergers and other major changes result in a high degree of volatility for an enterprise and its surroundings [11]. The assumed importance of EA is attributed to the need for an organization to adapt to quickly changing customer requirements and business goals.

---

[1] Business planning aspects include: goals, visions, strategies and governance principles.

[2] Business operation aspects include: business terms, organization structures, processes and data.

[3] Business automation aspects include: information systems and databases.

[4] Technological Infrastructure include: computers, operating systems and networks.

This need influences the entire chain of activities of an enterprise, from business processes to IT support. Some benefits of using EA, include:

- Readily available documentation of the enterprise.
- Ability to unify and integrate business processes across the enterprise.
- Ability to unify and integrate data across the enterprise and to link with external partners.
- Increased agility by lowering the "complexity barrier".
- Reduced solution delivery time and development costs by maximizing reuse of enterprise models; and
- Ability to create and maintain a common vision of the future shared by both the business and IT communities, driving continuous business/IT alignment.

The foregoing suggests that the need to deploy EA by telecom companies is vital for their survival. This is attributed to the current market dynamics whereby voice, SMS, and MMS services which were traditionally regarded as the core offerings of telecoms are now considered as commodities. Therefore, Telecoms may not experience growth if they cannot tap into other offering currently dictated by market dynamics and more precisely the mobile devices capabilities[5]. However, EA benefits suggest that the unit of analysis for measuring the value of EA as determined by Returns on Investments (ROI) is not only quantified in financial terms. Instead, many other aspects discussed in the next sections need to be considered. The aimed is to equip organizations with the ability to always be ready for change and also capture the value of such change.

EA is thus the suitable tool for enabling telecoms to have a thorough knowledge of the current-status of their organization within a given ecosystem. It helps in exploring future trends with regard to the ecosystem in various aspects (business, technical and infrastructural) in order to provide meaningful arguments for change [12]. However, although EA deployment in telecoms is widely spread, the need to qualitatively and quantitatively measure the value of its deployment at various stages of its implementation becomes critical. This paper addresses such shortcoming by proposing a framework that can be used for fast decision making. The next section discusses in general metrics required for measuring value at enterprise level.

3   EA's Value Measurement for Telecoms

A case study was carried out at two South African telecom companies referred-to as: Fixedcom and Mobilecom for confidentiality. Fixedcomm is one of the biggest telecom companies in Africa, it provides integrated communications solutions to the whole spectrum of clients. Mobilecomm is a South African based mobile telephone network operator and is active in 21 African countries. Our data collection questionnaire was formulated around some of the following themes: EA business drivers and requirements, EA development and implementation, return on investments (ROI) and EA

---

[5] Current smart phone capabilities are beyond mere voice text exchange and perfectly accommodate sophisticated applications not necessarily provided by Telecoms.

review mechanisms. We further conducted quantitative and qualitative analysis on data of which result contributed to the development of our framework [14]. Our analysis revealed that the measurement of enterprise architecture success within telecoms is based on the identification, qualification and quantification of a range of critical success factors' metrics that are relevant to the organization's success in all aspects. Some of EA's critical success factors obtained from our findings include amongst others the following key elements:

- *Value Goals*: Value is often defined by means of determining whether or not an entity does meet its goals and objectives of its existence. EA goals can be explicit and tangible. An EA that generates value is one that derives its goals from business goals and requirements, and in unison supporting IT strategy. It is therefore recommended that in measuring EA value, that EA goals be evaluated against business goals and requirements in conjunction with the IT strategy.
- *Baseline and Target Architecture Documentation*: Establishing a stable architecture might take a number of iterations depending on complexity of business processes, technology and data, meaning it is not a once-off exercise. Establishing the baseline architecture is the first step towards identifying challenges brought about by the current landscape. The target architecture can thus be seen as a solution that addresses current challenges with solution architecture being the vehicle through which the transition from 'current' to 'future' is carried out. It is therefore recommended that in order to realize EA value; the baseline architecture be carefully and thoroughly documented before paying much attention to the target architecture. Value can then be seen after transition by comparing the previous state to the current.
- *EA Maturity Index*: A more mature EA programme is more effective and will render more results generating even more value when compared to a less mature EA. EA maturity can be a biased factor when there's no maturity measurement system in place, however a valid measurement can present factual indicators rendering it objective. Therefore, it is imperative that all EA stakeholders take into account the maturity of the EA programme in order ascertain value. It can be said that measuring the level of observance to critical success factors can be used as value measurement factors.
- *ROI*: Some of the indicators of an effective EA are good returns on investments. If deployed correctly, EA will yield quantifiable benefits. ROI can be attained through reducing direct IT costs whilst increasing additional savings from risk mitigation and cost avoidance. Therefore, the degree to which EA yields ROI can be used as a measure to determine the value of EA.
- *Agility*: If implemented effectively, the agility of an EA will ultimately affect business agility. Also, business agility can be determined by the ability for business to embrace change and to meet market demands swiftly by reducing time to market for new products. Therefore business agility is one of the factors that can be employed to discover EA's value to the organization.

The Value Measurement Metrics are used to collect and to analyze data relating to the level of adherence to industry standards and best-practices at the respective cycle level for the stipulated processes. Results from the analysis are then appraised thereby indicating the level of *EA Maturity*. EA Maturity is an input to EA Value Measurement because it provides a certain level of confidence on the value or success of EA, thus EA Maturity is measured throughout the entire EA lifecycle.

While in this study we recommend a set of processes to be measured, the adherence scale and best-practices for each process will vary from one organization to another depending on the guidelines and best practices that the respective organization sub-scribes to. To this effect, stakeholders need to constantly perform a monitoring and evaluation exercise based collected and analyzed data. We term the data collection and analysis process as VMDCA (*Value Metrics Data Collection and Analysis*) which is used at all levels of measurement. This metrics seeks to provide appropriate mecha-nisms for measuring and monitoring value and post deployment impact. Table 2 below presents an extract VMDCA at both strategic and operation levels when engaging in the process of integrating a new product/service in an organization based on EA. Our proposed framework on which VMDCA relies is presented in the next section.

Table 2. An extract Value Metrics table

	Best practices	Best practice 1	Best practice 2	Best practice 3
Enterprise's Strategy				
Vision	Adherence Scale			
Business case	Adherence Scale			
Value proposition	Adherence Scale			
Customer engagement	Adherence Scale			
Enterprise' Management				
Business requirements	Adherence scale			
Solution development	Adherence scale			
Solution implementation	Adherence scale			
Validation	Adherence scale			

4 Proposed Telecoms EA Value Measurement Framework

Organizations focus on attaining predefined goals and objectives, mainly because of assumed value. The proposed framework provides a step-by-step guide which is to be used as a measurement process in order to determine EA value in both technical and business context. This process also involves a considerable amount of data collection and analysis at various levels. This framework is aimed at measuring the value which is yielded by the current EA. We hereby propose a framework (see Fig. 1 below) based on our findings as well some adaptation from the Enhanced Telecoms Operations Model (eTOM). The framework is intended to enable the EA team to demonstrate measurable deliverables and results.

It remains common knowledge that the end product of an organization's strategy as driven by its vision will either be products or services that customers will consume satisfactorily. The proposed EA value measurement framework is executed in a project/

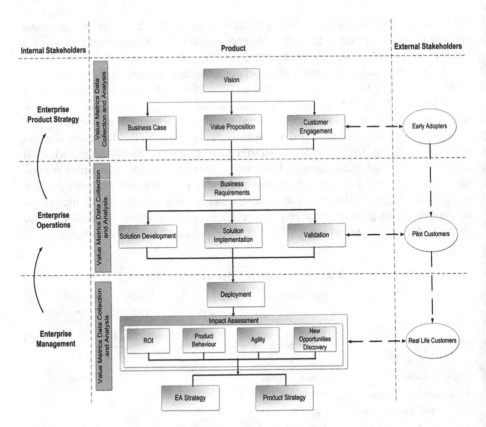

Fig. 1. Telecoms EA value measurement framework

iteration and continuous approach. Value is measured at each iteration level. The process of EA value measurement should be carried out and validated by the Architecture Review Board (ARB). Table 3 below presents the main concepts associated with the framework.

Our framework regards EA lifecycle from the perspective of product and services lifecycle management while considering the organization's vision and strategy as the primary drivers. EA Value Measurement is carried out from the following perspectives: (1) *Enterprise Product Strategy*, (2) *Enterprise Operations* and (3) *Enterprise Management*. Each of the perspective is discussed below.

(a) **Enterprise Product Strategy**

At the enterprise's strategic level, vision, mission and business strategies are formulated. This would normally drive the organization to rollout certain products or services. In order to validate the strategy, the following would be necessary:

- *Business Case:* A business case would be produced in order to capture the business objectives and goals, as well as to justify the reasoning behind the business strategy.

Table 3. Concepts of the value measurement framework for telecoms

Concept	Description
Internal stakeholders	Stakeholders internal to the organization that are involved at strategy, operation or management levels
Product	Refers to the intended offering to be created or improved and introduced to customers in the form of product and/or service
External stakeholders	Stakeholders that do not form part of EA and product lifecycles, however they are involved in consuming and validating the products and services throughout the lifecycles
Early adopters	Identified potential customers
Pilot customers	Identified group of potential consumers of whom input in highly valuable for the success of the intended product/service
Real life customers	End-consumers of the final product/service offered in real-life
Strategy value metrics	Metrics used for value measurement at strategy level
Operation value metrics	Metrics used for value measurement at enterprise operations level
Management value metrics	Metrics that is used for value measurement at enterprise management level

- **Value Proposition:** Proposed value would be the foundation for stakeholder (internal and external) buy-in. It stipulates the kind of contribution which the end-product or service would make to the organization or its customers.
- **Customer Engagement:** In order to substantiate value proposition, a market analysis is done thereby gathering real customer prospects (Early Adopters).

Measuring the value of EA starts at this level by establishing EA target goals (EA Value Goals). Thus EA value expectations and requirements can be driven by and mapped to strategic business objectives and goals, while business goals are clearly articulated in the value proposition as part of the business strategy which is a means through which the organization's vision is expressed. These goals and objectives are then supported and enabled by the IT strategy. EA value goals are regarded as the basis through which business and IT strategies alignment is achieved, therefore Key Performance Indicators (KPI's) are defined and appraised in order to measure the alignment of both strategies.

Using the Enterprise Strategy Value Measurement Metrics, data relating to the adherence of the organization's prescribed guidelines and best-practices is collected and analyzed; this would then render warnings about the efficacy of EA value goals.

(b) **Enterprise Operations**

Business Requirements: Business Requirements are derived from the business strategy, at the same time they also drive the development and implementation of solutions. The value of EA can be measured on how it enables an organization's increased operational efficiencies at reduced costs; this includes business functions;

processes and information systems. EA Value Measurement at this level also focuses on the manner in which the target EA (Solution) is to be implemented thereby indicating improvements in the future state from a performance, business, service, data, and technology perspective.

Solution Development: At an operational level, solutions that address the organization's products business capabilities can also be utilized to reveal EA value. These business capabilities should be clearly mapped to the strategy as stipulated in the business objectives. This can be done by:

- *Documenting the baseline architecture* - This allows for EA stakeholders to identify problem areas in the current landscape.
- *Documenting the target architecture* - The target architecture is regarded as an illustration of the answer to the current problem areas. At this stage; KPI's should be clearly defined and documented. These KPI's will be used to determine whether or not the business objectives have been fulfilled thereby demonstrating value.

Solution Implementation: After the solution has been implemented, comparisons are done taking into consideration the previous and current state of the EA landscape and fulfilment of business objectives identifying improvements brought by the proposed or implemented Enterprise Solution Architecture. This will be a demonstration of value. At this stage, the value of EA can be measured by quantifying the solution's collaboration and reuse of architecture building blocks. This helps to establish the organization's progress in making use and reuse of shared services (this refers to any architecture building blocks e.g. business processes, applications etc.). Effective use and reuse of shared services result into costs reduction. In consequence, the results of this exercise are to be used as an input when assessing ROI. The outputs from collaboration and reuse measurement provide an indication on EA efficiency. Efficiencies are to be used in order to measure ROI by mapping to EA outputs including; costs that have been saved and avoided as a result of, for example, the elimination of duplicate components that result into high costs.

Validation: Evidence to test and further support that customers' buy-in is gathered. It gives an indication as to whether or not the product would be successful or would require further improvements.

Using the Enterprise Operations Value Measurement Metrics, data relating to the adherence of the organization's prescribed guidelines and best-practices is collected and analyzed, presenting potential value.

(c) **Enterprise Management**

    Deployment: The product gets deployed or launched to the market; this is to be done in accordance with the organization's strategy.

Impact Assessment: Impact Assessment is carried out both internally and externally on a live environment with *Real Life Customers*, its purpose is to evaluate EA's effect on the following:

- *Product Behaviour* – the behaviour of the product in the market is assessed, giving an indication on the product's demand patterns.
- *ROI* - is measured internally by analysing and reporting the findings pertaining to the difference in IT portfolio investments through taking into consideration cost savings emanating from solution development and implementation. It can also be measured externally through the calculation of cash-flows received as a result of product sales and services consumption.
- *Agility* - can be perceived both internally and externally to the organization. It can first be measured through the flexibility of the organization's internal processes and later be measured through external processes. It is expressed by the time taken from conceptualizing and ultimately rolling out (deploying) products or services to the market.
- *New Opportunities Discovery* – the assessment of newly discovered opportunities as a result of an EA-driven product launch are assessed. This serves as an indication of how EA has enabled the organization to attain competitive advantage in the market.

Depending on the favorability of the EA Value Measurement results, either the EA Strategy (Enterprise Operations) or Product strategy (Enterprise Product strategy) might have to be reviewed in order to ensure continuous product improvement and value add. Thus measuring the value of EA cannot be done in linear approach, but it is iterative.

5 Conclusion and Future Research Work

In this paper, we have proposed a framework for measuring the value of EA deployment for Telecoms companies in South Africa. The suggested framework uses the golden thread of the deployment of a product/service by a telecom organization to its customer base. It is shown that at each level of the deployment lifecycle, a range of value metrics should be collected and analyzed in order to capture the value of such an endeavor. Such exercise regarded as a monitoring exercise is of tremendous importance in the decision making process. In fact, not all changes may be relevant to an organization. By subjecting companies to a rigorous process as advocated by the framework, analyzed data may provide insights as to whether to proceed with change or not. This would assist companies to embark on change based on tangible evidence. Although the proposed framework is product-centric, informed readers would find it easy to adapt it for any kind of EA endeavor within an organization. An EA initiative may be to optimize the current organizational process, infrastructure and even Unit. It is of our view that the framework can be easily tailored to meet such an endeavor.

As a matter of future work, our intention is to further decompose the framework so as to provide tangible metrics based on best practice so as to formalize data collection and analysis. Such a contribution will enable telecoms to be more rigorous when engaging in EA.

References

1. Losavio, F., Ortega, D., Pérez, M.: Comparison of EAI frameworks. J. Object Technol. **4**(4), 93–114 (2005)
2. Benson, R.J.: Enterprise architecture and information technology. In: Cooper, C.L. (ed.) The Blackwell Encyclopedia of Management. Blackwell Publishing, Oxford (2012)
3. Cao, G., Clarke, S., Lehaney, B.: A critique of BPR from a holistic perspective. Bus. Process Manage. J. **7**(4), 332–339 (2001)
4. Shaw, D.R., Holland, C.P., Kawalek, P., Snowdon, B., Warboys, B.: Elements of a business process management system: theory and practice. Bus. Process Manage. J. **13**(1), 91–107 (2007)
5. Chen, D., Doumeingts, G., Vernadat, F.: Architectures for enterprise integration and interoperability: past, present and future. Comput. Ind. **59**(7), 647–659 (2008)
6. Mkhomazi, S.S., Iyamu, T.: The social context of broadband infrastructure sharing. In: Proceedings of the 13th International Conference on Information Integration and Web-Based Applications and Service. pp. 403–407 (2011)
7. Schouwenaar, M., Martin, E.: Optimization of a telecommunications billing system. In: Proceedings of the 2003 Winter Simulation Conference, pp. 1843–1847 (2003)
8. Caldeira, M., Dhillon, G.: Are we really competent? Assessing organizational ability in delivering IT benefits. Bus. Process Manage. J. **16**(1), 5–28 (2010)
9. Zachman, J.: A framework for information systems architecture. IBM Syst. J. **26**(3), 84–92 (1987)
10. Schekkerman, J.: Enterprise architecture validation: achieving business-aligned and validate enterprise architecture (2004). http://www.enterprisearchitecture.Info
11. Niemann, K.: From Enterprise Architecture to IT Governance – Elements of Effective IT Management. Vieweg & Sohn Verlag, Wiesbaden (2006)
12. GAO.: Enterprise architecture, leadership remains key to establishing and leveraging architectures for organizational transformation (2006). http://www.gao.gov/new.items/d06831.pdf
13. Oyedijo, A.: Strategic agility and competitive performance in nigerian telecommunication industry: an empirical investigation. Am. J. Contemp. Res. **2**(3), 227–237 (2012)
14. Lukhele, C.F.: A Framework for Measuring the Value of Enterprise Architecture: A Case of Telecommunication Companies. Tshwane University of Technology (2014)

Understanding the Value of Evaluating ICT Models to Improve Medium and Small Enterprises

Anass Bayaga[1], Paul Tarwireyi[1(✉)], and Emmanual Adu[2]

[1] University of Zululand, Private Bag X1001,
Kwadlangezwa 3886, South Africa
{bayagaa, tarwireyip}@unizulu.ac.za
[2] University of Fort Hare, East London, South Africa
eadu@ufh.ac.za

Abstract. This research investigated evaluation models for understanding the value of Information and Communication Technology (ICT) Operational Risk Management (ORM) in Medium and Small Enterprises (MSEs). Multiple regression, Repeated-Measures Analysis of Variance (RM-ANOVA) and Repeated-Measures Multivariate Analysis of Variance (RM-MANOVA) were performed. The findings of the distribution revealed that only one variable made a significant percentage contribution to the level of ICT operation in MSEs, the Payback method ($\beta = 0.410$, $p < .000$). It may thus be inferred that the Payback method is the prominent variable, explaining the variation in level of evaluation models affecting ICT adoption within MSEs. Consequently, looking at (1) degree of variability explained and (2) predictors, the results revealed that the variable contributed approximately 88.4 % of the variations in evaluation models affecting ICT adoption within MSEs. The analysis of variance also revealed that the regression coefficients were real and did not occur by chance.

Keywords: ICT · Evaluation models · Medium and Small Enterprises (MSEs) · Operational risk management (ORM)

1 Introduction

This research presents the findings of the empirical investigation carried out to study the factors impacting on ICT and operational risk management (ICT ORM) within Medium and Small Enterprises (MSEs). An information system can provide business value for a firm in many different ways, including increased profitability and productivity. Some, but not all, of these business benefits can be quantified and measured [1, 8].

Inferring from the aforementioned quote, there is an indication that the IT Governance Institute described the central concept of IT as having a coherent set of activities with a set of shared core values. Moreover [16:7] argue that "modelling for management and control over IT processes is based on a method of evaluating the organisation, so it can be rated from a maturity level of non-existent (0) to optimised (5)." However, research notes that in reviewing the progress of the industry in the measurement of operational risk "…causal measurement and modelling of operational risk remains at the

© Institute for Computer Sciences, Social Informatics and Telecommunications Engineering 2015
A. Nungu et al. (Eds.): AFRICOMM 2014, LNICST 147, pp. 293–301, 2015.
DOI: 10.1007/978-3-319-16886-9_30

earliest stages" [2:2]. However, [10] studied this variable, while looking at the attitudes of end-users, but failed to correlate evaluation models with the attitudes of the end-users, suggesting that the use of this variable in their earlier work on MSEs did not receive the support for evaluation models impacting on ORM.

2 Background of Study

The definition of MSEs varies from country to country and is ideally defined specifically according to sector. The cut-off point in terms of size for this study was based on a recommendation from the African Development Bank, which defines MSEs as having less than 50 employees. This study deals with businesses[1] that aim to generate sustainable income streams. In the information society environment, successful enterprises produce high technology goods and services and transform human effort materials and other economic resources into product and services that meet customer needs [14]. In such a society, in order to be successful, MSEs need high quality information and must always provide superior value, better than competitors, when it comes to quality, price and services [11].

An information system can provide business value for a firm in many different ways, including increased profitability and productivity. Some, but not all, of these business benefits can be quantified and measured [2]. It has been pointed out that "one of the fundamental roles of banks and other financial intermediaries is to invest in assets which, because of their information-intensive nature, cannot be frictionlessly traded in the capital markets" [8]. The authors indicate that "the standard example of such an illiquid asset is a loan to a small or medium-sized company" [4]. First, some risks can be offset by hedging transactions in the capital market. Second, for those risks where direct hedging transactions are not feasible, another way for the bank to control its exposure is by altering its investment policies. Therefore, with illiquid risks, the bank's capital budgeting and risk management functions become linked" [5]. This reasoning suggests that capital budgeting models are used to determine whether an investment in information technology produces sufficient returns to justify its cost. Arguably, the principal capital budgeting models are the payback method, accounting rate of return on investment, net present value cost, cost benefits ratio, profitability index, and internal rate of return (see Table 1).

"Perhaps because the classical finance approach does not speak to their concerns with risk management, practitioners have developed alternative techniques for capital budgeting" [16]. Other models for evaluating information system investments involve non-financial considerations [12]. It has been argued that another important contribution is the Portfolio Theory [5].

It was suggested that it is possible to maximise the expected return of a portfolio of stocks but the risk level [is] measured by the probability of losing money. Recent studies define two major concepts that constitute the critical role of evaluation models in the management of financial institution portfolios [4]. Firstly, to assess and manage

---

[1] In this study 'business,' 'firm' 'organisation' and 'institutions' are used interchangeably.

Table 1. Evaluation models and ICT ORM adoption

A. Net Present Value (NPV) method is used to evaluate and align objectives of executive management and information systems projects.
B. Internal Rate of Return (IRR) method is used to evaluate and align objectives of executive management and information systems projects.
C. Portfolio analysis and scoring models are used to evaluate and align objectives of executive management and information systems projects.
D. Val IT framework is used to evaluate and align objectives of executive management and information systems projects.
E. COBIT framework is used to evaluate and align objectives of executive management and information systems projects.

risks, an institution must effectively determine the appropriate evaluation model necessary to absorb unexpected losses arising from its market, credit and operational risk exposures [5]. Secondly, profits that arise from various business activities need to be evaluated relative to capital necessary to cover the associated risks. There are few conceptual explanations on the association between risk management and capital adequacy and even fewer on empirical studies that show the relationship between an evaluation model and ITRM that affects the performance of MSEs [3]. Yet, others investigated how active management of financial institution exposure through loan sales market (such as the 'case study' used in this study) affects capital structure, lending, profits, and risks. Finally, effective risk management strategies should contribute to the financial institution's ability to assess not only the level of capital it would need in relation to assets and deposits, but also, in principle, mitigate the risk of financial institution failure [6].

Other studies support the above study by arguing that: "Performance measurement is essential for IT governance. It is supported by COBIT and includes setting and monitoring measurable objectives of what the IT processes need to deliver (process outcome) and how to deliver it (process capability and performance). Many surveys have identified that the lack of transparency of IT's cost, value and risks is one of the most important drivers for IT governance" [16]. Inferring from the above quote, the IT Governance Institute describe the central concept of IT as having a coherent set of activities with a set of shared core values. ITGI [8] arguing that "modelling for management and control over IT processes is based on a method of evaluating the organisation, so it can be rated from a maturity level of non-existent (0) to optimised (5)."

3 Research Problem

Literature notes that in reviewing the progress of the industry in the measurement of operational risk causal measurement and modelling of operational risk remains at the earliest stages. Thus evaluation models' affect the way an organisation operates from its values and its basic underlying assumption to technology diffusion. It is evident that evaluation models of an organisation either facilitate or impede the process of technology diffusion. However, the relevance of this variable in inter-organisational decision making has led the researcher of the current study to include this in the study of ORM adoption.

From the literature, it is expected that there will be a relationship between risk management practices and evaluation models. Hence, it is expected that good risk management involves good IT operational risk management.

4   Research Hypothesis

Consequently, an ICT operational risk model for MSEs was discussed and developed. Following the research objectives and the reviewed literature, the hypotheses that emerged included:

H1: there is a significant relationship between evaluation models and the likelihood of ICT ORM adoption within MSEs.

H0: there is no a significant relationship between evaluation models and the likelihood of ICT ORM adoption within MSEs.

5   Research Methodology

Simple descriptive and inferential statistical methods were incorporated into the statistical package for the social sciences (SPSS) programme for analysing the data. The variables were pre-coded in preparation for entry into the programme [15].

Despite the fact that the variables were descriptive in nature, they were assigned numeric codes to facilitate different statistical analysis [11]. Some of the measurement levels (scale of measurement) were nominal and others ordinal. After the data had been checked, the codes were entered into the programme and the process of data cleaning ensured.

Appropriate statistical procedures were then performed. Frequency counts and percentages were applied to the data relating to the demographic details of the respondents in order to determine the distribution of gender, age group, position, department and level of education. A bivariate analysis between the respondents' demographic characteristics and the relationship between; (1) ICT operational risk management and (2) performances of MSEs was, performed.

6   Data Analysis

Factor Analysis was used as the data reduction technique [12]. Factor Analysis was used to reduce a large number of related variables to a more manageable number, prior to using them in other analyses such as multiple regression or multivariate analysis of variance (MANOVA) [15].

In order to understand the degree of association between the performances of MSEs and the independent variables, multiple regressions, Repeated-Measures Analysis of Variance[2] RM-ANOVA and Repeated-Measures Multivariate Analysis of Variance - RM-MANOVA were performed [6]. Where a significant value was observed, either

---

[2] A four point Likert scale also cf. questionnaire.

Betas of multiple regression or significant levels of RM-ANOVA or RM-MANOVA ascertained these differences [15]. The outcomes of these analyses are described in subsequent sections.

One of the objectives of this study was to find the factors predicting ICT operational risk within MSEs. Multi- item constructs were used to capture the information about various types of variables to adopt ICT operational risk. The study was based upon a survey design to collect the primary data from 107 respondents using the simple random sampling technique. A one stage normative model associative in nature was developed based upon reviewing of previous research and in line with the research objectives.

6.1   Multivariate Regression

Generally, multivariate regression explains the relationship between multiple independent or multiple predictor variables and one dependent or criterion variable (Hypotheses). In multiple regressions, a dependent variable is modelled as a function of several independent variables with corresponding multiple regression coefficients, along with the constant term [15]. Multiple regressions require two or more predictor variables, which explain the term, multiple regressions [15]. The multiple regression equation explained above takes the following form:

$$y = b_1 x_1 + b_1 x_1 + \ldots + b_n x_n + c \tag{1}$$

In the multivariate case, when there is more than one independent variable, the regression line cannot be visualised in two dimensional spaces, but can be computed just as easily and is able to construct a linear equation containing all those variables. In general then, multiple regression procedures will estimate a linear equation of the form:

$$Y = a + b_1 {}^* X_1 + b_2 {}^* X_2 + \ldots + b_p {}^* X_p \tag{2}$$

Here, b_i's $(i = 1, 2 \ldots n)$ are the regression coefficients, which in multiple regression represents the value at which the criterion variable changes when the predictor variable changes [15]. For the purpose of the current paper, there are certain terminologies that help in understanding multiple regressions [15]. These terminologies are as follows.

The beta value in multiple regressions was used to measure how effectively the predictor variable influences the criterion variable [15]. In multiple regression (Presentation of data), it is measured in terms of standard deviation [15].

R, in multiple regressions is the measure of association between the observed value and the predicted value of the criterion variable [15]. R Square, or R^2, in multiple regressions is the square of the measure of association which indicates the percent of overlap between the predictor variables and the criterion variable [17].

7   Presentation of Research Findings

This section sought to determine the significant relationship between evaluation models and ICT adoption in MSEs. The object of this research question was to answer the question, (1) how well do the measures of evaluation models and ICT predict ORM adoption within MSEs? (2) Which is the best predictor of evaluation models and ICT in MSEs?

Table 2. Analysis of hypothesis

Model[a]		Unstandardized Coefficients		Standardized Coefficients	T	Sig.	Correlations			Collinearity Statistics	
		B	Std. Error	Beta			Zero-order	Partial	Part	Tolerance	VIF
1	Const	1.651	.345		4.780	.000					
	A	.430	.164	.410	2.618	.010	.258	.252	.246	.359	2.787
	B	-.164	.136	-.180	-1.205	.231	.143	-.119	-.113	.395	2.533
	C	.187	.103	.190	1.813	.073	.207	.178	.170	.802	1.247
	D-	-.114	.110	-.142	-1.034	.304	.113	-.102	-.097	.468	2.136
	E	.055	.113	.065	.487	.627	.132	.048	.046	.501	1.996

[a]A-Net Present Value method is used to evaluate and align objectives of executive management and information systems projects.
B-Internal Rate of Return (IRR) method is used to evaluate and align objectives of executive management and information systems projects.
C-Portfolio analysis and scoring models are used to evaluate and align objectives of executive management and information systems projects.
D-Val IT framework is used to evaluate and align objectives of executive management and information systems projects.
E-COBIT framework is used to evaluate and align objectives of executive management and information systems projects.

Table 3. Multivariate tests

Effect		Value	F	Hypothesis df	Error df	Sig.	Partial Eta Squared
Intert	Pillai's Trace	.980	967.9	5.000	98.0	.000	.980
	Wilks' Lambda	.020	967.9	5.000	98.0	.000	.980
	Hotelling's Trace	49.38	967.9	5.000	98.0	.000	.980
	Roy's Largest Root	49.38	967.9	5.000	98.0	.000	.980
Dep't	Pillai's Trace	.184	1.306	15.000	300.0	.197	.061
	Wilks' Lambda	.825	1.302	15.000	270.9	.020	.062
	Hotelling's Trace	.201	1.295	15.000	290.0	.204	.063
	Roy's Largest Root	.124	2.474[b]	5.000	100.0	.037	.110

Once more, about two-thirds (66.4 %, n = 71) agree that the Payback method is used to evaluate and align objectives of executive management and information systems projects.

About one-third (33.6 %, n = 36) disagree. Well over half (59.8 %, n = 102) agree that the Net Present Value method is used to evaluate and align objectives of executive management and information systems projects. Meanwhile, 40.2 % (n = 43) disagree. Nearly two-third (64.5 %, n = 69) agree that the Internal Rate of Return (IRR) method is used to evaluate and align objectives of executive management and information systems projects while 35.5 % disagree (Tables 2 and 3).

Ensuring Reliability and Validity.

A little over three-quarter (75.7 %, n = 81) agree that Portfolio analysis and scoring models are used to evaluate and align objectives of executive management and information systems projects; 24.3 % disagree.

Nearly a half (49.6 %, n = 53) agree that the Val IT framework is used to evaluate and align objectives of executive management and information systems projects. More than half (57 %, n = 61) agree that the COBIT framework is used to evaluate and align objectives of executive management and information systems projects; 43.0 % disagree.

Multiple regression analysis was utilized to determine the percentage contribution of some of the identified significant predictors of evaluation models affecting ICT adoption within MSEs.

The distribution revealed that only one variable made a significant percentage contribution to the level of ICT operations in MSEs; that is, A ($\beta = 0.410$, p < .000). It may thus be inferred that 'A' is the variable, prominent in explaining the variation in level of evaluation models affecting ICT adoption within MSEs.

In answering the two questions (1) degree of variability explained and (2) predictors, the results revealed that the variable contributed approximately 88.4 % of the variations in evaluation models affecting ICT adoption within MSEs. The analysis of variance also revealed that the regression coefficients were real and did not occur by chance.

It may therefore be inferred that relatively, 'An' impacts on evaluation models which affect ICT adoption within MSEs.

By implication, there seems to be enough evidence to suggest that evaluation models in ICT operation would become more effective if efforts were targeted towards A. Thus, the hypothesis was accepted.

For further analysis using Wilk's statistics, there was no significant effect of department $\Lambda = .825$, $(5, 15) = 1.30$, $p < .05$. Additionally, a one-way repeated measure ANOVA was conducted to compare scores on the various departments. There was a significant effect for evaluation models (Wilks' lamda $= 0.25$, $F (2, 28) = 41.17$, $p > .000$, multivariate partial eta squared $= 0.75$), noting that this result suggests a small effect size. This suggests that there is a significant relationship between departments and evaluation models in ICT operations.

Additionally, data was analysed using a mixed-design ANOVA with a within-subjects factor of subscale (years of service) and a between-subject factor of gender (male, female).

Mauchly's test indicated that the assumption of sphericity had been violated ($\chi 2 = 16.8$, $p < .001$), therefore degrees of freedom were corrected using Greenhouse-Geisser estimates of sphericity ($\varepsilon = 0.98$).

The results revealed no main effects of subscale, $F (1.91, 1350.8) = 378$, $p > .05$, $\eta p2 = .03$, and gender, $F (1, 709) = 78.8$, $p > .05$, $\eta p2 = .10$, were qualified by an interaction between subscale and gender, $F (1.91, 1351) = 30.4$, $p > .05$, $\eta p2 = .041$.

Furthermore, an ANCOVA [between-subjects factor: gender (male, female); covariate: Education] revealed no main effects of gender, $F (1, 732) = 2.00$, $p = .16$, $\eta p2 = .003$, or education, $F (1, 732) = 3.25$, $p = .072$, $\eta p2 = .004$, and no interaction between gender and education, $F (1, 732) = 0.016$, $p = .90$, $\eta p2 < .001$.

In any case, all other main effects and interactions were non-significant and irrelevant to the hypotheses, all $F \leq 0.94$, $p \geq .39$, $\eta p2 \leq .001$.

8   Discussions of Research Findings

Evaluation models are found to be important for ICT operational risk in MSEs. The plausible reason for the relevant importance of this variable in MSEs is due to A[3] and D[4] (cf. results). The respondents considered the evaluation models an important prerequisite when deciding on technology adoption. Thus, the organisation may pay more

---

[3] Payback method is used to evaluate and align objectives of executive management and information systems projects.

[4] Portfolio analysis and scoring models are used to evaluate and align objectives of executive management and information systems projects.

attention to the viable benefits, although not all the models in the study were agreed upon. This might be because the evaluation models process in MSEs is always short-term [7]. Also, evaluation models can be regarded as a substitution for ICT operation to ensure a financial institution's safety [9].

The findings of this study support the reviewed literature which suggests that evaluation models can act as motivators to encourage ICT operational risk [5]. This is because direct benefits are more viable and are easier to measure [5]. Therefore, this study supports the prior study of [5], that evaluation models are influential determinants of technology usage in MSEs. A similar finding is reported by a previous study of ICT operation [4] which found the relative advantage of evaluation models a significant factor of adoption within MSEs; the study however contrasted previous findings of [3].

In support of the current study's position, [9] noted that even the smallest of businesses now have the potential to trade in the global economy using ICT. Additionally [9] maintains that these changes in the nature of the competitive processes and commercial relationships provide significant strategic opportunities for the smaller organisation, arguably placing them on an equal footing with their larger competitors already established in the marketplace.

9   Conclusion

The study concludes that managers in MSEs need to be equipped to identify, analyse and manage ICT operation from a more diverse range of sources and contexts. If this is not carefully considered, MSEs Managers, irrespective of whether they engage in business or not, may find it more difficult to avoid the risks resulting from increased ICT global competition in their home markets.

References

1. Balbas, A.: Mathematical methods in modern risk measurement: a survey. Appl. Math. 101(2), 205–219 (2007)
2. Basel Committee on Banking Supervision. New Basel Capital Accord Operational Risk. Basel (2004)
3. Burget, C., Ruschendorf, L.: Consistent risk measures for portfolio vectors. Insur.: Math. Econ. 38, 289–297 (2006)
4. Calder, A.: Information Security based on ISO 27001. Van Haren, Amersfoort - NL (2006)
5. CAS – Casualty Actuarial Society, Overview of Enterprise Risk. NY (2003)
6. Cody, R.P., Smith, J.K.: Applied Statistics and the SAS Programming Language. Prentice, Upper Saddle River (2005)
7. Conner, F.W., Coviello, A.W.: Information security governance: A call to action. The Corporate Governance Task Force (2004). http://www.cyberpartnership.org/InfoSecGov4_04 Retrieved January 9, 2010
8. Froot, K.A., Stein, J.C.: Risk management, capital budgeting, and capital structure policy for financial institutions: An integrated approach. J. Financ. Econ. 47, 55–82 (1998)
9. Lam, J.: Emerging best practices in developing key risk indicators and ERM reporting. James Lam and Associates, Wellesley (2006)

10. Liebenberg, A., Hoyt, R.: The determinants of enterprise risk management: evidence from the appointment of chief risk officers. Risk Manage. Insur. Rev. 6(1), 37–52 (2003)
11. Meyers, L.S., Gamst, G., Guarino, A.J.: Applied Multivariate Research. Sage, Thousand Oaks (2006)
12. Raykov, T., Marcoulides, G.A.: An Introduction to Applied Multivariate Analysis. Rutledge, New York (2008)
13. South Africa. Department of Trade and Industry. Micro Finance Regulatory Council (MFRC) (2006). Retrieved February 21, 2009, from The DTI
14. Stoney, C.: Risk Management: a Guide to its Relevance and Application in Quality Management and Enhancement. Leeds Metropolitan University (2007)
15. Tabachnick, B.G.: Multivariate statistics: an introduction and some applications. Invited workshop presented to the American Psychology - Law Society, Jacksonville, FL (2008)
16. IT Governance Institute: ITGICobiT 4.., Executive Summary. IT Governance Institute (2007)
17. Tabachnick, B.G., Fidell, L.S.: Using Multivariate Statistics, 5th edn. Allyn and Bacon, Boston (2007)

Author Index

Printed in the United States
By Bookmasters